**W9-DBM-505**

I&T Collector's Series

FARM TRACTORS

1916-1925

Editorial

Editorial Director
Randy Stephens

Technical Editor
C.G. Ewing

Inventory/Production Manager
Terry Distin

Editorial Assistant
Shirley Renicker

Marketing

Marketing Director
Chris Charlton

Advertising Manager
Diane Wilmot

Advertising Assistant
Katherine Nelms

Graphic Designer
Anita Blattner

Sales & Administration

Sales & Marketing Manager
Roger Cobb

Customer Service & Administration Manager
Joan Jackson

Marketing Coordinator
Lynn Reynolds

Published by
Intertec Publishing Corporation

President
Jack Hancock

Group Vice President
Bill Wiesner

I&T Collector's Series

FARM TRACTORS

1916-1925

Cover Photo: Thomas Hart Benton
"Chilmark Hay" 1951
Courtesy of Forbes Magazines, Inc.
New York, New York

Library of Congress Catalog Number: 91-57971
International Standard Book Number: 0-87288-480-5

Printed in the United States of America by
Walsworth Press, Marceline, Missouri 64658

Special thanks to Farm Press Publications, Inc.

CONTENTS

PREFACE

Very few tractors of any kind except the big plowing and threshing units were built before 1912, and plowing or cultivating with power machinery was mostly a future possibility.

Two factors in 1915 might have been responsible for the rapid increase in power farming at this time. One was the increased loss of horses due to the war and to disease. The other was Henry Ford's offer to England of 5000 Fordson tractors.

Both coincide with the beginning of a growth pattern in farming, particularly mechanized farming. This book has its beginning in 1916 and takes the reader to 1925, recognized as the "Golden Years" of farm tractor development in America. In that ten years, as many tractors were built and sold as occurred in the following thirty years.

Before 1916, there had never been a national showcase or any other means to assess the national tractor market or its possibilities. Practically all tractors were hand built individually and to order and it was difficult to ascertain what might be available. There had never been an annual listing similar to the *Cooperative Tractor Catalog* where features could be compared.

1916

The 1916 listing contains 74 makes and 118 models which vary widely as to design. Some of the products shown cannot be confirmed as to whether or not they really existed. Many of the companies responding were builders of specialized equipment who modified it slightly to perform another job.

ADVANCE-RUMELY THRESHER CO.

Laporte, Indiana

All Purpose 8-16	1916-1918
All Purpose 12-24	1916-1917
Gas Pull 15-30	1916-1917
Oil Pull 15-30	1916-1917

All Purpose 8-16
Advance-Rumely Thresher Co., Laporte, Ind.

Type of traction, wheel; fuel, gasoline; guaranteed belt h. p., 16; guaranteed drawbar h. p., 8; motor, Advance-Rumely vertical; number of cylinders, 4; cast en bloc; speed of motor, 850 r. p. m.; bore, 4 inches; stroke, 5½ inches; 2 or 4-cycle, 4; transmission, gear; cooling system, water, forced; bearings, Hyatt; carburetor, Kingston vertical; ignition, Kingston jump spark; oiling system, force and splash; length over all, 197 inches; width over all, 79 inches; height over all 62 inches; number of wheels, 4; number of drive wheels, 1; diameter of drive wheels, 54 inches; face of drive wheels 26 inches; clutch, make and type, Advance-Rumely disk; control speeds, 1; speed on road 2 1-10 miles per hour; speed in furrow, 2.1 miles per hour; diameter of pulley, 14 inches; face of pulley, 6½ inches; capacity of fuel tank, 22 gallons; front axle, 2½ inches; rear axle, 2 inches; diameter of crankshaft, 2¼ inches; weight, 6,650 pounds.

All Purpose 12-24
Advance-Rumely Thresher Co., Laporte, Ind.

Type of traction, wheel; fuel, gasoline; guaranteed belt h. p., 24; guaranteed drawbar h. p., 12; motor, Advance-Rumely vertical; number of cylinders, 4; cast en bloc; speed of motor, 750 r. p. m.; bore, $4\frac{1}{2}$ inches; stroke, $6\frac{3}{4}$ inches; 2 or 4-cycle, 4; transmission, gear; cooling system, water forced; bearings, Hyatt; carburetor, Kingston vertical; ignition, Kingston jump spark; oiling system, force and splash; length over all, 217 inches; width over all, 96 inches; height over all, 71 inches; number of wheels, 4; number of drive wheels, 1; diameter of drive wheels, $63\frac{1}{2}$ inches; face of drive wheels, 26 inches; clutch, make and type, Advance-Rumely disk; control speeds, 1; speed on road, 2.3 miles per hour; speed in furrow, 2.3 miles per hour; diameter of pulley, 15 inches; face of pulley, 8 inches; capacity of fuel tank, 22 gallons; front axle, 3 inches; rear axle, 2 inches; diameter of crankshaft, $2\frac{1}{8}$ inches; weight, 8,900 pounds.

Gas Pull 15-30
Advance-Rumely Thresher Co., Laporte, Ind.

Type of traction, wheel; fuel, gasoline; guaranteed belt h. p., 30; guaranteed drawbar h. p., 15; motor, Advance-Rumely; number of cylinders, 2; speed of motor, 500 r. p. m.; bore, $7\frac{1}{2}$ inches; stroke, 8 inches; 2 or 4-cycle, 4; transmission, gear; cooling system, thermo-syphon; bearings, babbitt, carburetor, Kingston; ignition, Remy jump spark; oiling system, force and splash; length over all, 178 inches; width over all, 102 inches; height over all, 108 inches; number of wheels, 4; number of drive wheels, 2; diameter of drive wheels, $61\frac{1}{2}$ inches; face of drive wheels, 20 inches; clutch, make and type, Advance-Rumely shoe; control speeds, 2; speed on road, $2\frac{3}{4}$ miles per hour; speed in furrow, 2 miles per hour; diameter of pulley, 18 inches; face of pulley, 9 inches; capacity of fuel tank, 53 gallons; front axle, 2 inches; rear axle, $3\frac{5}{16}$ inches; diameter of crankshaft, $3\frac{1}{2}$ inches; weight, 11,000 pounds.

Oil Pull 15-30
Advance-Rumely Thresher Co., Laporte, Ind.

Type of traction, wheel; fuel, kerosene; guaranteed belt h. p., 30; guaranteed drawbar h. p., 15; motor, Advance-Rumely horizontal; number of cylinders, 1; speed of motor, 375 r. p. m.; bore, 10 inches; stroke, 12 inches; 2 or 4-cycle, 4; transmission, gear; cooling system, oil-forced circulation; bearings, babbitt; carburetor, Advance-Rumely; ignition, Bosch make and break; oiling system, force and splash; length over all, 192 inches; width over all, 94 inches; height over all, $123\frac{1}{2}$ inches; number of wheels, 4; number of drive wheels, 2; diameter of drive wheels, 70 inches; face of drive wheels, 24 inches; clutch, make and type, Advance-Rumely shoe; control speeds, 2; speed on road, $2\frac{1}{2}$ miles per hour; speed in furrow, 1.9 miles per hour; diameter of pulley, 30 inches; face of pulley, $9\frac{1}{2}$ inches; capacity of fuel tank, 36 gallons; capacity of water tank, 35 gallons; front axle, $2\frac{1}{2}$ inches; rear axle, $4\frac{3}{16}$ inches; diameter of crankshaft, $4\frac{7}{16}$ inches; weight, 16,000 pounds.

ALLIS-CHALMERS MANUFACTURING CO.

Milwaukee, Wisconsin

Allis-Chalmers 10-18   1916-1921

Allis-Chalmers 10-18
Allis-Chalmers Mfg. Co., Milwaukee, Wis.

Type of traction, wheel fuel, gasoline; guaranteed belt h. p., 18; guaranteed drawbar h. p., 10; motor, Allis-Chalmers; number of cylinders, 2; cast opposed; speed of motor, 720 r. p. m.; bore, $5\frac{1}{4}$ inches; stroke, 7 inches; 2 or 4-cycle, 4; transmission, gear; cooling system, radiator and pump; bearings, Babbitt; carburetor, Bennett; ignition, Kingston, impulse starter; oiling system, force, feed and splash; engine suspension, bolted; length over all, 140 inches; width over all, 77 inches; height over all, 75 inches; number of wheels, 3; number of drive wheels, 2; diameter of drive wheels, 56 inches; face of drive wheels, 12 inches; how mounted, solid; clutch, make and type, Allis-Chalmers, 2-shoe expanding; control speeds, 1; speed on road, $2\frac{1}{3}$ miles per hour; speed in furrow, $2\frac{1}{3}$ miles per hour; diameter of pulley, $14\frac{1}{2}$ inches; face of pulley, $6\frac{1}{2}$ inches; capacity of fuel tank, $17\frac{1}{2}$ gallons; rear axle, $2\frac{15}{16}$ inches; diameter of crankshaft, $2\frac{1}{2}$ inches; weight, 4,650 pounds; price, $750 f. o. b. factory.

AMERICAN TRACTOR CO.
Des Moines, Iowa

American Oil Tractor   1916

American Oil Tractor
American Tractor Co., Des Moines, Ia.

Type of traction, wheel; fuel, gasoline or kerosene; guaranteed belt h. p., 35; guaranteed drawbar h. p., 20; motor, vertical; number of cylinders, 4, cast separately; speed of motor, 700 r. p. m.; bore, 5 inches; stroke, 7 inches; 2 or 4-cycle, 4; transmission, gear; cooling system, water, copper tub radiator; bearings, roller and babbitt; carburetor, Bennett oil; ignition, K.-W. high tension magneto; oiling system, splash and force feed; engine suspension, on main frame; length over all, 148 inches; width over all, 80 inches; height over all, 72 inches; number of wheels, 4; number of drive wheels, 2; diameter of drive wheels, 60 inches; face of drive wheels, 16 inches; how mounted, spring; clutch, make and type, expanding; control speeds, 2; speed on road, 3 to 4 miles per hour; speed in furrow, $1\frac{3}{4}$ to $2\frac{1}{2}$ miles per hour; diameter of pulley, 20 inches; face of pulley, $8\frac{1}{2}$ inches; capacity of fuel tank, 25 gallons; capacity of water tank, 15 gallons; diameter of crankshaft, $2\frac{1}{2}$ inches; special equipment, 6 or 8-inch extension rims for drive wheels; weight, 6,300 pounds; price, $1,600 f. o. b. factory.

ANDREWS TRACTOR CO.

Minneapolis, Minnesota

Andrews 10-20   1916-1918

Andrews 10-20
Andrews Tractor Co., Minneapolis, Minn.

Type of traction, drum; fuel, gasoline; guaranteed belt h. p., 20; guaranteed drawbar h. p., 10; motor, double opposed; number of cylinders, 4, cast separately; speed of motor, 800 r. p. m.; bore, 4 inches; stroke, 5 inches; 2 or 4-cycle, 2; friction; cooling system, forced air; bearings, roller and babbitt; carburetor, Krice or Bennett; ignition, Bosch high tension magneto; oiling system, through gasoline feed; engine suspension, 3-point; legnth over all, 176 inches; width over all, 90 inches; height over all, 56 inches; number of wheels, 3; number of drive wheels, 1; diameter of drive wheels, 48 inches; face of drive wheels, 30 inches; how mounted, hub or roller bearings; clutch, make and type, friction; speed on road, 3 miles per hour; speed in furrow, 2½ miles per hour; diameter of pulley, 12 inches; face of pulley, 7 inches; capacity of fuel tank, 22 gallons; diameter of crankshaft, 1¾ inches; weight, 4,400 pounds; price, $640 f. o. b. factory.

AULTMAN & TAYLOR MACHINERY CO.
Mansfield, Ohio

A. & T. 18-36   1916-1919
A. & T. 25-50   1916-1919
A. & T. 30-60   1916-1919

A. & T. 18-36
Aultman & Taylor Machinery Co., Mansfield, O.

Type of traction, wheel; fuel, gasoline, kerosene or distillate; guaranteed belt h. p., 36; guaranteed drawbar h. p., 18; number of cylinders, 4, cast in pairs; speed of motor, 600 r. p. m.; bore, 5 inches; stroke, 8 inches; transmission, gear; cooling system, radiator; length over all, 166 inches; width over all, 90 inches; height over all, 125 inches; number of wheels, 4; number of drive wheels, 2; diameter of drive wheels, 70 inches; face of drive wheels, 20 inches.

A. & T. 25-50
Aultman & Taylor Machinery Co., Mansfield, O.

Type of traction, wheel; fuel, gasoline, kerosene or distillate; guaranteed belt h. p. 50; guaranteed drawbar h. p., 25; number of cylinders, 4; cast in pairs; bore, 6 inches; stroke, 9 inches; transmission, gear; cooling system, radiator; length over all, $184\frac{1}{2}$ inches; width over all, 106 inches; height over all, 136 inches; number of wheels, 4; number of drive wheels, 2; diameter of drive wheels, 78 inches; face of drive wheels, 20 inches; diameter of pulley, 24 inches; face of pulley, 11 inches; capacity of fuel tank, 50 gallons.

A. & T. 30-60
Aultman & Taylor Machinery Co., Mansfield, O.

Type of traction, wheel; fuel, gasoline, kerosene or distillate; guranteed belt h. p., 60; guaranteed drawbar h. p., 30; number of cylinders, 4; cast in pairs; speed of motor, 500 r. p. m.; bore, 7 inches; stroke, 9 inches; transmission gear; cooling system, tubular radiator; length over all, 218 inches; height over all, 138 inches; number of wheels, 4; number of drive wheels, 2; diameter of drive wheels, 90 inches; face of drive wheels, 24-36 inches; diameter of pulley, 24 inches; face of pulley, 11 inches; capacity of fuel tank, 60 gallons.

AVERY CO.
Peoria, Illinois

Avery 5-10	1916-1922
Avery 8-16	1916-1922
Avery 12-25	1916-1922
Avery 18-36	1916-1922
Avery 25-50	1916-1923
Avery 40-80	1916-1920

Avery 5-10
Avery Co., Peoria, Ill.

Type of traction, wheel; fuel, gasoline; guaranteed belt h. p., 10; guaranteed drawbar h. p., 5; motor, Avery vertical; number of cylinders, 4, cast en bloc; speed of motor, 1,200 r. p. m.; bore, 3 inches; stroke, 4 inches; 2 or 4-cycle, 4; tranmission, combination friction and double drive spur gear; cooling system, thermo-syphon; bearings, Avery babbitt and Hyatt roller; carburetor, Zephyr; ignition, Atwater-Kent; oiling system, internal pump and splash; length over all, 145 inches; width over all, 35 inches; height over all, ... inches; number of wheels, 3; number of drive wheels, 2; diameter of drive wheels, 38 inches; face of drive wheels, 5 inches; clutch, make and type, none; control speeds, 3; speed on road $3\frac{1}{2}$ to 4 miles per hour; speed in furrow, $1\frac{1}{3}$ to 2 miles per hour; diameter of pulley, $4\frac{3}{4}$ inches; face of pulley, $4\frac{1}{4}$ inches; capacity of fuel tank, 11 gallons; front axle, $1\frac{5}{8}$ inches; rear axle, 2 inches; diameter of crankshaft, $1\frac{3}{4}$ inches; weight, 1,700 pounds; price, $365 f. o. b. factory.

Avery 8-16
Avery Co., Peoria, Ill.

Type of traction, wheel; fuel, gasoline or kerosene; guaranteed belt h. p., 16; guaranteed draw-bar h. p., 8; motor, Avery opposed; number of cylinders, 2; cast separate; speed of motor, 600 r. p. m.; bore, $5\frac{1}{2}$ inches; stroke, 6 inches; 2 or 4-cycle, 4; transmission, gear; cooling system, thermo-syphon; bearings, Avery babbitted; carburetor, Kingston double; ignition, high tension; oiling system, internal gear, pump and splash; length over all, 130 inches; width over all, 56 inches; height over all, 53 inches; number of wheels, 4; number of drive wheels, 2; diameter of drive wheels, 50 inches; face of drive wheels, 12 inches; clutch, make and type, Avery steam engine and type; control speeds, 2; speed on road, 3 miles per hour; speed in furrow, $1\frac{3}{4}$ miles per hour; diameter of pulley, $19\frac{1}{2}$ inches; face of pulley, 7 inches; capacity of fuel tank, 14 gallons; front axle, 2 inches; rear axle, $2\frac{1}{2}$ inches; diameter of crankshaft, $2\frac{3}{4}$ inches; special equipment, reversible inner cylinder walls; valves in the head; 2-speed drive, spur gear transmission, revolving rear axle, no intermediate gear shaft or bearings, no pumps or fan; weight, 4,900 pounds; price, $760 cash, $800 time, f. o. b. factory.

Avery 12-25
Avery Co., Peoria, Ill.

Type of traction, wheel; fuel, gasoline or kerosene; guaranteed belt h. p., 25; guaranteed draw-bar h. p., 12; motor, Avery opposed; number of cylinders, 2, cast separately; speed of motor, 570 r. p. m.; bore $6\frac{1}{2}$ inches; stroke, 7 inches; 2 or 4-cycle, 4; transmission, gear; cooling system, thermo-syphon; bearings, Avery babbitted; carburetor, Kingston, double; ignition, high tension; oiling system, internal gear, pump and splash; length over all, 164 inches; width over all, 80 inches; height over all, 105 inches; number of wheels, 4; number of drive wheels, 2; diameter of drive wheels, 56 inches; face of drive wheels, 20 inches; clutch, make and type, Avery steam engine type in belt wheel; control speeds, 2; speed on road, $2\frac{3}{4}$ miles per hour; speed in furrow, $1\frac{3}{4}$ miles per hour; diameter of pulley, $19\frac{1}{2}$ inches; face of pulley, 7 inches; capacity of fuel tank, 20 gallons; front axle, 2 inches; rear axle, 3 inches; diameter of crankshaft, $3\frac{1}{4}$ inches; special equipment, valves in head; reversible inner cylinder walls; sliding frame, 2-speed, double driven, spur gear transmission, revolving rear axle, no intermediate gear, shaft or bearings, no pumps or fan; weight, 7,500 pounds; price, $1,195 cash, $1,280 time, f. o. b. factory.

Avery 18-36
Avery Co., Peoria, Ill.

Type of traction, wheel; fuel, gasoline or kerosene; guaranteed belt h. p., 36; guaranteed drawbar h. p., 18; motor, Avery opposed; number of cylinders, 4; cast, in pairs; speed of motor, 650 r. p. m.; bore, $5^{1}/_{2}$ inches; stroke, 6 inches; 2 or 4-cycle, 4; transmission, gear; cooling system, thermo-syphon; bearings, Avery babbitted; carburetor, Kingston, double, ignition, high tension; oiling system, internal gear, pump and splash; length over all, 152 inches; width over all, 84 inches; height over all, 105 inches; number of wheels, 4; number of drive wheels 2; diameter of drive wheels, 65 inches; face of drive wheels, 20 inches; clutch, make and type, Avery steam engine types in belt wheel; control speeds, 2; speed on road, 3 miles per hour; speed in furrow, 2 miles per hour; diameter of pulley, 18 inches; face of pulley, 8 inches; capacity of fuel tanks, 33 gallons; front axle, $2^{1}/_{2}$ inches; rear axle, 3 inches; diameter of crankshaft, $3^{1}/_{8}$ inches; special equipment, valves in the head; reversible inner cylinder walls; sliding frame, 2-speed, double drive, spur gear transmission, revolving rear axle; no intermediate gear, shaft or bearings, no pumps or fan; weight, 9,250; price, $1,775 cash, $1,900 time, f. o. b. factory.

Avery 25-50
Avery Co., Peoria, Ill.

Type of traction, wheel; fuel, gasoline or kerosene; guaranteed belt h. p., 50; guaranteed drawbar h. p., 25; motor, Avery opposed; number of cylinders, 4, cast in pairs; speed of motor, 500 r. p. m.; bore, $6^{1}/_{2}$ inches; stroke, 7 inches; 2 or 4-cycle, 4; transmission, gear; cooling system, thermo-syphon; bearings, Avery babbitted; carburetor, Kingston, double; ignition, high tension; oiling system, internal gear, pump and splash; length over all, 176 inches; width over all, $90^{1}/_{2}$ inches; height over all, 108 inches; number of wheels, 4; number of drive wheels, 2; diameter of drive wheels, 69 inches; face of drive wheels, 20 inches; how mounted, ...; clutch, make and type, Avery steam engine type in belt wheel; control speeds, 2; speed on road, 3 miles per hour; speed in furrow, 2 miles per hour; diameter of pulley, 22 inches; face of pulley, $8^{1}/_{2}$ inches; capacity of fuel tanks, 33 gallons; front axle, $2^{1}/_{2}$ inches; rear axle, $3^{1}/_{2}$ inches; diameter of crankshaft, $3^{3}/_{4}$ inches; special equipment, valves in the head; reversible inner cylinder walls; sliding frame, 2-speed, double drive, spur gear transmission, revolving rear axle, no intermediate gear shaft or bearings, no pumps or fans; weight, 12,500 pounds; price, $2,190 cash, $2,350 time, f. o. b. factory.

Avery 40-80
Avery Co., Peoria, Ill.

Type of traction, wheel; fuel, gasoline or kerosene; guaranteed belt h. p., 80; guaranteed draw-bar h. p., 40; motor, Avery opposed; number of cylinders, 4, cast in pairs; speed of motor, 500 r. p. m.; bore, $7\frac{3}{4}$ inches; stroke, 8 inches; 2 or 4-cycle, 4; transmission, gear; cooling system, thermo-syphon; bearing, Avery babbitted; carburetor, Kingston double; ignition, high tension; oiling system, internal gear, pump and splash; length over all, 215 inches; width over all $111\frac{1}{2}$ inches; height over all, 121 inches; number of wheels, 4; number of drive wheels, 2; diameter of drive wheels, $87\frac{1}{2}$ inches; face of drive wheels, 24 inches; clutch, make and type, Avery steam engine type in belt wheel; control speeds, 2; speed on road, 2 2-3 miles per hour; speed in furrow, $1\frac{3}{4}$ miles per hour; diameter of pulley, 26 inches; face of pulley, 10 inches; capacity of fuel tanks, 50 gallons; front axle, $3\frac{1}{2}$ inches; rear axle, 5 inches; diameter of crankshaft, $4\frac{1}{2}$ inches; special equipment, valves in the head, reversible inner cylinder walls; sliding frame, 2-speed, double drive, spur gear, transmission; revolving rear axle; no intermediate gear, shafts or bearings, no pumps or fan; weight, 22,000 pounds; price, $2,625 cash, $2,800 time, f. o. b. factory.

B. F. AVERY & SONS

Louisville, Kentucky

Louisville Motor Plow 10-20   1916-1917

Louisville Motor Plow 10-20
B.F. Avery & Sons, Louisville, Ky.

Type of traction, wheel; fuel, gasoline or kerosene; guaranteed belt h. p., 20; guaranteed drawbar h. p., 10; motor, opposed valve-in-head; number of cylinders, 2; cast en bloc; bore, 6 inches; stroke, 6 inches; 2 or 4-cycle, 4; transmission, gear; cooling system, radiator; bearings, bronze; ignition, high tension; oiling system, force feed; length over all, 156 inches; width over all, 84 inches; height over all, 67 inches; number of wheels, 3; number of drive wheels, 1; clutch, make and type, expanding drum; control speeds, 1; speed on road, $2\frac{1}{2}$ miles per hour; speed in furrow, $2\frac{1}{2}$ miles per hour; capacity of fuel tank, gasoline 15 gallons, kerosene 15 gallons; special equipment, 2 14-inch turning plows or 2 14-inch disks; weight, 5,000 pounds.

BATES TRACTOR CO.
Lansing, Michigan

Bates All Steel Oil   1916

Bates All Steel Oil
Bates Tractor Co., Lansing, Mich.

Type of traction, wheel; fuel, kerosene; guaranteed belt h. p., 16-30; guaranteed drawbar h. p., 10-20; motor, Bates; number of cylinders, 1-2; cast separately; speed of motor, 300-500 r. p. m.; bore, 7 inches; stroke, $8\frac{1}{2}$, $7\frac{1}{2}$ inches; 2 or 4-cycle, 4; transmission, gear; cooling system, fan; bearings, adjustable; carburetor, Bates; ignition, vibrating coil; oiling system, positive; engine suspension, on crank case; length over all, 90-102 inches; width over all, 63-75 inches; height over all, 99-90 inches; number of wheels, 4; number of drive wheels, 2; diameter of drive wheels, 50-60 inches; face of drive wheels, 20-24 inches; how mounted, solid; clutch, make and type, Bates; control speeds, 2; speed on road, $2\frac{1}{2}$-3 miles per hour; speed in furrow, 2-$2\frac{1}{4}$ miles per hour; diameter of pulley, 16-18 inches; face of pulley, 8 inches; capacity of fuel tank, 9-15 gallons; capacity of water tank, 10 gallons; diameter of crankshaft, 3 inches; special equipment, Bates plow carriage, 2 and 4-plows; weight, 5,000-8,000 pounds; price, $975-$1,650 f. o. b. factory.

BEEMAN GARDEN TRACTOR CO.
Minneapolis, Minnesota

Beeman Garden Tractor   1916

Beeman Garden Tractor
Beeman Garden Tractor Co., Minneapolis, Minn.

Type of traction, wheel; fuel, gasoline; guaranteed belt h. p., 3; guaranteed drawbar h. p., $1\frac{3}{4}$; motor, motorcyle type; number of cylinders, 1; speed of motor, 230 to 2,200 r. p. m.; bore, $3\frac{1}{2}$ inches; stroke, $4\frac{1}{2}$ inches; 2 or 4-cycle, 4; transmission, friction; cooling system, gravity, radiator and fan; bearings, bronze; carburetor, Schebler; ignition, standard magneto; oiling system, splash system; engine suspension, between drive wheels; length over all, 78 inches; width over all, 17 inches; height over all, 31 inches; number of wheels, 4; number of drive wheels, 2; diameter of drive wheels, 25 inches; face of drive wheels, $3\frac{1}{2}$ inches; how mounted, solid; clutch, make and type, friction; control speeds, 1; speeds on road, 1 to 3 miles per hour; speed in furrow, $\frac{3}{4}$ to $2\frac{1}{2}$ miles per hour; diameter of pulley, 4 inches; face of pulley, 4 inches; capacity of fuel tank, 1 gallon; capacity of water tank, $\frac{3}{4}$ gallon; center axle, $2\frac{1}{2}$ inches; diameter of crankshaft, $1\frac{1}{3}$ inches; special equipment, equipped for attaching any garden tool; weight, 449 pounds; price, $150 f. o. b. factory.

C. L. BEST GAS TRACTOR CO.
Oakland, California

Pony   1916
Tracklayer 30 H.P.   1916-1917
Tracklayer 40 H.P.   1916-1917

Pony
C.L. Best Gas Traction Co., Oakland, Cal.

Type of traction, crawler; fuel, distillate; guaranteed belt h. p., 16; guaranteed drawbar h. p., 8; motor. own; number of cylinders, 4; cast singly; speed of motor, 650 r. p. m.; bore, $4\frac{3}{8}$ inches; stroke, $5\frac{1}{4}$ inches; 2 or 4-cycle, 4; transmission, bevel gear and friction; cooling system, pump and radiator; bearings, babbitt; carburetor, Schebler float; ignition, K. W. high tension; oiling system, own; length over all, 96 inches; width over all, 48 inches; height over all, 48 inches; length of traction surface of crawlers, 66 inches; how mounted, spring; clutch, make and type, own; control speeds, 24; speed on road, $2\frac{3}{4}$ miles per hour; speed in furrow, $2\frac{3}{8}$ miles per hour; diameter of pulley, 10 inches; face of pulley, 4 inches; capacity of fuel tank, 15 gallons; capacity of radiator, 18 gallons; front axle, $2\frac{1}{8}$ inches; rear axle, $2\frac{1}{2}$ inches; diameter of crankshaft, $2\frac{1}{4}$ inches; price, $1,400 f. o. b. factory.

Tracklayer 30 H.P.
C.L. Best Gas Traction Co., Oakland, Cal.

Type of traction, crawler; fuel, distillate; guaranteed belt h. p., 30; guaranteed drawbar h. p., 16; motor, own; number of cylinders, 4; cast singly; speed of motor, 650 r. p. m.; bore, $5\frac{1}{4}$ inches; stroke, $6\frac{1}{4}$ inches, 2 or 4-cycle, 4; transmission, spur gear and friction; cooling system, pump fan and radiator; bearings, babbitt; carburetor, Schebler; ignition K. W. high tension; oiling system, own, splash; length over all, 126 inches; width over all, 76 inches; height over all, 62 inches; number of crawlers, 2; face of crawlers, 12 inches; length of traction surface crawlers, 120 inches; how mounted, spring; clutch, make and type, own; control speeds, 3; speed on road, $2\frac{3}{8}$ miles per hour; speed in furrow, $1\frac{3}{4}$ miles per hour; diameter of pulley, 12 inches; face of pulley, 8 inches; capacity of fuel tank, 25 gallons; capacity of radiator, 20 gallons; diameter of crankshaft, $2\frac{1}{2}$ inches; weight, 9,600 pounds.

Tracklayer 40 H.P.
C.L. Best Gas Traction Co., Oakland, Cal.

Type of traction, crawler; fuel, distillate; guaranteed belt h. p., 40; guaranteed drawbar h. p., 22; motor, own; number of cylinders, 4; cast singly; speed of motor, 450 r. p. m.; bore, $7\frac{3}{4}$ inches; stroke, 9 inches; 2 or 4-cycle 4; cooling system, pump, fan and radiator; bearings, babbitt; carburetor, Schebler; ignition, K. W. high tension; oiling system, Hancock force and splash; length over all, 268 inches; width over all, 87 inches; height over all, 120 inches; face of crawlers, 24 inches; how mounted, spring; clutch, make and type, own, internal expanding; control speeds 3; speed on road, $1\frac{5}{8}$ to $2\frac{3}{8}$ miles per hour; speed in furrow, $1\frac{5}{8}$ to $1\frac{3}{4}$ miles per hour; diameter of pulley, 18 inches; face of pulley, 10 inches; capacity of fuel tank, 80 gallons; capacity of radiator, 35 gallons; front axle, $2\frac{7}{8}$ inches; rear axle, $2\frac{7}{16}$ inches; diameter of crankshaft, $3\frac{1}{4}$ inches; weight, 28,000 pounds; price, $4,565 f. o. b. factory.

BORING TRACTOR CO.
Chicago, Illinois

Boring 35   1916-1920

Boring 35
Boring Tractor Co., Chicago, Ill.

Type of traction, wheel; fuel, gasoline or kerosene; guaranteed belt h. p., 20; guaranteed drawbar h. p., 10; motor, Waukesha; number of cylinders, 4; cast in pairs; speed of motor, .. r. p. m.; bore, $3\frac{3}{4}$ inches; stroke, $5\frac{3}{4}$ inches; 2 or 4-cycle, 4; transmission, chain; oiling system, automatic splash; length over all, 117 inches; width over all, $70\frac{1}{2}$ inches; number of drive wheels, 2; diameter of drive wheels, 54 inches; face of drive wheels, 10 inches; clutch, make and type, pivoting lever; control speeds, 2 forward, 2 reverse; speed on road, 1 to 9 miles per hour; speed in furrow, 1 to 6 miles per hour; diameter of pulley, 10 inches; face of pulley, 6 inches; capacity of fuel tank, 10 gallons; diameter of crankshaft, $1\frac{1}{4}$ inches; weight, 3,200 pounds.

BRILLION IRON WORKS
Brillion, Wisconsin

Brillion Front Wheel Pull   1916

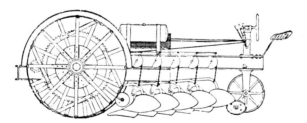

Brillion Front Wheel Pull
Brillion Iron Works, Brillion, Wis.

Type of traction, crawler; fuel, gasoline or kerosene; belt h. p., 30; guaranteed drawbar h. p., 22; motor, Brillion opposed; number of cylinders, 2; cast singly; speed of motor, 400 r. p. m.; bore, $6\frac{3}{4}$ inches; stroke, 8 inches; 2 or 4-cycle, 4; transmission, gear; cooling system, water cooled; bearings, babbitt; carburetor, Wilcox, Bennett; ignition, Atwater-Kent; oiling system, automatic; length over all, 144 inches; width over all, 80 inches; height over all, 66 inches; number of wheels, 3; number of drive wheels, 2; diameter of drive wheels, 60 inches; face of drive wheels, 10 inches; how mounted, 8-inch channel; clutch, make and type, Brillion hub shoe expanding; control speeds, 2; speed on road, 2, $3\frac{3}{4}$ miles per hour; speed in furrow, 1, 2 miles per hour; diameter of pulley, 16 inches; face of pulley, 6 inches; capacity of fuel tank, 30 gallons; capacity of water tank, 10 gallons; front axle, 3 inches; diameter of crankshaft, $3\frac{1}{4}$ inches; weight, 5,200 pounds; price, $885 f. o. b. factory.

BUCKEYE MANUFACTURING CO.
Anderson, Indiana

Buckeye Junior   1916
Buckeye C. T. 4   1916-1917

Buckeye Junior
Buckeye Mfg. Co., Anderson, Ind.

Type of traction, wheel and crawler; fuel, gasoline; guaranteed belt h. p., 16; guaranteed drawbar h. p., 8; motor, special valve in head, tractor motor; number of cylinders, 4; cast en bloc; speed of motor, 1,000 r. p. m.; bore, 3¾ inches; stroke, 5 inches; 2 or 4-cycle, 4; transmission, gear; cooling system, vertical tubular radiator; bearings, ball and roller; carburetor, float feed with clarifier; ignition, Dixie; oiling system, splash and force; engine suspension, 3-point; length over all, 122 inches; width over all, 72 inches; height over all, 61 inches; number of wheels, 3; number of drive wheels, 1; diameter of drive wheels or crawlers, 36 inches; face of drive wheels, 16 inches; how mounted, special mounting; clutch, make and type, Buckeye expansion; control speeds, 1; speed on road, 2½ miles per hour; speed in furrow, 2½ miles per hour; diameter of pulley, 12 inches; face of pulley, 6 inches; capacity of fuel tank, 10 gallons; capacity of water tank, 3 gallons; diameter of crankshaft, 2 inches; weight, 4,000 pounds; price, $650 f. o. b. factory.

Buckeye, C. T. 4
Buckeye Mfg. Co., Anderson, Ind.

Type of traction, crawler; fuel, gasoline or kerosene; guaranteed belt h. p., 32; guaranteed drawbar h. p., 16; motor, Buckeye valve in head; number of cylinders, 4; cast en bloc; speed of motor, 9 1,000 r. p. m.; bore, 4¾ inches; stroke, 6 inches; 2 or 4-cycle, 4; transmission, gear; cooling system vertical tubular; bearings, Timkin; carburetor, standard float feed; ignition, Dixie magneto, oiling system, splash and force; engine suspension, 3-point; length over all, 120 inches; width over all, 66 inches height over all, 60 inches; number of wheels, 2 crawlers; number of drive wheels, 2 crawlers; face of drive wheels, 1 1-6 inches, clutch, make and type, Buckeye multiple disk; control speeds, 2; speed on road, 2½ miles per hour; speed in furrow, 2½ miles per hour; diameter of pulley, 12 inches; face of pulley, 8 inches; capacity of fuel tank, 20 gallons; capacity of water tank, 8 gallons; diameter of crankshaft, 2½ inches; weight, 6,000 pounds; price, $1,500 f. o. b. factory.

BULL TRACTOR CO.

Minneapolis, Minnesota

Big Bull   1916

Big Bull
Bull Tractor Co., Minneapolis, Minn.

Type of traction, wheel, fuel, gasoline or kerosene; guaranteed belt h. p., 20; guaranteed draw-bar h. p., 7; motor, Bull double opposed; number of cylinders, 2, cast singly; speed of motor, 620 to 720 r. p. m.; bore, $5\frac{1}{4}$ inches; stroke, 7 inches; 2 or 4-cycle, 4; transmission, gear; cooling system, water, pump and radiator; bearings, Hyatt and plain; carburetor, Kingston; ignition, Kingston; oiling system, Detroit oiler and splash; engine suspension, 4-point; length over all, 167 inches; width over all 77 inches; height over all, 75 inches; number of wheels, 3; number of drive wheels, 1; diameter of drive wheel, 60 inches; face of drive wheel, 14 inches; how mounted, solid; clutch, make and type, external contracting; control speeds, 1; speed on road, $2\frac{1}{2}$ to 3 miles per hour; speed in furrow, $2\frac{1}{2}$ to 3 miles per hour; diameter of pulley, 12 inches; face of pulley, $6\frac{1}{2}$ inches; capacity of fuel tank, $18\frac{1}{2}$ gallons; capacity of water tank, $8\frac{1}{2}$ gallons; front axle, 1.68 inches; rear axle, 2.93 inches; diameter of crank-shaft, $2\frac{3}{4}$ inches; weight, 4,750 pounds; price, $645 f. o. b. factory.

BULLOCK TRACTOR CO.
Chicago, Illinois

Creeping Grip 12-20   1916-1917

Creeping Grip 12-20
Bullock Tractor Co., Chicago, Ill.

Type of traction, crawler; fuel, gasoline; guaranteed belt h. p., 20; guaranteed drawbar h. p., 12; motor, Gile horizontal; number of cylinders, 2, cast separately; speed of motor, 750 r. p .m.; bore, 6 inches; stroke, $6\frac{1}{2}$ inches; 2 or 4-cycle, 4; transmission, gear; cooling system, force pump, for cooling radiator; bearings, bronze; carburetor, Bennett; ignition, high tension magneto; oiling system, light force feed; length over all, 108 inches; width over all, 81 inches; height over all, 78 inches; number of wheels, 2 crawlers; number of drive wheels, 2 crawlers; face of drive wheels, 12 inches; clutch, make and type, Strite expanding shoe; control speeds, 1; speed on road, $2\frac{1}{2}$ miles per hour; speed in furrow, $2\frac{1}{4}$ miles per hour; diameter of pulley, 12 inches; face of pulley, 8 inches; capacity of fuel tank, $17\frac{1}{2}$ gallons; capacity of water tank, 40 gallons; rear axle, $2\frac{11}{16}$ inches; diameter of crankshaft, ... inches; weight, 7,200 pounds; price, $1,250 f. o. b. factory.

J. I. CASE THRESHING MACHINE CO.
Racine, Wisconsin

Case 10-20	1916-1919
Case 12-25	1916-1918
Case 20-40	1916-1920
Case 30-60	1916-1918

Case 10-20
J. I. Case Threshing Machine Co., Racine, Wis.

Type of traction, wheel.............; fuel, gasoline; guranteed belt h. p., 20; guaranteed drawbar h. p., 10; motor, Case vertical, valve in head; number of cylinders, 4; cast en bloc; speed of motor, 800 r. p. m.; bore, $4^1/4$ inches; stroke, 6 inches; 2 or 4-cycle, 4; transmission, gear; cooling system, pump and truck type radiator; bearings, bronze shell, babbitt lined, carburetor, Kingston; ignition, Heinze; oiling system, pump and splash; engine suspension, 4-point; length over all, 150 inches; width over all, 67 inches; height over all, 60 inches; number of wheels, 3; number of drive wheels, 2; diameter of drive wheels, 52 inches; face of drive wheels 22 and 10 inches; how mounted, solid; clutch, make and type, Case, cone; control speeds, 1; speed on road, 2 miles per hour; speed in furrow, 2 miles per hour; diameter of pulley, 17 inches; face of pulley, $6^1/2$ inches; capacity of fuel tank, 20 gallons; capacity of water tank, 10 gallons; diameter of crankshaft, $2^1/8$ inches; special equipment, wheel lugs; weight, 4,900 pounds; price, $890 f. o. b. factory.

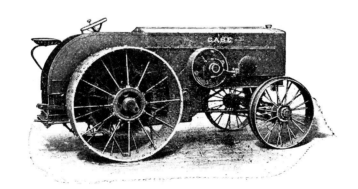

Case 12-25
J. I. Case Threshing Machine Co., Racine, Wis.

Type of traction, wheel ....; fuel, gasoline; guaranteed belt h. p., 25; guaranteed drawbar h. p., 12; motor, Case opposed, valve in head; number of cylinders, 2; cast singly; speed of motor, 600 r. p. m.; bore 7 inches; stroke, 7 inches; 2 or 4-cycle, 4; transmission, gear; cooling system, thermo-syphon; bearings, bronze shell, babbitt lined; carburetor, Kingston; ignition, Heinze; oiling system, force feed; engine suspension, 4-point; length over all, $148^3/4$ inches; width over all, 73 inches; height over all, 70 inches; number of wheels, 4; number of drive wheels, 2; diameter of drive wheels, 56 inches; face of drive wheels, 18 inches; how mounted, solid; clutch, make and type, Case expanding; control speeds, 2; speed on road, 2.2 miles per hour; speed in furrow, $1^3/4$ miles per hour; diameter of pulley, 22 inches; face of pulley, $7^1/2$ inches; capacity of fuel tank, 17 gallons; capacity of water tank, 15 gallons; diameter of crankshaft, $3^1/4$ inches; special equipment, wheel lugs, extension rims and 3-plow drawbar; weight, 9,000 pounds; price, $1,425 f. o. b. factory.

Case 20-40
J. I. Case Threshing Machine Co., Racine, Wis.

Type of traction, ... wheel; fuel, gasoline or kerosene; guaranteed belt h. p., 40; guaranteed drawbar h. p., 20; motor, Case opposed, valve in head; number of cylinders, 2; cast singly; speed of motor, 475 r. p. m.; bore, 8 inches; stroke, 9 inches; 2 or 4-cycle, 4; transmission, gear; cooling system, thermo-syphon; bearings, die cast and bronze shell; carburetor, Kingston; ignition, Heinze; oiling system, force feed; engine suspension, 4-point; length over all, 177 inches; width over all, 100 inches; height over all, 107 inches; number of wheels, 4; number of drive wheels, 2; diameter of drive wheels, 66 inches; face of drive wheels, 20 inches; how mounted, solid; clutch, make and type, Case expanding; control speeds, 2; speed on road, 3 miles per hour; speed in furrow, 2 miles per hour; diameter of pulley, 24 inches; face of pulley, 8½ inches; capacity of fuel tanks, 11 gallons gasoline, 26 gallons kerosene; capacity of water tank, 28 gallons; diameter of crankshaft, 3½ inches; special equipment, wheel lugs and extension rims; weight, 13,900 pounds; price, $2,100 f. o. b. factory.

Case 30-60
J. I. Case Threshing Machine Co., Racine, Wis.

Type of traction, wheel ....; fuel, gasoline or kerosene; guaranteed belt h. p., 60; guaranteed drawbar h. p., 30; motor, Case twin-cylinder, horizontal; number of cylinders, 2; cast singly; speed of motor, 365 r. p. m.; bore, 10 inches; stroke, 12 inches; 2 or 4-cycle, 4; transmission, gear; cooling system, pump and cooling tank; bearings, bronze shell, babbitt lined; carburetor, Kingston; ignition, Sumter; oiling system, force feed; engine suspension, 4-point; length over all, 223 inches; width over all, 105 inches; height over all, 126 inches; number of wheels, 4; number of drive wheels, 2; diameter of drive wheels, 72 inches; face of drive wheels, 24 inches; how mounted, solid; clutch, make and type, Case, expanding; control speeds, 1; speed on road, 2 miles per hour; speed in furrow, 2 miles per hour; diameter of pulley, 32 inches; face of pulley, 12½ inches; capacity of fuel tank, 90 gallons kerosene, 22 gallons gasoline; capacity of water tank, 170 gallons; diameter of crankshaft, 4½ inches; special equipment, extension rims for rear wheels; weight, 25,800 pounds; price, $2,650 f. o. b. factory.

CHASE MOTOR TRUCK CO.
Syracuse, New York

Chase 6-25   1916
Chase 35   1916

Chase 6-25
Chase Motor Truck Co., Syracuse, N.Y.

Type of traction drum; fuel, gasoline or kerosene; guaranteed belt h. p., 25; guaranteed drawbar h. p. 6; motor, ...; number of cylinders, 4; cast enbloc; speed of motor, 1200 r. p. m.; bore, $3\frac{1}{2}$ inches; stroke, $5\frac{1}{4}$ inches; 2 or 4-cycle, 4; transmission, spur gear; cooling system, water; bearings, bronze and plain; carburetor, Zenith; ignition, Bosch high tension; oiling system, pump and splash; engine suspension, 3 point; length over all, 144 inches; width over all, 76 inches; height over all, 58 inches; number of wheels, 3; number of drive wheels, 2; diameter of drive wheels, 48 inches; face of drive wheels, 22 inches; clutch, make and type, expanding jaw; control speeds, 3; speed on road, $1\frac{1}{2}$ to $2\frac{1}{2}$ miles per hour; speed in furrow, $1\frac{1}{2}$ to $2\frac{1}{2}$ miles per hour; diameter of pulley, 14 inches; face of pullley, 8 inches; capacity of fuel tank, 12 gallons; capacity of water tank, 5 gallons; front axle, 2 inches; rear axle, 3 inches; diameter of crankshaft, 2 inches; weight, 4,500 pounds.

Chase 35
Chase Motor Truck Co., Syracuse, N.Y.

Type of traction, drum; fuel, gasoline or kerosene; guaranteed belt h. p., 35; motor, Waukesha; number of cylinders, 4; cast in pairs; speed of motor, 800 r. p. m.; bore, $4\frac{1}{2}$ inches; stroke, $6\frac{3}{4}$ inches: 2 or 4-cycle, 4; transmission, chain; cooling system, radiator and pump; bearings, bronze and Timken; carburetor, Holly and Kingston; ignition, Remy; oiling system, force feed and splash; engine suspension, 4-point; length over all, 132 inches; width over all, 102 inches, height over all, 60 inches; number of drums, 3; number of drive drums, 2; diameter of drive drums, 36 inches; face of drive drums, 30 inches; clutch, make and type, Brown & Lipe; control speeds, 3; speed on road, 3 miles per hour; speed in furrow, $2\frac{1}{2}$ miles per hour; diameter of pulley, 14 inches; face of pulley, 8 inches; capacity of fuel tank, 25 gallons; capacity of water tank, 20 gallons; diameter of crankshaft, 2 inches; special equipment, orchard guards; weight, 6,000 pounds; price, $1,750 f. o. b. factory.

CLEVELAND HORSELESS FARM MACHINE CO.

Cleveland, Ohio

Baby Johnson   1916

Baby Johnson
Cleveland Horseless Farm Machine Co., Cleveland, O.

Type of traction, wheel; fuel, gasoline; guaranteed belt h. p., 29; guaranteed drawbar h. p., 27; motor, Continental; number of cylinders, 4, cast en bloc; speed of motor, 1000-2000 r. p. m.; bore, $3\frac{1}{2}$ inches; stroke, 5 inches; 2 or 4-cycle, 4; transmission, drum; cooling system, pump radiator and tank; bearings, ...; carburetor, K. D.; ignition Eiseman; oiling system, pump and splash; engine suspensions, 3-point; length over all, 140 inches; width over all, 74 inches; height over all, 58 inches; number of wheels, 3; number of driver wheels, 2; diameter of drive wheels, 36 inches; face of drive wheels, 24 inches; how mounted, spring; clutch, make and type, own make, disk; control speeds, 3; speed on road, 8-10 miles per hour; speed in furrow, $1\frac{1}{2}$-2 miles per hour; diameter of pulleys, 6 to 18 inches; face of pulley, 6 inches; capacity of fuel tank, 15 gallons; capacity of water tank, 10 gallons; front axle, 2 inches; rear axle, 2 inches; diameter of crankshaft, $2\frac{1}{4}$ inches; special equipment, $1\frac{1}{2}$-yard box and 65-foot cable for extracting tractor from stalled places; weight, 4,500 pounds; price, $1,250 f. o. b. factory.

C. O. D. TRACTOR CO.

Minneapolis, Minnesota

C. O. D. 13-25

1916-1919

C. O. D. 13-25

C. O. D. Tractor Co., Minneapolis, Minn.

Type of traction, wheel; fuel, gasoline and kerosene; guaranteed belt h. p., 25; guaranteed drawbar h. p., 13; motor, C. O. D. opposed; number of cylinders, 2; cast singly; speed of motor, 600 r. p. m.; bore, 6½ inches; stroke, 7 inches; 2 or 4-cycle, 2; transmission, gear; cooling system, water centrifugal circulating pump; bearings, bronze and babbitt; carburetor, Kingston, Bennett; ignition, Atwater, Kent batteries; oiling system, Detroit force feed; engine suspension, 3-point; length over all, 156 inches; width over all, 72 inches; height over all, 72 inches; number of wheels, 4; number of drive wheels, 2; diameter of drive wheels, 70 inches; face of drive wheels, 12 inches; how mounted, direct; clutch, make and type, C. O. D. cone; control speeds, 2; speed on road, 2½ miles per hour; speed in furrow, 2½ miles per hour; diameter of pulley, 18 inches; face of pulley, 8 inches; capacity of fuel tank, 18 gallons; capacity of water tank, 32 gallons; front axle, 2 inches; rear axle, 3 inches; diameter of crankshaft, 2¾ inches; special equipment, spade shaped corks for drive wheels; weight, 6,600 pounds; price, $785 f. o. b. factory.

COMMON SENSE TRACTOR CO.

Minneapolis, Minnesota

Common Sense 20-40

1916-1918

Common Sense 20-40

Common Sense Tractor Co., Minneapolis, Minn.

Type of traction, wheels; fuel, gasoline or kerosene; guaranteed belt h. p., 25; guaranteed drawbar h. p., 15; motor, vertical; number of cylinders, 4, cast en bloc; speed of motor, 960 r. p. m.; bore, 4½ inches; stroke, 5 inches; 2 or 4-cycle, 4; transmission, chain; cooling system, water forced draft; bearings, Hyatt; carburetor, Schebler; ignition, K.-W. high tension; oiling system, lever and splash; engine suspension, 3-point; length over all, 183 inches; width over all, 88 inches; height over all, 72 inches; number of wheels, 3; number of drive wheels, 1; diameter of drive wheels, 62 inches; face of drive wheels, 24 inches; how mounted, solid; clutch, make and type, Borge & Beck; control speeds, 4; speed on road, 1¾ to 3½ miles per hour; speed in furrow, 2½ miles per hour; diameter of pulley, 22 inches; face of pulley, 7½ inches; capacity of fuel tank, 37 gallons; capacity of water tank, 10 gallons; front axle, 2 inches; rear axle, 3 inches; diameter of crankshaft, 2 inches; weight, 6,000 pounds; price, $1,395 f. o. b. factory.

COMMONWEALTH TRACTOR CO.

Kansas City, Missouri

Neverslip   1916

Neverslip
Commonwealth Tractor Co., Kansas City, Mo.

Type of traction, crawler; fuel, gasoline or kerosene; guaranteed belt h. p., 20; guaranteed drawbar h. p., 12; motor, Gile opposed; number of cylinders, 2; cast separately; speed of motor, 700 r. p. m.; bore, 6 inches; stroke, $6^{1/2}$ inches; 2 or 4-cycle, 4; transmission, gear and chain; cooling system, water, gear driven pump; bearings, Hyatt; carburetor, Bennett; ignition, Dixie magneto; oiling system, Madison-Kipp, 6-point force feed; engine suspension, 3-point; length over all, 126 inches; width over all, 64 inches; height over all, with canopy 84 inches; number of wheels, 2 crawlers; number of drive wheels, 2 crawlers; length of crawler, 54 inches; face of drive wheels, 12 inches; how mounted, spring; clutch, make and type, expanding; control speeds, 4, 2 reverse; speed on road, $3^{1/4}$ miles per hour; speed in furrow, $2^{1/2}$ miles per hour; diameter of pulley, 10 inches; face of pulley, 8 inches; capacity of fuel tank, 16 gallons; capacity of water tank, 20 gallons; diameter of crankshaft, $2^{3/4}$ inches; weight, 5,400 pounds.

CORN BELT TRACTOR CO.

Minneapolis, Minnesota

Corn Belt   1916

Corn Belt
Corn Belt Tractor Co., Minneapolis, Minn.

Type of traction, wheel; fuel, gasoline; guaranteed belt h. p., 18; guaranteed drawbar h. p., 8; motor, Gile; number of cylinders, 2; cast opposed; speed of motor, 750 r. p. m.; bore, 5 inches; stroke, $6^{1/2}$ inches; 2 or 4-cycle, 4; transmission, friction; cooling system, water; bearings, ball and roller; carburetor, Kingston; ignition, Kingston high tension; oiling system, Madison Kipp; engine suspension, 4 point; length over all, 160 inches; width over all, 84 inches; height over all, 72 inches; number of wheels, 3; number of drive wheels, 1; diameter of drive wheels, 44 inches; face of drive wheels, 18 inches; how mounted, solid; clutch, make and type, own, expanding; control speeds, 10; speed on road, 1 to 5 miles per hour; speed in furrow $2^{1/4}$ to $2^{3/4}$ miles per hour; diameter of pulley, 12 inches; face of pulley, 7 inches; capacity of fuel tank, 20 gallons; capacity of radiator, 22 gallons; front axle, $2^{5/8}$ inches; rear axle, $2^{3/8}$ inches; diameter of crankshaft, $2^{5/8}$ inches; weight, 3,800 pounds; price, $750 f. o. b. factory.

DAUCH MANUFACTURING CO.

Sandusky, Ohio

Sandusky 15-35   1916-1921

Sandusky 15-35
Dauch Mfg. Co., Sandusky, O.

Type of traction, wheel; fuel, gasoline or kerosene; guaranteed belt h. p., 35; guaranteed drawbar h. p., 15; motor, own; number of cylinders, 4; cast singly; speed of motor, 750 r. p. m.; bore, 5 inches; stroke, 6½ inches; 2 or 4-cycle, 4; transmission, spur gear; cooling system, pump, fan and radiator; bearings, babbitt; carburetor, Kingston; ignition, Kingston; oiling system, force and splash; engine suspension, 4 point; length over all, 147 inches; width over all, 84 inches; height over all, 72 inches; number of wheels, 4; number of drive wheels, 2; diameter of drive wheels, 56 inches; face of drive wheels, 16 inches; how mounted, spring; clutch, make and type, own, expanding; control speeds, 4; speed on road, 2 to 5½ miles per hour; speed in furrow, 2 to 3 miles per hour; diameter of pulley, 15 inches; face of pulley, 9 inches; capacity of fuel tank, 35 gallons; capacity of water tank, 25 gallons; front axle, 2 inches; rear axle, 3 inches; diameter of crankshaft, 2½ inches; weight, 8,000 pounds; price, $2,000 f. o. b. factory.

DAYTON DICK CO.

Quincy, Illinois

Leader 9-15   1916
Leader 12-18   1916-1918
Leader 25-40   1916-1918

Leader 9-15
Dayton-Dick Co., Quincy, Ill.

Type of traction, wheel; fuel, gasoline or kerosene; guaranteed belt, h. p., 15; guaranteed drawbar h. p., 9; motor, opposed; number of cylinders, 2; cast separately; speed of motor, 750 r. p. m.; bore, 5¾ inches; stroke, 6 inches; 2 or 4-cycle, 4; transmission, gear; cooling system, open and enclosed types; bearings, bronze and babbitt; carburetor, Kingston-Bennett; ignition, Kingston; oiling system, Detroit force feed; height over all, 60 inches; number of wheels, 4; number of drive wheels, 2; diameter of drive wheels, 48 inches; face of drive wheels, 12 inches; how mounted, spring in front; clutch, make and type, shoe; control speeds, 3; speed on road, 3½ miles per hour; speed in furrow, 2-2½ miles per hour; diameter of pulley, 14 inches; face of pulley, 7 inches; capacity of fuel tank, 18 gallons; capacity of water tank, 9 gallons enclosed, 30 gallons open; diameter of crankshaft, 2½ inches; weight, 3,800 pounds; price, $525 f. o. b. factory.

Leader 12-18
Dayton-Dick Co., Quincy, Ill.

Type of traction, wheel; fuel, gasoline or kerosene; guaranteed belt h. p., 18; guaranteed drawbar h. p., 12; motor, opposed; number of cylinders, 2; cast separately; speed of motor, 750 r. p. m.; bore, 6¼ inches; stroke, 6 inches; 2 or 4-cycle, 4; transmission, chain; cooling system, open and enclosed types; bearings, bronze and babbitt; carburetor, Kingston-Bennett; ignition, Kingston; oiling system, Detroit force feed; height over all, 70 inches; number of wheels, 4; number of drive wheels, 2; diameter of drive wheels, 54 inches; face of drive wheels, 16 inches; how mounted, spring in front; clutch, make and type, cone; control speeds, 3; speed on road, 3½ miles per hour; speed in furrow, 2, 2½ miles per hour; diameter of pulley, 14 inches; face of pulley, 7 inches; capacity of fuel tank, 18; capacity of water tank, 9 gallons open, 30 gallons enclosed; diameter of crankshaft, 2½ inches; weight, 5,000 pounds; price, $890 f. o. b. factory.

Leader 25-40
Dayton-Dick Co., Quincy, Ill.

Type of traction, crawler; fuel, gasoline or kerosene; guaranteed belt h. p., 40; guaranteed drawbar h. p., 25; motor, vertical; number of cylinders, 4; cast separately; speed of motor, 750 r. p. m.; bore, 7 inches; stroke, 7 inches; 2 or 4-cycle, 4; transmission, chain; cooling system, open and inclosed type; bearings, bronze and babbitt; carburetor, Kingston-Bennett; ignition, Kingston; oiling system, Detroit force feed; height over all, 66 nches; number of wheels, 4; number of drive wheels, 2; diameter of drive wheels, 54 inches; face of drive wheels, 16 inches; how mounted, spring in front; clutch, make and type, cone; control speeds, 3; speed on road, 3½ miles per hour; speed in furrow, 2, 2½ miles per hour; diameter of pulley, 14 inches; face of pulley, 7 inches; capacity of fuel tank, 18 gallons; capacity of water tank, 9 gallons enclosed and 30 gallons open; diameter of crankshaft, 2½ inches; weight, 6,000 pounds; price, $1,550 f. o. b. factory.

DENNING TRACTOR CO.
Cedar Rapids, Iowa

Denning 10-18   1916-1917

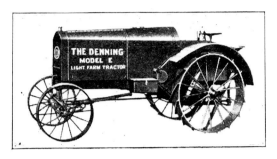

Denning 10-18
Denning Tractor Co., Cedar Rapids, Ia.

Type of traction, wheel; fuel, gasoline or kerosene; guaranteed belt h. p., 18; guaranteed drawbar h. p., 10; motor, Waukesha; number of cylinders, 4; cast en bloc; speed of motor, 1200 r. p. m.; bore, $3\frac{1}{2}$ inches; stroke, $5\frac{1}{4}$ inches; 2 or 4-cycle, 4; transmission, friction; cooling system, pump and Perfex radiator; bearings, plain or New Departure; carburetor, Bennett; ignition, Dixie magneto; oiling system, pump; engine suspension, 3-point; length over all, 120 inches; width over all, 56 inches; height over all, 61 inches; number of wheels, 4; number of drive wheels, 2; diameter of drive wheels, 46 inches; face of drive wheels, 10 inches; how mounted, spring; clutch, make and type, Rockwood; control speeds, variable; speed on road, $1\frac{3}{4}$ to $3\frac{1}{2}$ miles per hour; speed in furrow, $1\frac{3}{4}$ to $3\frac{1}{2}$ miles per hour; diameter of pulley, 10 inches; face of pulley, 6 inches; capacity of fuel tanks, 15 and 5 gallons; capacity of water tank, 7 gallons; diameter of crankshaft, 2 inches; special equipment, 8-inch extension rims; weight, 3,600 pounds; price, $800 f. o. b. factory.

DILL TRACTOR MANUFACTURING CO.
Harrisburg, Arkansas

Dill 20   1916-1918

Dill 20
Dill Tractor Mfg. Co., Harrisburg, Ark.

Type of traction, wheel or drum; fuel, gasoline; guaranteed belt ....; guaranteed drawbar h. p., 20; motor, Continental; number of cylinders, 4; cast singly; speed of motor, 800-1,500 r. p. m.; bore, $4\frac{1}{2}$ inches; stroke, $5\frac{1}{2}$ inches; 2 or 4-cycle, 4; transmission, spur gear and chain; cooling system, pump and radiator; bearings, Hyatt roller; carburetor, Carter; ignition, Bosch; oiling system, pump; engine suspension, 4 point; length over all, 192 inches; width over all, 104 inches; height over all, 68 inches; number of wheels, 4; diameter of drive wheels, 42 inches; face of drive wheels, 36 inches; how mounted, ...; clutch, make and type, Cotton; control speeds, 4; capacity of fuel tank, 12 gallons; rear axle, $2\frac{13}{16}$ inches; diameter of crankshaft, $1\frac{7}{8}$ inches; weight, 4,400 pounds; price, $2,400 f. o. b. factory.

EAGLE MANUFACTURING CO.
Appleton, Wisconsin

Eagle 12-22   1916-1921

Eagle 12-22
Eagle Mfg. Co., Appleton, Wis.

Type of traction, wheel; fuel, gasoline or kerosene; guaranteed belt h. p., 25; guaranteed drawbar h. p., 12; motor, ...; number of cylinders, 2; cast ....; speed of motor, 400 r. p. m.; bore, ... inches; stroke, ... inches; 2 or 4-cycle, 4; transmission, gear and chain; length over all, 120 inches; width over all, 70 inches; height over all, 60 inches; number of wheels, 4; number of drive wheels, 2; diameter of drive wheels, 44 inches; face of drive wheels, 14-12 inches; speed on road, 2½ miles per hour; speed in furrow, 2 miles per hour; diameter of pulley, 20 inches; face of pulley, 9 inches; capacity of fuel tanks, 20 gallons; capacity of water tank, 8 gallons; weight, 5,200 pounds; price, $1,000 f. o. b. factory.

ELECTRIC WHEEL CO.
Quincy, Illinois

Light All Work   1916-1917

Light All Work
Electric Wheel Co., Quincy, Ill.

Type of traction, wheel; fuel, gasoline or kerosene; guaranteed belt h. p., 25; guaranteed drawbar h. p., 12; motor, Model upright; number of cylinders, 4; cast singly; speed of motor, 750 r. p. m.; bore, 5 inches; stroke, 6 inches; 2 or 4-cycle, 4; transmission, gear; cooling system, radiator and fan; bearings, bronze, babbitt and roller; carburetor, Kingston; ignition, Swiss high tension magneto; oiling system, pump and splash; engine suspension, 3-point; length over all, 125 inches; width over all, 66 inches; height over all, 69 inches; number of wheels, 4; number of drive wheels, 2; diameter of drive wheels, 48 inches; face of drive wheels, 12 inches; clutch, make and type, friction disk; control speeds, 3; speed on road, 2½-3 miles per hour; speed in furrow, 2 4-10 miles per hour; diameter of pulley, 12 inches; face of pulley, 7 inches; capacity of fuel tank, 15 gallons; capacity of water tank, 12 gallons; diameter of crankshaft, 1⅞ inches; special equipment, extension for drivers (extra) and self-steering device (extra); weight, 4,800 pounds; price, $975 f. o. b. factory.

EMERSON-BRANTINGHAM CO.

Rockford, Illinois

Emerson Model L	1916
Big Four 20	1916
Big Four 30	1916

Emerson Model L
Emerson-Brantingham Co., Rockford, Ill.

Type of traction, wheel; fuel, gasoline and kerosene; guaranteed belt h. p., 20; guaranteed drawbar h. p., 12; motor, Big Four vertical; number of cylinders, 4; cast in pairs; speed of motor, 800 r. p. m.; bore, $4\frac{1}{2}$ inches; stroke, 5 inches; 2 or 4-cycle, 4; transmission, gear; bearings, Hyatt; carburetor, Bennett; ignition, K. W. Magneto high tension; oiling system, splash; engine suspension, 3-point; length over all, 180 inches; width over all, 96 inches; height over all, 63 inches; number of wheels, 3; number of drive wheels, 1; diameter of drive wheels, 60 inches; face of drive wheels, 24 inches; how mounted, spring; clutch, make and type, cone; control speeds, 2; speed on road, $1\frac{2}{3}$-$2\frac{1}{3}$ miles per hour; speed in furrow, $1\frac{2}{3}$-$2\frac{1}{3}$ miles per hour; diameter of pulley, $12\frac{1}{2}$ inches; face of pulley, 7 inches; capacity of fuel tank, 25 gallons; capacity of water tank, 9 gallons; diameter of crankshaft, $2\frac{3}{16}$ inches; weight, 5,000 pounds; price, $1,040 cash, $1,100 on time f. o. b. factory.

Big Four 20
Emerson-Brantingham Co., Rockford, Ill.

Type of traction, wheel; fuel, gasoline or kerosene; guaranteed belt h. p., 35; guaranteed drawbar h. p. 20; motor, own, vertical; number of cylinders, 4; cast in pairs; speed of motor, 700 r. p. m.; bore, 5 inches; stroke, 7 inches; 2 or 4-cycle, 4; transmission, gear; cooling system, radiator; bearings, Hyatt; carburetor, Bennett; ignition, K. W. high tension; oiling system, splash; engine suspension, 3-point; length over all, 196 inches; width over all, 76 inches; height over all, ...inches; number of wheels, 4; number of drive wheels, 2; diameter of drive wheels, 72 inches; face of drive wheels, 16 inches; how mounted, spring; clutch, make and type, cone; control speeds, 2; speed on road, 2.52-1.88 miles per hour; speed in furrow, 2.52-1.88 miles per hour; diameter of pulley, 16 inches; face of pulley, 9 inches; capacity of fuel tank, 35 kerosene, 5 gasoline gallons; capacity of radiator, 15 gallons; diameter of crankshaft, $2\frac{11}{16}$ inches; special equipment ....; weight, 10,800 pounds.

Big Four 30
Emerson-Brantingham Co., Rockford, Ill.

Type of traction, wheel; fuel, kerosene; guaranteed belt h. p., 55; guaranteed drawbar h. p., 30; motor, Big Four; number of cylinders, 4; cast, in pairs; 2 or 4-cycle, 4; transmission, gear; cooling system, radiator; length over all, 258 inches; width over all, 117 inches; height over all, 131 inches; number of wheels, 4; number of drive wheels; 2; diameter of drive wheels, $57\frac{1}{2}$ inches; face of drive wheels, 30 inches; control speeds, 4; speed on road, 3.33 miles per hour; speed in furrow, 2.22 miles per hour; diameter of pulley, $23\frac{1}{2}$ inches; face of pulley, 9 inches; capacity of fuel tank, 78 gallons; capacity of water tank, 170 gallons; weight, 22,725 pounds.

FAIRMONT GAS ENGINE AND RAILWAY MOTOR CAR CO.

Fairmont, Minnesota

Fairmont   1916

Fairmont
Fairmont Gas Engine and Railway Motor Car Co., Fairmont, Minn.

Type of traction, wheel; fuel, gasoline or kerosene; guaranteed belt h. p., 26; guaranteed drawbar h. p., 16; motor, Fairmont; number of cylinders, 1; speed of motor, 500 r. p. m.; bore, 8 inches; stroke, $8\frac{1}{2}$ inches; 2 or 4-cycle, 2; transmission, chain and gear; cooling system, thermo-syphon; bearings, babbitt and bronze; carburetor, Fairmont; ignition, jump spark; oiling system, splash; engine suspension, direct to main frame; length over all, 141 inches; width over all, 62 inches; height over all, 60 inches; number of wheels, 4; number of drive wheels, 2; diameter of drive wheels, 44 inches; face of drive wheels, 14 inches; clutch, make and type, cone in flywheel; control speeds, 2; speed on road, 3 miles per hour; speed in furrow, $1\frac{3}{4}$ miles per hour; diameter of pulley, 24 inches; face of pulley, $6\frac{1}{2}$ inches; capacity of fuel tank, 12 gallons; capacity of water tank, 30 gallons; front axle, $2\frac{1}{8}$ inches; rear axle, 4 inches; diameter of crankshaft, $2\frac{1}{2}$ inches; special equipment, special easy seat for driver, accommodates two persons; weight, 4,800 pounds.

36   1916

FARM ENGINEERING CO.
Sand Springs, Oklahoma

Little Chief   1916-1918

Little Chief
Farm Engineering Co., Sand Springs, Okla.

Type of traction, wheel; fuel, gasoline or kerosene; guaranteed belt h. p., 40; guaranteed drawbar h. p., 20; motor, own; number of cylinders, 4; cast enbloc; speed of motor, 800 r. p. m.; bore, $5\frac{1}{2}$ inches; stroke, 6 inches; 2 or 4-cycle, 4; transmission, spur gear; cooling system, pump and radiator; bearings, Hyatt roller; carburetor, ownll, 60 inches; height over all, 61 inches; number splash; length over all, $152\frac{1}{2}$ inches; width over a; ignition, Bosch high tension; oiling system, of wheels, 4; number of drive wheels, 2; diameter of drive wheels, 50 inches; face of drive wheels, 20 inches; clutch, make and type, multiple disk; control speeds, 4; speed on road, 4 miles per hour; speed in furrow, $2\frac{1}{4}$ miles per hour; diameter of pulley, 12 inches; face of pulley, 10 inches; capacity of fuel tank, 30 gallons; capacity of water tank, 30 gallons; diameter of crankshaft, $2\frac{3}{4}$ inches; special equipment, ...; weight, 4,500 pounds; price,$1,500 f. o. b. factory.

FARM HORSE TRACTOR WORKS
Hartford, South Dakota

Farm Horse Tractor 15-26   1916-1919

Farm Horse Tractor 15-26
Farm Horse Tractor Works, Hartford, S.D.

Type of traction, wheel; fuel, gasoline; guaranteed belt h. p., 30; guaranteed drawbar h. p., 15; motor, Model; number of cylinders, 4; cast singly; speed of motor, 800 r. p. m.; bore, 5 inches; stroke, 6 inches; 2 or 4-cycle, 4; transmission, spur gear and chain; cooling system, radiator; bearings, babbitt; carburetor, Kingston; ignition, Remy and Dixie; oiling system, splash; engine suspension, 4 point; length over all, 144 inches; width over all, 81 inches; height over all, 96 inches; number of wheels, 4; number of drive wheels, 2; diameter of drive wheels, 48 inches; face of drive wheels, 24 inches; how mounted, spring; clutch, make and type, Strite; control speeds, 3; speed on road, $2\frac{1}{2}$ to $3\frac{1}{2}$ miles per hour; speed in furrow, $2\frac{1}{2}$ to $3\frac{1}{2}$ miles per hour; diameter of pulley, 14 inches; face of pulley, 7 inches; capacity of fuel tank, 20 gallons; front axle, 2 inches; rear axle, $2\frac{11}{16}$ inches; diameter of crankshaft, $1\frac{7}{8}$ inches; price, $895 f. o. b. factory.

FOUR DRIVE TRACTOR CO.
Big Rapids, Michigan

Fitch Four Drive   1916-1918

Fitch Four Drive
Four Drive Tractor Co., Big Rapids, Mich.

Type of traction, wheel; fuel, gasoline or kerosene; guaranteed belt h. p., 35; motor, Waukesha heavy duty; number of cylinders, 4; bore, 4 inches; stroke, $5\frac{3}{4}$ inches; 2 or 4-cycle, 4; transmission, gear; cooling system, water pump; bearings,. . . . .; carburetor, Stromberg, Schebler & Bennett; ignition, Bosch, Splitdori high tension; oiling system, splash; engine suspension, 3-point; length over all, 72 inches; width over all, 68 inches; height over all, ... inches; number of wheels, 4; number of drive wheels, 4; diameter of drive wheels, 42-36 inches; face of drive wheels, 12 inches; clutch, make and type, dry disc; control speeds, 3; speed on road, 7, $4\frac{1}{2}$, 2 miles per hour; speed in furrow, 2 miles per hour; capacity of fuel tank, 20 gallons; weight, 3,000 pounds; price, $1,000; f. o. b. factory.

GRAY TRACTOR MANUFACTURING CO.
Minneapolis, Minnesota

Gray Model B   1916
Gray 18-36   1916-1921

Gray Model B
Gray Tractor Mfg. Co., Minneapolis, Minn.

Type of traction, wide drive drum; fuel, gasoline; guaranteed belt h. p., 25; guaranteed drawbar h. p. 15; motor, Waukesha vertical; number of cylinders, 4; cast in pairs; speed of motor, 800 r. p. m.; bore, $4\frac{1}{4}$ inches; stroke, $6\frac{3}{4}$ inches; 2 or 4-cycle, 4; transmission, chain; cooling system, water driven by centrifugal pump; bearings, Hyatt; carburetor, Wilcox-Bennett, ignition, K. W. high tension; oiling system, automatic splash; engine suspension, 4-point; length over all, 174 inches; width over all, 76 inches; height over all, 60 inches; number of wheels, 3; number of drive wheels, drive drum; diameter of drive wheels, 52 inches; face of drive wheels, 48 inches; how mounted, spring; clutch, make and type, Raybestos face cone; control speeds, 3; speed on road, 18-10 to 23-10 miles per hour; speed in furrow, 23-10 miles per hour; diameter of pulley, 11 inches; face of pulley, 7 inches; capacity of fuel tank, 30 gallons; capacity of water tank, 12 gallons; rear axle, 2 inches; diameter of crankshaft, 2 inches; special equipment, harrow arms attachment; weight, 5,500 pounds; price, $1,650 f. o. b. factory.

Gray 18-36
Gray Tractor Mfg. Co., Minneapolis, Minn.

Type of traction, wide drive drum; fuel, gasoline; guranteed belt h. p., 35; guaranteed drawbar h. p., 20; motor, Waukesha vertical; number of cylinders, 4; cast in pairs; speed of motor, 800 r. p. m.; bore, $4^{3}/4$ inches; stroke, $6^{3}/4$ inches; 2 or 4-cycle, 4; transmission, chain; cooling system, water driven by centrifugal pump; bearings, Hyatt; carburetor, Wilcox-Bennett; ignition, K. W. high tension; oiling system, automatic splash; engine suspension, 4-point; length over all, 203 inches; width over all, 96 inches; height over all, 72 inches; number of wheels, 3; number of drive wheels, 1 drive drum; diameter of drive wheel, 60 inches; face of drive wheel, 60 inches; how mounted, spring; clutch, make and type, Raybestos face cone; control speeds, 3; speed on road, $1^{1}/2$ to 2.1 miles per hour; speed in furrow, 2.1 miles per hour; diameter of pulley, 12 inches; face of pulley, 9 inches; capacity of fuel tank, 40 gallons; capacity of water tank, 15 gallons; rear axle, $2^{1}/2$ inches; diameter of crankshaft, 2 inches; special equipment, harrow arms attachment; weight, 8,000 pounds; price, $2,150 f. o. b. factory.

HAPPY FARMER TRACTOR CO.

Minneapolis, Minnesota

Happy Farmer   1916

Happy Farmer
Happy Farmer Tractor Co., Minneapolis, Minn.

Type of traction, wheel; fuel, gasoline; guaranteed belt h. p., 16; guaranteed drawbar h. p., 8; motor, opposed; number of cylinders, 2; bore, 5 inches; stroke, $6^{1}/2$ inches; 2 or 4-cycle, 4; transmission, gear; cooling system, water; bearings, bronze; carburetor, Bennett; ignition, Atwater-Kent; oiling system, pump feed; engine suspension, 4-point; length over all, 156 inches; width over all, 78 inches; number of wheels, 3; number of drive wheels, 2; diameter of drive wheels, 56 inches; face of drive wheels, 10 inches; how mounted, axle to frame; clutch, make and type, wood shoe; control speeds, 1; speed on road, $2^{1}/2$ miles per hour; speed in furrow, $2^{1}/2$ miles per hour; diameter of pulley, 11 inches; face of pulley, 6 inches; capacity of fuel tank, 15 gallons; capacity of water tank, 9 gallons; rear axle, 2 inches; diameter of crank shaft, $2^{1}/4$ inches; weight, 3,200 pounds; price, $550 f. o. b. factory.

HART-PARR CO.
Charles City, Iowa

Little Devil 25-22	1916-1917
Crop Maker 17-27	1916-1917
Oil King 23-35	1916-1919
Steel King	1916
Old Reliable 38-60	1916-1918

Little Devil 25-22
Hart-Parr Co., Charles City, Ia.

Type of traction, wheel; fuel; kerosene; guaranteed belt h. p., 22; guaranteed drawbar h. p., 15; motor, Hart-Parr horizontal; number of cylinders, 2; cast en bloc; speed of motor, 600 r. p. m.; bore, 5½ inches; stroke, 7 inches; 2 or 4-cycle, 2; transmission, gear; cooling system, thermo syphon water; bearings, Gurney ball and babbitt bushings; carburetor, Hart-Parr kerosene; ignition, Kingston; oiling system; automatic force feed; engine suspension, 3-point; length over all, 104 inches; width over all, 95½ inches; height over all, 84 inches; number of wheels, 3; number of drive wheels, 1; diameter of drive wheels, 64 inches; face of drive wheels, 26 inches; how mounted, solid; clutch, make and type, floating plate type; control speeds, 2; speed on road, 3⅓-2¼ miles per hour; speed in furrow, 3⅓-2¼ miles per hour; diameter of pulley, 16 inches; face of pulley, 7 inches; capacity of fuel tank, 23¾ gallons; capacity of water tank, 13¼ gallons; diameter of crankshaft, 2 3-16 inches; weight, 6,647 pounds.

Crop Maker 17-27
Hart-Parr Co., Charles City, Ia.

Type of traction, wheel; fuel, kerosene; guaranteed belt h. p., 27; guaranteed drawbar h. p. 17; motor, Hart-Parr vertical; number of cylinders, 1; speed of motor, 500 r. p. m.; bore, 8½ inches; stroke, 10 inches; 2 or 4-cycle, 4; transmission, gear; cooling system, oil cooled; bearings, U. S. ball, babbitt bushing; carburetor, Hart-Parr; ignition, Naxon coil jump spark! oiling system, Madison-Kipp automatic; engine suspension, 4-point; length over all, 107¾ inches; width over all, 72 inches; height over all, 125 inches; number of wheels, 4; number of drive wheels, 2; diameter of drive wheels, 74 inches; face of drive wheels, 12½ inches; how mounted, solid; clutch, make and type, floating plate type; control speeds, 2; speed on road, 1¾-2½ miles per hour; speed in furrow, 1¾-2½ miles per hour; diameter of pulley, 22 inches; face of pulley, 7 inches; capacity of fuel tank, 30 gallons; capacity of water tank, 20 gallons; diameter of crankshaft, 3¾ inches; special equipment, hold fast lugs; weight, 11,900 pounds.

Oil King 23-35
Hart-Parr Co., Charles City, Ia.

Type of traction, wheel; fuel, kerosene; guaranteed belt h. p., 35; guaranteed drawbar h. p., 23; motor, Hart-Parr vertical; number of cylinders, 1; speed of motor, 500 r. p. m.; bore, 10 inches; stroke, 10 inches; 2 or 4-cycle, 4; transmission, gear; cooling system, oil cooled; bearings, U. S. ball and babbitt bushing; carburetor, Hart-Parr; ignition, Naxon coil jump spark, oiling system, Madison-Kipp automatic; engine suspension, 4-point; length over all, $107^3/4$ inches; width over all, 72 inches; height over all, 125 inches; number of wheels, 4; number of drive wheels, 2; diameter of drive wheels, 74 inches; face of drive wheels, $12^1/2$ inches; how mounted, solid; clutch, make and type, floating plate type; control speeds, 2; speed on road, 1.8-2.6 miles per hour; speed in furrow, 1.8-2.6 miles per hour; diameter of pulley, $23^1/2$ inches; face of pulley, 9 inches, capacity of fuel tank, 30 gallons; capacity of water tank, 30 gallons; diameter of crankshaft, $3^3/4$ inches; special equipment, hold fast lugs; weight, 12,000 pounds.

Steel King
Hart-Parr Co., Charles City, Ia.

Type of traction, wheel; fuel, kerosene; guaranteed belt h. p., 40; guaranteed drawbar h. p., 27; motor, Hart-Parr vertical; number of cylinders, 2; cast separately; speed of motor, 400 r. p. m.; bore, 8 inches; stroke, 12 inches; 2 or 4-cycle, 4; transmission, gear; cooling system, oil cooled; bearings, Hess Bright ball with babbitt blushing; carburetor, Hart-Parr; ignition, K. W. high and low tension; oiling system, Madison-Kipp automatic; engine suspension, 4-point; length over all, 191 inches; width over all, 95 inches; number of wheels, 3; number of drive wheels, 2; diameter of drive wheels, 73 inches; face of drive wheels, 20 inches; how mounted, spring; clutch, make and type, 3 friction blocks; control speeds, 2; speed on road, 2.2—4 miles per hour; speed in furrow, 2 2-10 miles per hour; diameter of pulley. 30 inches; face of pulley, 9 inches; capacity of fuel tank, 50 gallons; capacity of water tank, 50 gallons; diameter of crankshaft, $3^3/4$ inches; weight, 15,870 pounds.

Old Reliable 38-60
Hart-Parr Co., Charles City, Ia.

Type of traction, wheel; fuel, kerosene; guaranteed belt h. p., 60; guaranteed drawbar h. p., 38; motor, Hart-Parr horizontal; number of cylinders, 2; cast separately; speed of motor, 300 r. p. m.; bore, 10 inches; stroke, 15 inches; 2 or 4-cycle, 4; transmission, gear; cooling system, oil cooled; bearings, Hart-Parr babbitt bushings; carburetor, Hart-Parr; ignition, K. W. high and low tension; oiling system, Madison Kipp automatic; engine suspension, 4-point; length over all, 200 inches; width over all, 106 inches; height over all, 148 inches; number of wheels, 4; number of drive wheels, 2; diameter of drive wheels, 66 inches; face of drive wheels, 24 inches; how mounted, solid; clutch, make and type, 3 friction blocks; control speeds, 1; speed on road, 2 3-10 miles per hour; speed in furrow, 2 3-10 miles per hour; diameter of pulley, 40 inches; face of pulley, 12 inches; capacity of fuel tank, 50 gallons; capacity of water tank, new 50 gallons, old 24 gallons; front axle, 3 inchees; rear axle, 5 inches; diameter of crankshaft, 4 inches; weight 20,100 pounds.

HOKE TRACTOR CO.

South Bend, Indiana

Hoke   1916

Hoke
Hoke Tractor Co., South Bend, Ind.

Type of traction, wheel; fuel, gasoline; guaranteed belt h. p., 21; motor, Waukesha; number of cylinders, 4; cast en bloc; speed of motor, 800 r. p m.; bore, 4¼ inches; stroke, 5¾ inches; 2 or 4-cycle, 4; transmission, chain; cooling system, pump water; bearings, Bower roller; carburetor, air friction; ignition, Eisemann high tension; oiling system, force feed; engine suspension, 3-point; height over all, 72 inches; number of wheels, 3; number of drive wheels, 2; diameter of drive wheels, 60 inches; face of drive wheels, 12 inches; how mounted, spring; clutch, make and type, Hoke expanding; control speeds, 1; speed on road, 2 to 4 miles per hour; speed in furrow, 2½ miles per hour; diameter of pulley, 10 inches; face of pulley, 8 inches; capacity of fuel tank, 20 gallons; capacity of water tank, 8 gallons; special equipment, plows, connecting iron for binder, mower, etc.

HOLT MANUFACTURING CO.

Peoria, Illinois and Stockton, California

Caterpillar 25-45   1916-1919
Caterpillar 50-75   1916-1919

Caterpillar 25-45
Holt Mfg. Co., Peoria, Ill., and Stockton, Cal.

Type of traction, Caterpillar track; fuel, gasoline; guaranteed belt h. p., 45; guaranteed drawbar h. p., 25; motor, Holt valve in head; number of cylinders, 4; cast singly; speed of motor, 600 r. p. m.; bore, .. inches; stroke, .. inches; 2 or 4-cycle, ..; transmission, gear; cooling system, water; bearings, Hyatt; carburetor, Kingston; ignition, K. W.; oiling system, splash, force feed; engine suspension, 4-point; length over all, 153 inches; width over all, $74\frac{1}{2}$ inches; height over all, 70 inches; width of caterpillar tracks, 13 inches; how mounted, spring; clutch, make and type, Holt dry disk; control speeds, 4, 2 reverse; speed on road, $2\frac{1}{8}$ to $3\frac{1}{2}$ miles per hour; speed in furrow $2\frac{1}{8}$ miles per hour; diameter of pulley, 14 inches; face of pulley, 9 inches; capacity of fuel tank, $48\frac{1}{2}$ gallons; capacity of water tank, 9 gallons; diameter of crankshaft, $2\frac{13}{16}$ inches; special equipment, electric lights; weight, 13,500 pounds; price, $3,000 f. o. b. factory.

Caterpillar 50-75
Holt Mfg. Co., Peoria, Ill., and Stockton, Cal.

Type of traction, Caterpillar track; fuel, gasoline; belt h. p., 75; guaranteed drawbar h. p., 50; motor, Holt valve in head; number of cylinders, 4; cast singly; speed of motor, 550 r. p. m.; bore, $7\frac{1}{8}$ inches; stroke, 8 inches; 2 or 4-cycle, 4; transmission, chain; cooling system, water; bearings, Hyatt; carburetor, Kingston; ignition, Kiv. high tension; oiling system, force and splash; engine suspension, 4-point; length over all, 240 inches; width over all, 104 inches; height over all, 120 inches; how mounted, spring; clutch, make and type, Holt dry disk; control speeds, 3; speed on road, $2\frac{1}{8}$-3 miles per hour; speed in furrow, $2\frac{1}{8}$ miles per hour; diameter of pulley, 22 inches; face of pulley, 14 inches; capacity of fuel tank, 74 gallons; capacity of water tank, 53 gallons; diameter of crankshaft, $3\frac{1}{8}$ inches; special equipment, electric lights and Stewart vacuum feed; weight, 23,600 pounds; price, $4,500 single speed and $4,750 double speed, f. o. b. factory.

HUBER MANUFACTURING CO.

Marion, Ohio

Huber 20-40   1916
Huber 30-60   1916

Huber 20-40
Huber Mfg. Co., Marion, O.

Type of traction, wheel; fuel, gasoline or kerosene; guaranteed belt h. p. 40; guaranteed drawbar h. p., 20; motor, Huber opposed; number of cylinders, 2; cast singly; speed of motor, 550 r. p. m.; bore, 8 inches; stroke, 9 inches; 2 or 4-cycle, 4; transmission, chain; cooling system, water; bearings, Huber; carburetor Kingston; ignition, Stor pump spark; oiling system, splash; length over all, 179 inches; width over all, 87 inches; height over all, 94 inches; number of wheels, 4; number of drive wheels, 2; diameter of drive wheels, 68 inches; face of drive wheels, 20 inches; how mounted, solid; clutch, make and type, Huber, balanced; control speeds, 3; speed on road, $3\frac{1}{4}$ miles per hour; speed in furrow, 2 miles per hour; diameter of pulley, 21 inches; face of pulley, 9 inches; capacity of fuel tank, 45 gallons; capacity of water tank, 48 gallons; front axle, $2\frac{1}{4}$ inches; rear axle, $3\frac{1}{2}$ inches; diameter of crankshaft, $3\frac{1}{2}$ inches; weight, 12,500 pounds; price, $1,800 f. o. b. factory.

Huber 30-60
Huber Mfg. Co., Marion, O.

Type of traction, wheel; fuel, gasoline or kerosene; guaranteed belt h. p., 60; guaranteed drawbar h. p., 30; motor, Huber vertical; number of cylinders, 4; cast singly; speed of motor, 550-600 r. p. m.; bore, $7\frac{1}{4}$ inches; stroke, 8 inches; 2 or 4-cycle, 4; transmission, chain; cooling system, water; bearings, Huber; carburetor, Kingston; ignition, Remy; oiling system, splash; length over all, 254 inches; width over all, 116 inches; height over all, 106 inches; number of wheels, 4; number of drive wheels, 2; diameter of drive wheels, 96 inches; face of drive wheels, 30 inches; how mounted, solid; clutch, make and type, Huber balanced; control speeds, 3; speed on road, $3\frac{1}{2}$ miles per hour; speed in furrow, 2 miles per hour; diameter of pulley, 24 inches; face of pulley, 12 inches; capacity of fuel tank, 65 gallons; capacity of water tank, 95 gallons; front axle, 3 inches; rear axle, 5 inches; diameter of crankshaft, $3\frac{1}{4}$ inches, weight, 23,200 pounds; price, $3,000 f. o. b. factory.

HUME MANUFACTURING CO.
Hume, Illinois

Hume, Jr.   1916
Hume 20-30   1916

Hume, Jr.
Hume Mfg. Co., Hume, Ill.

Type of Traction, wheel; fuel, gasoline; guaranteed belt h. p., 12; guaranteed drawbar h. p., 18; motor, Waukesha; number of cylinders, 4; cast en bloc; speed of motor, 1200 r. p. m.; bore, $3\frac{1}{2}$ inches; stroke, $5\frac{1}{4}$ inches; 2 or 4-cycle, 4; transmission, gear; cooling system, centrifugal water pump; bearings, Hyatt roller and U. S. ball; carburetor, Kingston; ignition, Eisemann high tension; oiling system, automatic splash; engine suspension, 3-point; length over all, 144 inches; width over all, $66\frac{1}{2}$ inches; height over all, 84 inches; number of wheels, 3; number of drive wheels, 2; diameter of drive wheels, 66 inches; face of drive wheels, 16 inches; how mounted, live axle; clutch, make and type, Hume non-grab expanding; control speeds, 2; speed on road, $2\frac{3}{4}$ miles per hour; speed in furrow, $2\frac{3}{4}$ miles per hour; diameter of pulley, 9 inches; face of pulley 6 inches; capacity of fuel tank, 25 gallons; front axle, $1\frac{3}{4}$ inches; rear axle, $2\frac{3}{4}$ inches; diameter of crankshaft, 2 inches; special equipment, self steering device, Perfex radiator; weight, 4,200 pounds price, $895 f. o. b. factory.

Hume 20-30
Hume Mfg. Co., Hume, Ill.

Type of traction, wheel; fuel, gasoline; guaranteed belt h. p., 30; guaranteed drawbar h. p., 20; motor, Waukesha; number of cylinders, 4; cast en bloc; speed of motor, 800 r. p. m.; bore, $4\frac{3}{4}$ inches; stroke, $6\frac{3}{4}$ inches; 2 or 4-cycle, 4; transmission, gear; cooling system, centrifugal water pump; bearings, U. S. ball; carburetor, Holly; ignition, Eisemann; oiling system, automatic splash; engine suspension, 4-point; length over all, 150 inches; width over all, 74 inches; height over all, 97 inches; number of wheels, 3; number of drive wheels, 2; diameter of drive wheels, 72 inches; face of drive wheels, 18 inches; how mounted, dead axle; clutch, make and type, Waukesha; control speeds, 1; speed on road, $2\frac{1}{4}$ miles per hour; speed in furrow, $2\frac{1}{4}$ miles per hour; diameter of pulley, 10 inches; face of pulley, 7 inches; capacity of fuel tank, 25 gallons; front axle, $2\frac{3}{4}$ inches; rear axle, $3\frac{1}{2}$ inches; diameter of crankshaft, 2 inches; special equipment, Perfex radiator, weight, 7,000 pounds; price, $1,350 f. o. b. factory.

IMPERIAL MACHINERY CO., INC.
Minneapolis, Minnesota

Imperial   1916-1917

Imperial
Imperial Machinery Co., Inc., Minneapolis, Minn.

Type of traction, wheel; fuel, gasoline; guaranteed belt h. p., 75; guaranteed drawbar h. p., 40; motor, Imperial; number of cylinders, 4; cast in pairs; speed of motor, 400 r. p. m.; bore, $7\frac{1}{2}$ inches; stroke, 9 inches; 2 or 4-cycle, 4; cooling system, standard radiator and fan; bearings, babbitt; carburetor, Kingston; ignition, high tension magneto; oiling system, sight feed, force pump; length over all, 209 inches; width over all, 110 inches; number of wheels, 4; number of drive wheels, 2; diameter of drive wheels, 96 inches; face of drive wheels, 24 or 30 inches; clutch, make and type, Imperial internal expanding; control speeds, 3; speed on road, 3 miles per hour; speed in furrow, $2\frac{1}{4}$ miles per hour; diameter of pulley, 30 inches; face of pulley, 12 inches; capacity of fuel tank, 70 gallons; capacity of water tank, 40 gallons; rear axle, $5\frac{1}{2}$ inches; diameter of crankshaft, $3\frac{1}{4}$ to $4\frac{3}{4}$ inches; weight, 21,000 pounds, price, $3,000 f. o. b. factory.

INDEPENDENT HARVESTER CO.
Plano, Illinois

Independent   1916-1917

Independent
Independent Harvester Co., Plano, Ill.

Type of traction, wheel; fuel, kerosene; guaranteed belt h. p., 20; guaranteed drawbar h. p., 12; number of cylinders, 4; speed of motor, 900 r. p. m.; 2 or 4-cycle, 4; transmission, gear; cooling system, Perfex radiator; bearings, Hyatt roller, carburetor, Bennett; ignition, magneto; number of wheels, 4; number of drive wheels, 2; diameter of drive wheels, 54 inches; face of drive wheels, 10 inches; speed on road, 3 miles per hour; speed in furrow, $2\frac{3}{4}$ miles per hour; diameter of pulley, 14-16 inches; face of pulley, 5 inches; capacity of fuel tank, 21 gallons; weight, 3,500 pounds; price, $1,000 f. o. b. factory.

INTERNATIONAL GAS ENGINE CO.
Cudahy, Wisconsin

Ingeco Farm Type   1916

46   1916

Ingeco Farm Type
International Gas Engine Co., Cudahy, Wis.

Type of traction, wheel; fuel, kerosene; guaranteed belt h. p., 20; guaranteed drawbar h. p., 10; motor, Ingeco opposed; number of cylinders, 2; cast separately; speed of motor, 650 r. p. m.; bore, 5¾ inches; stroke, 7 inches; 2 or 4-cycle, 4; transmission, chain; cooling system, radiator fan and pump; bearings, babbitt; carburetor, Kingston; ignition, Dixie high tension; oiling system, force feed; engine suspension, rests on channels; length over all, 168 inches; width over all, 72 inches; height over all, 72 inches; number of wheels, 4; number of drive wheels, 1; diameter of drive wheels, 69 inches; face of drive wheels, 16 inches; how mounted, solid; clutch, make and type, ...; control speeds, 1; speed on road, 3 miles per hour; speed in furrow, 2½ miles per hour; diameter of pulley 14 inches; face of pulley, 8 inches; capacity of fuel tank, 25 gallons; capacity of water tank, 11 gallons; diameter of crankshaft, 2¾ inches; weight, 5,000 pounds; price, $700 f. o. b. factory.

INTERNATIONAL HARVESTER CO.

Chicago, Illinois

Mogul 8-16	1916-1917
Mogul 12-25	1916-1917
Titan 15-30	1916-1917
Titan 30-60	1916-1917

Mogul 8-16
International Harvester Co., Chicago, Ill.

Type of traction, wheel; fuel, gasoline, kerosene, distillate, naphtha or motor spirits; guaranteed belt h. p., 16; guaranteed drawbar h. p., 8; speed of motor, 400 r. p. m.; 2 or 4-cycle, 4; transmission, ...; oiling system, mechanically oiled; length over all, 135 inches; width over all, 56 inches; height over all, 61 inches; number of wheels, 4; number of drive wheels, 2; diameter of drive wheels, ...; diameter of pulley, 20 or more inches; capacity of fuel tank, 19 gallons; capacity of water tank, 35 gallons; front axle, ...inches; rear axle, ...inches; diameter of crankshaft, ...inches; special equipment, self steering device, pulleys, extension rims, etc.; weight, 5,000 pounds.

Mogul 12-25
International Harvester Co., Chicago, Ill.

Type of traction, wheel; fuel, kerosene, distillate, naphtha, motor spirits or gasoline; guaranteed belt h. p., 25; guaranteed drawbar h. p., 12; number of cylinders, 2; speed of motor, 550 r. p. m.; length over all, 162 inches; width over all, 81 inches; height over all, 100 inches; number of wheels, 4; number of drive wheels, 2; how mounted, spring; diameter of pulley, 18 inches; capacity of fuel tank, 30 gallons kerosene; weight, 9,850 pounds.

Titan 15-30
International Harvester Co., Chicago, Ill.

Type of traction, wheel; fuel, kerosene, distillate and all high grade fuels; guaranteed belt h. p., 30; guaranteed drawbar h. p., 15; number of cylinders, 4; speed of motor, 575 r. p. m.; 2 or 4-cycle, 4; oiling system, force feed; length over all, 140½ inches; width over all, 85 inches; height over all, 118 inches; number of wheels, 4; number of drive wheels, 2; diameter of pulley, 22 inches; capacity of fuel tank, 29 gallons; special equipment, steering device, pulleys, extension tires and lugs; weight, 9,580 pounds.

Titan 30-60
International Harvester Co, Chicago, Ill.

Four wheels, driving from two rear wheels. Length 202 inches, width 205 inches, height 132 inches. Weight 20,830 lbs. Diameter of drive wheel 72 inches, face 24 inches. Horizontal twin cylinder, valve-in-head motor, 9x14, r.p.m. 335 normal. Special kerosene mixer carburetor. Low tension ignition. Rotary pump, fan and radiator. Madison-Kipp force sight feed lubrication. One speed forward and reverse, 2.08 m.p.h. Sliding gear speed change.

JOLIET OIL TRACTOR CO.
Joliet, Illinois

Steel Mule 13-30   1916-1918

Steel Mule 13-30
Joliet Oil Tractor Co., Joliet, Ill.

Two wheels and one crawler, driving from crawler in rear center. Recommended for three 14″ plows, 28″ thresher. Height 68¾ inches, face of crawler 15 inches; total traction surface 720 sq. in. Weight 5,600 lbs. Price $985. Vertical four cylinder motor, cast en bloc, 4x6, r.p.m. 900 normal, valve-in-head. Bennett kerosene carburetor. Dixie high tension independent magneto with impulse starter. Centrifugal pump, fan and tubular radiator. Babbitt transmission bearings. Force sight feed lubrication. Two forward, one reverse speed, 2¼ to 3½ m.p.h. Selective sliding gear speed change, enclosed. Chain final drive. Machined steel gearing.

K. C. HAY PRESS CO.
Kansas City, Missouri

K.C. Prairie Dog   1916

K. C. Prairie Dog
K. C. Hay Press Co., Kansas City, Mo.

Type of traction, wheel; fuel, gasoline or kerosene; guaranteed belt h. p., 25; guaranteed drawbar h. p., 12; motor, Waukesha; number of cylinders, 4; cast in pairs; speed of motor, 800 r. p. m.; bore, $4\frac{1}{4}$ inches; stroke, $5\frac{3}{4}$ inches; 2 or 4-cycle, 4; transmission, gears; cooling system, pump circulation; bearings, Hyatt roller; carburetor, Schebler; ignition, Eisemann magneto; oiling system, splash; engine suspension, 3-point; length over all, 180 inches; width over all, 88 inches; height over all, 72 inches; number of wheels, 3; number of drive wheels, 1; diameter of drive wheels, 60 inches; face of drive wheels, 18 inches; how mounted, spring; clutch, make and type, positive expanding; control speeds, 3; speed on road, 5 miles per hour; speed in furrow, 2 1-3 miles per hour; diameter of pulley, 22 inches; face of pulley, 8 inches; capacity of fuel tank, 22 gallons; capacity of water tank, 5 gallons; front axle, $2\frac{1}{4}$ inches; rear axle, $2\frac{7}{16}$ inches; diameter of crankshaft, 2 inches; weight, 5,500 pounds; price, $1,000 f. o. b. factory.

KILLEN-STRAIT MANUFACTURING CO.
Appleton, Wisconsin

Strait's Tractor, Model 3   1916-1918
Strait's Motor Tractor   1916

Strait's Tractor, Model 3
Killen-Strait Mfg. Co., Appleton, Wis.

Type of traction, crawler; fuel, gasoline; guaranteed belt h. p., 25; guaranteed drawbar h. p., 15; motor, Waukesha vertical; number of cylinders, 4; cast in pairs; speed of motor in r. p. m., 900; bore, $4\frac{1}{4}$ inches; stroke, $5\frac{3}{4}$ inches; 2 or 4-cycle, 2; transmission, gear; cooling system, radiator; bearings, bronze; carburetor, Holly; ignition, high tension magneto; length over all, 130 inches; width over all, $71\frac{1}{2}$ inches; clutch, make and type, cone faced with raybestos; control speed, 2; speed on road, $1\frac{1}{2}$ to $3\frac{1}{2}$ miles per hour; speed in furrow, 2 miles per hour; diameter of pullye, 10 inches; face of pulley, 7 inches; capacity of fuel tank, 12 gallons; capacity of water tank, $8\frac{1}{2}$ gallons; weight, 6,000 pounds.

Strait's Motor Tractor
Killen-Strait Mfg. Co., Appleton, Wis.

Type of traction, crawler; fuel, gasoline or kerosene; guaranteed belt h. p., 50; guaranteed draw-bar h. p., 30; speed of motor, 900 r. p. m.; bore, 4¾; stroke, 6¾; 2 or 4-cycle, 4; transmission, gear; bearings, babbitt; carburetor, Holly; ignition, high tension; oiling system, automatic; length over all, 156 inches; width over all, 72, 84, 96 inches; height over all, 72 inches; how mounted, spring; clutch, make and type, sliding cone, raybestos faced; control speeds, 3; speed on road, 2 to 3 miles per hour; speed in furrow, 2 to 3 miles per hour; diameter of pulley, 10 inches; face of pulley, 7½ inches; capacity of fuel tank, 30 gallons; capacity of water tank, 15 gallons; weight, 9,000 pounds.

JOHN LAUSON MANUFACTURING CO.

New Holstein, Wisconsin

Lauson 15-25   1916-1919
Lauson 20-35   1916

Lauson 15-25
John Lauson Mfg. Co., New Holstein, Wis.

Four wheels, driving from two front wheels. Recommended for three 14" plows, 24" thresher. Length 133 inches, width 74 inches, height 91 inches. Diameter of drive wheels 54 inches, face 12 inches. Weight 5,000 lbs. Vertical four cylinder motor, cast en bloc, 4x6, r. p. m. 950 normal, valve-in-head. Kingston kerosene and gasoline carburetor. Dixie high tension independent magneto. Centrifugal pump, fan and Perfex cellular radiator. Splash lubrication. Enclosed speed change. Machined semi-steel gearing. Hyatt roller transmission bearings.

Lauson 20-35
John Lauson Mfg. Co., New Holstein, Wis.

Type of traction, wheel; fuel, gasoline or kerosene; guaranteed belt h. p., 35; guaranteed drawbar h. p., 20; motor, valve in head, vertical; number of cylinders, 4; speed of motor, 700 r. p. m.; bore, 4¾ inches; stroke, 6 inches; 2 or 4-cycle, 4; transmission, gear; cooling system, honeycomb radiator; bearings, Hyatt roller; carburetor, Kingston; ignition, Dixie magneto; oiling system, splash and force feed; engine suspension, 4-point; length over all, 161 inches; width over all, 84 inches; height over all, 103 inches; number of wheels, 4; number of drive wheels, 2; diameter of drive wheels, 66 inches; face of drive wheels, 16 inches; how mounted, solid; clutch, make and type, Lauson; control speeds, 2; speed on road, 2½ miles per hour; speed in furrow, 2½ miles per hour; diameter of pulley, 20 inches; face of pulley, 8 inches; capacity of fuel tank, 20 gallons; capacity of water tank, 12 gallons; special equipment, enclosed dust proof hood hinged on both sides and large roomy cab; weight, 7,300 pounds.

LION TRACTOR CO.

Minneapolis, Minnesota

Lion   1916-1917

Lion
Lion Tractor Co., Minneapolis, Minn.

Type of traction, wheel; fuel, gasoline; guaranteed belt h. p., 16; guaranteed drawbar h. p., 8; motor, Gile opposed; number of cylinders, 2; speed of motor, 750 r. p. m.; bore, 5 inches; stroke, 6½ inches; 2 or 4-cycle, 4; transmission, gear; cooling system, auto type, water; bearings, bronze and babbitt; carburetor, Bennett; ignition, Kingston magneto and batteries; oiling system, Madison-Kipp; length over all, 124 inches; width over all, 78 inches; height over all, 65 inches; number of wheels, 3; number of drive wheels, 2; diameter of drive wheels, 60 inches; face of drive wheels, 10 inches; how mounted, underslung axle; clutch, make and type, Bierman internal expanding; control speeds, 2; speed on road, 3-3½ miles per hour; speed in furrow, 2 1-3 miles per hour; diameter of pulley, 12 inches; face of pulley, 6 inches; capacity of fuel tank, 12 gallons; front axle, 2⅝ inches; diameter of crankshaft, 2¼ inches; special equipment, Bennett carburetor air cleaner; weight, 3,600 pounds; price, $565 f. o. b. factory.

MAYER BROS. CO.

Mankato, Minnesota

Little Giant Model A   1916-1926
Little Giant Model B   1916-1927

Little Giant Model A
Mayer Bros. Co., Mankato, Minn.

Four wheels, driving from two rear wheels. Recommended for five to six 14″ plows, length 150 inches, width 75 inches, height 72 inches. Diameter of drive wheels 54 inches, face 20 inches. Weight 8,700 lbs. Price $2300. Vertical four cylinder motor, cast in pairs, $5^1/_4 \times 6$, r.p.m. 750 normal, L-Head. Schebler or H&N gasoline, kerosene and distillate carburetor. K-W or Dixie high tension independent magneto. Centrifugal pump, fan and Perfex cellular radiator. Pressure feed and splash lubrication. Three forward and one reverse speeds, $1^1/_2$ to 6 m.p.h. Selective sliding gear speed change, enclosed. Bevel gear final drive, enclosed. Machined chrome steel. Nine Hyatt roller bearings in transmission and Hyatt rollers in all wheels. Coil springs in drive axle.

Little Giant Model B
Mayer Bros. Co., Mankato, Minn.

Type of traction wheel; fuel, gasoline, alcohol or kerosene; guaranteed belt h. p., 22; guaranteed drawbar h. p., 16; motor, Mayer Bros. L-Head; number of cylinders, 4; cast pairs; speed of motor, 900 r. p. m.; bore, $4\frac{1}{4}$ inches; stroke, 5 inches; 2 or 4-cycle; 4; transmission, gear; cooling system, water; bearings, Hyatt; carburetor, buyer's choice; ignition, K. W.; oiling system, force feed and splash; engine suspension, 3-point; length over all, 130 inches; width over all, 55 inches; height over all, 60 inches; number of wheels, 4; number of drive wheels, 2; diameter of drive wheels, 54 inches; face of drive wheels, 14 inches; how mounted, springs; clutch, make and type, cone; control speeds, 4; speed on road, 6 miles per hour; speed in furrow, $3-1\frac{1}{2}$ miles per hour; diameter of pulley, 9 inches; face of pulley, 7 inches; capacity of fuel tank, 25 gallons main, reserve 5 gallons; capacity of water tank, 8 gallons; diameter of crankshaft, 2 inches; special equipment, head and tail lights and extension rims; weight, 5,200 pounds; price, $1,250 f. o. b. factory.

McINTYRE MANUFACTURING CO.
Columbus, Ohio

Farmer Boy 10-20   1916-1917

Farmer Boy 10-20
McIntyre Mfg. Co., Columbus, Ohio.

Three wheeled, driving from one rear wheel. Recommended for two or three 14″ plows, 28″ thresher. Diameter of drive wheel 50 inches, face 12 inches. Length 130 inches, width 52 inches, height 50 inches. Weight 3,200 lbs. Price $850. Waukesha vertical four cylinder L-Head motor, cast en bloc, $3\frac{3}{4} \times 5\frac{1}{4}$, r.p.m. 1,000 normal. Kingston double gasoline or kerosene carburetor. High tension independent magneto, automatic. Centrfiugal pump, fan and Candler cellular radiator. Pressure feed and splash lubrication. One speed forward and reverse, 1 to 4 m.p.h. Bevel gear speed change, enclosed. Spur gear final drive. Machine steel gearing. S K F ball countershaft and transmission bearings. Roller bearings in drive wheel.

MINNEAPOLIS STEEL & MACHINERY CO.
Minneapolis, Minnesota

Twin City 15-30   1916-1919
Twin City 25-45   1916-1920
Twin City 40-65   1916-1925
Twin City 60-95   1916-1918

Twin City 15-30
Minneapolis Steel & Machinery Co., Minneapolis, Minn.

Type of traction, wheel; fuel, kerosene, distillate or gasoline; guaranteed belt h. p., 30; guaranteed drawbar h. p., 15; motor, Twin City vertical; number of cylinders, 4; cast in pairs; speed of motor, 650 r. p. m.; bore, $4\frac{3}{4}$ inches; stroke, 7 inches; 2or 4-cycle, 4; transmission, gear; cooling system, water forced; bearings, babbitt; carburetor, Bennett; ignition, K. W. high tension; oiling system, Detroit force feed; length over all, 180 inches; width over all, 60 inches; height over all, 120 inches; number of wheels, 4; number of drive wheels, 2; diameter of drive wheels, 60 inches; face of drive wheels, 14 inches; how mounted, spring; clutch, make and type, contracting band; control speeds, 2; speed on road, $1\frac{3}{4}$ to $3\frac{1}{2}$ miles per hour; speed in furrow, $1\frac{3}{4}$ to $3\frac{1}{2}$ miles per hour; diameter of pulley, 16 inches; face of pulley, 7 inches; capacity of fuel tank, 32 gallons; capacity of water tank, 50 gallons; rear axle, $3\frac{1}{2}$ inches; diameter of crankshaft, $2\frac{1}{2}$ inches; weight, 7,650 pounds.

Twin City 25-45
Minneapolis Steel & Machinery Co., Minneapolis, Minn.

Type of traction, wheel; fuel, gasoline, kerosene or distillate; guaranteed belt h. p., 45; guaranteed drawbar h. p., 25; motor, Twin City vertical; number of cylinders, 4; cast in pairs; speed of motor, 600 r. p. m.; bore, 6 inches; stroke, 8 inches; 2 or 4-cycle, 4; transmission, gear; cooling system, water; bearings, babbitt; carburetor, Bennett; ignition, high tension; oiling system, Detroit force feed; length over all, 220 inches; width over all, 80 inches; height over all, 125 inches; number of wheels, 4; number of drive wheels, 2; diameter of drive wheels, 84 inches; face of drive wheels, 20 inches; how mounted, springs; clutch, make and type, contracting band; control speed, 2; speed on road, $1\frac{3}{4}$-$3\frac{1}{2}$ miles per hour; speed in furrow, $1\frac{3}{4}$ to $3\frac{1}{2}$ miles per hour; diameter of pulley, 20 inches; face of pulley, $8\frac{1}{2}$ inches; capacity of fuel tank, 66 gallons; capacity of water tank, 86 gallons; rear axle, 4 inches; diameter of crankshaft, 3 inches; weight, 15,500 pounds.

Twin City 40-65
Minneapolis Steel & Machinery Co., Minneapolis, Minn.

Type of traction, wheel; fuel, kerosene, distillate or gasoline; guaranteed belt h. p., 65; guaranteed drawbar h. p., 40; motor, Twin City vertical; number of cylinders, 4; cast singly; speed of motor, 500 r. p. m.; bore, $7\frac{1}{4}$ inches; stroke, 9 inches; 2 or 4-cycle, 4; transmission, gear; cooling system, water; bearings, babbitt; carburetor, Bennett; ignition, high tension; oiling system, Detroit force feed; length over all, 238 inches; width over all, 98 inches; height over all, 122 inches; number of wheels, 4; number of drive wheels, 2; diameter of drive wheels, 84 inches; face of drive wheels, 24 inches; how mounted, springs; clutch, make and type, Twin City contracting band; control speeds, 1; speed on road, 2 miles per hour; speed in furrow, 2 miles per hour; diameter of pulleys, $23\frac{1}{4}$ inches; face of pulley, $10\frac{1}{2}$ inches; capacity of fuel tank, 86 gallons; capacity of water tank, 115 gallons, rear axle, 5 inches; diameter of crankshaft, $3\frac{1}{2}$ inches; weight, 23,300 pounds.

Twin City 60-95

Minneapolis Steel & Machinery Co., Minneapolis, Minn.

Type of traction, wheel; fuel, kerosene, gasoline or distillate; guaranteed belt h. p., 95; guaranteed drawbar h. p., 60; motor, Twin City vertical; number of cylinders, 6; cast singly; speed of motor, 500 r. p. m.; bore, $7\frac{1}{4}$ inches; stroke, 9 inches; 2 or 4-cycle, 4; transmission, gear; cooling system, water; bearings, babbitt; carburetor, Bennett; ignition, high tension; oiling system, Detroit force feed; length over all, $262\frac{1}{2}$ inches; width over all, $110\frac{1}{2}$ inches; height over all, 122 inches; number of wheels, 4; number of drive wheels, 2; diameter of drive wheels, 84 inches; face of drive wheels, 30 inches; how mounted, spring; clutch, make and type, contracting band; control speeds, 1; speed on road, 2 miles per hour; speed in furrow, 2 miles per hour; diameter of pulley, $23\frac{1}{4}$ inches; face of pulley, $10\frac{1}{2}$ inches; capacity of fuel tank, 86 gallons; capacity of water tank, 120 gallons; rear axle, $5\frac{3}{4}$ inches; diameter of crankshaft, $3\frac{1}{2}$ inches; special equipment; weight, 27,100 pounds.

MINNEAPOLIS THRESHING MACHINE CO.

Hopkins, Minnesota

Minneapolis 15   1916
Minneapolis 20   1916-1918
Minneapolis 25   1916
Minneapolis 40   1916-1918

Minneapolis 15

Minneapolis Threshing Machine Co., Hopkins, Minn.

Type of traction, wheel; fuel, gasoline; guaranteed drawbar h. p., 15; motor, vertical; number of cylinders, 4; cast en bloc; speed of motor, 750 r. p. m.; bore, $4\frac{1}{4}$ inches; stroke, 7 inches; 2 or 4-cycle, 4; transmission, gear; length over all, 168 inches; width over all, 72 inches; height over all, ... inches; number of wheels, 3; number of drive wheels, 2; diameter of drive wheels, 56 inches; face of drive wheels, 10 and 20 inches; control speeds, 2; speed on road, 3 miles per hour; speed in furrow, $2\frac{1}{4}$ miles per hour; diameter of pulley, 15 inches; face of pulley, $6\frac{1}{2}$ inches; capacity of fuel tank, $18\frac{1}{2}$ gallons; weight, 5,600 pounds.

Minneapolis 20
Minneapolis Threshing Machine Co., Hopkins, Minn.

Type of traction, wheel; fuel, gasoline or kerosene; guaranteed drawbar h. p., 20; motor, horizontal; number of cylinders, 4; cast separately; speed of motor, 650 r. p. m.; bore, 5¾ inches; stroke, 7 inches; 2 or 4-cycle, 4; transmission, gear; carburetor, standard make; ignition, K. W. high tension; oiling system, pump and splash; length over all, 167 inches; width over all, 96 inches; height over all, 110½ inches; number of wheels, 4; number of drive wheels, 2; diameter of drive wheels, 62 inches; face of drive wheels, 20 inches; control speeds; 2; speed on road, 2¼ miles per hour; speed in furrow, 2 miles per hour; diameter of pulley, 20 inches; face of pulley, 10 inches; capacity of fuel tank, 30 gallons; rear axle, 3 7-16 inches; diameter of crankshaft, 3 inches; weight, 12,000 pounds.

Minneapolis 25
Minneapolis Threshing Machine Co., Hopkins, Minn.

Type of traction, wheel; fuel, gasoline or kerosene; guaranteed drawbar h. p., 25; motor, vertical; number of cylinders, 4; cast separately; speed on motor, 550 r. p. m.; bore, 6 inches; stroke, 8 inches; 2 or 4-cycle, 4; transmission, gear; cooling system, water; carburetor, standard make; ignition, K. W. high tension; oiling system, force feed and splash; number of wheels, 4; number of drive wheels, 2; diameter of drive wheels, 85 inches; face of drive wheels, 24 inches; speed on road, 2½ miles per hour; diameter of pulley, 28 inches; face of pulley, 10 inches; weight, 17,000 pounds.

Minneapolis 40
Minneapolis Threshing Machine Co., Hopkins, Minn.

Type of traction, wheel; fuel, gasoline or kerosene; guaranteed drawbar h. p., 40; motor, horizontal; number of cylinders, 4; cast in pairs; speed of motor, 500 r. p. m.; bore, $7\frac{1}{4}$ inches; stroke, 9 inches; 2 or 4-cycle, 4; transmission, gear; cooling system, water; bearings, brass; carburetor, Standard make; ignition, K. W. high tension; oiling system, force feed and splash; length over all, 206 inches; width over all, 108 inches; height over all, 136 inches; number of wheels, 4; number of drive wheels, 2; diameter of drive wheels, 85 inches; face of drive wheels, 30 inches; control speeds, 2; speed on road, $2\frac{1}{2}$ miles per hour; speed in furrow, 2 miles per hour; diameter of pulley, 24 inches; face of pulley, $10\frac{1}{4}$ inches; capacity of fuel tank, 80 gallons; diameter of crank shaft, $3\frac{3}{4}$ inches; weight, 22,500 pounds.

MOLINE PLOW CO.

Moline, Illinois

Moline Universal Model D   1916-1923

Moline Universal Model D
Moline Plow Co., Moline, Ill.

Type of traction, wheel; fuel, gasoline; guaranteed belt h. p., 10-12; guaranteed drawbar h. p., 5-6; motor, Moline universal; number of cylinders, 2; cast en bloc; speed of motor, 800-1200 r. p. m.; bore, $4\frac{3}{4}$ inches; stroke, 6 inches; 2 or 4-cycle, 4; transmission, gear; cooling system, water and air, honeycomb radiator, pump and fan; bearings, Hyatt; carburetor, Holly; ignition, Dixie high tension; oiling system, automatic force feed; engine suspension, 2-point; length over all, 133 inches; width over all, 54 inches; height over all, 53 inches; number of wheels, 2; number of drive wheels, 2; diameter of drive wheels, 52 inches; face of drive wheels, 9 inches; how mounted, solid; clutch, make and type, cone faced with asbestos; speed on road, $\frac{1}{2}$ to 3 miles per hour; speed in furrow, $\frac{1}{2}$ to 3 miles per hour; diameter of pulley, 8 inches; face of pulley, 7 inches; capacity of fuel tank, 6 gallons; capacity of water tank, 5 gallons; diameter of crankshaft, $2\frac{1}{2}$ inches; special equipment, extension rims; weight, 2,800 pounds; price, $700.00, with rear truck $735.00, with 2 14-inch bottoms, $790.00 f. o. b. factory.

NATIONAL PULLEY & MANUFACTURING CO.
Chicago, Illinois

Paramount 10-20   1916
Paramount 12-25   1916

Paramount 10-20
National Pulley & Mfg. Co., Chicago, Ill.

Type of traction, wheel; fuel, gasoline, kerosene or distillate; guaranteed belt h. p., 18-20; guaranteed drawbar h. p., 9-10; motor, Waukesha or Beaver; number of cylinders, 4; speed of motor, 850 to 1,200 r. p. m.; bore, $3\frac{1}{2}$, $3\frac{3}{4}$ inches; stroke, $5\frac{1}{4}$, 5 inches; 2 or 4-cycle, 4; transmission, gear; cooling system, force circulation; bearings, Hyatt; carburetor, Bennett; ignition, Dixie high tension; oiling system, splash; engine suspension, crosswise to tractor frame; length over all, 144 inches; width over all, 72 inches; height over all, 60 inches; number of wheels, 3; number of drive wheels, 1; diameter of drive wheels, 54 inches; face of drive wheels, 24 inches; how mounted, solid; clutch, make and type, ...; control speeds, 2; speed on road, $2\frac{1}{4}$, 3 miles per hour; speed in furrow, $2\frac{1}{4}$, $2\frac{1}{2}$ miles per hour; diameter of pulley, 7 inches; face of pulley, 7 inches; capacity of fuel tank, 15 gallons; capacity of water tank, 30 gallons; front axle, 2 inches; rear axle, 3 inches; diameter of crankshaft, 2 inches; special equipment, floating drawbar, extra large gears, Bennett air cleaner; weight, 3,800 pounds; price, gasoline $785, kerosene, $800 f. o. b. factory.

Paramount 12-25
National Pulley & Mfg. Co., Chicago, Ill.

Type of traction, wheel; fuel, gasoline, distillate or kerosene; guaranteed belt h. p., 25; guaranteed drawbar h. p., 12; motor, Waukesha; number of cylinders, 4; cast in pairs; speed of motor, 750 to 1,000 r. p. m.; bore, $4\frac{1}{4}$ inches; stroke, $5\frac{3}{4}$ inches; 2 or 4-cycle, 4; transmission, gear; cooling system, force circulation; bearings, Hyatt; carburetor, Bennett; ignition, Dixie high tension; oiling system, splash; engine suspension, to frame; length over all, 144 inches; width over all, 78 inches; height over all, 60 inches; number of wheels, 3; number of drive wheels, 1; diameter of drive wheels, 54 inches; face of drive wheels, 24 inches; how mounted, solid; clutch, make and type, expansion shoe; control speeds, 2; speed on road, $2\frac{1}{4}$, 3 miles per hour; speed in furrow, $2\frac{1}{4}$, $2\frac{1}{2}$ miles per hour; diameter of pulley, 10 inches; face of pulley, 7 inches; capacity of fuel tank, 15 gallons; capacity of water tank, 30 gallons; front axle, 2 inches; rear axle, 3 inches; diameter of crankshaft, 2 inches; special equipment, floating drawbar, extra large gear faces in transmission; weight, 4,000 pounds; price, gasoline $900, kerosene $950 f. o. b. factory.

NEW AGE TRACTOR CO.

Minneapolis, Minnesota

New Age

1916-1917

New Age
New Age Tractor Co., Minneapolis, Minn.

Type of traction, wheel; fuel, gasoline, guaranteed belt h. p., 18; guaranteed drawbar h. p., 10. motor, Gile; number of cylinders, 2; cast separately; speed of motor 800 r. p. m.; bore, 5 inches; stroke, $6\frac{1}{2}$ inches; 2 or 4-cycle, 4; transmission, gear; cooling system, water, circulating pump and fan; bearings, Hyatt; carburetor, Bennett; ignition, Kingston; oiling system, force feed; engine suspension, 2-point; length over all, 160 inches; width over all, 76 inches; height over all, 64 inches; number of wheels, 3; number of drive wheels, 2; diameter of drive wheels, 60 inches; face of drive wheels, 10 inches; how mounted, solid; clutch, make and type, Bierman; control speeds, 1; speed on road, $2\frac{1}{2}$ miles per hour; speed in furrow, $2\frac{1}{2}$ miles per hour; diameter of pulley, 12 inches; face of pulley, 6 inches; capacity of fuel tank, 15 gallons; capacity of water tank, 3 gallons; diameter of crankshaft, $2\frac{3}{4}$ inches; weight, 4,000 pounds.

NILSON FARM MACHINE CO.

Minneapolis, Minnesota

Nilson 25 hp

1916-1917

Nilson 25 H.P.
Nilson Farm Machine Co., Minneapolis, Minn.

Type of traction, wheel; fuel, gasoline or kerosene; guaranteed belt h. p., 40; guaranteed drawbar h. p., 24; motor, Waukesha; number of cylinders, 4; cast in pairs; speed of motor, 800 r. p. m.; bore, $4\frac{3}{4}$ inches; stroke, $6\frac{3}{4}$ inches; 2 or 4-cycle, 4; transmission, chain; cooling system, Perfex radiator; bearings, Hyatt; carburetor, Kingston; ignition, K. W. impulse starter; oiling system, automatic splash; engine suspension, 3-point; length over all, 165 inches; width over all, 82 inches; number of wheels, 3; number of drive wheels, 1; diameter of drive wheels, 52 inches; face of drive wheels, 23 inches; how mounted, spring; clutch, make and type, Bierman; control speeds, 2; speed on road, 5, 6 miles per hour; speed in furrow, $2\frac{1}{3}$ miles per hour; diameter of pulley, 18 inches; face of pulley, 8 inches; capacity of fuel tank, 24 gallons; rear axle, $2\frac{7}{8}$ inches; diameter of crankshaft, $1\frac{1}{4}$ inches; price, $1,485 f. o. b. factory.

OLIN GAS ENGINE CO.

Buffalo, New York

Olin

1916

Olin
Olin Gas Engine Co., Buffalo, N.Y.

Type of traction, crawler; fuel, gasoline or kerosene; guaranteed belt h. p., 25; guaranteed drawbar h. p., 13; motor, Peerless; number of cylinders, 4; cast in pairs; speed of motor, 400 to 650 r. p. m.; bore, 5 inches; stroke, 6 inches; 2 or 4-cycle, 4; transmission, ...; cooling system, honeycomb radiator; bearings, Hyatt and die cast; carburetor, Kingston; ignition, Kingston; oiling system, force feed; engine suspension, steel channel; length over all, 132 inches; width over all, 48-72 inches; height over all, 63 inches; number of wheels, 2 and crawler; number of drive wheels, 1 crawler; clutch, make and type, Bierman expanding shoe; control speeds, 1; speed on road, $1\frac{1}{2}$-3 miles per hour; speed in furrow, $1\frac{1}{2}$-3 miles per hour; diameter of pulley, 13 inches; face of pulley, 10 inches; capacity of fuel tank, 20 gallons; diameter of crankshaft, $1\frac{3}{4}$ inches; weight, 4,800 pounds; price, $1,200 f. o. b. factory.

PARRETT TRACTOR CO.

Chicago, Illinois

Parrett All Purpose

1916

Parrett All Purpose
Parrett Tractor Co., Chicago, Ill.

Type of traction, wheel; fuel, gasoline or kerosene; guaranteed belt h. p., 20; guaranteed drawbar h. p., 10; motor, Buda vertical; number of cylinders, 4; cast en bloc; speed of motor, 900 r. p. m.; bore, $4\frac{1}{4}$ inches; stroke, $5\frac{1}{2}$ inches; 2 or 4-cycle, 4; transmission, gear; cooling system, pump; bearings, babbitt; carburetor, Kingston; ignition, high tension; oiling system, splash and pump; engine suspension, 3-point; length over all, 108 inches; width over all, 72 inches; height over all, 96 inches; number of wheels, 4; number of drive wheels, 2; diameter of drive wheels, 60 inches; face of drive wheels, 10 inches; how mounted, ...; clutch, make and type, cone; control speeds, 2; speed on road, 4 miles per hour; speed in furrow, $2\frac{3}{8}$ miles per hour; diameter of pulley, 15 inches; face of pulley, 7 inches; capacity of fuel tank, 18 gallons; capacity of water tank, 5 gallons; front axle, ... inches; rear axle, $2\frac{5}{8}$ inches; diameter of crankshaft, $2\frac{1}{8}$ inches; special equipment, one set of lugs; weight, 5,000 pounds; price, $1,075 f. o. b. factory.

PEORIA TRACTOR CO.

Peoria, Illinois

Peoria   1916

Peoria

Peoria Tractor Co., Peoria, Ill.

Type of traction, wheel; fuel, kerosene; guaranteed belt h. p., 20; guaranteed drawbar h. p., 8; motor, Beaver; number of cylinders, 4; cast in pairs; speed of motor, 700-1,000 r. p. m.; bore, 3¾ inches; stroke, 5 inches; 2 or 4-cycle, 4; transmission, spur gear; cooling system, Eureka radiator; bearings, babbitt; carburetor, Stromberg; ignition, Eisemann magneto; oiling system, Beaver; engine suspension, 4 point; length over all, 164 inches; width over all, 66 inches; height over all, 68 inches; number of wheels, 3; number of drive wheels, 1; diameter of drive wheels, 60 inches; face of drive wheels, 18 inches; clutch, make and type, own, expanding shoe; control speeds, 2; speed on road, 1 to 3 miles per hour; speed in furrow, 2½ to 3 miles per hour; diameter of pulley, 12 inches; face of pulley, 6 inches; capacity of fuel tank, 12 gallons; capacity of water tank, 5 gallons; front axle, 2 inches; rear axle, 4½ inches; diameter of crankshaft, 2 inches; weight, 3,950 pounds; price, $685 f. o. b. factory.

PIONEER TRACTOR CO.

Winona, Minnesota

Pioneer Pony   1916
Pioneer Junior   1916
Pioneer 40-75   1916

Pioneer Pony

Pioneer Tractor Co., Winona, Minn.

Type of traction, wheel; fuel, gas or kerosene; guaranteed belt h. p., 30; guaranteed drawbar h. p., 15; motor, own; number of cylinders, 4; cast, pairs; speed of motor, 650 r. p. m.; bore, 5 inches; stroke, 6 inches; 2 or 4-cycle, 4; transmission, spur gear; cooling system, radiator; bearings, babbitt; carburetor, Kingston; ignition, K-W; oiling system, force; length over all, 158 inches; width over all, 96 inches; height over all, 64 inches; number of wheels, 4; number of drive wheels, 1; diameter of drive wheels, 60 inches; face of drive wheels, 24 inches; how mounted, solid; clutch, make and type, Pioneer contracting; control speeds, 3; speed on road, 2¼-4 miles per hour; speed in furrow, 2 miles per hour; diameter of pulley, 10; inches; face of pulley, 8 inches; capacity of fuel tank, 33 gallons; diameter of crankshaft, 2½ inches; weight, 6,000 pounds; price, $765.00 f. o. b. factory.

Pioneer Junior
Pioneer Tractor Co., Winona, Wis.

Type of traction, wheel; fuel, gas or kerosene; guaranteed belt h. p., 45; guaranteed drawbar h. p., 20; motor, own; number of cylinders, 4; cast, pairs; speed of motor, 625 r. p. m.; bore, 6 inches; stroke, 7 inches; 2 or 4-cycle, 4; transmission, spur gear; cooling system, radiator; bearings, babbitt; carburetor, Kingston; ignition, K-W high tension; oiling system, Detroit force feed; length over all, 157 inches; width over all, 87 inches; height over all, 64 inches; number of wheels, 4; number of drive wheels, 2; diameter of drive wheels, 72 inches; face of drive wheels, 20 inches; how mounted, spring; clutch, make and type, Pioneer multiple disk; control speeds, 5; speed on road, 2-5½ miles per hour; speed in furrow, 2-2¼ miles per hour; diameter of pulley, 14 inches; face of pulley, 10 inches; capacity of fuel tank, 60 gallons; rear axle, 3 7-16 inches; diameter of crankshaft, 3 inches; weight, 11,000 pounds; price, $1,750 f. o. b. factory.

Pioneer 40-75
Pioneer Tractor Co., Winona, Wis.

Type of traction, wheel; fuel, gas or kerosene; guaranteed belt h. p., 75; guaranteed drawbar h. p., 40; motor, Hoe Opp; number of cylinders, 4; cast, pairs, speed of motor, 625 r. p. m.; bore, 6 inches; stroke, 7 inches; 2 or 4-cycle, 4; transmission, spur gear; cooling system, radiator; bearings, Todd babbitt; carburetor, Kingston; ignition, K-W high tension; oiling system, Detroit force feed; engine suspension, ; length over all, 237 inches; width over all, 120 inches; height over all, 144 inches; number of wheels, 4; number of drive wheels, 2; diameter of drive wheels, 96 inches; face of drive wheels, 24 inches; how mounted, spring clutch; make and type, Pioneer multiple disk; control speeds, 4; speed on road, 2-6 miles per hour; speed in furrow, $1^7/8$-$2^1/4$ miles per hour; diameter of pulley, $17^1/2$ inches; face of pulley, 15 inches; capacity of fuel tank, 25 gallons; rear axle, 4 7-16 inches; diameter of crankshaft, $3^1/2$ inches; weight, 22,000 pounds; price, $2,850 f. o. b. factory.

ROCK ISLAND PLOW CO.
Rock Island, Illinois

Heider  1916

Heider
Rock Island Plow Co., Rock Island, Ill.

Type of traction, wheel; fuel, kerosene, gasoline or motor spirits; guaranteed belt h. p., 20; guaranteed drawbar h. p. 10; motor, Waukesha; number of cylinders, 4; cast in pairs; speed of motor, 100 to 800 r. p. m.; bore, 4½ inches; stroke, 6¾ inches; 2 or 4-cycle, ..; transmission, friction; cooling system, Perfex radiator; bearings, U. S. ball; carburetor, Kingston; ignition, Kingston magneto and batteries; oiling system, splash; engine suspension, 4-point; length over all, 144 inches; width over all, 74 inches; height over all, 96 inches; number of wheels, 4; number of drive wheels, 2; diameter of drive wheels, 57 inches; face of drive wheels, 10 inches; how mounted, solid; clutch, make and type, friction; control speeds 7; speed on road, 4 miles per hour; speed in furrow, 2¼ miles per hour; diameter of pulley, 14 inches; face of pulley, 7 inches; capacity of fuel tank, 26 gallons; capacity of water tank, 10 gallons; diameter of crankshaft, 2 inches; special equipment, extra mud lugs; weight, 5,800 pounds; price, $995 f. o. b. factory.

THE RUSSELL & CO.
Massillon, Ohio

Russell 12-24   1916-1919

Russell 12-24
The Russell & Co., Massillon, O.

Type of traction, wheel; fuel, gasoline or kerosene; guaranteed belt h. p., 24; guaranteed drawbar h. p., 12; motor, own; number of cylinders, 4; cast singly; speed of motor, 950 r. p. m.; bore, $4\frac{1}{4}$ inches; stroke, $5\frac{1}{2}$ inches; 2 or 4-cycle, 4; transmission, sliding jaw clutch; cooling system, Perfex radiator; bearings, roller; carburetor, Kingston dual; ignition, Bosch high tension; oiling system, Madison-Kipp; engine suspension, 4 point; length over all, 139 inches; width over all, 67 inches; height over all, 74 inches; number of wheels, 4; number of drive wheels, 2; diameter of drive wheels, 53 inches; face of drive wheels, 10 inches; how mounted, spring; clutch, make and type, own, 2-shoe; control speeds, 4; speed on road, $2\frac{1}{2}$ to $3\frac{3}{4}$ miles per hour: speed in furrow, $2\frac{1}{2}$ miles per hour; diameter of pulley, $12\frac{1}{2}$ inches; face of pulley, 7 inches; capacity of fuel tank, 20 gallons; front axle, $2\frac{1}{4}$ inches; rear axle, $2\frac{3}{8}$ inches; diameter of crankshaft, $1\frac{5}{8}$ inches; weight, 5,500 pounds.

SAMSON IRON WORKS
Stockton, California

Samson Sieve Grip 12-25   1916-1917

Samson Sieve Grip 12-25
Samson Iron Works, Stockton, Cal.

Type of traction, wheel; fuel, distillate; guaranteed belt h. p., 25; guaranteed drawbar h. p., 10; motor, enclosed tractor type; number of cylinders, 4; cast in pairs; speed of motor, 650 r. p. m.; bore, $4\frac{1}{4}$ inches; stroke, $6\frac{3}{4}$ inches; 2 or 4-cycle, 4; transmission, ...; cooling system, radiator and pump; bearings, interchangeable; carburetor, Holly; ignition, high tension; oiling system, pump and splash; engine suspension, set in frame; length over all, 138 inches; width over all, 52 inches; height over all, 48 inches; number of wheels, 3; number of drive wheels, 2 sieve grip; diameter of drive wheels, 44 inches; face of drive wheels, 18 inches; how mounted, drop axle; clutch, make and type, Samson; control speeds, 1; speed on road, $3\frac{1}{2}$ miles per hour; speed in furrow, $2\frac{1}{4}$ miles per hour; diameter of pulley, 14 inches; face of pulley, 8 inches; capacity of fuel tank, 24 gallons; diameter of crankshaft, 2 inches; weight, 5,000 pounds; price, $1,250 f. o. b. factory.

SIMPLEX TRACTOR CO.
Minneapolis, Minnesota

Simplex 15-30   1916-1917

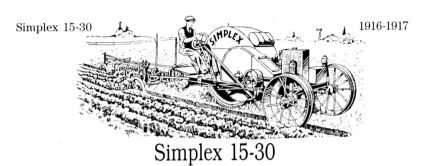

Simplex 15-30
Simplex Tractor Co., Minneapolis, Minn.

Type of traction, wheel; fuel, gas; guaranteed belt h. p., 30; guaranteed drawbar h. p., 15; motor, Simplex horizontal; number of cylinders, 4; cast in pairs; speed of motor, 750 r. p. m.; bore, 5 inches; stroke, 5 inches; 2 or 4-cycle, 4; transmission, gears; cooling system, radiator, fan and pump; bearings, Hyatt; carburetor, Kingston; ignition, Kingston with compulsion starter; oiling system, splash and pump; length over all, 144 inches; width over all, 68 inches; number of wheels, 3; number of drive wheels, 1; diameter of drive wheels, 60 inches; face of drive wheels, 26 inches; how mounted, spring; clutch, make and type, Simplex expanding; control speeds, 3; speed on road, 3 miles per hour; speed in furrow, 2 3-10 miles per hour; diameter of pulley, 14 inches; face of pulley, 9¾ inches; capacity of fuel tank, 25 gallons; capacity of water tank, 15 gallons; diameter of crankshaft, 2½ inches; weight, 5,500 pounds; price, $950 f. o. b. factory.

STANDARD DETROIT TRACTOR CO.
Detroit, Michigan

Standard Detroit 10-20   1916-1917

Standard Detroit 10-20
Standard Detroit Tractor Co., Detroit, Mich.

Type of traction, wheel; fuel, gasoline; guaranteed belt h. p., 20; guaranteed drawbar h. p., 10; motor, Beaver; number of cylinders, 4; speed of motor, 1,100 r. p. m.; bore, 3¾ inches; stroke, 5 inches; 2 or 4-cycle, 4; transmission, chain; cooling system, radiator; bearings, Hyatt; carburetor, Kingston; ignition, Dixie magneto; oiling system, splash and force; engine suspension, 3-point; length over all, 174 inches; width over all, 60 inches; height over all 60 inches; number of wheels 4; number of drive wheels 2; diameter of drive wheels 44 inches; face of drive wheels together 54 inches; clutch, make and type, Bierman friction; control speeds, 2; speed on road, 3½ miles per hour; speed in furrow, 3 miles per hour; diameter of pulley, 10 inches; face of pulley, 7 inches; capacity of fuel tank, 20 gallons; front axle, 1¾ inches; rear axle, 2 inches; diameter of crankshaft, 2¼ inches; weight, 3,945 pounds; price, $1,065 f. o. b. factory.

STRITE TRACTOR CO.
Minneapolis, Minnesota

Strite Three Point 25   1916-1917

Strite Three Point 25
Strite Tractor Co., Minneapolis, Minn.

Type of traction, wheel; fuel, kerosene or gasoline; guaranteed belt h. p., 25; guaranteed drawbar h. p., 12; motor, Waukesha; number of cylinders, 4; cast en bloc; speed of motor, 800 r. p. m.; bore, $4\frac{1}{4}$ inches; stroke, $5\frac{3}{4}$ inches; 2 or 4-cycle, 4; transmission, ...; cooling system, water; bearings, Waukesha; carburetor, Bennett; ignition, Dixie; engine suspension, 3-point; length over all, 204 inches; width over all, 96 inches; height over all, 72 inches; number of wheels, 3; number of drive wheels, 1; diameter of drive wheel, 72 inches; face of drive wheel, 20 inches; how mounted, spring; clutch, make and type, Bierman; control speeds, 3; speed on road, 4 miles per hour; speed in furrow, $2\frac{1}{2}$ miles per hour; diameter of pulley, 9 inches; face of pulley, 6 inches; capacity of fuel tank, 25 gallons; capacity of water tank, 25 gallons; weight, 4,200 pounds; price, $985 f. o. b. factory.

SULLIVAN TRACTOR CO.
Oakland, California

Sullivan   1916

Sullivan
Sullivan Tractor Co., Oakland, Cal.

Type of traction, crawler; fuel, distillate; guaranteed belt h. p., 10; guaranteed drawbar h. p., 8-10; motor, Beaver; number of cylinders, 4; cast in pairs; speed of motor, 800 r. p. m.; bore, $4\frac{3}{4}$ inches; stroke, $5\frac{1}{2}$ inches; 2 or 4-cycle, 4; transmission, ...; cooling system, pump and radiator; carburetor, Master; ignition, Eisemann high tension; length over all, 108 inches; width over all, 58 inches; height over all, 50 inches; number of wheels, 2 crawlers; number of drive wheels, 2 crawlers; diameter of crawlers, 24 inches; face of crawlers, 12 inches; clutch, make and type, planetary transmission; control speeds, 2; speed on road, $2\frac{3}{4}$ miles per hour; speed in furrow, $2\frac{3}{4}$ miles per hour; capacity of fuel tank, 20 gallons; diameter of crankshaft, $2\frac{1}{8}$ inches; weight, 4,000 pounds; price, $1,250 f. o. b. factory.

SWEENEY TRACTOR CO.
Kansas City, Missouri

Sweeney's Iron Horse   1916

Sweeney's Iron Horse
Sweeney Tractor Co., Kansas City, Mo.

Type of traction, drum; fuel, gasoline; guaranteed belt h. p., 25; motor, Continental L-Head; number of cylinders, 6; cast en bloc; speed of motor, 1,000 r. p. m.; bore, $3\frac{1}{2}$ inches; stroke, 5 inches; 2 or 4-cycle, 4; transmission, chain; cooling system, pump radiator and fan; bearings, bronze and babbitt; carburetor, Kingston; ignition, Eiseman high tension; oiling system, force feed and splash; engine suspension, 3-point; length over all, 156 inches; width over all, 68 inches; height over all, 56 inches; number of wheels, 2; number of drive wheels, 1 drum drive; diameter of drive wheel, 48 inches; face of drive wheel, 54 inches; how mounted, solid; clutch, make and type, direct expanding, fiber shoe; control speeds, 3; speed on road, $3\frac{1}{4}$ miles per hour; speed in furrow, $2\frac{1}{2}$ miles per hour; diameter of pulley, 10 inches; face of pulley, 10 inches; capacity of fuel tank, 25 gallons; capacity of water tank, $5\frac{1}{2}$ gallons; diameter of crankshaft, $2\frac{1}{4}$ inches; special equipment, Bennett air cleaner; weight, 5,000 pounds; price, $985 f. o. b. factory.

TOM THUMB TRACTOR CO.
Minneapolis, Minnesota

Tom Thumb 12-20   1916-1918

Tom Thumb 12-20
Tom Thumb Tractor Co., Minneapolis, Minn.

Type of traction, crawler; fuel, kerosene or gasoline; guaranteed belt h. p., 20; guaranteed draw-bar h. p., 12; motor, Waukesha; number of cylinders, 4; cast en bloc; speed of motor, 800 r. p. m.; bore, $4\frac{1}{4}$ inches; stroke, $5\frac{3}{4}$ inches; 2 or 4-cycle, 4; transmission, friction; cooling system, Perfex radiator and pump; bearings, Hyatt; carburetor, Bennett; ignition, Dixie high tension impulse starter; oiling system, splash; engine suspension, 4-point; length over all, 128 inches; width over all, 88 inches; height over all, 66 inches; number of wheels, 2 and crawler; number of drive wheel, 1 crawler; diameter of drive wheel, $24\frac{3}{4}$ inches; face of drive wheel, 16 inches; clutch, make and type, 2-shoe expanding; control speeds, 2; speed on road, $2\frac{3}{4}$ miles per hour; speed in furrow, $2\frac{1}{4}$ miles per hour; diameter of pulley, 16 inches; face of pulley, 7 inches; capacity of fuel tank, 15 gallons kerosene, 5 gallons gasoline; diameter of crankshaft, 2 inches; weight, 4,500 pounds.

WAITE TRACTOR CO.
Elgin, Illinois

Waite   1916

Waite
Waite Tractor Co., Elgin, Ill.

Type of traction, wheel; fuel, gasoline, kerosene or distillate; guaranteed belt h. p., 16; guaranteed drawbar h. p., 8; motor, Waukesha vertical; number of cylinders, 4; cast en bloc; speed of motor, 1,000 r. p. m.; bore, $3\frac{1}{2}$ inches; stroke, $5\frac{1}{4}$ inches; 2 or 4-cycle, 4; transmission, friction; cooling system, radiator, thermo syphon; bearings, Hyatt New Departure and Timken; carburetor, Kingston; ignition, Dixie high tension; oiling system, pump, constant level; engine suspension, 3-point; length over all, 128 inches; width over all, 58 inches; height over all, 68 inches; number of wheels, 4; number of drive wheels, 2; diameter of drive wheels, 42 inches; face of drive wheels, 8 inches; how mounted, springs; clutch, make and type, friction; control speeds, 9; speed on road, 4-10 miles per hour; speed in furrow, $3\frac{1}{2}$ miles per hour; diameter of pulley, 9 iches; face of pulley, 8 inches; capacity of fuel tank, 20 gallons; capacity of water tank, 7 gallons; diameter of crankshaft, 2 inches; special equipment, drawbar and spring seat; weight, 2,700 pounds; price, $800 f. o. b. factory.

WALLIS TRACTOR CO.

Racine, Wisconsin

Wallis Cub

1916

Wallis Cub
Wallis Tractor Co., Racine, Wis.

Type of traction, wheel; fuel, gasoline, kerosene or distillate; guaranteed belt h. p., 44 2-10; guaranteed drawbar h. p., 26; motor, Wattes T-head vertical; number of cylinders, 4; cast in pairs; speed of motor, 650 r. p. m.; bore, 6 inches; stroke, 7 inches; 2 or 4-cycle, 4; transmission, gear; cooling system, water; bearings, bronze shell, babbitt lined; carburetor, Bennett XX; ignition, K. W. high tension; oiling system, automatic; engine suspension, 3-point; length over all, $102\frac{1}{2}$ inches; width over all, 74 inches; height over all, 87 inches; number of wheels, 3; number of drive wheels, 2; diameter of drive wheels, 60 inches; face of drive wheels, 20 inches; how mounted, spring clutch, make and type, clamping plate; control speeds, 2; speed on road, $3\frac{1}{2}$ miles per hour; speed in furrow, 2 4-10 miles per hour; diameter of pulley, 14 inches; face of pulley, 9 inches; capacity of fuel tank, 33 gallons; capacity of water tank, 16 gallons; diameter of crankshaft, $2\frac{3}{4}$ inches, special equipment, dust separator or carburetor extra rims, Model XX kerosene carburetor, umbrella top; head lights; weight, 8,365 pounds; price, $1,850 f. o. b. factory.

WATERLOO GASOLINE ENGINE CO.

Waterloo, Iowa

Waterloo

1916

Waterloo
Waterloo Gasoline Engine Co., Waterloo, Ia.

Type of traction, wheel; fuel, kerosene; guaranteed belt h. p., 24; guaranteed drawbar h. p., 12; motor, horizontal; number of cylinders, 2, cast en bloc; speed of motor, 750 r. p. m.; bore, 6 inches; stroke, 7 inches; 2 or 4-cycle, 4; transmission, gear; cooling system, pump and radiator; bearings, die cast and bronze; carburetor, Schebler; ignition, Dixie high tension magneto; oiling system, force sight feed; engine suspension, 3-point; length over all, 132 inches; width over all, 72 inches; height over all, 63 inches; number of wheels, 4; number of drive wheels, 2; diameter of drive wheels, 52 inches; face of drive wheels, 10 inches; clutch, make and type, cone; control speeds 2; speed on road, 2¼-3 miles per hour; speed in furrow, 2¼ miles per hour; diameter of pulley, 14 inches; face of pulley, 8 inches; capacity of fuel tank, 20 gallons; capacity of water tank, 12 gallons; diameter of crankshaft, 2½ inches; weight, 4,800 pounds; price, $750 f. o. b. factory.

WILLMAR TRACTOR & MANUFACTURING CO.

Willmar, Minnesota

Little Oak

1916

Little Oak
Willmar Tractor & Mfg. Co., Willmar, Minn.

Type of traction, wheel; fuel, gasoline or kerosene; guaranteed belt h. p., 44; guaranteed drawbar h. p., 22; motor, Westman; number of cylinders, 4; cast separately; speed of motor, 600 r. p. m.; bore, 5⅝ inches; stroke, 7½ inches; 2 or 4-cycle, 4; transmission, chain; cooling system, water and fan; bearings, high speed and babbitt; carburetor, Kingston; ignition, Remy; oiling system, splash; engine suspension, 4-point; length over all, 43½ inches; height over all, 36 inches; number of wheels, 4; number of drive wheels, 2; diameter of drive wheels, 69 inches; face of drive wheels, 14 inches; how mounted, spring; clutch, make and type, shoe; control speeds, 3; speed on road, 4 miles per hour; speed in furrow, 3 miles per hour; diameter of pulley, 30 inches; face of pulley, 8 inches; capacity of fuel tank, 50 gallons; capacity of water tank, 70 gallons; front axle, 2½ inches; rear axle, 3 inches; diameter of crankshaft, 2⅜ inches; weight, 1,300 pounds; price, $1,400 f. o. b. factory.

Lincoln, Ill.

Electric Wheel Co.,
   Quincy, Ill.

Gentlemen:

I have used my ALLWORK Tractor for different kinds of work with good success. In plowing or preparing a seed bed the tractor certainly will do better work and do it quicker than horses.

The ALLWORK has plenty of power and will pull three 14-inch plows from 6 to 9 inches deep in any kind of soil. I use kerosene to operate the machine and cannot tell it from gasoline. My son, twelve years old, has run my tractor the greater part of the time, and has plowed as much as twelve acres a day plowing 8 inches deep. We have run our ALLWORK thirteen hours without stopping the engine and when we stopped it the motor was cool enough that we could hold our hands on any of the four cylinders. We plowed 105 acres last spring and can safely say that we did not use over one and a half gallons of water cooling after the radiator had been filled. I believe it is the only tractor for this country as it is so light and powerful.

Yours truly,
                     HENRY PAULUS.

Allwork Kerosene Tractor

GUARANTEED to operate successfully on kerosene and to develop 12 h.p. at drawbar and 25 h.p. at belt pulley. The Light ALLWORK Tractor is giving perfect satisfaction on hundreds of farms throughout the country today and every user is a booster. The ALLWORK has a large tractor motor with 4 cylinders, 5-inch bore and 6-inch stroke, which enables it to pull three plows easily under adverse conditions and still have plenty of reserve power. Motor develops its rated horse power at only 700 to 750 R.P.M. with no vibration; two speed transmission; all gears thoroughly enclosed and run in bath of oil; motor sets crosswise on frame and power is transmitted to drawbar through direct spur gears; automobile type steering insures easy handling; perfect oscillating front axle which gives three point suspension; cooling system is positive and motor cannot get hot; weighs 4,800 lbs; will work on plowed ground without packing soil; runs 18-inch Ensilage Cutter and 28-inch Separator; pulls 8-foot Road Grader.

The ALLWORK is simple, durable and powerful, and sells at a moderate price. Write for illustrated catalog with full description.

Electric Wheel Company
Box 264.   Quincy, Ill.

ALLIS-CHALMERS 10-18 H.P. FARM TRACTOR

Back of the Allis-Chalmers Tractor are the Allis-Chalmers name and reputation of 60 years as designers and builders of high grade machinery. The purchasers of this tractor are assured of the same service that the Allis-Chalmers Manufacturing Company gives all its customers on every product it manufactures.

The only tractor that has a one-piece steel heat-treated frame—no rivets to work loose—will not sag under heaviest strains. Allis-Chalmers motor bearings never get out of line through frame weakness.

Important improvements insure absolute protection of working parts from dust and grit. Special attention has been given to the design of the belt pulley—long bearings of large diameter preserve perfect alignment.

Dealers in unallotted territory will find our proposition a highly profitable one. Write for full particulars of how we help the dealer to make sales.

ALLIS-CHALMERS
Manufacturing Co.
Milwaukee, Wisconsin

1917

In 1917, 94 models of 65 makes not included in 1916 were added.

THE ADAMS CO.
Marysville, Ohio

Adams No. 1, 8-12   1917-1921
Adams No. 2, 11-16   1917-1921

Adams No. 1, 8-12
The Adams Company, Marysville, O.

Four wheels, driving from two rear wheels. Recommended for 1 to 2 14″ plows. Length 136 inches, width 68 inches, height 70 inches. Diameter of drive wheels 36 inches, face 9 inches. Weight 4,000 lbs. Price $545. Any standard stationary one cylinder motor. Chain final drive. Machined cast steel gearing.

Adams No. 2, 11-16
The Adams Company, Marysville, O.

Four wheels, driving from two rear wheels. Recommended for two to three 14″ plows. Length 146 inches, width 74 inches, height 84 inches. Diameter of drive wheels 50 inches, face 12 inches. Weight 5,500 lbs. Price $695. Any standard stationary one cylinder motor. Chain final drive. Machined cast steel gearing.

ADVANCE-RUMELY THRESHER CO.

LaPorte, Indiana

Oil Pull 30-60   1917-1924

Oil Pull 30-60
Advance-Rumely Thresher Co., Laporte, Ind.

Four wheels, driving from two rear wheels. Recommended for eight 14″ plows, 40×64 thresher. Length 228 inches, width 114 inches, height 132 inches. Drive wheels 80 inches diameter, 30 inch face. Weight 26,000 lbs. Advance-Rumely two cylinder horizontal opposed motor, 10×12, r.p.m. 375 normal. Secor-Higgins special carburetor burning any oil fuel. Bosch low tension dual magneto starting on battery. Oil or water cooling circulated by centrifugal pump, special multi-section radiator air circulation by exhaust. Madison-Kipp force sight feed oiler, gears running in oil bath. Final drive spur gear to wheel, single speed. Steel and semi-steel cast gears. Babbitt bearings in transmission, and drive wheels, cast iron bearings in front wheels.

ALBAUGH-DOVER CO.

Chicago, Illinois

Albaugh-Dover "Square Turn"   1917

Albaugh-Dover "Square Turn"
Albaugh-Dover Co., Chicago, Ill.

Two drive wheels and small stub steering wheel. Recommended for three 14″ plows, 28x32 thresher. Length 180 inches, width 95 inches, height 76 inches. Drive wheels 62 inches diameter, face 12 inches. Weight 6,500 lbs. Price $1285. Waukesha vertical L-Head four cylinder motor cast in pairs, $4\frac{3}{4}x6\frac{3}{4}$, r. p. m. 950 normal. Bennett dual gasoline or kerosene carburetor. Dixie high tension independent magneto, manual control, with impulse starter. Centrifugal pump, fan and Perfex cellular radiator. Waukesha automatic splash cylinder lubrication, gears running in oil bath. Noxspeed change gearing, speed regulated by throttle. Final drive spur pinion. Cast steel and cast iron gears. Ten Hyatt roller transmission bearings. Six Hyatt roller and Bantam ball bearings in axles.

ALBERT LEA TRACTOR & MANUFACTURING CO.

Albert Lea, Minnesota

Sexton "B" 10-25   1917
Sexton "C" 15-45   1917

Sexton "B" 10-25
Albert Lea Tractor & Mfg. Co., Albert Lea, Minn.

Four wheels driving from two rear wheels. Recommended for two to three 14″ plows, 24″ thresher. Length 144 inches, width 59 inches, height 64 inches. Diameter of drive wheels 54 inches, face 10 inches. Weight 4,750 lbs. Price $1035. Waukesha TU4 vertical four cylinder motor, cast en block, L-Head, $3\frac{1}{2}x5\frac{1}{4}$, r. p. m 1000 normal. Kingston dual gasoline or kerosene carburetor. Dixie high tension independent magneto with Gould storage battery starting system. Centrifugal pump, fan and Perfex cellular radiator. Waukesha automatic splash lubrication. Sliding gear speed change, enclosed. Spur gear final drive. Cut wrought steel gearing. Hyatt roller transmission bearings. Coil springs in front.

3 Horse
Work—Plus
1 Horse
Cost—Minus

THE UniTractor

A Dealer's
Opportunity

Make the Farmer's Ford Do
Double Duty

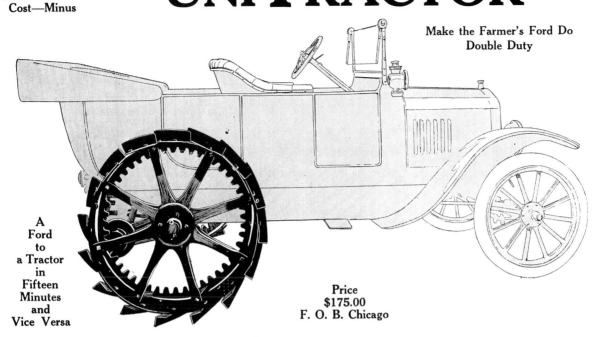

A
Ford
to
a Tractor
in
Fifteen
Minutes
and
Vice Versa

Price
$175.00
F. O. B. Chicago

The UniTractor Company 376 N. CICERO AVENUE Chicago

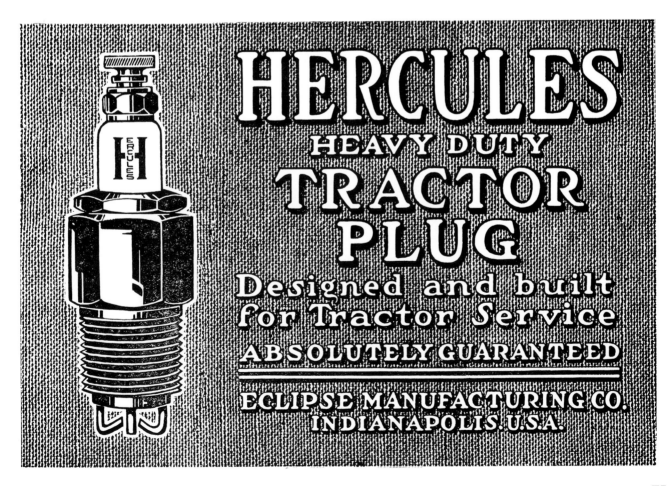

HERCULES
HEAVY DUTY
TRACTOR
PLUG
Designed and built
for Tractor Service
ABSOLUTELY GUARANTEED

ECLIPSE MANUFACTURING CO.
INDIANAPOLIS U.S.A.

Sexton "C" 15-45
Albert Lea Tractor & Mfg. Co., Albert Lea, Minn.

Four wheels, driving from two rear wheels. Recommended for three to four 14" plows, 28" to 30" thresher. Length 158 inches, width 67 inches, height 67 inches. Diameter of drive wheels 54 inches, face 14 inches. Weight 5,000 lbs. Price $1485. Doman vertical four cylinder motor, cast in pairs, $4\frac{3}{4}$x6, r. p. m. 800 normal, L-Head. Kingston dual gasoline or kerosene carburetor. Dixie high tension independent magneto, with Gould storage battery starting system. Centrifugal pump, fan and Perfex cellular radiator. Doman force feed and splash lubrication. Sliding spur gear speed change, enclosed. Spur gear final drive. Cut wrought steel gearing. Hyatt roller transmission bearings. Coil springs in front.

APPLETON MANUFACTURING CO.

Batavia, Illinois

Appleton 14-28   1917-1918

Appleton 14-28
Appleton Mfg. Co., Batavia, Ill.

Four wheel, driving from two rear wheels. Recommended for three 14" plows, 28" thresher. Length 162 inches, width $67\frac{1}{2}$ inches, height 61 inches. Drive wheels 54 inches diameter, face 12 inches. Coil springs front and rear axle. Weight 5,000 lbs. Price $1500. Buda vertical L-Head 4 cylinder motor, cast en bloc, $4\frac{1}{4}$x$5\frac{1}{2}$, r.p.m. 900 normal. Schebler float feed gasoline carburetor. High tension ignition. Centrifugal pump, fan and Perfex cellular radiator. Buda force feed oiling. Roller pinion final drive. Speed change sliding spur gear. Semi steel cast gearing, speed change enclosed. Hyatt roller and ball transmission bearings. Hyatt roller bearings in rear axle.

AUSTIN DRAINAGE EXCAVATOR CO.
Chicago, Illinois

Austin Multipedal 8-15   1917
Austin Multipedal 18-35   1917-1918

Austin Multipedal 8-15
Austin Drainage Excavator Co., Chicago, Ill.

Two crawlers. Recommended for two or three 14" plows. Diameter of crawlers 30 inches, face 12 to 16 inches, total area traction surface 2,000 square inches. Length 108 inches, width 72 inches, height 57 inches. Weight 5,600 lbs. Buda four cylinder vertical motor, cast in pairs, $4^1/_4 \times 5^1/_2$, 800 r. p. m. normal, L-Head. Linga gasoline and kerosene carburetor. High tension ignition. Rotary pump, fan and tubular radiator. Pressure feed and splash lubrication. Enclosed speed change gearing, chain final drive. Machine cut, hardened steel gearing.

Austin Multipedal 18-35
Austin Drainage Excavator Co., Chicago, Ill.

Two crawlers. Recommended for four to six 14" plows. Diameter of crawlers 30 inches, face 12 and 36 inches, 7,000 square inches traction surface. Length 120 inches, width 116 inches, height 90 inches. Weight 10,500 lbs. Buffalo four cylinder vertical motor, cast in pairs, 5×6, 800 r. p. m. normal, L-Head. Linga gasoline and kerosene carburetor, high tension ignition. Rotary pump, fan and tabular radiator. Pressure feed and splash lubrication. Enclosed speed change gearing, chain final drive. Machine cut steel gearing.

BEAN SPRAY PUMP CO.

San Jose, California

Bean Trackpull 6-10   1917-1921

Bean Trackpull 6-10
Bean Spray Pump Co., San Jose, Cal.

Crawler in front, two rear wheels. Recommended for two 14″ plows. Length 102 inches, width 72 inches, height 46 inches. Crawler 12 inch face, 432 sq. in. traction surface. Weight 2,750 lbs. Price 975. LeRoi vertical L-Head four cylinder motor, cast en bloc, $3\frac{1}{2}$x$4\frac{1}{2}$, r.p.m. 1,200 normal. Mayer distillate carburetor. High tension independent magneto, manual control. Centrifugal pump, fan and Perfex cellular radiator. LeRoi pressure feed and splash lubrication. One speed forward and reverse, 2 to $2\frac{1}{4}$ m.p.h. Internal gear and pinion final drive, enclosed. Steel gears rough cast and machined. New Departure ball transmission bearings. Hyatt roller bearings in track.

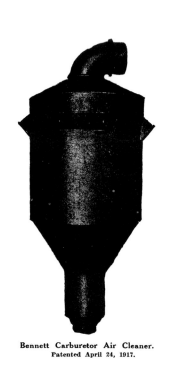

Bennett Carburetor Air Cleaner.
Patented April 24, 1917.

THE tractors giving the most efficient service this season are those equipped with a Bennett Air Cleaner and a Bennett Kerosene Carburetor.

Whether you are a farmer, dealer, distributor or manufacturer the tractors you use or sell should be Bennett Equipped.

The Bennett Air Cleaner solves the dust problem; the Bennett Carburetor gives you a smooth-running motor with kerosene fuel.

Look at the detailed tractor specifications in this book and note how many of the important tractor manufacturers are using Bennett air cleaners and carburetors.

Our service department is willing to help you.

Wilcox-Bennett Carburetor Co.

Minneapolis, Minnesota

Specialists in Kerosene Carburetion.

Bennett Kerosene Carburetor

C. L. BEST GAS TRACTION CO.

Oakland, California

Tracklayer 37-75   1917
Tracklayer 45-90   1917

Tracklayer 37-75

C. L. Best Gas Traction Co., Oakland, Cal.

Two crawlers, small front steering wheel. Recommended for twelve 14″ plows, largest thresher. Length 280 inches, width 120 inches, height 120 inches. Crawlers 54 inches diameter, 24 inch face, 4,320 sq. in. traction surface. Weight 32,000 lbs. Price $5400. Vertical four cylinder motor, cast singly, 8x9, r.p.m. 500 normal, overhead valve. Schebler distillate carburetor. High tension independent magneto, automatic. Rotary pump, fan and tubular radiator. Pressure feed lubrication to all bearings. Two speeds forward and one reverse, $1\frac{1}{2}$ to $2\frac{1}{2}$ m.p.h. Progressive sliding bevel gear speed change, enclosed. Bevel gear final drive, enclosed. Chrome steel machined bearings. Transmission bearings, babbitt. Bronze bushings in drive axles.

Tracklayer 45-90

C. L. Best Gas Traction Co., Oakland, Cal.

Two crawlers, small front steering wheel. Recommended for eight 14″ plows, any thresher. Length 269 inches, width 104 inches, height 120 inches. Crawlers 54 inches diameter, 24 inch face, 2,976 sq. in. traction surface. Weight 28,000 lbs. Price $5000. Vertical motor, four cylinder, cast separately, $7^{3}/_{4}\times9$, r. p. m. 435 normal, overhead valves. Schebler distillate carburetor. High tension independent magneto, automatic. Rotary pump, fan and tubular radiator. Pressure feed to all bearings. Two speeds forward and one reverse, $1\frac{1}{2}$ to $2\frac{1}{2}$ m.p.h. Progressive sliding bevel gear speed change, enclosed. Bevel gear final drive, enclosed. Chrome steel machined gears. Babbitt transmission bearings. Bronze bushings in axles.

BORING TRACTOR

A Carrying Tractor

The exclusive patented design of the Boring Tractor enables it to carry a great many of the standard farm machines now being pulled.

These tools are easily and quickly attached. They are lifted free and clear from the ground when not in use, or when being carried from place to place.

Upkeep of tools and roadbed obviously is reduced as a result of carrying such accessories as plows, disks, cultivators, mowers, seeders, saw-tables, cotton and tobacco tools. First cost, too, naturally is less, since the farmer finds lacking many wheels, levers, springs, toggles, of drawn or pulled tools.

Agility, ease of handling, pulling power are all enhanced by this carrying feature of the Boring Tractor.

The Boring Tractor will successfully cultivate two standard corn rows at a time, using any standard type shovels. The operator cultivates two rows; then pivots and returns on the next two.

One man drives and cultivates, guiding the gangs with his feet.

One man can operate the Boring Cultivator as easily as one man can operate a standard two-row horse-drawn

MOTOR-PLOW   TRACTOR   CULTIVATOR

Liberal agreements will be written with distributors at advantageous points in Missouri, Iowa, Dakotas, Kansas, Nebraska, Texas, Tennessee, Georgia.

Boring Tractor

Rockford, Illinois

For Profits, Sales and Satisfaction

Better plowing—cheaper plowing—more rapid plowing. These are the big items facing the farm business man today—the items whose solution means satisfaction to the farmer —sales to the dealer. It is these problems which the

TRACFORD

"The Tractor Universal"

$125 F. O. B. Detroit

meets to the greatest satisfaction of the man on the average American farm—the man who wants power farming at less than big-tractor expense. The TRACFORD attachment converts any Ford into a **guaranteed light** tractor with a draw-bar pull of 1000 pounds on high gear—2000 pounds on low gear.

Ample in power—economical in operation as the Ford car itself—able to plow throughout the entire day on high gear without over-heating—the TRACFORD is a big profit maker for both buyer and seller.

If you are a farm owner or farm operator, the TRACFORD gives you a flexible power unit which can be converted into a work or pleasure car at will. If you are an implement dealer, the TRACFORD is a wonderful selling opportunity for you. Write us direct for information on available territory, terms, and full details on our proposition.

Ask for "The Tracford Catechism." It explains every technical and practical question you may want to ask.

Standard-Detroit Tractor Co.
1506 West Fort Street, Detroit, Mich.

BORING TRACTOR CO.

Rockford, Illinois

Boring 35   1917-1918

Boring 35
Boring Tractor Co., Rockford, Ill.

Three wheels, driving from two front wheels. Recommended for two 14" plows or 24" thresher. Diameter of drive wheels 54 inches, face 10 inches. Length 144 inches, width 74 and 97 inches, height 74½ inches. Weight 3,600 lbs. Waukhesha four cylinder vertical motor, cast in pairs, 4¼x5¾, 1200 r. p. m. normal, L-Head. Gasoline and kerosene carburetor, high tension ignition. Centrifugal pump, fan and Perfex cellular radiator. Two speeds forward, one reverse, speed change gearing enclosed and running in oil. All gears drop forged machine cut. Hyatt roller transmission and drive axle bearings.

BUCKEYE MANUFACTURING CO.

Anderson, Indiana

Buckeye Giant Baby 10-20   1917

Buckeye Giant Baby 10-20
Buckeye Mfg. Co., Anderson, Ind.

Two crawlers. Recommended for three 14" plows. Length 108 inches, width 52 inches, height 42 inches. Face of crawlers 13 inches, total area traction surface 1,456 square inches. Erd four cylinder motor, cast en bloc, 4x6, r. p. m. 900 normal, valve-in-head. Tillotson gasoline or kerosene carburetor. Kingston high tension magneto, variable, with impulse starter. Centrifugal pump, fan and Modine cellular radiator. Erd oiling system. Sliding gear speed change, enclosed. Direct final drive, enclosed. Machined alloy steel gearing. Roller transmission bearings.

1917   81

The New BIG BULL

A *Real* Kerosene Tractor and a Practical *Three-Plow* Outfit

THREE big new features—*plus* the time-tested, proven original Bull design, the sub-soiling feature, the self-steering feature, the leveling device, the flexibility, sturdiness, simplicity and all other features which have made it the world's most popular tractor—all these things make it surely worth your while to investigate the Big Bull before you buy **any** tractor.

The Clapper Kerosene Vaporizer—a new and exclusive Big Bull feature—which vaporizes the liquid kerosene before it enters the combustion chamber and makes perfect combustion possible—enables the Big Bull motor to produce as much power from a gallon of kerosene as from a gallon of gasoline, and is, we believe, the most efficient, economical, simple and easy-to-operate kerosene device on the market.

Power on the Land Wheel in addition to the Big Bull sub-soiling wheel running in the furrow bottom. Also a larger motor—developing full 12 h. p. at the drawbar and 24 h. p. at the belt.

POSITIVE CIRCULATING OILING SYSTEM oils connecting rod bearings through hollow crank shaft. Insures positive lubrication with no attention except to keep oil reservoir filled. A big saving in oil consumption.

ACT QUICK!—If you want to be sure of getting a BIG BULL for this season's work. **Write for free sub-soiling book,** Big Bull catalog and three months' FREE subscription to the Monthly Tractor Bulletin.

BULL TRACTOR CO.

776 UNIVERSITY AVE. S.E.　　　　　　　　　　　　　**MINNEAPOLIS, MINNESOTA**

Announcing the

Wallis "Cub Junior"

PULLS ITS OWN WEIGHT at the Drawbar

"Mightiest of Light Weight Tractors."

A MARVEL OF
Simplicity, Power and Speed.
"Just Like the Cub—Only Smaller"

Since the earliest days of modern tractor construction, engineers the world over have been striving to perfect a machine which will develop a pull at the draw bar equal to its own weight.

At last this great engineering dream has been realized in the production of the Wallis "Cub Junior" pictured above.

Although this small tractor weighs but 3,000 lbs., it developed a draw bar pull of 3,250 lbs. in a recent dynamometer test conducted by the Hyatt Roller Bearing Company. That was accomplishing what was heretofore considered impossible.

This miracle of the tractor industry shows a mechanical efficiency of over 74% as compared

to 50% in most tractors.

Think what this superiority in design—superiority in construction—superiority in performance means in daily farm work.

If you are interested in handling a small tractor this year make it a point to get complete information about the "Cub Junior," before taking on an agency.

BRANCHES
MINNEAPOLIS
INDIANAPOLIS
BALTIMORE
ST. LOUIS

J·I·Case Plow Works—Racine, Wis.
GENERAL SELLING AGENTS

BRANCHES
DALLAS
OMAHA
KANSAS CITY
OKLAHOMA CITY

BULL TRACTOR CO.
Minneapolis, Minnesota

Big Bull 12-24   1917-1924

Big Bull 12-24
Bull Tractor Co., Minneapolis, Minn.

Three wheel, one front steering wheel, drive wheel in furrow, auxiliary drive on left rear wheel. Recommended for three 14" plows, 26x38 thresher. Length 167 inches, width 78 inches, height 78 inches. Drive wheel 60 inches diameter, 14 inch face. Weight 4,850 lbs. Price $875. Toro horizontal opposed two cylinder motor, cast singly, $5\frac{1}{2}x7$, r.p.m. 750 normal, L-Head. Kingston dual kerosene and gasoline carburetor. Kingston high tension independent magneto with impulse starter. Centrifugal pump, fan and tubular radiator. Toro pressure feed lubrication. One speed forward and reverse, 2.4 m.p.h. Spur gear final drive. Drop forged and semi-steel, machined and rough cast gearing. Babbitt transmission bearings. Two Hyatt roller bearings in drive axle.

J. I. CASE PLOW WORKS
Racine, Wisconsin

Cub Junior 15-30   1917-1919
Cub 26-52   1917

Cub Junior 15-30
J. I. Case Plow Works, Racine, Wis.

Three wheels, driving from two rear wheels. Recommended for two to three 14" plows, 26" thresher. Length 172 inches, 60 inches wide, height 64 inches. Diameter of drive wheels 48 inches, face 12 inches. Vertical four cylinder motor, cast en bloc, $4\frac{1}{4}x5\frac{3}{4}$, r.p.m. 900 normal, overhead valves, Bennett dual gasoline or kerosene carburetor. K-W high tension independent magneto, manual control, with impulse starter. Centrifugal pump, fan and cellular radiator. Pressure feed and splash lubrication. Selective sliding spur gear speed change, enclosed. Final drive spur gear. Drop forged machined steel gearing. Six Hyatt transmission bearings and four in drive wheels, two in front.

Case 20-40   Case 12-25   Case 10-20   Case 9-18

EVERY ONE A KEROSENE TRACTOR. ALSO A LARGER MODEL CASE 30-60 OIL TRACTOR

Why Case Tractors are in Popular Demand

The demand for Case tractors this season has kept the Case factories working day and night. Not only have Case tractors been sold in the United States and Canada in large numbers but heavy foreign sales have been made as well. Why this demand for Case tractors? Why are farmers insisting on Case tractors?

Today there are many makes of tractors on the market. But there are also makeshifts and experiments among them. Farmers are careful in choosing their tractors. Too many farmers have learned the lesson of "orphaned" machines. Now they turn to a company who for three-quarters of a century has faithfully served farmers in all parts of

the world, a company that proudly boasts of four generations of satisfied customers. Farmers know and honor the Case name. It stands for quality—honest value—fair dealing.

In the tractor field Case holds a position second to none. We are the pioneer builders of tractors. Our experience, our facilities, our corps of skilled engineers have brought the tractor to a high state of development. All materials used in Case tractors are tested in our laboratories. They are built complete in the Case shops. In simplicity, in accessibility, in power and all around usefulness Case tractors are leaders. Literature describing Case tractors will gladly be sent on request.

J. I. CASE T. M. CO., Inc., 847 Liberty St., Racine, Wis.

Coleman WORM DRIVE Tractor

The Gearless Transmission Power Shaft — showing clutch brake, shifting fork, and triple thrust ball bearings—the only moving parts except the motor and differential. No gears except the final worm are in mesh on direct drive. Every moving part is completely enclosed and running in oil bath.

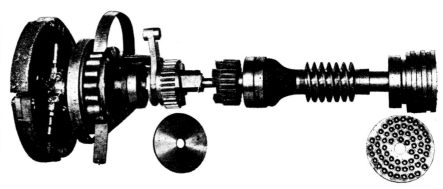

See illustration and condensed specifications on opposite page.

The Coleman Worm Drive Tractor is a light weight compact machine designed to overcome the difficulties of continuous strain, working in dust and sand, and the high cost of fuel. These difficulties are best met by the highest type of engineering and shop practice, using the best known methods of power production and transmission in the tractor itself.

The high speed motor is admittedly the most efficient, the objection to its use in tractor work having been that in reducing the high speed to tractor requirements, too much power was lost. With a worm drive, the greater the reduction, the higher the efficiency. By eliminating cast iron and using machined steel gearing and bronze master gear, enclosed in oil baths, the highest possible fuel economy is obtained.

Write for complete information and technical photographs of the Coleman Worm Drive Tractor.

Winslow Mfg. Co.,   16th & Walnut Sts.   Kansas City, Mo

Cub 26-52

J. I. Case Plow Works, Racine, Wis.

Three wheels, driving from two rear wheels. Recommended for four to six 14" plows, 32" thresher. Length 171 inches, 74 inches wide, height 72 inches. Diameter drive wheels 60 inches, face 20 inches. Coil springs both front and rear. Vertical four cylinder motor, cast in pairs, 6x7, r.p.m. 650 normal, L-Head. Bennett dual gasoline or kerosene carburetor. K-W high tension independent magneto, manual control, with impulse starter. Centrifugal pump, fan and cellular radiator. Pressure feed and splash lubrication. Selective sliding spur gear speed change, enclosed. Final drive spur gear. Drop forged machined steel gearing. Seven Hyatt transmission bearings.

J. I. CASE THRESHING MACHINE CO.

Racine, Wisconsin

Case 9-18   1917

Case 9-18

J. I. Case T. M. Co., Racine, Wis.

Four wheel, driving from two rear wheels. Recommended for two 14" plows, 20" thresher without feeder or wind stacker. Drive wheels 48 inches diameter, 10 inch face. Length 123 inches, width 58 inches, height 61 inches. Weight 3,770 lbs. Price $900. Four cylinder vertical valve-in-head motor, cast en bloc, $3\frac{7}{8}$x5, 900 r.p.m. normal. Kingston gasoline or kerosene carburetor. Kingston high tension independent magneto with impulse starter. Centrifugal pump, fan and cellular radiator. Madison Kipp force sight pressure feed and splash lubrication. Two speeds forward, one reverse, $2\frac{1}{4}$ to $3\frac{1}{2}$ m.p.h. Enclosed sliding spur gear speed change, enclosed spur gear final drive. Machined and rough cast chilled semi-steel and forged gears. Four Hyatt roller transmission and two Hyatt roller drive axle bearings.

CHALLENGE TRACTOR CO.

Minneapolis, Minnesota

Challenge 12-20   1917

Challenge 12-20
Challenge Tractor Company, Minneapolis, Minn.

Three wheels, driving from two rear wheels. Recommended for two to three 14″ plows, 24″ thresher. Length 126 inches, 79 inches wide, height 66 inches. Diameter of drive wheels 60 inches, face 10 inches. Weight 3,900 lbs. Price $885. Opposed two cylinder motor, $5\frac{1}{2}$x$6\frac{1}{2}$, r.p.m. 750 to 800 normal. Bennett gasoline carburetor. Dixie high tension independent magneto with impulse starter. Centrifugal pump, fan and radiator. Madison-Kipp force sight feed oiler to all bearings. Sliding spur gear speed change, enclosed. Final drive roller pinion. Machined steel gearing.

CHASE MOTOR TRUCK CO.

Syracuse, New York

Chase 8-16   1917-1918

Chase 8-16
Chase Motor Truck Company, Syracuse, N.Y.

Three wheels, driving from two rear wheels. Recommended for two 14″ plows. Diameter of drive wheels 48 inches, face 22 inches. Price $1000. Waukesha four cylinder motor, cast en bloc, $3\frac{1}{2}$x$5\frac{1}{4}$, r.p.m. 1,000 normal. Holley gasoline carburetor. Kingston high tension independent magneto. Centrifugal pump, fan and Perfex cellular radiator. Waukesha automatic splash lubrication. Sliding gear speed change, enclosed. Roller pinion final drive. Machined manganese steel gearing. Bronze transmission and drive axle bearings.

"COMMON SENSE"

Gas Tractors

4-Cylinder—25 H. P. Belt, 15 H. P. Drawbar
8-Cylinder—35 H. P. Belt, 20 H. P. Drawbar

A Practical 4-Plow, 1-Man Outfit

WE KNOW of one farmer who has the right idea (he is also a successful business man). He says:

"A tractor has harder work, greater strains, and heavier pulls to meet than an automobile. So what I want is a tractor that is built like a fine automobile—then it will stand up to the racket."

That is the idea behind the "Common Sense"—"built like a fine automobile—to stand up to the racket."

The "Common Sense" 8, with hood raised showing motor.

The 8-Cylinder "Common Sense"

Combines Advanced Engineering Principles With Proved Practical Features and Fewer Working Parts

A tractor needs an 8-cylinder motor, far more than does an automobile.

An automobile motor has the momentum of the whole car to help it. The tractor has no rolling momentum—the motor must do every bit of the work. So a tractor motor that is built to run at high speed and keeps up its own momentum delivers the smoothest power.

The load a tractor pulls isn't what wears it out. That is steady. It is power delivered in jerks that wears it out.

The 8-cylinder motor gives an absolutely steady pull to meet the steady load. The result is longer life to every wearing part. The connecting rod bearings, the clutch, the transmission gears, the drive shaft, the drive chains—all give double the service, when they transmit a power that has no jerks in it.

The whole machine is built up to the standard of unrelenting care you'll find in the best automobile factories.

The "Common Sense" will plow 20 to 25 acres a day—and do it on 1½ gallons of gaso-

line to the acre, and 3 quarts of cylinder oil per day. Figure the low cost per acre for yourself.

The "Common Sense" will cost you more to buy—and the additional money it will make for you through years of faithful service, because of its inbred quality, will be mighty big dividends on the investment.

It is a pleasure to furnish complete information about "Common Sense" Tractors—and perhaps we can help you make a decision on the tractor best fitted to suit your needs.

Common Sense Gas Tractor Company, 650 9th St. S. E. Minneapolis, Minnesota

---

MODEL K

CLIMAX ENGINEERING CO

KEROSENE

TRACTOR ENGINES

A New Design, a Real Tractor Engine

4 cylinder, L-Head, 4¾ and 5 in. bore, 6½ in. stroke, cylinders in pairs, separate heads, large water jackets, pressure lubricating system, enclosed variable speed governor, dust excluding devices throughout, centrifugal pump. Full specifications, prices and deliveries upon request.

KEROSENE ECONOMY with GASOLINE FLEXIBILITY

CLIMAX
ENGINEERING CO.
CLINTON, IOWA.

THE COMMON SENSE GAS TRACTOR CO.

Minneapolis, Minnesota

Common Sense 20-50   1917-1920

Common Sense 20-50
The Common Sense Gas Tractor Co., Minneapolis, Minn.

Three wheels, driving from one rear wheel. Recommended for four to six 14″ plows, 32″ thresher. Length 156 inches, width 78 inches, height 66 inches. Diameter of drive wheels 62 inches, face 24 inches. Weight 5,900 lbs. Price $1850. Herschell-Spillman vertical eight cylinder motor, cast en bloc, $3\frac{1}{4}x5$, r. p. m. 1,200 normal, L-Head. Schebler gasoline carburetor. K-W high tension independent magneto, with impulse starter. Centrifugal pump, fan and Todd tubular radiator. Pressure feed lubrication. Sliding spur gear speed change, enclosed. Chain final drive, semi-enclosed. Machined steel gearing. Hyatt roller transmission bearings.

CORN BELT TRACTOR CO.

Minneapolis, Minnesota

Corn Belt 7-18   1917

Corn Belt 7-18
Corn Belt Tractor Co., Minneapolis, Minn.

Four wheel, driving from two front wheels. Recommended for two 14″ plows or 24″ thresher. Length 150 inches, width 90 inches, height 72 inches. Weight 4,000 lbs. Price $750. Horizontal opposed two cylinder motor, $5\times6^{1/2}$, 750 r. p. m. normal. Gasoline carburetor, high tension dual ignition. Centrifugal pump, fan and tubular radiator. Chain final drive. Hess Bright bearings in transmission.

DAUCH MANUFACTURING CO.

Sandusky, Ohio

Sandusky 10-20   1917-1921

Sandusky 10-20
Dauch Manufacturing Co., Sandusky, Ohio.

Four wheels, driving from two rear wheels. Recommended for two or three 14″ plows, 24″ thresher. Length 140 inches, width 74 inches, height 58 inches. Diameter of drive wheels 48 inches, face 12 inches. Weight 4,600 lbs. Price $1095. Level springs both front and rear. Vertical four cylinder motor, cast en bloc, $4\frac{1}{4} \times 5\frac{1}{4}$, r.p.m. 1,000 normal, L-Head. Kingston dual gasoline or kerosene carburetor. Dixie & Sevison high tension independent magneto with impulse starter. Centrifugal pump, fan and Candler cellular radiator. Pressure feed and splash lubrication. Two speeds forward and one reverse, 2 to 3 m.p.h. Spur gear speed change, enclosed. Internal worm final drive, machined steel gearing. SKF ball and six Hyatt roller transmission bearings. Bronze drive axle bearings.

Tractor Insurance

We have originated a special policy for the sole purpose of providing good protection anywhere, against hazards of fire, explosion, self-ignition, lightning, tornado and the perils of transportation, for the benifit of tractor owners.

We are ready to meet the requirements of farmer, municipality, manufacturer, distributer and dealer.

Special proposition for dealers and distributers.

Real insurance service is furnished by our Tractor and Automobile Department without cost.   It can be yours for the asking.

Consult our agents, or write us your needs today, and let us help you.

HANOVER FIRE INSURANCE CO.

Home Office   *Western Dept.*   *Pacific Coast Dept.*
NEW YORK   *CHICAGO*   *SAN FRANCISCO*
34 Pine St.   *Insurance Exchange*   *411 Sansome St.*

DAYTON-DICK CO.

Quincy, Illinois

Leader 15-25 1917

Leader 15-25
Dayton-Dick Co., Quincy, Ill.

Four wheels, driving from two rear wheels. Recommended for three or four 14″ plows, 30x32 thresher. Length 134 inches, width 60 inches, height 60 inches. Diameter of drive wheels 48 inches, face 12 inches. Weight 5,000 lbs. Price $1150. Erd vertical four cylinder motor, cast en bloc, 4x6, r.p.m. 750 normal, valve-in-head. Kingston float feed gasoline or kerosene carburetor. Kingston high tension independent magneto, with impulse starter. Centrifugal pump, fan and Perfex cellular radiator. Pressure feed oil bath lubrication. Two speeds forward and reverse, $2\frac{1}{2}$ to $3\frac{1}{2}$ m. p. h. Sliding spur gear speed change, enclosed. Internal gear final drive. Machined steel gearing. Bronze and babbitt bearings.

EAGLE MANUFACTURING CO.

Appleton, Wisconsin

Eagle 16-30 1917-1921

Eagle 16-30
Eagle Manufacturing Co., Appleton, Wis.

Four wheels, driving from two rear wheels. Recommended for four to five 14″ plows, 34″ thresher. Length 141 inches, width 70 inches, height 78 inches. Diameter of drive wheels 52 inches, face 12 inches. Weight 7,100 lbs. Price $1300. Horizontal two cylinder motor, cast en bloc, 8x8, r.p.m. 425 normal, valve-in-head. Linga kerosene carburetor. Dixie high tension magneto, with impulse starter. Centrifugal pump, fan and Perfex cellular radiator. Madison-Kipp force sight feed lubrication. Sliding spur gear speed change, enclosed. Spur gear final drive, enclosed. Cast semi-steel gearing. Five Hyatt roller transmission bearings.

ELGIN TRACTOR CORP.

Elgin, Illinois

Elgin 9-18   1917

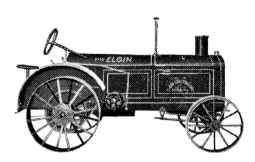

Elgin 9-18
Elgin Tractor Corporation, Elgin, Ill.

Four wheels, driving from two rear wheels. Recommended for two 14" plows, 24" thresher. Length 128 inches, width 54 inches, height 68 inches. Diameter of drive wheels 42 inches, face 8 inches. Weight 2,900 lbs. Price $825. Buda vertical four cylinder motor, cast en bloc, $3\frac{3}{4}$x$5\frac{1}{8}$, r.p.m. 900 normal, L-Head. Kingston float feed gasoline carburetor. High tension independent magneto, fixed. Thermo-syphon water cooled Perfex cellular radiator. Buda constant level splash lubrication. Friction speed change, enclosed, 0 to $3\frac{1}{2}$ m.p.h., with sprocket change, to 8 m.p.h. Two chain final drive. Nickel steel gearing. Six Hyatt roller transmission bearings.

G. W. ELLIOTT & CO.

DeSmet, South Dakota

Dakota No. 1, 7-10   1917
Dakota No. 2, 14-18   1917

Dakota No. 1, 7-10

G. W. Elliott & Co., DeSmet, S. D.

Three wheel, drive wheel in rear center. Recommended for two 14" plows, 18" thresher. Drive wheel 36 inches diameter, 48 inch face. Length 132 inches, width 70 inches, height 66 inches. Weight, 2,800 lbs. Price $935. Waukesha four cylinder vertical L-Head motor, cast en bloc, $3\frac{3}{4}$x$5\frac{1}{4}$, 850 r.p.m. normal. Kingston gasoline carburetor. Kingston high tension independent magneto, manual control, with impulse starter. Rotary pump, fan and exhaust air circulation, and tubular radiator. Waukesha automatic splash lubrication. One speed forward and reverse, 2 to 4 m.p.h Chain final drive. Machined steel and cast iron gearing. Babbitt bearings throughout.

Dakota No. 2, 14-18
G. W. Elliott & Co., DeSmet, S. D.

Three wheel, drive wheel in rear center. Recommended for four 14″ plows, 26″ thresher. Drive wheels 42 inches diameter, 60 inch face. Length 156 inches, width 79 inches, height 78 inches. Waukesha four cylinder vertical L-Head motor, cast in pairs $4^{1}/_{2} \times 6^{3}/_{4}$, 750 r.p.m. normal. Kingston double gasoline and kerosene carburetor. Kingston high tension independent magneto, manual control, with impulse starter. Rotary pump, fan and exhaust air circulation, and tubular radiator. Waukesha automatic splash lubrication. One speed forward and reverse, 2 to 4 m.p.h. Chain final drive. Machined steel and cast iron gearing. Babbitt bearings.

EMERSON-BRANTINGHAM IMPLEMENT CO.

Rockford, Illinois

E-B 9-16	1917-1919
E-B 12-20	1917-1920
Big Four 20-35	1917-1920
Reeves 40-60	1917-1918

E-B 9-16
Emerson-Brantingham Implement Co., Rockford, Ill.

Four wheels, driving from two rear wheels. Recommended for two 14″ plows. Length $150^{1}/_{2}$ inches, width 72 inches, height 76 inches. Diameter of drive wheels 54 inches, face 8 inches. Weight 4,000 lbs. Price $875. Four cylinder vertical L-Head motor, cast en bloc, $4^{1}/_{8} \times 4^{1}/_{4}$, 800 r.p.m. normal. Bennett dual gasoline or kerosene carburetor. K-W high tension independent magneto, manual control. Centrifugal pump, fan and Perfex cellular radiator. Pressure feed and splash lubrication. Two forward and one reverse speeds, 1.72 to 2.33 m.p.h. Selective sliding spur and bevel gear speed change, enclosed. Spur final drive. Machined steel gears. Hyatt transmission bearings.

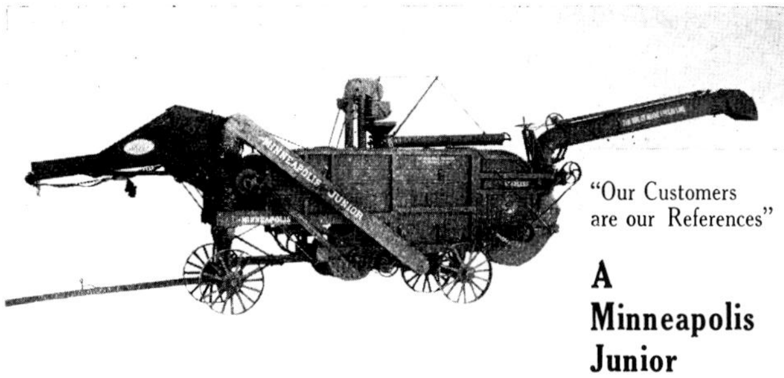

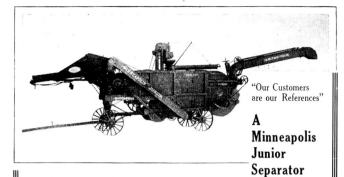

"Our Customers are our References"

A Minneapolis Junior Separator with any medium power tractor makes an ideal outfit and will be a source of profit to the man who owns one. Doubly fortunate will he be if his tractor is also of "*The Great Minneapolis Line.*"

CATALOG AND TESTIMONIAL BOOKS FREE

Minneapolis Threshing Machine Co.

HOPKINS, MINN.

Built up to a Standard Not down to a price

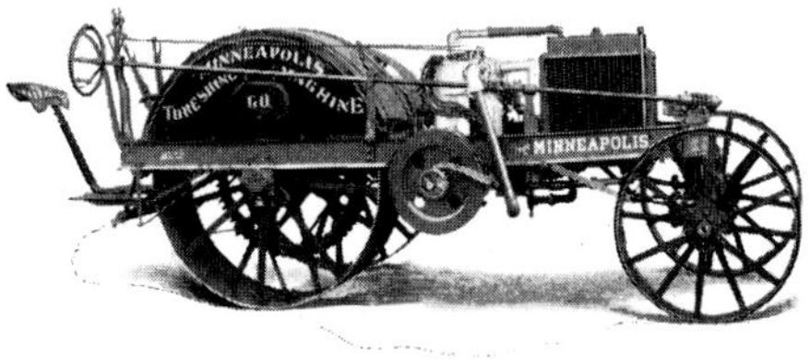

10-20 PLOW BOY — ALL STANDARD TRACTOR — 13-30 PLOW MAN

A RECORD OF SUCCESS

THE original Plow Boy All-Standard Tractor was developed by engineers of established reputation in the construction of successful tractors.

By utilizing all this previous experience and absolutely standardizing every feature of our tractor, we have produced a machine of unqualified success. Although we have refined various details, there has been no occasion for a single radical change.

This record is the result of the hardest kind of service in the field and is backed by the hearty endorsement of farmers, dealers and export buyers.

Every working unit is standard including the powerful 4-Cylinder Buda Motor, Hyatt Roller Bearings, Combination One-Case Transmission, Flexible Coil Radiator with Triple Cooling System, Oscillating Front Axle, French & Hecht Wheels with removable bushings, Automobile Control, Automatic Steering Appliance, etc., etc.

Write for Catalog and detailed information.

INTERSTATE ENGINE & TRACTOR Co.

WATERLOO IOWA

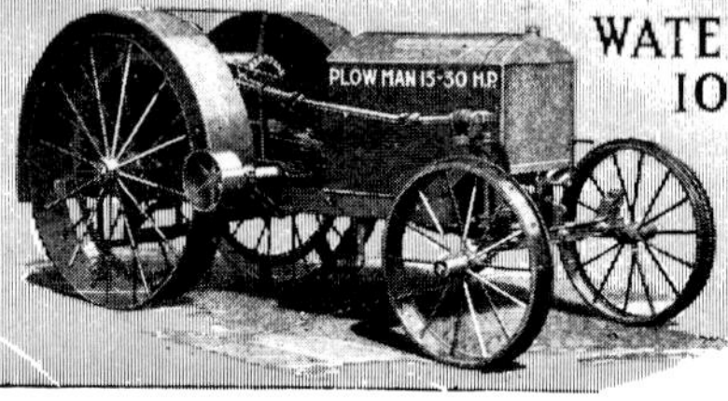

Spark Plug Specifications for various makes of TRACTORS

Champion Toledo

Dependable Spark Plugs

The explosion in the engine's cylinders determine the power of a tractor.

To insure that all the latent power in every cylinder-full of gas mixture will be set-off, be sure to use Champion Toledo Dependable Spark Plugs.

The success of these Toledo-made plugs is evidenced by the fact that four out of every five of all gasoline motors leave their factories equipped with them.

There is a Champion Toledo plug designed especially for every type of engine.

Champion Spark Plug Company

501 UPTON AVENUE — TOLEDO, OHIO

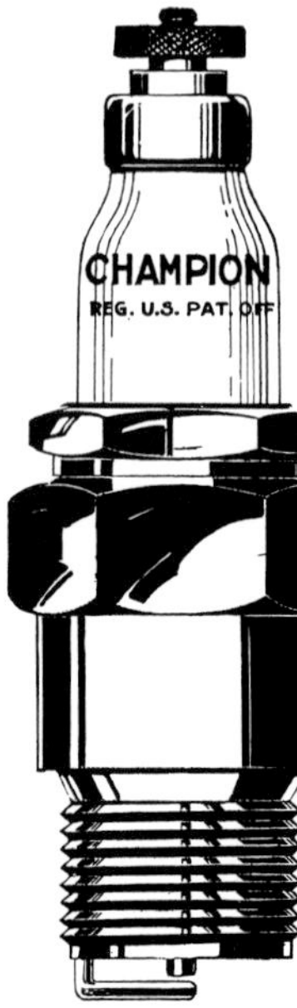

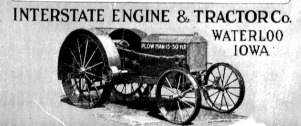

Allis Chalmers Co., "Allis Chalmers," Milwaukee, Wis., 2-pc. Stone ⅞".
Aultman-Taylor Mchy. Co., "Aultman Taylor," Mansfield, O., 2-pc. Stone ½".
Advance Rumely Thresher Co., "All Purpose," LaPorte, Ind., Con. ⅞".
C. L. Best Gas Traction Co., "Pony," Oakland, Cal., Con. ½".
Buckeye Mfg. Co., "Buckeye," Anderson, Ind., Con. ½" or ⅞".
Buckeye Traction Ditcher, Findlay, O., Con. ½" long. Heavy Duty ½".
Bull Tractor, "Bull," "Little Bull," "Big Bull," Minneapolis, Minn., 2-pc. Stone ½" Reg. ½".
Bulkley Rider Tractor Corp., Los Angeles, Cal., Con. ⅞".
Central Locomotive Car Wks., Chicago, Ill., 2-pc. Stone ⅞".
Common Sense Tractor Co., "Common Sense," Minneapolis, Minn., Reg. ⅞".
Denning Tractor Co., "Denning," Cedar Rapids, Ia., Con. or Heavy Duty ⅞".
Dill Tractor Co., "Dill," Harrisburg, Ark., Reg. or Con. ½".
Eagle Mfg. Co., "Eagle," Appleton, Wis., Reg. ½".
Elec. Wheel Co., "All Work," Quincy, Ill., Heavy Duty or 2-pc. Stone, ½" or ⅞".
Emerson-Brantingham, "Big Four," "Emerson Model L," Minneapolis, Minn., Heavy Duty ½".
Fairbanks-Morse, "Fairbanks-Morse," Chicago, Ill., Reg. ½".
Fairmont Mch. Co., "Fairmont," Fairmont, Minn., Reg. ⅞".
Federal Bridge & Struct. Co., Waukesha, Wis., 2-pc. Stone and Con., ½" or ⅞".
Gray Tractor Co., "Gray," Minneapolis, Minn., Reg. ⅞".
Gould Shapley & Muir, Brantford, Can., 2-pc. Stone ½".
Happy Farmer Tractor Co., "Happy Farmer," Minneapolis, Minn., Reg. ½".
Holt Mfg. Co., "Baby Caterpillar," Peoria, Ill., 2-pc. Stone ½".
International Harvester Co., "I. H. C. Mogul," "I. H. C. Mogul, Jr., "I. H. C. Titan," Chicago, Ill., Con. ⅞".
Joliet Oil Tractor Co., "Bates Steel Mule," Joliet, Ill., Heavy Duty ⅞", Con. ⅞" long.
Kinnard-Haines, "Kinnard," Minneapolis, Minn., Con. ½" long.
Lion Tractor Co., "Lion," Minneapolis, Minn., Reg. ½".
Minneapolis Steel Mchy. Co., "Minneapolis," Minneapolis, Minn., Reg. ½" or ⅞".
Moline Plow Co., "Moline Universal," Moline, Ill., 2-pc. Stone ½".
Peoria Tractor Co., "Peoria," Peoria, Ill., 1-pc. Stone ½" or ⅞".
Pioneer Tractor Mfg. Co., "Pioneer," Winona, Minn., 2-pc. Stone ½".
Red Wing Motor Co., Red Wing, Minn., Reg. ⅞".
Toro Motor Co., Minneapolis, Minn., Reg. ½" or 2-pc. Stone ½".
Elgin Tractor Corporation, "Elgin," Elgin, Ill., 2-pc. Stone ⅞".
Wallis Tractor Co., "Wallis Cub," Racine, Wis., Con. ⅞".
Waterloo Gas Eng. Co., "Waterloo Boy," Waterloo, Ia., ½" Extra Long.
Wilcox Motor Car Co., Minneapolis, Minn., Reg. ½".

E-B 12-20
Emerson-Brantingham Implement Co., Rockford, Ill.

Four wheel, driving from two rear wheels. Recommended for three 14" plows, 24x32 thresher. Length $154\frac{1}{2}$ inches, width $77\frac{1}{2}$ inches, height 86 inches. Weight 6,500 lbs. Price $1140. Drive wheels 60 inches diameter, 12 inch face. Four cylinder vertical L-Head motor, cast in pairs, $4\frac{1}{2}$x5, 800 r.p.m. normal. Bennett dual gasoline or kerosene carburetor. K-W high tension independent magneto, manual control. Centrifugal pump, fan and Perfex cellular radiator. Pressure feed and splash lubrication. Three forward and one reverse speeds, 1.66 to 4.75 m.p.h. Selective spur and bevel speed change, enclosed. Spur final drive. Machined and rough steel and semi-steel gearing. Hyatt transmission bearings.

Big Four 20-35
Emerson-Brantingham Implement Co., Rockford, Ill.

Four wheel, driving from two rear wheels. Recommended for five 14" plows, 28×48 thresher. Length $196\frac{1}{2}$ inches, width $181\frac{1}{8}$ inches, height $116\frac{1}{4}$ inches. Weight 9,800 lbs. Price $1800. Drive wheels 72 inches diameter, face 16 inches. Four cylinder vertical motor, cast in pairs, 5×7, L-Head, 700 r.p.m. normal. Bennett dual gasoline or kerosene carburetor. K-W high tension independent magneto with manual control. Centrifugal pump, fan and Perfex cellular radiator. Pressure feed and splash lubrication. Two speeds forward, one reverse, 1.71 to 2.76 m.p.h. Sliding spur and bevel selective speed change, enclosed. Spur final drive. Machined and rough steel and semi steel gears. Hyatt roller transmission bearings.

Reeves 40-60
Emerson-Brantingham Implement Co., Rockford, Ill.

Four wheel, driving from two rear wheels. Recommended for eight to ten 14″ plows, 36x60 thresher. Length 198 inches, width 112 inches, height 130 inches. Weight 23,500 lbs. Price $2925. Four cylinder L-Head motor, cast separately, $7\frac{1}{4}$x9, r.p.m. 500 normal. Bennett dual gasoline or kerosene carburetor. K-W high tension independent magneto with impulse starter. Plunger pump, fan and tubular radiator. Detroit force sight feed lubrication. One forward and one reverse speed, 2 m.p.h. Spur final drive. Babbitt transmission and drive axle bearings.

FOUR DRIVE TRACTOR CO.

Big Rapids, Michigan

Fitch Model 20-30   1917-1919

Fitch Model 20-30
Four Drive Tractor Co., Big Rapids, Mich.

Drives on all four wheels, Recommended for three to four 14″ plows. Length 113 inches, width 68 inches, height 68 inches. Weight 4,400 lbs. Price $2000. Waukesha four cylinder vertical motor, cast en bloc, $4 \times 5^{3}/_{4}$, 800 r.p.m. normal. Any standard gasoline carburetor. Dixie high tension independent magneto. Centrifugal pump, fan and Wright tubular radiator. Waukesha automatic splash lubrication. Three speeds forward, one reverse, 1 to $4^{1}/_{2}$ m.p.h. Muncie Gear Works transmission, enclosed. Worm in rear, gear in front. Final drive, all enclosed. Machined cut, hardened and ground nickel steel gearing. Timken roller bearings in transmission and drive axles.

GEHL BROS. MANUFACTURING CO.
West Bend, Wisconsin

Gehl 12-25   1917-1918

Gehl 12-25
Gehl Bros. Mfg. Co., West Bend, Wis.

Three wheels, driving from one rear drum. Recommended for three 14″ plows and 30″ thresher. Length 162 inches, width 86 inches, height 59 inches. Diameter of drum 48 inches, face 42 inches. Weight 4,200 lbs. Price $1150. Waukesha vertical four cylinder motor, cast in pairs, $4\frac{1}{2} \times 6\frac{3}{4}$, r. p. m. 900 normal, L-Head. Kingston kerosene carburetor. Kingston high tension independent magneto, variable, with impulse starter. Centrifugal pump, fan and Ideal cellular radiator. Waukesha automatic splash lubrication, gears running in oil. Sliding gear speed change, enclosed. Spur gear final drive, enclosed. Machined steel gearing. Hyatt roller transmission bearings. Coil springs in front.

GILE TRACTOR & ENGINE CO.
Ludington, Michigan

Gile Model L 10-20   1917-1918
Gile Model K 12-25   1917

Gile Model L 10-20
Gile Tractor & Engine Company, Ludington, Mich.

Three wheels, driving from two rear wheels. Recommended for two 14″ plows. Length 135 inches, width 88 inches, height 68 inches. Diameter of drive wheels 60 inches, face 12 inches. Weight 4,500 lbs. Price $735. Horizontal opposed two cylinder motor, cast separately, $5\frac{1}{2} \times 6\frac{1}{2}$, r. p. m. 750 normal, L-Head. Bennett gasoline carburetor. High tension automatic magneto. Centrifugal pump, fan and Modine cellular radiator. Madison-Kipp force sight feed and splash lubrication. Spur speed change, enclosed. Roller pinion final drive, open. Cut Nikrome steel gearing. Hyatt roller transmission bearings.

Gile Model K 12-25
Gile Tractor & Engine Company, Ludington, Mich.

Two crawlers. Recommended for three 14″ plows. Length 95 inches, width 68 inches, height 70 inches. Diameter of crawlers 30 inches, face 12 inches. Total area traction surface 1,200 square inches. Weight 6,000 lbs. Price $1470. Horizontal opposed two cylinder motor, cast separately, $6 \times 6^{1}/_{2}$, r. p. m. 750 normal, L-Head. Bennett gasoline carburetor. High tension independent magneto, automatic. Plunger pump, fan and Modine cellular radiator. Madison-Kipp force sight feed lubrication. Spur gear speed change, enclosed. Roller pinion final drive. Cut Nikrome steel gearing. Hyatt roller transmission bearings. Helical springs in drive axle.

GOLDEN GATE GAS TRACTOR CO.
Berkeley, California

Golden Gate 10-20   1917

Golden Gate 10-20
Golden Gate Gas Tractor Co., Berkeley, Cal.

Four wheels, driving from two rear wheels. Recommended for three 14″ plows, 20″ thresher. Length 120 inches, width 50 inches, height 54 inches. Diameter of drive wheels 54 inches, face $12^{1}/_{2}$ inches. Weight 4,500 lbs. Price $1750. Four cylinder vertical motor, cast en bloc, $4^{3}/_{4} \times 5^{1}/_{2}$, r.p.m. 750 normal, L-Head. Stromberg distillate carburetor. Bosch high tension magneto. Centrifugal pump, fan and Perfex cellular radiator. Splash lubrication. Spur gear final drive, enclosed. Finished hardened alloy steel gearing. Timken roller transmission bearings.

1917   99

THE GRAIN BELT TRACTOR CO.

Minneapolis, Minnesota

Grain Belt 15-35   1917-1918

Grain Belt 15-35
The Grain Belt Tractor Co., Minneapolis, Minn.

Four wheels, driving from two rear wheels. Recommended for four 14" plows, 28" thresher. Length 156 inches, width 78 inches, height 108 inches. Diameter of drive wheels 60 inches, face 18 inches. Weight 5,700 lbs. Price $1150. Waukesha vertical four cylinder motor, cast in pairs, $4\frac{1}{2}$x$6\frac{3}{4}$, r. p. m. 850 normal, L-Head. Bennett gasoline carburetor. K-W high tension independent magneto, with impulse starter. Centrifugal pump, fan and radiator. Waukesha automatic splash lubrication. Sliding gear speed change, enclosed. Spur gear final drive, enclosed. Machined steel gearing. Hyatt roller transmission bearings. Speed $2\frac{1}{2}$ to 4 m. p. h.

HACKNEY MANUFACTURING CO.

St. Paul, Minnesota

Orchard 7-13   1917
Corn & Cotton 8-14   1917
Auto Plow No. 3, 16-32   1917
Auto Tractor 17-32   1917
Auto Plow No. 4, 20-40   1917

Orchard 7-13
Hackney Mfg. Co., St. Paul, Minn.

Four wheels and one crawler drive. Recommended for two 14" plows, 24" thresher. Length 70 inches, width 46 inches, height 48 inches. Diameter of drive wheels 30 inches, face 10 inches. Weight 2,800 lbs. Price $800. Vertical two cylinder motor, cast en bloc, $4\frac{1}{2}$x6, r.p.m. 600 normal. Ensign gasoline carburetor. High tension independent magneto. Centrifugal pump, fan and cellular radiator. Splash lubrication. Spur gear speed change, enclosed. Spur gear final drive. Machined steel gearing. Hyatt roller transmission bearings.

Corn & Cotton 8-14
Hackney Mfg. Co., St. Paul, Minn.

Four wheels, driving from one rear wheel. Recommended for two 14" plows. 24" thresher. Length 100 inches, width 48 inches, height 54 inches. Diameter of drive wheel 48 inches, face 8 inches. Weight 2,500 lbs. Price $750. Vertical two cylinder motor, cast en bloc, $4\frac{1}{2} \times 7$, r.p.m. 600 normal. Ensign gasoline and kerosene carburetor. Centrifugal pump, fan and cellular radiator. Splash lubrication. Spur gear speed change, enclosed. Spur gear final drive. Machined steel gearing.

Auto Plow No. 3, 16-32
Hackney Mfg. Co., St. Paul, Minn.

Three wheels, driving from two front wheels. Recommended for three 14" plows, 28" thresher. Length 180 inches, width 84 inches, height 84 inches. Diameter of drive wheels 66 inches, face 14 inches. Weight 7,400 lbs. Price $1000. Vertical four cylinder motor, cast separately, 5×6, r.p.m. 750 normal, L-Head. Kingston gasoline carburetor. Coil springs in front. High tension dual magneto. Centrifugal pump, fan and cellular radiator. Splash lubrication. Sliding spur gear speed change, enclosed. Chain final drive. Drop forged machined gearing.

Auto Tractor 17-32
Hackney Mfg. Co., St. Paul, Minn.

Three wheels, driving from two front wheels. Recommended for three 14" plows, 28" thresher. Length 176 inches, width 84 inches, height 84 inches. Diameter of drive wheels 66 inches, face 14 inches. Weight 6,000 lbs. Price $800. Coil spring in front. Vertical four cylinder motor, cast, separately, 5×6, r.p.m. 750 normal, L-Head. Kingston gasoline carburetor. High tension independent magneto. Centrifugal pump, fan and cellular radiator. Splash lubrication. Sliding spur gear speed change, enclosed. Chain final drive. Drop forged machined gearing.

Auto Plow No. 4, 20-40
Hackney Mfg. Co., St. Paul, Minn.

Three wheels, driving from two front wheels. Recommended for four 14" plows, 30" thresher. Length 176 inches, width 84 inches, height 84 inches. Diameter of drive wheels 66 inches, face 14 inches. Weight 8,200 lbs. Price $1200. Coil spring drive axle. Vertical four cylinder motor, cast in pairs, $4\frac{3}{4} \times 7$, r.p.m. 700 normal, L-Head. Ensign gasoline or kerosene carburetor. High tension independent magneto. Centrifugal pump, fan and cellular radiator. Pressure feed lubrication. Sliding spur gear speed change, enclosed. Chain final drive. Drop forged machined gearing.

HERBERT TRACTOR CO.

Detroit, Michigan

Herbert 16-32   1917

Herbert 16-32

Herbert Tractor Company, Detroit, Michigan

Four wheels, driving from two rear wheels. Recommended for three 14″ plows. Length 126 inches, width 60 inches, height 60 inches. Diameter of drive wheels 48 inches, face 12 inches. Weight 3,000 lbs. Price $795. Waukesha four cylinder vertical motor, cast en bloc, $3\frac{3}{4} \times 5\frac{1}{4}$ r.p.m. 1,200 normal, L-Head. Kingston kerosene carburetor. Eisemann high tension independent magneto, fixed. Pump, fan and cellular radiator. Waukesha automatic splash lubrication. "H" plate speed change, enclosed. Machined high carbon steel gears. New departure ball and Hyatt roller transmission bearings. Hyatt drive wheel bearings.

HURON TRACTOR CO.

Detroit, Michigan

Huron Four 12-25   1917

Huron Four 12-25

Huron Tractor Company, Detroit, Mich.

Four wheels, driving from two rear wheels. Recommended for three 14″ plows, 28″ thresher. Length 126 inches, width 71 inches, height 67 inches. Diameter of drive wheels 48 inches, face 12 inches. Weight 3,800 lbs. Price $1060. Waukesha vertical four cylinder motor, cast in pairs, $4\frac{1}{4} \times 5\frac{3}{4}$, r.p.m. 1,000 normal, L-Head. Kingston dual kerosene and gasoline carburetor. Dixie high tension independent magneto. Pump, fan and Modine cellular radiator. Hyatt roller bearings throughout. Waukesha automatic splash lubrication. Three speeds forward and one reverse, 1 to 5 m.p.h. Selective sliding spur gear speed change, enclosed. Internal spur gear final drive, enclosed. Machined steel gearing.

ILLINOIS SILO & TRACTOR CO.

Bloomington, Illinois

Illinois 8-16   1917

Illinois 8-16

Illinois Silo & Tractor Co., Bloomington, Ill.

Four wheels, driving from two rear wheels. Recommended for two 14" plows. Diameter of drive wheels 48 inches, face $7\frac{1}{2}$ inches. Length 90 inches, width 60 inches, height 60 inches. Sterling four cylinder vertical motor, cast en bloc, $3 \times 4\frac{1}{4}$, 1,200 r. p. m. normal, valve-in-head. Zenith gasoline carburetor. High tension ignition. Plunger pump, fan and Eureka cellular radiator. Force and splash lubrication. Enclosed speed change and final drive, all gears machined. Hyatt roller bearings in drive axle, coil spring mounted both front and rear.

INTERNATIONAL HARVESTER CO.

Chicago, Illinois

Titan 10-20   1917-1922
Mogul 10-20   1917-1920

Titan 10-20

International Harvester Co., Chicago, Ill.

Four wheel, driving from two rear wheels. Drive wheel 54 inches, face 10 inches. Length 147 inches, width 60 inches, height $66\frac{3}{4}$ inches. Weight 5,525 lbs. Price $950. Horizontal two cylinder valve-in-head motor, $6\frac{1}{2} \times 8$, 500 r.p.m. normal. Special kerosene mixer-carburetor. High tension magneto. Thermo-Syphon water cooling. Madison-Kipp force sight feed lubrication. Two forward and one reverse speeds, 1.87 to 2.5 m.p.h. Sliding selective speed change, enclosed. Chain final drive.

We Guarantee Mogul and Titan Tractors To Operate On Kerosene

In spite of the fact that for some years past Mogul and Titan tractors have operated successfully on kerosene in the hands of average farmers, we still find a vague doubt in the minds of many possible tractor dealers and buyers that any internal combustion tractor will operate successfully and continuously on kerosene.

It is not difficult to find the source of this doubt. The issue is one upon which few people except trained engineers have any definite data. The average farmer, untrained in technical engineering theory or practice, might easily be swayed from

one side to another by the plausible talk of clever salesmen.

We found it necessary to devise a simple, not to be misunderstood method of proving that Mogul and Titan tractors would operate successfully on kerosene in all ordinary circumstances. In order to remove the last shadow of doubt from the mind of any man who was wavering between buying a Mogul or Titan or a gasoline tractor, because he was not sure that our tractors would live up to the promises made for them, we incorporated in the warranty which goes to every purchaser of one of our tractors a definite guarantee that Mogul and Titan tractors would operate successfully on kerosene.

We wish to emphasize the statement that the above guarantee applies to all of the Mogul and Titan tractors described on pages 51 to 53.

International Harvester Company of America

(Incorporated)

Chicago   **U. S. A.**

Four Machines in One—and each machine has Special Features

FIRST OF ALL, The Kardell "Four-in-One" is an 18-horse-power Tractor designed for use on farms of from 100 to 500 acres. On such farms it is supreme. It does more work and better work, and does it at less expense. The secret is its lightness and its "positive grip wheels." The wheels dig in and grip like a horse's hoof. Instead of the usual heavy parts, the Kardell "Four-in-One" comprises the very lightest and simplest units possible, without sacrificing durability. In performance and wearing qualities, this Tractor stands out from among all others as a machine of service—service that costs less.

SECOND, the Kardell "Four-in-One" is a super-efficient motor plow. It CARRIES its special plow member UNDER the main frame—instead of dragging the PLOWS BEHIND. This patented idea revolutionizes plowing by reducing the draft ONE-THIRD. The three-plow unit is quickly and easily attached to the frame by means of securely hinged stirrups.

The plow bottoms are hitched directly to front end of main frame by an adjustable spring. This spring positively prevents damage resulting from collision with rocks or stumps, because it automatically disengages the clutch whenever such obstacles are encountered.

THIRD, the Kardell "Four-in-One" is a reliable three-ton truck. A patented extension frame, with rear wheels and springs connected, converts it into a 5,000 pound motor-vehicle capable of a speed of 8 miles an hour. Thus converted, the Kardell "Four-in-One" will carry a four-ton load as efficiently as any truck on the market. Sectional steel bands, which are furnished for attaching to the webbed treads of the traction wheels, serve as tires for travel on roads or city streets.

FOURTH, the Kardell "Four-in-One" is a 30-horse-power "all around" engine. It furnishes motive power sufficient to do any work on the farm, from churning to filling silos. And none of its power is wasted.

Here Are The Selling Advantages of
THE KARDELL
"FOUR-IN-ONE"
TRACTOR

Every farmer with 100 or more acres will soon be in the market for a tractor—if he is not already.

And every farmer who can think in terms of the Tractor is the kind of farmer who is anxious to use "efficiency" equipment in every department of his work.

Now then—here's a tractor, simpler, better, more economical than the usual heavy type—and this tractor is readily converted into a truck, a plow or a stationary engine.

The "simplicity" feature overcomes all fear on the part of the farmer who hesitates to invest in complicated machinery. The "durability" feature means long wear under all kind of service. The "economy" feature means most of all. This feature is the big one in the Kardell superiority. There's a proof of it in our instructive literature. There are actual figures showing just how the Kardell Four-in-One will save $1,370 a year on a 200-acre farm.

There is a detailed description of this improved machine, showing exactly how it surpasses every implement in its class for performance and economy.

If you are at all interested in Tractors, either as a dealer or a consumer, send now for this literature by filling out and mailing the coupon. Mail it today.

Price of Tractor with Motor Plow and Gangs **$1250**
Price of Truck Attachment **225**

The Kardell Tractor & Truck Co.
Dept. 20
3145 Locust St.
St. Louis, Mo.

Coupon
Kardell Tractor Co.,
Dept. 20
3145 Locust St. St. Louis, Mo.
Please send me your FREE literature describing the Kardell Four-in-One.

Name _____
Address _____
I am interested as a consumer ( )
I am interested as a dealer ( )

Mogul 10-20
International Harvester Co., Chicago, Ill.

Four wheels, driving from two rear wheels. Recommended for three 14″ plows. Length 135 inches, width 56 inches, height 70 inches. Weight 5,500 lbs. Drive wheels 54 inches diameter, face 10 inches. Single cylinder 8½x12 motor, r.p.m. 400 normal. Special kerosene-distillate carburetor. High tension magneto. Hopper cooled. Madison-Kipp force sight feed lubrication. Transmission enclosed. Flexible chain final drive. Drop forged carbonized steel gears. Roller transmission and drive axle bearings.

INTERSTATE ENGINE & TRACTOR CO.

Waterloo, Iowa

Plow Boy 10-20   1917
Plow Man 13-30   1917-1919

Plow Boy 10-20
Interstate Engine and Tractor Company, Waterloo, Ia.

Four wheels, driving from two rear wheels. Recommended for two 14″ plows. Length 156 inches, width 70 inches, height 70 inches. Diameter of drive wheels 60 inches, face 10 inches. Weight 3,800 lbs. Price $875. Waukesha vertical four cylinder motor, cast en bloc, 3½x5¼, r.p.m. 1,200 normal, L-Head. Kingston gasoline or kerosene carburetor. Dixie high tension independent magneto with impulse starter. Pump, fan and Perfex cellular radiator. Six Hyatt roller transmission bearings. Waukesha automatic splash lubrication. Sliding gear speed change, enclosed. Roller pinion final drive. Cast steel gearing.

Plow Man 13-30
Interstate Engine and Tractor Company, Waterloo, Ia.

Four wheels, driving from two rear wheels. Recommended for three 14" plows. Length 156 inches, width 70 inches, height 70 inches. Diameter of drive wheels 60 inches, face 10 inches. Weight 3,800 lbs. Price $995. Buda vertical four cylinder motor, cast in pairs, $4\frac{1}{2}x5\frac{1}{2}$, r.p.m. 900 normal, L-Head. Kingston gasoline or kerosene carburetor. Dixie high tension independent magneto, with impulse starter. Pump, fan and Perfex cellular radiator. Hyatt roller transmission bearings. Buda automatic splash lubrication. Sliding gear speed change, enclosed. Roller pinion final drive. Cast steel gearing.

KANSAS CITY HAY PRESS CO.
Kansas City, Missouri

Prairie Dog 10-20   1917

Prairie Dog 10-20
Kansas City Hay Press Co., Kansas City, Mo.

Three wheels, driving from one rear center drive wheel. Recommended for two 14" plows. Length 156 inches, width $74\frac{1}{2}$ inches, height 65 inches. Diameter of drive wheels 48 inches, face 18 inches. Weight 3,000 lbs. Price $850. Waukesha four cylinder motor, cast en bloc, $3\frac{3}{4}x5\frac{1}{4}$, r.p.m 950 normal, L-Head. Bennett gasoline carburetor. Dixie high tension independent magneto with impulse starter. Centrifugal pump, fan and Perfex cellular radiator. Waukesha automatic splash lubrication. Selective sliding bevel gear speed change, enclosed. Enclosed gear final drive. Machined steel gearing. Seven Hyatt roller transmission and two Hyatt roller rear wheel bearings.

KARDELL TRACTOR & TRUCK CO.

St. Louis, Missouri

Four In One 20-32

1917-1919

Four in One 20-32

Kardell Tractor & Truck Co., St. Louis, Mo.

Three wheeled convertible truck and tractor unit, driving from two front wheels. Recommended for three 14" plows. Diameter of drive wheels 60 inches, face 12 inches. Length 158 inches, width 84 inches, height 84 inches. Weight 7,300 lbs. Price $1250. Waukesha four cylinder vertical L-Head motor, cast en bloc, $4\frac{1}{4}x5\frac{3}{4}$, r.p.m. 1,000 normal. Bennett dual gasoline and kerosene carburetor. Dixie high tension independent magneto, with impulse starter. Centrifugal pump, fan and radiator. Waukesha automatic splash lubrication. Two speeds forward, one reverse, 1 to 8 miles per hour. Enclosed speed change gearing. Chain final drive. Machined alloy steel heat treated gears. Hyatt roller transmission bearings. Drive axle mounted on coil and elliptic springs.

KILLEN-STRAIT MANUFACTURING CO.

Appleton, Wisconsin

Strait 15-20
Strait 25-50

1917-1918
1917

Strait 15-30

Killen-Strait Mfg. Co., Appleton, Wis.

Two crawlers and one rear wheel. Recommended for two to three 14" plows. Face of drive wheel 17 inches. Length 154 inches, width 70 inches, height 70 inches. Weight 6,000 lbs. Erd vertical four cylinder motor, cast en bloc, 4x6, r.p.m. 1,000 normal, L-Head. Holley gasoline or kerosene carburetor. Coil springs in front and rear. K-W high tension independent magneto. Centrifugal pump, fan and tubular radiator. Babbitt transmission bearings. Erd constant level splash lubrication. One forward and one reverse, $2\frac{1}{4}$ m.p.h. Sliding spur gear speed change, enclosed. Spur gear final drive. Machined steel gearing.

Strait 25-50
Killen-Strait Mfg. Co., Appleton, Wis.

Three crawlers. Recommended for four to six 14" plows. Length 156 inches, width 72 inches, height 72 inches. Face of crawlers 18 inches, 24 inches and 30 inches. Weight 9,600 lbs. Waukesha vertical four cylinder motor, cast in pairs, $4\frac{3}{4} \times 6\frac{3}{4}$, r.p.m. 900 normal, L-Head. Holley gasoline or kerosene carburetor. K-W high tension independent magneto, with impulse starter. Centrifugal pump, fan and tubular radiator. Babbitt transmission bearings. Waukesha automatic splash lubrication. One forward and reverse speeds, $2\frac{1}{4}$ m.p.m. Sliding spur gear speed change, enclosed. Spur gear final drive. Machined steel gearing. Coil springs front and back.

KINKEAD TRACTOR CO.

Minneapolis, Minnesota

| K. T. 16, 12-25 | 1917 |
| K. T. 17, 12-30 | 1917 |

K. T. 16, 12-25
Kinkead Tractor Co., Minneapolis, Minn.

Three wheels, driving from one rear wheel. Recommended for three 14" plows, 28" thresher. Diameter of drive wheel 60 inches, face 24 inches, height 65 inches. Weight 4,500 lbs. Price $850. Waukesha four cylinder vertical motor, cast in pairs, $4\frac{1}{4} \times 5\frac{3}{4}$ r.p.m. 850 normal, L-Head. Schebler gasoline carburetor. Dixie high tension independent magneto with impulse starter. Centrifugal pump, fan and cellular radiator. Two speeds forward, one reverse, $2\frac{1}{4}$ to 3 m.p.h. Babbitt transmission bearings. Waukesha automatic splash lubrication. Spur gear speed change, enclosed.

K. T. 17, 12-30
Kinkead Tractor Co., Minneapolis, Minn.

Four wheels, driving from two rear wheels. Recommended for three 14″ plows, 28″ thresher. Diameter of drive wheels 54 inches, face 12 inches. Height 60 inches. Weight 4,000 lbs. Price $1250. Waukesha four cylinder vertical motor, cast in pairs, $4\frac{1}{2}$x$6\frac{3}{4}$, r.p.m. 850 normal, L-Head. Schebler kerosene carburetor. Dixie high tension independent magneto with impulse starter. Centrifugal pump, fan and cellular radiator. Hyatt roller transmission and drive axle bearings. Waukesha automatic splash lubrication. Two speeds forward, one reverse, 2 to 3 m.p.h. Bevel and spur gear speed change, enclosed. Machined chrome steel gearing.

LaCROSSE TRACTOR CO.

LaCrosse, Wisconsin

Happy Farmer 8-16   1917
Happy Farmer 12-24   1917-1919

Happy Farmer 8-16
LaCrosse Tractor Co., LaCrosse, Wis.

Three wheels, driving from two rear wheels. Recommended for two 14″ plows, 18″ thresher. Length $152\frac{1}{2}$ inches, width 72 inches, height 62 inches. Diameter of drive wheel 56 inches, face 10 inches. Weight 3,500 lbs. Price $585. Gile horizontal two cylinder motor, 5x$6\frac{1}{2}$, r.p.m. 750 normal, L-Head. Bennett gasoline carburetor. Atwater-Kent high tension dual magneto, automatic. Centrifugal pump, fan and Perfex cellular radiator. Babbitt transmission bearings. Madison-Kipp force sight feed lubrication. One forward and reverse speeds, $2\frac{1}{4}$ m.p.h. Sliding spur gear speed change, enclosed. Roller pinion final drive. Machined steel gearing.

Happy Farmer 12-24
LaCrosse Tractor Co., LaCrosse, Wis.

Three wheels, driving from two rear wheels. Recommended for three 14″ plows, 24″ thresher. Length 142 inches, width $82\frac{1}{2}$ inches, height 62 inches. Diameter of drive wheels 56 inches, face 10 inches. Weight 3,700 lbs. Price $735. Horizontal two cylinder motor, cast in pairs, $5\frac{3}{4}$x7, r.p.m. 750 normal, overhead valves. Kingston kerosene carburetor. Atwater-Kent high tension dual magneto, automatic. Centrifugal pump, fan and Modine cellular radiator. Madison-Kipp force sight feed lubrication. One forward and reverse, $2\frac{1}{2}$ m.p.h. Sliding spur gear speed change, enclosed. Roller pinion final drive. Machined steel and semi-steel gearing. Four transmission and two drive axle Hyatt roller bearings.

La Crosse Happy Farmer Tractors—Models A and B
The Tractors of Great Promise and Wonderful Fulfillment
A Marked Success Where Other Tractors Fail.

Models of simplicity—not a pound of superfluous weight—more power than guaranteed and none of it wasted—designed right—built honestly, of the best materials—adapted to general farm purposes—sold at a fair price—afford a fair profit to the dealer—backed by an absolutely reliable company.

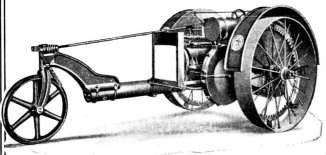

Model "A" 8-16 h. p. **$685** F. O. B. La Crosse, Wis.
1500 lbs. Guaranteed D. B. Pull See Specifications

Model "B" 12-24 h. p. **$835** F. O. B. La Crosse, Wis.
2000 lbs. Guaranteed D. B. Pull See Specifications

PRICES SUBJECT TO CHANGE WITHOUT NOTICE

MODEL "B" IS THE MOST SUCCESSFUL KEROSENE BURNER EVER BUILT
Both Models Perfectly Adapted for Plowing, Disking, Drilling, Pulling Binder, Cutting Ensilage, Running Shredder, Sheller, Feed Grinder, Farm Thresher, Road Building, etc.
Convincing Literature Free—Send for It
Distributors for prompt service in all parts of the United States and Canada

LA CROSSE TRACTOR CO.   LA CROSSE, WISCONSIN

DRIVES LIKE A HORSE

The "Line Drive" Tractor

Drives like a horse. Is started, stopped, backed up and turned right or left with a pair of lines just as anyone would drive a team. A proved success. On the market four years and every machine giving perfect satisfaction.

For field or road work, the "Line Drive" has no equal in simplicity and adaptability to all requirements.

The adaptability and versatility of the "Line Drive" for army work has also been fully demonstrated.

Are you interested? If so please write

THE Line-Drive Tractor (Inc)
MILWAUKEE, WIS.

Sales Office, 525B M. & M. Bank Bldg.

C-W Water Circulator
Cast Aluminum

The
ORIGINAL
Only Guaranteed
Efficient
Water
Cooler

Weight 4 lbs.

ADOPTED
Standard
Equipment
by Largest
Ford Truck
and Tractor
Mfgrs.

Shipped complete ready to install
NO MACHINE WORK NECESSARY
Designed for the

Ford Engine

Write for Manufacturers Prices

Code
"CRUMWI" U. S. A.
Crum-Wiley Mfg. Co.
Peru, Ind.

THE LINE DRIVE TRACTOR, INC.
Milwaukee, Wisconsin

Line Drive 15-25   1917

Line Drive 15-25
The Line Drive Tractor, Inc., Milwaukee, Wis.

Four wheels, driving from two front wheels. Recommended for three 14″ plows, 32″ thresher. Length 161 inches, width $91\frac{1}{2}$ inches, height 72 inches. Diameter of drive wheels 66 inches, face 12 inches. Weight 5,000 lbs. Price $1185. Waukesha vertical four cylinder motor, cast in pairs, $4\frac{1}{4}$x$5\frac{3}{4}$, r.p.m. 900 normal, L-Head. Kingston-Bennett gasoline and kerosene carburetor. Dixie-Eisemann high tension independent magneto. Centrifugal pump, fan and Perfex cellular radiator. Hyatt roller transmission bearings. Waukesha automatic splash lubrication. Two forward and reverse speeds, $2\frac{1}{2}$ to 4 m.p.h. Sliding spur gear speed change, enclosed. Spur gear final drive. Machined cast steel gearing.

LINN MANUFACTURING CO.
Morris, New York

Linn 85   1917
Linn 85
Linn Mfg. Co., Morris, N. Y.

Two crawlers. Recommended for four 14″ plows. Length 174 inches, width 54 inches, height 60 inches. Diameter crawlers 29 inches, face 10 inches, total area traction surface 800 square inches. Weight 7,500 lbs. Price $2000. Continental vertical four cylinder motor, cast in pairs, $4\frac{1}{2}$×$5\frac{1}{2}$, r.p.m. 1,000 normal, L-Head. Schebler gasoline carburetor. High tension magneto. Centrifugal pump, fan and Bush tubular radiator. Continental force feed and splash lubrication. Spur gear speed change, enclosed. Internal gear final drive, enclosed. Machined steel gearing. Ball transmission bearings.

The Atlas Tractor

"The Original Square Turn Tractor"

"Turns in Its Own Length"

TWO MODELS: **2400 4000** Draw Bar Pull

TO THE DEALER

It is of vital importance to you when selling a tractor, that you know that it has been thoroughly tried out. The Atlas Tractor (formerly The Hume) has been manufactured for five years and has proven entirely satisfactory in the hands of the owners, which means additional sales and profits for you.

Lyons Atlas Company, builders of the Atlas Tractor, are the largest and oldest manufacturers of gas and crude oil engines in America, having one of the most complete equipments of any concern in the country. Think what this means to you. Complete information on request.

Lyons Atlas Company

INDIANAPOLIS, INDIANA.

Builders of Tractors and Heavy-Oil Engines.

The Manzel Force Feed Oiler

For

Tractors

6 Feed Left Hand Ratchet Drive Oiler

Puts the Oil Where it's Needed, When it's Needed and in Just the Proper Quantities.

The ideal oiler for tractors. It will handle heavy or light oil in any temperature. It may be run in either direction and at any speed and can be accurately adjusted to supply just the amount of oil needed for each cylinder or bearing, each feed being adjusted independently.

Made with either rotary or ratchet drive.
One to fifty feeds.
Cast-iron, sheet steel or sheet brass reservoirs.

We Make a Specialty of Equipment Business

We can furnish anything you may require in the line of force feed oilers. Our immense facilities enable us to quote attractive prices and to make prompt delivery. Let us quote on your requirements for the coming season.

Manzel Brothers Co.

286-288 Babcock Street

Buffalo, New York

6 Feed Rotary Drive Oiler (Rear View)

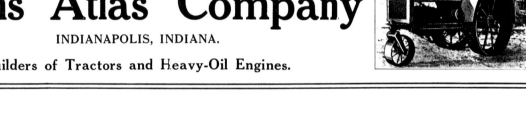

AMERICA'S STANDARD FOUR-CYCLE ENGINE

KERMATH

TRACTOR MOTORS

4 CYCLE CYLINDERS

10 H. P. — 16 H. P. 20 H. P.

All at 1000 R. P. M.

Made also in stationary and marine types

$225 and up

Quantity Prices on Application

KERMATH MFG. CO.

Boydell Bldg.
DETROIT, MICH.

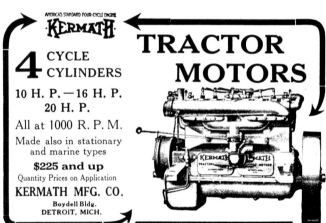

Pfanstiehl Starter Coil

A supplementary vibrating coil to interrupt the primary ignition circuit several times for each opening of the magneto or distributor circuit breaker, thus supplying a shower or series of sparks to the spark plugs and making starting easier with cold, lean or low grade fuel mixtures.

May be used with any standard ignition system.

Pfanstiehl Company, North Chicago, Illinois, U.S.A.

LOCOMOTIVE FINISHED MATERIAL CO.

Atchison, Kansas

Sunflower 15-30   1917

Sunflower 15-30
Locomotive Finished Material Co., Atchison, KS

Four wheels, driving from two rear wheels. Recommended for four 14″ plows. Diameter of drive wheels 50 inches, face 14 inches. Length 143 inches, width 72 inches, height 72 inches. Weight 6,250 lbs. Model four cylinder vertical valve-in-head motor, 5x6, r.p.m. 800 normal. Kingston gasoline carburetor. Kingston high tension independent magneto, with impulse starter. Centrifugal pump, fan and Perfex cellular radiator. Force feed and splash lubrication. Selective sliding spur gear enclosed speed change. Spur gear final drive, enclosed. All gears cut and machined cast steel. Bronze transmission bearings. Roller bearings in drive axle.

LYONS ATLAS CO.

Indianapolis, Indiana

Atlas 12-18   1917
Atlas 20-30   1917

Atlas 12-18
Lyons Atlas Co., Indianapolis, Ind.

Three wheels, driving from two rear wheels. Recommended for three 14″ plows. Length 136 inches, width 67 inches, height 76 inches. Diameter of drive wheels $66\frac{5}{8}$ inches, face 16 inches. Weight 4,500 lbs. Price $1150. Waukesha vertical four cylinder motor, cast en bloc, $3\frac{1}{2}x5\frac{1}{4}$, r.p.m. 850-1,100 normal, L-Head. Kingston gasoline carburetor. High tension variable magneto. Contrifugal pump, fan and Perfex cellular radiator. Waukesha automatic splash lubrication. One speed forward and reverse, $2\frac{1}{2}$ to $2\frac{3}{4}$ m.p.h. Spur gear final drive. Cast manganese gearing. Six Hyatt roller transmission bearings.

1917   113

PLAIN FACTS

About Farm Tractors in General and in Particular About the
LITTLE GIANT TRACTOR

On page 3 of the Cooperative Tractor Catalog will be found illustration of LITTLE GIANT TRACTORS, Model "A" and Model "B," and under lines No. 110-111 will be found general and detailed specifications.

It is impossible in the brief space of this article or the other space assigned to us in this tractor catalog, to give more than a short description of the LITTLE GIANT TRACTOR, and our purpose is not to do more than arouse the reader's interest sufficiently to give us the opportunity of sending full descriptive matter on the subject.

In design, material, workmanship and practical durability the LITTLE GIANT TRACTOR will compare favorably with the highest priced automobile made, and in these respects is as much superior to any other tractor as the highest priced automobile is to the cheapest in the market.

Tractor duty is far heavier than automobiles, commercial trucks or racing cars. Tractor material and workmanship should be equal to if not superior to either. Cast iron, cheap steel and like material, including sloppy workmanship, have no proper place in either.

No intelligent farmer could be induced to buy an automobile built almost entirely of cast iron and other low grade material. Yet for years farmers have been spending their hard-earned money for tractors built in this manner, from which they have received very little, if any, satisfaction.

The LITTLE GIANT TRACTOR is simpler than the Ford or any other automobile made, and will last as long under proper usage as any two or three automobiles. Not a particle of cast iron is used in its construction, hence we claim it is "EVERY OUNCE A TRACTOR."

Tractor sales are the next big proposition, and the wide-awake dealer of today who is successful in selling automobiles is going to be the successful tractor dealer of tomorrow.

No conscientious dealer can afford to jeopardize his business interests or lose the friendship of his customers by selling a tractor or any other article that will not give satisfaction to the user, or cause unreasonable expense to the dealer for trouble and service.

LITTLE GIANT TRACTORS sold in any neighborhood bring repeat orders without solicitation or expense. This is the kind of business that the dealer is looking for and this is the kind of a tractor that the farmer wants.

Good territories are open for LITTLE GIANT TRACTOR agencies with proper kind of dealers, from whom we respectfully solicit correspondence.

MAYER BROTHERS COMPANY

It's the Standard—
America's Lowest Priced Tractor Per Horse Power

22 H. P. ON THE DRAWBAR
AND PLENTY OF RESERVE POWER

The Standard Tractor gives more horse power per hundred pounds of weight than any other tractor on the market. All operations are controlled from the seat—it starts from the seat, and from this position the plows can be adjusted for depth while the tractor is moving.

The Standard Tractor
(A Successful One Man Tractor)

has the weight located just over the drive wheels, giving a maximum of traction. The drawbar is so placed that the heavier the load the harder the tractor will grip the ground. It is equipped with a dual carburetor—fuel can be changed from gasoline to kerosene by merely turning a switch. All high speed gears run in a bath of oil.

This is a machine of proven ability. It will be a big season for tractors. Write for catalog and full information. Our exclusive dealer sales proposition will interest you.

Standard Tractor Co.

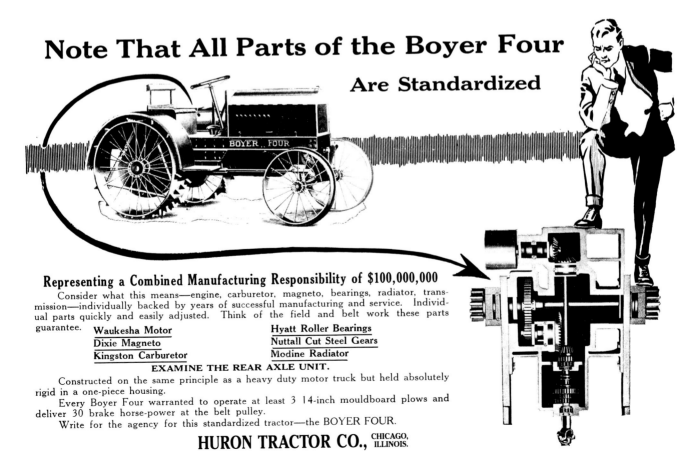

Note That All Parts of the Boyer Four
Are Standardized

Representing a Combined Manufacturing Responsibility of $100,000,000

Consider what this means—engine, carburetor, magneto, bearings, radiator, transmission—individually backed by years of successful manufacturing and service. Individual parts quickly and easily adjusted. Think of the field and belt work these parts guarantee.

Waukesha Motor
Dixie Magneto
Kingston Carburetor

Hyatt Roller Bearings
Nuttall Cut Steel Gears
Modine Radiator

EXAMINE THE REAR AXLE UNIT.

Constructed on the same principle as a heavy duty motor truck but held absolutely rigid in a one-piece housing.

Every Boyer Four warranted to operate at least 3 14-inch mouldboard plows and deliver 30 brake horse-power at the belt pulley.

Write for the agency for this standardized tractor—the BOYER FOUR.

HURON TRACTOR CO., CHICAGO, ILLINOIS.

Atlas 20-30
Lyons Atlas Company, Indianapolis, Ind.

Three wheels, driving from two rear wheels. Recommended for four 14" plows. Length 150 inches, width 74 inches, height 97 inches. Diameter of drive wheels 73 inches, face 16 inches. Weight 7,000 lbs. Price $1745. Waukesha vertical four cylinder motor, cast in pairs, $4\frac{3}{4}$x$6\frac{3}{4}$, r.p.m. 800 normal, L-Head. Kingston gasoline carburetor. High tension variable magneto. Centrifugal pump, fan and Perfex cellular radiator. Bronze transmission bearings. Waukesha automatic splash lubrication. One speed forward and reverse, $2\frac{1}{2}$ to $2\frac{3}{4}$ m.p.h. Spur gear final drive. Cast semi-steel gearing.

McFARLAND & WESTMONT TRACTOR CO.

Sauk City, Wisconsin

Wisconsin 14-25   1917

Wisconsin 14-25
McFarland & Westmont Tractor Co., Sauk City, Wis.

Four wheels, driving from two rear wheels. Recommended for three 14" plows, 28" thresher. Length 140 inches, width 65 inches, height 70 inches. Diameter of drive wheels 52 inches, face 14 inches. Weight 4,800 lbs. Price $1485. Waukesha vertical four cylinder motor, cast in pairs, $4\frac{1}{4}$x$5\frac{3}{4}$, r.p.m. 1,000 normal, L-Head. Senrab kerosene and gasoline carburetor. Eisemann high tension independent magneto, variable, with impulse starter. Centrifugal pump, fan and Modine cellular radiator. Hyatt roller transmission bearings. Waukesha automatic splash lubrication. Two forward and one reverse speeds, $1\frac{1}{4}$ to 5 m.p.h. Selective sliding spur gear speed change, enclosed. Roller pinion final drive. Cast steel gearing.

1917

MONARCH TRACTOR CO.

Watertown, Wisconsin

Neverslip 12-20
Neverslip 18-30

1917-1919
1917-1919

Neverslip 12-20
Monarch Tractor Company, Watertown, Wis.

Two crawlers. Recommended for three 14″ plows. Length 114 inches, width 64 inches, height 72 inches. Face of crawlers 12 inches, total traction area 1,440 sq. in. Weight 5,600 lbs. Price $1200. Horizontal two cylinder motor, cast separately, 6×6, r.p.m. 800 normal. Bennett Duplex gasoline or kerosene carburetor. High tension independent magneto, with impulse starter. Pump, Perfex cellular radiator. Hyatt roller transmission bearings. Madison-Kipp force sight feed splash lubrication. Enclosed speed change. Chain final drive. Machined chrome steel gearing.

Neverslip 18-30
Monarch Tractor Company, Watertown, Wis.

Two crawlers. Recommended for four 14″ plows, 32″ thresher. Length 126 inches, width 66 inches, height 75 inches. Face of crawler 12 inches. Total area traction 1,440 sq. in. Weight 6,100 lbs. Price $1650. Vertical four cylinder motor, cast in pairs, 4¾x7, r.p.m. 650 normal, L-Head. Bennett gasoline or kerosene carburetor. K-W high tension independent magneto, with impulse starter. Pump, Perfex cellular radiator. Detroit force sight feed lubrication. Hyatt roller transmission bearings. Spur gear speed change, enclosed. Roller pinion final drive. Machined steel gearing.

NILSON TRACTOR CO.
Minneapolis, Minnesota

Nilson Senior 35 H.P.   1917

Nilson Senior 35 H.P.
Nilson Tractor Co., Minneapolis, Minn.

Five wheels, driving from three rear wheels. Recommended for four 14" plows, 30" thresher. Length 156 inches, width 89 inches, height 69 inches. Diameter of drive wheels 52 inches, face 23 inches. Weight 5,900 lbs. Price $1635. Waukesha vertical four cylinder motor, cast in pairs, $4\frac{3}{4} \times 6\frac{3}{4}$, r.p.m. 800 normal, L-Head. Kingston gasoline carburetor. K-W high tension independent magneto with impulse starter. Centrifugal pump, fan and Perfex cellular radiator. Waukesha automatic splash lubrication. Speed change, enclosed. Chain final drive. Machined cast steel gearing. Two Hyatt roller bearings in rear axle. Six Hyatt roller transmission bearings. Coil springs drive axle, semi-elliptic front axle.

PARRETT TRACTOR CO.
Chicago, Illinois

Parrett 12-25   1917-1918

Parrett 12-25
Parrett Tractor Company, Chicago, Ill.

Four wheels, driving from two rear wheels. Recommended for three 14" plows, 28" thresher. Weight 5,200 lbs. Price $1190. Diameter drive wheels 60 inches, face 10 inches. Buda vertical four cylinder motor, cast en bloc, $4\frac{1}{4} \times 5\frac{1}{2}$, r.p.m. 900 normal, L-Head. Kingston gasoline or kerosene carburetor. Dixie high tension magneto with impulse starter. Centrifugal pump, fan and Perfex cellular radiator. Pressure feed lubrication. Two forward and one reverse, $\frac{1}{2}$ to 5 m.p.h. Spur gear speed change, enclosed. Spur gear final drive. Cast and machined steel and semi-steel gearing.

PHOENIX MANUFACTURING CO.
Eau Claire, Wisconsin

Phoenix Centiped 32-50   1917

Phoenix Centiped 32-50
Phoenix Manufacturing Company, Eau Claire, Wis.

Four wheels, driving from two rear wheels. Recommended for road use. Diameter of drive wheels 34 inches, face 12 inches. Weight 16,800 lbs. Price $4600. Model four cylinder vertical motor, cast separately, $5\frac{1}{2}$x7, r. p. m. 750 normal, L-Head. Kingston gasoline carburetor. High tension independent, variable magneto. Plunger pump, fan and Kells radiator. Detroit force sight feed and splash lubrication. Spur gear speed change, enclosed. Chain final drive. Machined nickel steel gearing. Spiral springs in drive axle.

PIONEER TRACTOR CO.
Winona, Minnesota

Pioneer Special 17-34   1917-1918
Pioneer 30-60   1917-1919

Pioneer Special 17-34
Pioneer Tractor Co., Winona, Minn.

Three wheel, driving from two rear wheels. Recommended for four 14″ plows or 26″ to 28″ thresher. Diameter of drive wheel 60 inches, face 18 inches. Length 169 inches, width 74 inches, height 64 inches. Weight 8,000 lbs. Price $1350. Four cylinder horizontal opposed motor, cast in pairs, $5\frac{1}{2}$x6, 700 r. p. m. normal, L-Head. Kingston dual gasoline or kerosene carburetor. K-W or Dixie high tension independent magneto with impulse starter. Centrifugal pump, fan and Todd cellular radiator. Own force feed lubrication. Selective sliding gear speed change, enclosed. Enclosed final drive. Machine cut steel gears. Rear axle coil spring mounted.

Pioneer 30-60
Pioneer Tractor Co., Winona, Minn.

Three wheel, driving from two rear wheels. Recommended for ten 14″ plows, 36″ to 40″ thresher. Drive wheels 96 inches diameter, face 24 inches. Length 237 inches, width 120 inches, height 118 inches. Weight 23,600 lbs. Price $3200 Four cylinder horizontal opposed motor, cast in pairs, 7x8, 600 r. p. m. normal, L-Head. Kingston dual gasoline or kerosene carburetor. K-W or Dixie high tension independent magneto, with impulse starter. Centrifugal pump, fan and Todd cellular radiator. Detroit force sight feed lubrication. Selective sliding gear speed change, enclosed.

PLANTATION EQUIPMENT CO.
St. Louis, Missouri

Ultimate 8-16	1917
Ultimate 12-25	1917
Ultimate 16-32	1917

Ultimate 8-16
Plantation Equipment Co., St. Louis, Mo.

Four wheel, driving from two rear wheels. Recommended for two to three 14" plows. Drive wheel 54 inches diameter, 10 inch face. Length 132 inches, width 63 inches, height 54 inches. Weight 2,500 lbs. Price $850. Continental four cylinder motor. Bosch high tension ignition. Pump, fan and Harrison tubular radiator. Splash lubrication. Four speeds forward and reverse, 1 to 5 m.p.h. Cotta transmission, entirely enclosed and running in oil. All gears machined cut steel. Ball bearings in transmission.

Ultimate 12-25
Plantation Equipment Co., St. Louis, Mo.

Four wheel, driving from two rear wheels. Recommended for three to four 14" plows. Diameter of drive wheels 54 inches, face 12 inches. Length 132 inches, width 64 inches, height 54 inches. Weight 3,500 lbs. Price $950. Continental four cylinder motor, $3\frac{3}{4}$x5, 1,000 r.p.m. normal. Gasoline carburetor. Bosch high tension ignition. Pump, fan and Harrison tubular radiator. Four speeds forward and reverse, 1 to 5 m.p.h. Cotta transmission, entirely enclosed and running in oil. All gears machined cut steel. Ball transmission bearings.

Ultimate 16-32
Plantation Equipment Co., St. Louis, Mo.

Four wheels, driving from two rear wheels. Recommended for four to five 14" plows. Drive wheels 54 inches diameter, 12 inch face. Length 132 inches, width 65 inches, height 54 inches. Weight 4,500 lbs. Price $1050. Continental four cylinder motor. Gasoline carburetor. Bosch high tension ignition. Pump, fan and Harrison tubular radiator. Four speeds forward and reverse, 1 to 5 m.p.h. Cotta transmission, all enclosed. All gears machine cut. Ball transmission bearings.

REED FOUNDRY & MACHINE CO.

Kalamazoo, Michigan

Reed 12-25 1917-1920

Reed 12-25
Reed Foundry & Machine Co., Kalamazoo, Mich.

Four wheels, driving from two rear wheels. Recommended for two plows. Waukesha motor. Selective transmission. Height 66 inches.

ROCK ISLAND PLOW CO.

Rock Island, Illinois

Heider Model "D" 9-16 1917-1929
Heider Model "C" 12-20 1917-1927

Heider Model "D" 9-16
Rock Island Plow Co., Rock Island, Ill.

Four wheels, driving from two rear wheels. Recommended for two 14" plows, 18" thresher. Length 130 inches, width 68 inches, height 60 inches. Diameter of drive wheels 54 inches, face 8 inches. Weight 4,000 lbs. Price $795. Waukesha vertical four cylinder motor, cast in pairs, $4\frac{1}{4}x5\frac{3}{4}$, r.p.m. 800 normal, L-Head. Kingston vertical gasoline or kerosene carburetor. Dixie high tension independent magneto, variable, with impulse starter. Centrifugal pump, fan and Perfex cellular radiator. Waukesha automatic splash lubrication. U. S. ball transmission bearings. Spur friction speed change, open. Friction final drive. Cast grey iron gearings.

Proven by 9 Years Actual Field Work

In taking on a tractor agency you want to be sure of at least three main points. First—That the tractor has shown its ability to stand up under hard work by years of actual service. Second—That it is backed by a company with a known reputation for standing back of its products. Third—That its merits are well known to the farmers as a result of consistent advertising and demonstrations. The machines that come up to these specifications are

MODEL "C" **12-20 H. P.** | # HEIDER TRACTORS | **MODEL "D"** **9-16 H. P.**

NOTICE THESE POINTS OF MERIT

Burns Kerosene or Gasoline
Friction Transmission
7 Speeds Forward, 7 Reverse

No Gears to Strip
Heavy Duty Waukesha Motor
Road speed 1 to 4 miles per hour

4 Wheels, 4 Cylinders
Model "C" pulls Three Plows
Model "D" pulls Two Plows

STUDY THE SPECIFICATIONS ON OPPOSITE PAGE

Remember that Heider Tractors are manufactured, sold and backed by a company that has built Farm Tools of Quality for 62 years.

SEND FOR CATALOGS ON BOTH

HEIDER TRACTORS
AND
ROCK ISLAND FARM TOOLS

INCLUDING

Plows
Spreaders
Discs
Drags
Drills
Planters

Seeders
Cultivators
Hay Rakes
Hay Loaders
Stalk Cutters
and

Cream Separators
Litter Carriers
Engines
Wagons
Buggies
Gears

ROCK ISLAND TRACTOR PLOWS

ROCK ISLAND PLOW COMPANY. Rock Island Ill.

"THE OLD RELIABLE RUSSELL LINE"

Backed by seventy-five years' experience in building only **good** farm machinery. Forty years' experience building traction machinery. The Russell line has always meant satisfaction to the user and profit to the seller. All Russell machinery is built of quality material throughout and thoroughly tested before leaving the factory. **We** stand the cost of experimenting—not the farmer.

Kerosene Tractors, 12-24, 20-40, 30-60. All standard four-wheel, kerosene burning, quality machines.
Steam Tractors, 6x8, 7½x10, 8x10, 8¼x12, 9x10, 10x13. Either Standard or Universal Boilers.
Steam Road Rollers and Saw Mill Machinery.
Threshers, Stackers, Feeders and Attachments.

The "Russell Junior" Thresher is built for those farmers who make the most profit from their crops, who insist that they be threshed at the right time, and who have the power to operate this "baby thresher" with a "man's size capacity" for good work. Every tractor dealer should be ready to supply this demand. Send for prices and full description.

The Russell & Company
Massillon, Ohio

Heider Model "C" 12-20
Rock Island Plow Co., Rock Island, Ill.

Four wheels, driving from two rear wheels. Recommended for three 14" plows, 24" thresher. Length 144 inches, width 74 inches, height 96 inches. Diameter of drive wheels 57 inches, face 10 inches. Weight 6,000 lbs. Price $1095. Waukesha vertical four cylinder motor, cast in pairs, $4\frac{1}{2}$x$6\frac{3}{4}$, r.p.m. 750 normal, L-Head. Kingston vertical gasoline or kerosene carburetor. Dixie high tension independent magneto, variable, with impulse starter. Centrifugal pump, fan and Perfex cellular radiator. Waukesha automatic splash lubrication. U. S. ball transmission bearings. Spur friction speed change, open. Friction final drive. Cast steel gearing.

THE RUSSELL & CO.
Massillon, Ohio

Russell 20-40   1917-1919
Russell 30-60   1917-1926

Russell 20-40
The Russell & Company, Massillon, Ohio

Four wheels, driving from two rear wheels. Recommended for five 14" plows, 50" thresher. Length 167 inches, width 66 inches, height 84 inches. Diameter of drive wheels 60 inches, face 16 inches. Weight 9,500 lbs. Vertical four cylinder motor, cast separately, 5x7, r.p.m. 750 normal, L-Head. Kingston dual gasoline or kerosene carburetor. Kingston high tension independent magneto, variable, with impulse starter. Centrifugal pump fan and Perfex cellular radiator. Detroit force sight feed and splash lubrication. American roller and New Departure ball transmission bearings. Coil springs both front and rear. Sliding spur gear speed change, enclosed. Spur gear final drive. Cast semi-steel gearing.

Russell 30-60

The Russell & Company, Massillon, Ohio

Four wheels, driving from two rear wheels. Recommended for eight 14″ plows, 30x60 thresher. Length 222 inches, width 108 inches, height 130 inches. Diameter of drive wheels 84 inches, face 22 inches. Weight 22,000 lbs. Vertical four cylinder motor, cast separately, 8x10, r.p.m. 525 normal, L-Head. Kingston dual gasoline or kerosene carburetor. Bosch high tension coil ignition. Centrifugal pump, fan and Russell tubular radiator. Madison-Kipp force sight feed lubrication. Babbitt transmission bearings. Coil springs both front and rear. Sliding spur gear speed change, enclosed. Spur final drive. Cast semi-steel gearing.

SAMSON SIEVE-GRIP TRACTOR CO.

Stockton, California

Sieve-Grip 6-12   1917
Sieve-Grip 12-25   1917

Sieve-Grip 6-12

Samson Sieve-Grip Tractor Co., Stockton, Cal.

Three wheels, driving from two rear wheels. Recommended for two 14″ plows. Diameter of drive wheel 40 inches, face 14 inches. Total length 138 inches, width 54 inches, height 50 inches. Weight 4,200 lbs. Price $775.00. One cylinder valve-in-head horizontal motor 7x9, 450 r.p.m. normal. Holley distillate vaporizer. Atwater-Kent ignition. Centrifugal pump, fan and radiator. Gravity and splash lubrication. Two speeds forward and one reverse, 1¼ to 3 m.p.h. Spur gear speed change. Roller pinion final drive. Cast steel gearing. Babbitt transmission bearings. Roller bearings in the drive axle.

Madison Kipp Lubricators

PROPER lubrication is the one big element necessary to *lasting* power.

In the quality of our lubricators is reflected our feeling of responsibility to the tractor industry—to make the tractor buyer's investment produce *lasting* returns.

MADISON KIPP LUBRICATOR CO.
MADISON, WISCONSIN

Two out of every three are *Kipp-Equipt*

$195 and a FORD
Makes a Guaranteed Powerful
STAUDE MAK-A-TRACTOR

Changes a Ford into a powerful tractor in 20 minutes, without damaging or changing appearance of Ford. Easy to operate. Plows 5 to 7 acres per day, and is equally successful in all other farm work, road work, and heavy hauling.

You can change from a Ford to a tractor or from a tractor to a Ford in 20 minutes

You can plow in the morning, do heavy hauling in the afternoon, and go pleasure riding in the evening. You can work 24 hours a day for late plowing, or late harvesting. Work in the scorching sun without fear of horses dropping dead. Raise the Ford Top, and you are in the shade.

IT DOES THE WORK OF FOUR HORSES

You can sell your horses and save the expense of feeding them—save housing and caring for them—save veterinary bills—save losses of time through horses' sickness—save losses of money through their death.

The Staude Mak-A-Tractor will do any work done by tractors costing several times as much. It works close to fences, and turns in a small radius.

SPECIAL FEATURES

Special Staude Radiator—six times as efficient as Ford Radiator for cooling. Patent Force Feed Oiling System eliminates lubrication trouble. 38-in. Tractor Wheels with 8-in. Base. Internal gear bolted integral to wheels, mesh into driving pinions which replace Ford rear wheels. 72 Staude Concave Creepers dig into soft soil, giving maximum traction without lost power. Very high clearance.

FULLY GUARANTEED

Combines with any Ford touring car or roadster in 20 minutes. Guaranteed to start and run continuously on high gear, and to do the work of 4 strong, sturdy horses when used with any Ford car in good condition.

Ford power multiplied 100%—speed reduced proportionately through gear reduction in the Staude Mak-A-Tractor itself. Positively no strain on engine.

SEND FOR FREE BOOK

Be sure to send for it and read the many interesting facts about the wonderful Staude Mak-A-Tractor. **Send today.**

E. G. STAUDE
MANUFACTURING CO.
St. Paul, Minn.

Sieve-Grip 12-25
Samson Sieve-Grip Tractor Co., Stockton, Cal.

Three wheels, driving from two rear wheels. Recommended for three 14" plows. Diameter of drive wheels 44 inches, face 18 inches. Length 145 inches, width 60 inches, height 53 inches. Weight 5,500 lbs. Price $1350.00. Four cylinder vertical L-Head motor, cast en bloc, $4\frac{1}{2}x6\frac{3}{4}$, 650 r.p.m. normal. Holley distillate carburetor. Bosch duplex high tension ignition. Centrifugal pump, fan and radiator. Pressure feed and splash lubrication. Two speeds forward and reverse, $\frac{1}{2}$ to 4 m.p.h. Enclosed bevel gear speed change gearing. Roller pinion final drive. Machined and rough cast steel gearing. Babbitt transmission bearings. Roller bearings in drive axle.

SAWYER-MASSEY CO.

Hamilton, Ontario, Canada

Sawyer-Massey 10-20	1917
Sawyer-Massey 16-32	1917
Sawyer-Massey 25-50	1917

Sawyer-Massey 10-20
Sawyer-Massey Company, Hamilton, Can.

Four wheels, driving from two rear wheels. Recommended for three 14" plows, 20" thresher. Diameter of drive wheels 40 inches, face 14 inches. Length 133 inches, width 61 inches, height 67 inches. Waukesha 4 cylinder vertical L-Head motor, cast in pairs, $4\frac{1}{2}x5\frac{3}{4}$, 880 r.p.m. normal. Wilcox-Bennett kerosene carburetor. K-W high tension independent magneto. Centrifugal pump, fan and tubular radiator. Waukesha automatic splash lubrication. Bevel gear speed change. Spur gear final drive. Steel and semi-steel bevel and pinions, bevels cut. New Departure ball and babbitt transmission bearings. Babbitt drive axle bearings.

Sawyer-Massey 16-32
Sawyer-Massey Company, Hamilton, Can.

Four wheels, driving from two rear wheels. Recommended for five 14" plows, 28" thresher. Length 174 inches, width $80\frac{1}{2}$ inches, height 112 inches. Four cylinder vertical valve-in-head motor, cast singly, $5\frac{1}{4}x7$, 680 r.p.m. normal. Wilcox-Bennett kerosene carburetor. K-W high tension independent magneto. Centrifugal pump, fan and tubular radiator. Detroit sight force feed and splash lubrication. Enclosed spur gear speed change. Spur gear final drive. Steel and semi-steel bevels and pinion, bevels cut. New Departure ball and babbitt transmission bearings. Babbitt drive axle bearings.

Sawyer-Massey 25-50
Sawyer-Massey Company, Hamilton, Can.

Four wheels, driving from two rear wheels. Recommended for six or seven 14" plows, 32" thresher. Diameter of drive wheels 68 inches, face 30 inches. Length 185 inches, width 108 inches, height 120 inches. Weight 17,500 lbs. Four cylinder vertical valve-in-head motor, cast singly, $6\frac{1}{4} \times 8$, 600 r.p.m. normal. Wilcox-Bennett kerosene carburetor. Atwater-Kent ignition. Centrifugal pump, fan and tubular radiator. Detroit force sight feed and splash lubrication. Spur gear final drive. Steel and semi-steel bevels and pinions, bevels cut. New Departure ball and babbitt transmission bearings. Babbitt drive axle bearings.

SHORT TURN TRACTOR CO.

Minneapolis, Minnesota

Short Turn 25   1917-1919

Short Turn 25
Short Turn Tractor Company, Minneapolis, Minn.

One drum. Recommended for two 14" plows. Diameter of drum 48 inches, face 24 inches. Length 98 inches, width 78 inches, height 54 inches. Weight 4,000 lbs. Price $1000.00. Four cylinder vertical, L-head motor, cast en bloc, $3\frac{1}{2} \times 5\frac{1}{4}$, 1000 r.p.m. normal. Wilcox-Bennett combination gasoline and kerosene carburetor. High tension independent magneto, manual control. Pump, fan and Todd cellular radiator. Splash lubrication. Two speeds forward and one reverse, 2 to $3\frac{1}{2}$ m.p.h. Bevel gear enclosed speed change. Chain final drive. Crucible steel gears. Babbitt transmission bearings.

SOUTHERN CORN BELT TRACTOR CO.

Atchison, Kansas

Corn Belt 7-18   1917

Corn Belt 7-18
Southern Corn Belt Tractor Co., Atchison, Kansas

Three wheels, driving from one front wheel. Recommended for two 14" plows, 20" thresher. Length 156 inches, width 86 inches-100 inches, height 76 inches. Diameter of drive wheel 44 inches, face 18 inches. Weight 3,700 lbs. Price $750.00. Gile horizontal opposed 2 cylinder motor, $5 \times 6\frac{1}{2}$, 700-900 r.p.m. normal. Bennett gasoline carburetor. High tension automatic magneto. Centrifugal pump, fan and tubular radiator. Madison-Kipp force sight feed lubrication.

Be A Tractor Expert

The Automobile and Tractor Business offers ambitious men wonderful opportunities to enjoy lasting success and big pay. I have successfully trained thousands who came to me without any previous experience. The **Rahe Method of Practical Automobile Training and Experience** is recognized as the most thorough, complete and efficient. Complete equipment. Three Big Buildings and Tractor Farms. All kinds of motors for my students' training and practice. Tractors of both types—Kerosene and Gasoline.

Big Demand For Tractor Experts

The man with proper training to handle automobiles and tractors is in demand. Hundreds of my graduates are making big money as Testers, Demonstrators, Drivers and Operators, Oxy-Acetylene Welders, Salesmen, Dealers, etc. Many more are employed in the big factories and assembling plants. A large number are in business for themselves as Garage Owners, Factory Representatives, Tractor Experts, Demonstrators, etc.

Only A Few Weeks Required

My method of training is all simple and easy—**the actual doing. No books—no printed lessons.** Implement dealers' sons find my course of training fascinating and invaluable. Dealers are recognizing the absolute necessity of trained men to further the sale of automobiles and tractors. My simplified and practical training is specially devised to answer this demand.

80 Page Catalog Postpaid I will gladly send my new 80-page Catalog to any Dealer or young man interested in making more money. This book is the finest ever issued by a trade or technical school in the country Tells all about my Method of Training, Equipment, opportunities, etc. etc. Send for it NOW.

H. J. RAHE, President,
RAHE'S AUTOMOBILE TRAINING SCHOOL
(The World's Greatest)

587 E. 11th St., – – – Kansas City, Mo.

FREE COURSE IN TRACTOR ENGINEERING

I have a limited number of Free Scholarships for Complete Training in Tractor Engineering available right now. Those enrolling for my regular course of training in all branches of the automobile business at this time will receive this added instruction without extra cost. The value of the Free Scholarship is $50. Big Tractor Testing and Practice Field. All kinds of Power Farming Machinery. My students get practical training and experience.

128

1917

STANDARD TRACTOR CO.
St. Paul, Minnesota

Standard 22-45   1917-1919

Standard 22-45
Standard Tractor Company, St. Paul, Minn.

Four wheels, driving from two rear wheels. Recommended for four 14" plows, 30" thresher. Diameter of drive wheels 69 inches, face 14 inches. Length 168 inches, width 100 inches, height 87 inches. Weight 8,000 lbs. Price $1500.00. Waukesha 4 cylinder vertical L-Head motor, cast in pairs, $4\frac{3}{4}$x$6\frac{3}{4}$, 900 r.p.m normal. Kingston kerosene carburetor. Dixie high tension independent magneto, with impulse starter. Centrifugal pump, fan and tubular radiator. Waukesha automatic splash lubrication. Two speeds forward, one reverse, 3 m.p.h. Spur gear speed change, enclosed. Spur gear and chain final drive. Machined steel gears. Babbitt transmission and drive axle bearings. Drive axle mounted on coil springs.

STINSON TRACTOR CO.

Minneapolis, Minnesota

Stinson 15-30   1917

Stinson 15-30
Stinson Tractor Company, Minneapolis, Minn.

Three wheels, driving from two rear wheels. Recommended for three to four 14″ plows. Length 156 inches, width 78 inches, height 60 inches. Diameter of drive wheels 61 inches, face 12 inches. Weight 5,200 lbs. Vertical four or eight cylinder motor, cast en bloc, 4x6 or $3\frac{1}{4}$x5, 925 r.p.m. normal, L-Head. Kingston gasoline or kerosene carburetor. High tension magneto, with impulse starter. Centrifugal pump, fan and cellular radiator. Pressure feed lubrication. Hyatt roller transmission bearings. Sliding spur gear speed change, enclosed. Spur gear final drive, enclosed. Machined steel gearing.

VAIL-RENTSCHLER TRACTOR CO.

Hamilton, Ohio

Vail Oil 9-18   1917

Vail Oil 9-18
Vail-Rentschler Tractor Co., Hamilton, O.

Four wheels driving from two rear wheels. Recommended for two 14″ plows. Diameter of drive wheels 48 inches, face 10 inches. Length 124 inches, width 56 inches, height 56 inches. Weight 3,300 lbs. Horizontal 2 cylinder parallel, valve-in head motor, cast en bloc, $4\frac{3}{4}$x7, 600 r.p.m. normal. Vail kerosene carburetor. Dixie high tension independent magneto, with impulse starter. Centrifugal pump, fan and cellular radiator. Gravity lubrication. Two speeds forward and reverse, $1\frac{3}{4}$ to 3 m.p.h. Sliding spur gear enclosed speed change. Spur gear and pinion enclosed final drive. Cast steel gearing. Die cast babbitt transmission bearings.

WATERLOO GASOLINE ENGINE CO.

Waterloo, Iowa

Waterloo Boy N 12-25   1917-1918

Waterloo Boy N 12-25

Waterloo Gasoline Engine Co., Waterloo, Iowa

Four wheels, driving from two rear wheels. Recommended for three 14″ plows. Diameter of drive wheels 52 inches, face 12 inches. Length 141 inches, width 76 inches, height 66 inches. Weight 5,000 lbs. Price $850.00. Two cylinder horizontal opposed, valve-in-head motor, $6^{1}/_{2} \times 7$, 750 r.p.m. normal. Schebler kerosene carburetor. Dixie high tension independent magneto, manual control, with impulse starter. Centrifugal pump, fan and Modine cellular radiator. Pressure feed and splash lubrication. Two speeds forward and one reverse. Sliding gear enclosed speed change. Internal spur final drive. Semi-steel gearing. Nine Hyatt roller transmission and two Hyatt roller drive axle bearings.

WESTERN TRACTOR CO.

Tulsa, Oklahoma

Western 8-15   1917

Western 8-15

Western Tractor Co., Tulsa, Okla.

Four wheels, driving from two front wheels. Recommended for two 14″ plows, 24″ thresher. Diameter of drive wheels 60 inches, face 10 inches. Length 132 inches, width 64 inches, height 66 inches. Weight 4,200 lbs. Price $735.00. Toro vertical 2 cylinder motor, cast separately, $5^{1}/_{4} \times 6^{1}/_{2}$, 750 r.p.m. normal, L-Head. Bennett gasoline carburetor. Dixie high tension independent magneto, variable, with impulse starter. Bunting phosphor bronze transmission bearings. Centrifugal pump, fan and Perfex, or Modine-Racine cellular radiators. Madison-Kipp force sight feed lubrication. Selective sliding spur gear speed change enclosed. Roller pinion final drive. Machined steel gearing.

WICHITA TRACTOR CO.

Wichita, Kansas

Wichita 8-16   1917-1920

Wichita 8-16

Wichita Tractor Co., Wichita, Kansas

Four wheels, driving from two rear wheels. Recommended for two 14″ plows. Diameter of drive wheels 56 inches, face 10 inches. Length 128 inches, width 72 inches, height 61 inches. Weight 3,275 lbs. Price $750.00. Gile 2 cylinder horizontal opposed motor, $5 \times 6^{1}/_{2}$, 750 r.p.m. normal. Kingston gasoline carburetor. Atwater-Kent ignition. Centrifugal pump, fan and Perfex cellular radiator. Madison-Kipp force sight feed lubrication. One speed forward and reverse. $2^{1}/_{4}$ m.p.h. Roller pinion final drive.

WINSLOW MANUFACTURING CO.

Kansas City, Missouri

Coleman 10-20   1917

Coleman 10-20

Winslow Manufacturing Company, Kansas City, Mo.

Four wheels, driving from two rear wheels. Recommended for two 14″ plows. Diameter of drive wheels 42 inches, face 10 inches. Weight 3,900 lbs. Price $985.00. Erd 4 cylinder vertical, valve-in-head motor, cast en bloc, 4x6, 1000 r.p.m. normal. Schebler gasoline carburetor. Dixie high tension independent magneto. Pump, fan and Perfex cellular radiator. Worm final drive enclosed. Worm, tool steel, master gear, bronze, both finished. Ball and roller transmission bearings. Roller drive axle bearings.

WORTHINGTON PUMP & MACHINERY CORP.

Cudahy, Wisconsin

Ingeco 10-20   1917-1918

Ingeco 10-20

Worthington Pump and Machinery Corporation, Cudahy, Wis.

Four wheels, driving from two rear wheels. Recommended for three 14″ plows. Diameter of drive wheels 60 inches, face 12 inches. Length 140 inches, width 72 inches, height 66 inches. Weight 5,600 lbs. Price $850.00. Two cylinder opposed valve-in-head motor, 6x7, 710 r.p.m. normal. Schebler gasoline and kerosene carburetor. High tension independent magneto, manual control. Centrifugal pump, fan and Perfex cellular radiator. Detroit force sight feed lubrication. One speed forward and reverse, 1 to 2¾ m.p.h. Spur gear final drive, enclosed. Steel gearing. Babbitt bearings.

YUBA CONSTRUCTION CO.

San Francisco, California

Ball Tread 12-20   1917-1918
Ball Tread 20-35   1917-1918

Ball Tread 12-20
Yuba Construction Co., San Francisco, Cal.

Two crawlers. Recommended for four 14″ plows. Face of crawler 13 inches. Total area traction surface, 1,050 sq. inches. Length 145 inches, width 55 inches, height 55 inches. Weight 6,750 lbs. Price $2200. Waukesha 4 cylinder vertical L-Head motor, cast in pairs, $4\frac{1}{2} \times 6\frac{3}{4}$, 700 r.p.m. normal. Distillate carburetor. High tension ignition. Centrifugal pump, fan and radiator. Three speeds forward, one reverse.

Ball Tread 20-35
Yuba Construction Co., San Francisco, Cal.

Two crawlers. Recommended for six 14″ plows. Face of crawler 17 inches. Total area traction surface of crawler 1,680 sq. in. Length $184\frac{7}{8}$ inches, width $73\frac{1}{2}$ inches, height 61 inches. Weight 10,250 lbs. Price $3450. Wisconsin 4 cylinder vertical L-Head motor, cast in pairs, $5\frac{1}{4} \times 7$, 700 r.p.m. normal. Distillate carburetor. High tension ignition. Two speeds forward, one reverse.

1918

The 1918 story must inevitably lead us back to the Ford Motor Co. and the Fordson tractor, which was introduced to the American farmer in 1918. The Fordson tractor borrowed its ignition system from the Model T Ford car. It was too short and the hitch was too far forward, which developed in it having the reputation for being a man-killer, which might have been true if it was not carefully handled.

Like the Model T, the Fordson tractor was loved and hated. It was built with a worm gear final drive which prevented it from being towed. The ignition system used the same low tension flywheel magneto as the Model T, and the same individual buzz coils. It burned the same gasoline as the Model T.

The Fordson tractor was produced off and on in the United States for ten years. In 1929, Henry Ford moved tractor production to Cork, Ireland, and in 1932 to Dagenham, England. In 1938 (or perhaps later), someone produced an unsigned and unidentified sheet which lists produced Fordson tractor motor numbers by months in the United States, Cork and Dagenham. The sheet is interesting but confusing (see page 421). At first glance, it seems to show a total of 830,000 tractors, but more careful study raises doubts as to what (tractors or motor numbers) are being reported. It is interesting to note that copies of the unidentified sheet are still extant in sales organizations after more than 50 years.

Another interesting part of the dealings between Fordson tractor operations in the United States and England, is that they were apparently pioneers in tractor trading (importing and exporting) between the continents.

The 1918 listing includes 87 models of 74 makes not shown in 1917.

ACME HARVESTING MACHINE CO.

Peoria, Illinois

Acme 12-25   1918

Traction Wheels: Four-wheel type, with drive on two rear wheels, 54 x 12, interchangeable with crawlers.
No. of Plows Recommended: Three 14-in
Length: 144 in.; **Width:** 76 in.; **Height:** 102 in.; **Weight:** 6006 lbs.
Acres Plowed in 10-hr. Day: 10.
Motor: Beaver; $4\frac{1}{2}$ x 6; valve-in-head, 4 cylinders, cast en bloc.
Lubrication: Force feed and splash system.
Carburetor: Kingston.
Ignition System: K-W high tension magneto.
Cooling System: Eureka radiator with pump and fan.
Bearings: Timken roller in speed change gears and own on drive axle.
Transmission: Sliding selective gears, $2\frac{1}{4}$ to $3\frac{1}{8}$ m.p.h. forward.
Final Drive: Open spur gear.
Belt Pulley: 14 x 7; 900 r.p.m.

ACME 12-25
Acme Harvesting Machine Co., Peoria, Ill.

ACME 12-25

Acme Harvesting Machine Co., Peoria, Ill.

Traction Wheels: Four wheels, with crawlers in rear, 12 x 35, interchangeable with wheels.
No. of Plows Recommended: Three 14-in.
Length: 144 in.; Width: 76 in.; Height: 102 in.; Weight: 6000 lbs.
Acres Plowed in 10-hr. Day: 10.
Motor: Beaver; $4\frac{1}{2}$ x 6, valve-in-head, 4 cylinders, cast en bloc.
Lubrication: Force feed and splash system.
Carburetor: Kingston.
Ignition System: K-W high tension magneto.
Cooling System: Eureka radiator with pump and fan.
Bearings: Timken roller in speed change gears and own on drive axle.
Transmission: Sliding selective gears, $2\frac{1}{4}$ to $3\frac{1}{8}$ m.p.h. forward.
Final Drive: Open spur gear.
Belt Pulley: 14 x 7; 900 r.p.m.

ADAMS CO.

Marysville, Ohio

Adams No. 2, 11-16

Traction Wheels: Four wheels; two drive wheels in rear, 50 x 12.
No. of Plows Recommended: Two or three 14-in.
Length: 146 in.; Width: 74 in.; Height: 84 in.; Weight: 5500 lbs.
Motor: Jacobs; horizontal, 1 cylinder.
Ignition System: Webster low tension magneto.
Cooling System: Hopper and tank combination.
Bearings: Babbitted throughout transmission and plain on drive axle.
Transmission: Chain, 2 to 3 m.p.h. forward.
Final Drive: Chains.
Belt Pulley: 16 or 24 x 7 or 10; 300 r.p.m.

1918

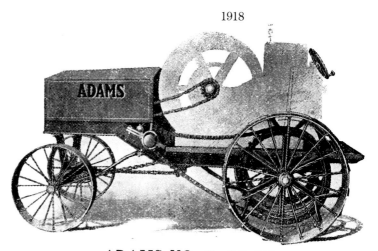

ADAMS NO. 2, 11-16

Adams Co., Marysville, O.

What Others Claim
Advance-Rumely
Guarantees

ADVANCE-RUMELY THRESHER CO.
Incorporated

LaPorte, - - **Indiana**

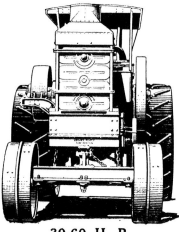

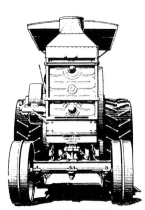

30-60 H. P.   18-35 H. P.   14-28 H. P.

ADVANCE-RUMELY

ADVANCE-RUMELY THRESHER CO.

La Porte, Indiana

Advance-Rumely 8-16   1918
Rumely Oil Pull 14-28   1918

ADVANCE-RUMELY 8-16
Advance-Rumely Thresher Co., La Porte, Ind.

Traction Wheels: Three wheels with one drive wheel, 56 x 26, in front.
No. of Plows Recommended: Two 14-in.
Length: 192 in.; **Width:** 105 in.; **Height:** 63 in.; **Height:** 5600 lbs.; **Price:** $1200.
Turning Radius: 15 ft.; **Acres Plowed in 10-hr. Day:** 3 to 4.
Motor: Own; 4 x 5½, vertical L-head, 4 cylinders, cast en bloc.
Lubrication: Madison-Kipp force feed and splash.
Carburetor: Kingston double bowl.
Ignition System: Kingston high tension magneto with impulse starter.
Cooling System: Circulating pump.
Bearings: Hyatt roller throughout transmission.
Transmission: Enclosed gears, 2.1 m.p.h. forward.
Final Drive: Spur gears.
Belt Pulley: 16 x 6½; 425 r.p.m. and 1780 feet per minute at normal engine speed.

Traction Wheels: Four wheels, with two drive wheels, 56 x 18. in rear.
No. of Plows Recommended: Three to five 14-in.
Length: 155 in.; **Width:** 80¼ in.; **Height:** 99 in.; **Weight:** 9600 lbs.; **Price:** $2400.
Turning Radius: 17 ft.; **Acres Plowed in 10-hr. Day:** 8 to 12.
Motor: Own; 7 x 8½, horizontal, 2 cylinders, cast en bloc.
Lubrication: Force feed and splash.
Carburetor: Secor-Higgins.
Ignition System: Low tension magneto.
Starting Equipment: Air starter.
Bearings: Hyatt roller in transmission and on drive axle.
Cooling System: Circulating pump.
Transmission: Spur gear enclosed, 2.1 to 3 m.p.h. forward; 2.65 m.p.h. reverse.
Final Drive: Open.
Belt Pulley: 23 x 8½; 530 r.p.m. and 3190 feet per minute at normal engine speed.

RUMELY OIL PULL 14-28
Advance-Rumely Thresher Co., La Porte, Ind.

1918   137

THE YANKEE

Rated
12-25

Develops
15-30

The Tractor Anyone Can Run

Single lever control. Automobile type steering device. Four cylinder valve-in-head, **Kerosene** burning motor. Three speeds forward and reverse. Full floating draw bar. The only comfortable seat on a tractor. Hardened steel gears. Forced feed oiling. Hyatt bearings.

Sells Itself and Stays Sold

You want a tractor that sells on its all-around merit—not on freak features. Here's a tractor that catches the farmer's eye at a glance—Simple, strong and sensible—and it will serve him for years.

Attractive Proposition for Dealers in Open Territory. Write Us.

American Tractor Corporation
Peoria, Illinois

AMERICAN TRACTOR CORP.

Peoria, Illinois

Yankee 12-25

1918-1920

YANKEE 12-25
American Tractor Corporation, Peoria, Ill.

Traction Wheels: Four wheels, two rear, 48 x 12, affording traction, with face-spade lugs.
No. of Plows Recommended: Three 14-in.
Length: 123½ in.; **Width:** 72½ in.; **Height:** 71 in.; **Weight:** 4400 lbs.; **Price:** $1585.
Turning Radius: 8½ ft.; **Acres Plowed in 10-hr. Day:** 10.
Motor: Erd; 4 x 6, overhead valve, 4 cylinders, cast en bloc.
Lubrication: Combination circulating pump and splash.
Carburetor: Kingston float feed.
Ignition System: Kingston high tension magneto.
Cooling System: Modine Spirex radiator, centrifugal water pump and fan.
Bearings: Hyatt roller on drive axle; Bunting bronze and Hyatt roller in transmission.
Transmission: Selective, sliding gear, 1½ to 5¼ m.p.h. forward; 1½ m.p.h. reverse.
Final Drive: Internal drive bull gear.
Belt Pulley: 11 x 7; 925 r.p.m. and 2680 feet per minute at normal engine speed.

ANDREWS TRACTOR CO.

Minneapolis, Minnesota

Andrews 12-25

1918-1919

Traction Wheels: Three wheels with drum drive member in rear, 40 x 38.
No. of Plows Recommended: Two and three 14-in.
Length: 176 in.; **Width:** 90 in.; **Height:** 56 in.; **Weight:** 5000 lbs; **Price:** $1000.
Turning Radius: 24 ft.
Motor: Verac; 4 x 5, 2-cycle, 4 cylinders, cast singly.
Lubrication: Force feed through drilled crankshaft.
Carburetor: Krice
Ignition System: Bosch high tension magneto.
Cooling System: Air.
Bearings: Own babbitt throughout transmission and roller on drive axle.
Transmission: Friction, 0 to 5 m.p.h. forward; 3 m.p.h. reverse.
Final Drive: Chain.
Belt Pulley: 12 x 7; 1000 r.p.m. and 3142 feet per minute at normal engine speed.

ANDREWS 12-25
Andrews Tractor Co., Minneapolis, Minn.

Wear on Tractor Bearings
Will Wear Out Tractor Gears
Unless They Are Adjustable

When the Bearings are New

Correctly cut gears work closely together, just as those here shown. Every part of the contact face of each tooth does its share of work. Pressure is smooth and steady as the gears turn. Friction is minimized by true, rolling contact and wear is even, so that the shape of the working surface is unchanged.

What Happens if the Bearings Have No Take-Up for Wear

If the bearings in your transmission are allowed to become loose, the gears separate. Wear on the tooth face is no longer even, and the surface wears out of shape. This destroys the rolling contact, causing friction and wear goes on more and more rapidly. Even though the wear on the bearings is no more than the thickness of this paper the teeth take on a shape like that shown at the left.

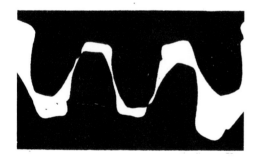

Bearings Must Be Correctly Adjusted

Once gears are worn out of shape, they can not be restored to efficiency even with a new set of bearings. The teeth will no longer mesh properly, on account of alteration in their shape. Therefore, the ultimate result is replacement of the gears as well as the bearings—unless the gears are mounted on bearings that can be easily adjusted to take up wear at the beginning of each season.

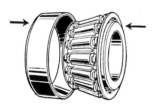

There are a lot of interesting facts about bearings told in the booklet, "Timken Bearings for Farm Tractors." Send for your copy and learn how important good bearings are to tractor operation.

 THE TIMKEN ROLLER BEARING CO.
Canton, Ohio

TIMKEN BEARINGS
FOR MOTOR CAR, TRUCK & TRACTOR

AVERY CO.
Peoria, Illinois

Avery Motor Cultivator 5-10   1918
Avery Motor Planter 5-10   1918

Traction Wheels: Three wheels, driving from two rear wheels, 42 x 6.
Length: 184 in.; **Width:** 112 in.; **Weight:** 3050 lbs.
Acres Cultivated in 10-hr. Day: 16 to 18.
Motor: Own; 3 x 4, vertical, 4 cylinders, cast en bloc.
Lubrication: By ring oiler, splash to cylinders, gravity to gearing.
Carburetor: Zephyr.
Ignition System: Atwater-Kent.
Cooling System: Thermo-syphon.
Transmission: Friction, 1 to 3 m.p.h. forward; 1 to 3 m.p.h. reverse.
Final Drive: Spur gear.
Belt Pulley: 9 x 6; 1000 r p.m.

AVERY MOTOR CULTIVATOR 5-10
Avery Co., Peoria, Ill.

Traction Wheels: Three wheels, driving from two rear wheels, 42 x 6.
Length: 184 in.; **Width:** 112 in.; **Weight:** 3050 lbs.
Acres Planted in 10-hr. Day: 16 to 18.
Motor: Own; 3 x 4, vertical, 4 cylinders, cast en bloc.
Lubrication: By ring oiler, splash to cylinders, gravity to gearing.
Carburetor: Zephyr.
Ignition System: Atwater-Kent.
Cooling System: Thermo-syphon.
Transmission: Friction, 1 to 3 m.p.h. forward; 1 to 3 m.p.h. reverse.
Final Drive: Spur gear.
Belt Pulley: 9 x 6; 1000 r.p.m.

AVERY MOTOR PLANTER 5-10
Avery Co., Peoria, Ill.

BEEMAN GARDEN TRACTOR CO.
Minneapolis, Minnesota

Beeman Garden Tractor   1918-1926

Traction Wheels: Drives on two wheels, 25 x 3½.
No. of Plows Recommended: One 7-in. and other garden tools.
Length: 86 in.; **Width:** 17¼ in.; **Height:** 39 in.; **Weight:** 525 lbs.; **Price:** $285.
Turning Radius: 6 ft.; **Acres Plowed in 10-hr. Day:** 1½.
Motor: Own; 3½ x 4½, vertical, 4-cycle, 1 cylinder.
Lubrication: Splash system.
Carburetor: Kingston.
Ignition System: Heinze high tension magneto.
Cooling System: Water, radiator and fan.
Transmission: External and internal clutch, ¾ to 3 m.p.h. forward.
Final Drive: Gears to bull wheels.
Belt Pulley: 4½ x 3¾; 230 to 2000 r.p.m.

BEEMAN GARDEN TRACTOR
Beeman Garden Tractor Co., Minneapolis, Minn.

1918   141

BELTRAIL TRACTOR CO.
St. Paul, Minnesota

Belt-Rail, Model B, 12-20   1918-1919

Traction Wheels: Drives by 21 x 48 crawler in rear, with two non-drive wheels in front.
No. of Plows Recommended: Two 14-in.
Length: 114 in.; **Width** 72 in.; **Height:** 54 in.; **Weight:** 4400 lbs.
Turning Radius: 9 ft.; Acres plowed in 10-hr. Day: 10.
Motor: Waukesha; 3¾ x 5¼, vertical, 4 cylinders, cast en bloc.
Lubrication: Splash system.
Carburetor: Kingston.
Ignition System: Dixie high tension magneto.
Cooling System: Sparks-Withington radiator and circulating pump.
Bearings: Timken roller on steering wheel axles.
Transmission: Gear drive, 2¼ to 3½ m.p.h. forward; 2¼ m.p.h. reverse.
Belt Pulley: 10 x 6; 950 r.p.m. and 2500 feet per minute at normal engine speed.

BELT-RAIL, MODEL B, 12-20
Beltrail Tractor Co., St. Paul, Minn

C. L. BEST GAS TRACTION CO.
San Leandro, California

Tracklayer, Model 75, 40-70   1918-1919
Tracklayer Model 40, 20-35   1918-1919

TRACKLAYER, MODEL 75, 40-70
C. L. Best Gas Traction Co., San Leandro, Cal.

Traction Wheels: Two crawlers, each 78 x 30.
No. of Plows Recommended: Eight to twelve 14-in.
Length: 268 in.; **Width:** 103 in.; **Height:** 120 in.; **Weight:** 28000 lbs.; **Price:** $5750.
Turning Radius: 23 ft ; Acres Plowed in 10-hr. Day: 20 to 30.
Motor: Own; 7¾ x 9, 4-cycle, 4 cylinders, cast separately.
Lubrication: McCord oiler, constant level splash.
Carburetor: Ensign.
Ignition System: K-W magneto with impulse starter.
Cooling System: Water pump, fan and radiator.
Bearings: Babbitt on transmission and bronze on drive axle.
Transmission: Selective gears, 1½ to 2¾ m.p.h. forward; 1⅝ m.p.h. reverse.
Final Drive: Internal gear.
Belt Pulley: 16 × 10; 600 r.p.m. and 2650 feet per minute at normal engine speed.

Traction Wheels: Two crawlers, each 66 x 18.
No. of Plows Recommended: Four to six 14-in.
Length: 130 in.; Width: 77 in.; Height: 80 in.; Weight: 11750 lbs.; Price: $4100.
Turning Radius: 8 ft.; Acres Plowed in 10-hr. Day: 10 to 15.
Motor: Own; $6\frac{1}{4}$ x $6\frac{1}{4}$, 4-cycle, 4 cylinders, cast separately.
Lubrication: Splash system throughout.
Carburetor: Ensign.
Ignition System: K-W magneto with impulse starter.
Cooling System: Water pump, fan and radiator.
Bearings: Babbitt throughout transmission and bronze on rear axle.
Transmission: Selective gears, $1\frac{3}{4}$ to $2\frac{1}{2}$ m.p.h. forward; $1\frac{5}{8}$ m.p.h. reverse.
Final Drive: Internal gear.
Belt Pulley: 16 x 10; 600 r.p.m. and 2650 feet per minute at normal engine speed.

TRACKLAYER, MODEL 40, 20-35
C. L. Best Gas Traction Co., San Leandro, Cal.

BLUMBERG MOTOR MANUFACTURING CO.

San Antonio, Texas

Blumberg Steady Pull 12-24   1918-1919

BLUMBERG STEADY PULL 12-24
Blumberg Motor Mfg. Co., San Antonio, Tex.

Traction Wheels: Four wheels, with two, 42 x 6, drive wheels in rear.
No. of Plows Recommended: Three 12-in.
Length: 132 in.; Width 60 in.; Height: 60 in.; Weight: 3300 lbs.
Turning Radius: 22 ft.; Acres Plowed in 10-hr. Day: 7.
Motor: Own; $3\frac{3}{4}$ x 5, valve-in-head, 4 cylinders, cast en bloc.
Lubrication: Splash system.
Carburetor: Stromberg.
Ignition System: Dixie high tension magneto.
Cooling System: Centrifugal pump, fan and Perfex radiator.
Transmission: Foote-Strite gears, $1\frac{3}{4}$ to 3 m.p.h. forward; 2 m.p.h. reverse.
Final Drive: Internal gear.
Belt Pulley: 14 x 6; 600 r.p.m.

BRILLION IRON WORKS
Brillion, Wisconsin

Brillion 12-22   1918

Traction Wheels: Two front drive wheels, 60 x 10.
No. of Plows Recommended: Three 14-in.
Length: 144 in.; **Width:** 70 in.; **Height:** 74 in.; **Weight:** 4800 lbs.
Turning Radius: 14 ft.; **Acres Plowed in 10-hr. Day:** 7.
Motor: Field; $3\frac{3}{4}$ x 5, opposed, 4 cylinders, cast en bloc.
Lubrication: Force feed and splash.
Carburetor: Kingston kerosene.
Ignition System: Dixie high tension magneto with impulse starter.
Cooling System: Modine cellular radiator, pump and fan.
Bearings: Hyatt roller in transmission and plain on drive axle.
Transmission: Spur gear, 2 to 5 m.p.h. forward.
Final Drive: Open gears.
Belt Pulley: 8 x 8; 1000 r.p.m. and 2100 feet per minute at normal engine speed

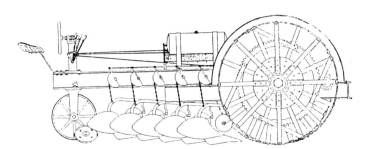

BRILLION 12-22
Brillion Iron Works, Brillion, Wis.

BUCKEYE MANUFACTURING CO.
Anderson, Indiana

Trundaar 20-35   1918-1919

TRUNDAAR 20-35
Buckeye Mfg. Co., Anderson, Ind.

Traction Wheels: Crawler on each side, 72 x 15.
No. of Plows Recommended: Four 14-in.
Length: 113 in.; **Width:** 74 in.; **Height:** 58 in.; **Weight:** 9500 lbs.
Turning Radius: 12 ft.; **Acres Plowed in 10-hr. Day:** 10.
Motor: Waukesha; $4\frac{3}{4}$ x $6\frac{3}{4}$, vertical, 4 cylinders, cast in pairs.
Lubrication: Splash and pump force feed.
Carburetor: Deppe.
Ignition System: K-W high tension magneto.
Cooling System: Force pump.
Bearings: Bronze in transmission and on rear axle.
Transmission: Sliding gear, 1 to 4 m.p.h. forward; 2 m.p.h. reverse.
Final Drive: Multiple disc clutch on each rear tread driver.
Belt Pulley: 10 x 8; 950 r.p.m. and 2650 feet per minute at normal engine speed.

The Cleveland Tractor

THERE'S not another tractor like **the Cleveland**—either in design, construction, performance or salability.

The Cleveland travels on its own tracks and can go almost anywhere. It travels through gullies and over ditches—even through wet clay or the loose sand and gumbo of the South.

The power of this little machine is tremendous in proportion to its size—20 horsepower at the pulley belt and 12 at the bar. Its great capacity and small size are combined with a degree of economy, both in upkeep and operation, that is truly remarkable.

Today, more than ever before, **The Cleveland Tractor** is a real necessity.

It is needed on every farm in the country.

It offers the only dealer opportunity of its kind.

The Cleveland Tractor Co., Cleveland, Ohio, U. S. A.

J. I. CASE THRESHING MACHINE CO.
Racine, Wisconsin

Case 9-18 Model B   1918

CASE 9-18 MODEL B
J. I. Case Threshing Machine Co., Racine, Wis.

Traction Wheels: Four wheels, two drive wheels in rear, 42 x 9.
No. of Plows Recommended: Two 14-in.
Length: 108 in.; **Width:** 58 in.; **Height:** 58 in.; **Weight:** 3310 lbs.
Turning Radius: 11 ft.
Motor: Own; $3\frac{7}{8}$ x 5, vertical valve-in-head, 4 cylinders, cast en bloc.
Lubrication: Circulating splash system.
Carburetor: Kingston.
Ignition System: Kingston high tension magneto, impulse starter.
Cooling System: Pump circulating system.
Bearings: Hyatt roller on drive axle.
Transmission: Sliding gear, $2\frac{1}{4}$ to $3\frac{1}{2}$ m.p.h. forward.
Final Drive: Enclosed spur gears.
Belt Pulley: $14\frac{1}{4}$ x $5\frac{1}{4}$.

CLEVELAND TRACTOR CO.
Cleveland, Ohio

Cleveland 12-20   1918-1921

CLEVELAND 12-20
Cleveland Tractor Co., Cleveland, O.

Traction Wheels: One crawler on each side.
No. of Plows Recommended: Two 14-in.
Length: 96 in.; **Width:** 50 in.; **Height:** 52 in.; **Weight:** 3175 lbs.; **Price:** $1385.
Turning Radius: 6 ft.; **Acres Plowed in 10-hr. Day:** 8 to 10.
Motor: Weidely; $3\frac{3}{4}$ x $5\frac{1}{2}$, 4-cycle, 4 cylinders, cast en bloc.
Lubrication: Force feed system.
Carburetor: Kingston.
Ignition System: Eisemann high tension magneto.
Cooling System: Water pump, radiator and fan.
Bearings: Hyatt roller on drive axle and bronze in transmission.
Transmission: Sliding gear, 1 to $3\frac{1}{2}$ m.p.h. forward; 1 to $3\frac{1}{2}$ m.p.h. reverse.
Final Drive: Internal gear and pinion.
Belt Pulley: 8 x 6; 1250 r.p.m. and 2600 feet per minute at normal engine speed.

We make it *easy* for you to *sell* the

Farmer Boy 10-20 TRACTOR

$1150
f. o. b.
Columbus

Will *you* be one of 200 live Distributors to make better than $15,000 *this year?*

One light farm tractor has been perfected to the point where *big men* can afford to enter the industry.

We need men of broad, clear vision—*business men*—confident of their ability to successfully organize and direct a sales force—*graduate dealers*—of self-proven capability — fellows who won't be satisfied with a $15,000 a year income.

For such as these, we have a definite, appealing, compelling message.

We will show the way—guide—help them to a success beyond any present conception of tractor sales possibilities.

If you are such a man, *we want you—need you—now*. *Today* is not too soon for you to enlist for the profit drive—to prepare to go "over the top" with us, in tractor sales.

We will show you a sales *franchise* of priceless worth backed by an intensive merchandising-advertising campaign, insuring positive, pre-determined *results* so big you'll doubt your own figures.

The **Farmer Boy (10-20) Tractor** is a *development*—not an experiment. It is built on lines approved by four years' *experience* and actual *performance*.

The **Farmer Boy (10-20) Tractor** *has* made *good* under the most trying quality and stability tests—is *in practical use* in farming operations where none but the best *material* and *mechanical* construction can survive.

The **Farmer Boy (10-20) Tractor** is just what every farmer needs—it is of preferred type, size and capacity—sturdily built—simple in construction and operation—extremely flexible in working scope.

The **Farmer Boy (10-20) Tractor** is made from "standard" units:

"Waukesha"—4-cyl.—Heavy Duty Truck.

"Kingston"—Double-bowl (Gasoline-Kerosene) carburetor.

"Borg & Beck"—Multiple disc clutch.

"K. W."—High tension magneto—impulse starter.

"Modine Spirex"—Radiator.

"Hyatt"—Roller Bearing.

"S. K. F."—Ball Bearings.

Full details of our exceptional distributor proposition are ready.

Our franchise will be offered **only** to men with adequate financial backing, the earmarks of success, the energy and ambition to become **dominating factors** in their respective territories. Knowledge of and experience in the tractor industry are not essential. The **prime requisites** of our $15,000 a year men are push, pep, enthusiasm and quick, direct thinking.

If **you** measure up within 50 per cent. of these specifications you can become a **100 per cent producer.** And—if you have **the makings** of the man we're after—you'll not let the sun go down on your decision to MAIL THIS COUPON.

INFORMATION COUPON.

The Columbus Tractor Co.,
 1912 Goodale St., Columbus, Ohio, U.S.A.

Gentlemen: — Without obligation on my part, forward full details of your Farmer Boy (10-20) Tractor offer.

NAME...

ADDRESS......................................

CITY.............. STATE..............

Present Business....Approx. Backing$....

**Our Big Ohio Plant Where the Daily Output
Insures Immediate Shipment of
Farmer Boy Tractors.**

The Columbus Tractor Company, 1912 Goodale St., Columbus, Ohio, U.S.A.

COLUMBUS TRACTOR CO.
Columbus, Ohio

Farmer Boy 10-20   1918

FARMER BOY 10-20
Columbus Tractor Co., Columbus, O.

Traction Wheels: Three-wheel tractor, one wheel in rear, 50 x 12, affording traction.
No. of Plows Recommended: Two 14-in.
Length: 130 in.; **Width:** 52 in.; **Height:** 50 in.; **Weight:** 3,200 lbs.; **Price:** $1,050.
Turning Radius: 6 ft.; **Acres Plowed in 10-hour day:** 6.
Motor: Waukesha. $3\frac{3}{4}$ x $5\frac{1}{4}$, valve in head, 4 cylinders, cast en bloc.
Lubrication: Circulating splash.
Carburetor: Kingston double bowl.
Ignition System: K-W high tension magneto with impulse starter.
Cooling System: Fan and Modine radiator.
Bearings: SKF ball in transmission and Hyatt roller on drive axle.
Transmission: Bevel gear, 1 to 4 m. p. h. forward, 1 to 4 m. p. h. reverse.
Final Drive: Spur gear.
Belt Pulley: 10 x 6, 1,000 r. p. m. and 2,400 feet per minute at normal engine speed.

DEPUE BROS. MANUFACTURING CO.
Clinton, Iowa

Depue 20-30   1918

DEPUE 20-30
Depue Bros. Mfg. Co., Clinton, Ia.

Traction Wheels: Four-wheel tractor, driven by all four wheels, each 100 x 10.
No. of Plows Recommended: Three or four 14-in.
Length: 140 in.; **Width:** 66 in.; **Height:** 102 in.; **Weight:** 8000 lbs.; **Price:** $2500.
Turning Radius: 16 ft.; **Acres Plowed in 10-hr. Day:** 15 to 20.
Motor: Buda; $4\frac{1}{4}$ x $5\frac{1}{2}$, L-head, 4 cylinders, cast en bloc.
Lubrication: Splash system.
Carburetor: Stromberg.
Ignition System: Dixie high tension magneto.
Cooling System: Perfex radiator, pump and fan.
Bearings: Timken roller in transmission and on drive axle.
Transmission: Selective sliding gear, $1\frac{1}{2}$ to 5 m.p.h. forward; $1\frac{1}{2}$ m.p.h. reverse.
Final Drive: Bevel gears.
Belt Pulley: 12 x 10; 600 r.p.m. and 3000 feet per minute at normal engine speed.

LIGHT ALLWORK TRACTOR ELECTRIC WHEEL CO. QUINCY, ILL.

Allwork
Kerosene   Tractor

ALLWORK ALWAYS

Burns Kerosene or Gasoline

THE BIG SUCCESS IN LIGHT TRACTORS

HAS more power for its weight than any other four-wheel tractor. Only 4800 pounds and develops 3000 pounds draw-bar pull on high gear and 4000 pounds on low gear. Has the largest engine on any tractor pulling 3 plows. Four cylinder, 5 x 6, 700 R. P. M. Mounted crosswise on the frame. Direct spur-gear drive, no intermediate. Belt pulley direct from crank-shaft extension. Here is the light tractor with an unusual record. It has demonstrated its success with satisfied owners everywhere. It is backed by a long-established organization that can give you quick, dependable service.

Write for Special Folder

Electric Wheel Company
Box 14A, Quincy, Ill.

ELECTRIC WHEEL CO.
Quincy, Illinois

All Work Kerosene 14-28   1918-1923

Traction Wheels: Four wheels, two traction wheels in rear, 48 x 12.
No. of Plows Recommended: Three 14-in.
Length: 125 in.; **Width:** 66 in.; **Height:** 69 in.; **Weight:** 5000 lbs.; **Price:** $1460.
Turning Radius: 12 ft.; **Acres Plowed in 10-hr. Day:** 10.
Motor: Own; 5 x 6, vertical, 4 cylinders, cast separately.
Lubrication: Constant level splash.
Carburetor: Kingston automatic.
Ignition System: Kingston high tension magneto.
Starting and Lighting Equipment: Double impulse starting coupling.
Cooling System: Perfex radiator, fan, water pump.
Bearings: Own babbitt in transmission and roller on drive axle.
Transmission: Selective sliding gear, 1.75 to 3 m.p.h. forward; 1.75 m.p.h. reverse.
Final Drive: Enclosed and self-oiling spur gears.
Belt Pulley: 12 x 7; 800 r.p.m. and 2514 feet per minute at normal engine speed.

ALL WORK KEROSENE 14-28
Electric Wheel Co., Quincy, Ill.

ELGIN TRACTOR CORP.
Piqua, Ohio

Elgin 17-27   1918

Traction Wheels: Four wheels, two traction wheels in rear, 42 x 10.
No. of Plows Recommended: Two 14-in.
Length: 128 in.; **Width:** 56 in.; **Height:** 68 in.; **Weight:** 3300 lbs.; **Price:** $1250.
Turning Radius: 25 ft.; **Acres Plowed in 10-hr. day:** 9.
Motor: Rutenber; $4\frac{1}{8}$ x $5\frac{1}{2}$, vertical L-head, 4 cylinders, cast in pairs.
Lubrication: Force feed system.
Carburetor: Kingston.
Ignition System: Dixie high tension magneto with impulse starter.
Bearings: Hyatt roller in transmission and Timken roller on drive axle.
Transmission: Friction.
Final Drive: Double chain.
Belt Pulley: 10 x 8; 900 r.p.m.

ELGIN 17-27
Elgin Tractor Corporation, Piqua, O.

EVANS MANUFACTURING CO.
Hudson, Ohio

Hudson, Model M, 12-20

1918-1919

HUDSON, MODEL M, 12-20
Evans Mfg. Co., Hudson, O.

Traction Wheels: Four wheels, two drive members in rear, 48 x 10.
No. of Plows Recommended: Two or three 14-in.
Length: 132 in.; **Width:** 56 in.; **Height:** 54 in.; **Weight:** 3000 lbs.
Turning Radius: 11 ft.; **Acres Plowed In 10-hr. Day:** 6.
Motor: Buda; $3\frac{3}{4}$ x $5\frac{1}{2}$, L-head, cylinders cast en bloc.
Lubrication: Splash and force feed.
Carburetor: Rayfield.
Ignition System: Bosch high tension magneto.
Cooling System: Candler cellular radiator, pump and fan.
Bearings: Timken roller throughout.
Transmission: Selective gear, $2\frac{1}{4}$ to 4 m.p.h. forward; $2\frac{1}{4}$ m.p.h. reverse.
Final Drive: Machine cut gears enclosed in oil.
Belt Pulley: 24 x 8; 415 r.p.m. and 2940 feet per minute at normal engine speed.

FAGEOL MOTORS CO.
Oakland, California

Fageol 6-15

1918-1919

Traction Wheels: Four-wheel tractor, with two driving wheels, 48 inches in diameter, in rear, with spokes extended.
No. of Plows Recommended: Two 12 or 14-in.
Length: 110 in.; **Width:** 53 in.; **Height:** 42 in.; **Weight:** 2750 lbs.; **Price:** $1250.
Motor: Overland; $3\frac{3}{8}$ x 5, vertical L-head, 4 cylinders, cast en bloc.
Lubrication: Impulse pump and splash.
Carburetor: Tillotson.
Ignition System: Berling high tension magneto.
Cooling System: Ten-gal. cast radiator and centrifugal pump.
Bearings: Fafnir radial ball in transmission and Timken on drive axle.
Transmission: One speed, $2\frac{1}{3}$ to $2\frac{3}{4}$ m.p.h. forward; same reverse.
Final Drive: Live axle and expanding clutch, 25 x 4 inches.
Belt Pulley: 6 x 5; 1000 r.p.m. and 1500 feet per minute at normal engine speed.

FAGEOL 6-15
Fageol Motors Co., Oakland, Cal.

FAIRBANKS, MORSE & CO.
Chicago, Illinois

Fair-Mor 10-20   1918-1920
Fair-Mor 12-25   1918

Traction Wheels: Four-wheel type, with two drive members, 48 x 10, in rear.
No. of Plows Recommended: Two 14-in.
Length: 120 in.; **Width:** 57 in.; **Height:** 66 in.; **Weight:** 3750 lbs.
Turning Radius: 13 ft.
Motor: 6 x 7, horizontal, 2 cylinders, cast en bloc.
Lubrication: Force feed system.
Carburetor: Atomizer.
Ignition System: Dixie high tension magneto.
Cooling System: Radiator and circulating pump.
Transmission: Sliding gear, $1\frac{1}{2}$ to $2\frac{1}{4}$ m.p.h. forward.
Belt Pulley: 18 x $6\frac{1}{2}$; 600 r.p.m.

FAIR-MOR 10-20
Fairbanks, Morse & Co., Chicago, Ill.

Traction Wheels: Four wheels, with two drives, 56 x 18, in rear.
No. of Plows Recommended: Three 14-in.
Length: 140 in.; **Width:** 78 in.; **Height:** 78 in.; **Weight:** 5500 lbs.
Turning Radius: 22 ft.
Motor: $6\frac{1}{2}$ x 8, horizontal, 2 cylinders, cast en bloc.
Lubrication: Force feed system.
Carburetor: Atomizer.
Ignition System: Dixie high tension magneto.
Cooling System: Radiator and circulating pump.
Transmission: Sliding gear, 2 to $2\frac{1}{2}$ m.p.h. forward.
Belt Pulley: 20 x 8; 500 r.p.m.

FAIR-MOR 12-25
Fairbanks, Morse & Co., Chicago, Ill.

FARM HORSE TRACTION WORKS
Hartford, South Dakota

Farm Horse 15-26

1918-1919

Traction Wheels: Four wheels, with two drive members in rear, 52x24.
No. of Plows Recommended: Three and four 14-in.
Length: 120 in.; **Width:** 84 in.; **Height:** 72 in.; **Weight:** 4800 lbs.; **Price:** $1285.
Turning Radius: 20 ft.; **Acres Plowed in 10-hr. Day:** 10.
Motor: Climax; 5 x 6½, L-head, 4 cylinders, cast en bloc.
Lubrication: Force feed.
Carburetor: Kingston.
Ignition System: Dixie.
Cooling System: Water and radiator.
Bearings: Hyatt roller in transmission and own on drive axle.
Transmission: Sliding gear, 2½ to 3½ m. p. h. forward; 2½ m.p.h. reverse.
Final Drive: Chain.
Belt Pulley: 14 x 8; 800 r.p.m. and 2800 feet per minute at normal engine speed.

FARM HORSE 15-26
Farm Horse Traction Works, Hartford, S. D.

A. B. FARQUHAR CO., LTD.
York, Pennsylvania

Farquhar 18-35

1918-1923

FARQUHAR 18-35
A. B. Farquhar Co., Ltd., York, Pa.

Traction Wheels: Four wheels; two drive members, 84 x 20, in rear.
No. of Plows Recommended: Four or five 14-in.
Length: 216 in.; **Width:** 98 in.; **Height:** 118 in.; **Weight:** 16000 lbs.
Motor: Own; 6 x 8, vertical, 4 cylinders, cast in pairs.
Lubrication: Detroit force feed oiler.
Carburetor: Kingston kerosene and gasoline.
Ignition System: K-W high tension magneto.
Cooling System: Tubular radiator, gear pump and fan.
Bearings: Plain in transmission and on drive axle.
Transmission: Gears, 1 to 2.3 m.p.h. forward.
Final Drive: Spur gears.
Belt Pulley: 32 x 9; 275 r.p.m.

FRICK 12-25 KEROSENE TRACTOR

Price $1350.00—F. O. B. Waynesboro, Pa.

A Dependable Tractor built by a Dependable Firm. The Frick is uniquely practical in design with maximum power, light in weight consistent with durability. Suitable to Plow, Harrow, Haul and Drive Grain Thresher, Saw Mill, Corn Sheller, Ensilage Cutter or other Farm Machinery.

Self Steering—travels in furrow.
Operator has unobstructed view ahead.
Fuel—kerosene or gasoline, kerosene preferred.
Belt Pulley is covered and connected direct to Motor Crank by Friction Clutch—no power lost by bevel or indirect gearing.

We solicit good agents for unoccupied territory. Write promptly if interested.

FRICK CO., Inc., Waynesboro, Pa.

684

THE BUSH MANUFACTURING CO.
HARTFORD, CONN.

Radiators for Tractors and Stationary Power Plants

Distributors, Indiana and Ohio:
McCOLLOUGH MOTOR SUPPLY CO., Chicago, Ill.

HENRY FORD & SON
Dearborn, Michigan

Fordson 22   1918-1926

FORDSON 22
Henry Ford & Son, Dearborn, Mich.

Traction Wheels: Two steering wheels in front and two drive members, 42 x 12, in rear.
No. of Plows Recommended: Two 14 in.
Length: 102 in.; **Width:** 63 in.; **Height:** 55 in.; **Weight:** 2500 lbs.
Turning Radius: 21 ft.; **Acres Plowed in 10-hr. Day:** 10.
Motor: Own; 4 x 5, vertical, 4 cylinders, cast en bloc.
Lubrication: Splash system.
Carburetor: Holley.
Ignition System: Magneto and vibrator.
Cooling System: Thermo-syphon.
Bearings: Gurney ball in transmission and Hyatt roller on drive axle.
Transmission: Spur gear, 1 to 8 m.p.h. forward; 2¾ m.p h. reverse.
Final Drive: Worm.
Belt Pulley: 9 x 6; 1000 r.p.m. and 2500 feet per minute at normal engine speed.

FRICK CO.
Waynesboro, Pennsylvania

Frick 12-25   1918-1920

Traction Wheels: Four wheels; two drive wheels, 60 x 10, in rear.
No. of Plows Recommended: Three 14-in.
Length: 158½ in.; **Width** 77½ in.; **Height:** 66 in.; **Weight:** 5800 lbs.
Turning Radius: 12½ ft.; **Acres Plowed in 10-hr. Day:** 10.
Motor: Erd; 4 x 6, valve-in-head, vertical, 4 cylinders, cast en bloc.
Lubrication: Automatic splash system.
Carburetor: Kingston with Bennett air cleaner.
Ignition System: Kingston high tension magneto with impulse starter.
Cooling System: Perfex radiator with centrifugal pump and fan.
Bearings: Hyatt roller in transmission and babbitt on drive axle.
Transmission: Sliding gear, 2.3 to 3.8 m.p.h. forward; 2 m.p.h. reverse.
Final Drive: Master gear and pinions.
Belt Pulley: 13 x 7; 900 r.p.m. and 3075 feet per minute at normal engine speed.

FRICK 12-25
Frick Co., Waynesboro, Pa.

GENERAL MOTORS TRUCK CO.
Pontiac, Michigan

GMC Samson 12-25   1918

Traction Wheels: Three-wheel type, two rear; special sieve grip wheels affording traction.
No. of Plows Recommended: Three 14-in.
Length: 160 in.; **Width:** 64½ in.; **Height:** 56 in.; **Price:** $1750.
Turning Radius: 12½ ft.; **Acres Plowed In 10-hr. Day:** 10.
Motor: GMC; 4¾ x 6; L-head, 4 cylinders, cast en bloc.
Lubrication: High pressure force feed on all bearings.
Carburetor: Marvel, automatic jet.
Ignition System: Eisemann, high tension, fixed spark magneto.
Starting and Lighting Equipment: Remy optional.
Cooling System: Centrifugal circulating pump.
Bearings: Own make, plain in transmission and roller on drive axle.
Transmission: Constant mesh gears and sliding clutch, 1½ to 2½ m.p.h. forward; 1½ to 3½ m.p.h. reverse.
Final Drive: Through patented roller pinion.
Belt Pulley: 14 in. x 8 in.; 700 r.p.m. and 2600 feet per minute at normal engine speed; belt pulley is not standard equipment, but is furnished when desired.

GMC SAMSON 12-25
General Motors Truck Co., Pontiac, Mich.

GILE TRACTOR & ENGINE CO.
Ludington, Michigan

Gile Model Q 15-35   1918-1919

Traction Wheels: Four wheels; two drive wheels in rear, 60 x 12.
No. of Plows Recommended: Three 14-in.
Length: 150 in.; **Width:** 73 in.; **Height:** 87 in.
Turning Radius: 24 ft.
Motor: Own, 4¾ x 6½, vertical, valve-in-head, 4 cylinders, cast en bloc.
Lubrication: Madison-Kipp force feed lubricator.
Carburetor: Bennett.
Ignition System: Dixie high tension magneto.
Cooling System: Perfex honeycomb radiator.
Transmission: Own spur gear.
Final Drive: Spur gears and live rear axle.
Belt Pulley: 18 x 8.
Bearings: Hyatt roller on countershaft and SKF ball in transmission and on drive axle.

GILE MODEL Q 15-35
Gile Tractor & Engine Co., Ludington, Mich.

The MILLION DOLLAR AUTOMOBILE and TRACTOR SCHOOL

SWEENEY'S

Endorsed by Leading Manufacturers and Publications

Read what some of the publications and manufacturers say about the Sweeney School:

AVERY COMPANY says: "We always endorse the Sweeney School. We have had the pleasure of selling our tractors to some of your students, and find their knowledge of machinery is far greater than the average mechanic's."

MOTOR AGE, one of the biggest magazines published for the automobile trade, gives Sweeney School a three-page unsolicited endorsement. It says: "Sweeney's method of teaching proves that intensive training in this school beats serving apprenticeship in a garage."

COUNTRY GENTLEMAN, the biggest publication of its kind in the world, gives Sweeney School a big write-up. It says: "States and governments should encourage this kind of school and training."

At the time these magazines were published, we had not carried a single line of advertising with them.

If you are mechanically inclined, learn the Automobile and Tractor business. Be able to repair your own machines, or earn big money as salesman or repairman. Unlimited opportunities for the trained mechanic. They are never out of a job. There are more jobs than men to fill them.

Every farmer should be a mechanic. Power farming is coming to be a necessity. Every farmer will have his own tractor and automobile and will save time and money if he can make his own repairs.

The Sweeney method of teaching the Automobile and Tractor business means we give you the actual experience in shop and tractor field. It is the only successful way, and I have built my school up to be the biggest in the world by using this method of teaching.

Write today for my big free catalogue that tells how I have trained hundreds of men to become expert Automobile and Tractor men, who are in business for themselves, or holding good positions.

The Automobile and Tractor business is growing faster than any business in the world. Get in it, and grow with it.

Sweeney Automobile and Tractor School

370 Union Station Plaza   **Kansas City, Mo.**

GRAY TRACTOR CO., INC.
Minneapolis, Minnesota

Gray 18-36   1918-1921

Traction Wheels: Three-wheel tractor, with one rear drum wheel 54 in. x 54 in., affording traction.
No. of Plows Recommended: Four 14-in.
Length: 168 in.; Width: 81 in.; Height: 62 in.; Weight: 6200 lbs.
Motor: Waukesha; $4\frac{3}{4}$ x $6\frac{3}{4}$; vertical L-head, 4 cylinders, cast in pairs.
Lubrication: Constant level splash and pump circulation.
Carburetor: Bennett.
Ignition System: K-W high tension magneto.
Starting and Lighting Equipment: Lighting equipment special.
Cooling System: Water, pump circulation and cellular radiator.
Bearings: Hyatt roller in transmission and own on drive axle.
Transmission: Sliding gear, 2 to $2\frac{1}{2}$ m.p.h. forward; 2 m.p.h. reverse.
Final Drive: Chain enclosed.
Belt Pulley: 11 x 8; 900 r.p.m. and 2600 feet per minute at normal engine speed.

GRAY 18-36
Gray Tractor Co., Inc., Minneapolis, Minn.

HART-PARR CO.
Charles City, Iowa

New Hart-Parr   1918-1919

Traction Wheels: Four-wheel tractor, with two drive members, 52 x 10, in rear.
No. of Plows Recommended: Three 14-in
Length: 138 in.; Width: 75 in.; Height: 60 in.; Weight: 5000 lbs.
Turning Radius: 13 ft.
Motor: Own; $6\frac{1}{2}$ x 7; horizontal, 2 cylinders, cast twin.
Lubrication: Madison-Kipp force feed lubricator.
Carburetor: Schebler.
Ignition System: High tension magneto with impulse starter.
Cooling System: Forced circulation with auto type radiator and fan.
Bearings: Hyatt roller and SKF ball in transmission and own on drive axle.
Transmission: Spur gear, 2 to 3 m.p.h. forward; 1.5 m.p.h. reverse.
Final Drive: Cast internal gear.
Belt Pulley: 14 x $8\frac{1}{2}$; 750 r.p.m. and 2600 feet per minute at normal engine speed.

NEW HART-PARR
Hart-Parr Co., Charles City, Ia.

HOLLIS TRACTOR CO.
Pittsburgh, Pennsylvania

Hollis "M" 15-25

1918-1920

HOLLIS "M" 15-25
Hollis Tractor Co., Pittsburgh, Pa.

Traction Wheels: Four-wheel tractor, with two traction members in rear, 30 x 9, equipped with patented absorption tires.
No. of Plows Recommended: Three 14-in.
Length: 136 in.; **Width:** 30 in.; **Height:** 67 in.; **Weight:** 2500 lbs.; **Price:** $975.
Turning Radius: 4½ ft.; **Acres Plowed in 10-hr. Day:** 10.
Motor: Light; 3¼ x 4½; vertical, 4 cylinders, cast en bloc.
Lubrication: Splash and force feed system.
Carburetor: Zenith.
Ignition System: Dixie high tension magneto.
Starting and Lighting Equipment: Impulse starter and acetylene lighting.
Cooling System: Frame and tubular radiator.
Bearings: Hyatt roller on drive axle and own bronze in transmission.
Transmission: Planetary; 1¾ to 7 m.p.h. forward; 1¾ to 7 m.p.h. reverse.
Final Drive: Balance bevel gear, enclosed and running in oil.
Belt Pulley: 14 x 8; 800 r.p.m. and 2800 feet per minute at normal engine speed.

HOLT MANUFACTURING CO.
Peoria, Illinois

Caterpillar 70-120

1918-1921

Traction Wheels: Crawler on each side, giving 1776 or 2200 square inches of traction, also steering wheel in front.
Length: 252 in.; **Width:** 104 in.; **Height:** 120 in ; **Weight:** 24,800 lbs.
Turning Radius: 25 ft.
Motor: Own; 7½ x 8; L-head, 6 cylinders, cast singly.
Lubrication: Force and splash system.
Carburetor: Kingston.
Ignition System: K-W high tension magneto.
Starting and Lighting Equipment: Special lighting.
Cooling System: Fan, radiator and centrifugal pump.
Bearings: Hyatt roller on drive axle and own babbitt in transmission.
Transmission: Gear and chain, 2⅛ to 3 m.p.h. forward; 2⅛ m.p.h. reverse.
Final Drive: Enclosed chain.
Belt Pulley: 22 x 12; 460 r.p.m. and 2649 feet per minute at normal engine speed.

CATERPILLAR 70-120
Holt Mfg. Co., Peoria, Ill.

HUBER MANUFACTURING CO.
Marion, Ohio

Huber Light Four

1918-1928

HUBER LIGHT FOUR
Huber Mfg. Co., Marion, O.

Traction Wheels: Four wheels, with two drives in rear, 60 x 10.
No. of Plows Recommended: Three 14-in.
Length: 150 in.; **Width:** 80 in.; **Height:** 70 in.; **Weight:** 5000 lbs.; **Price:** $1285.
Turning Radius: $11\frac{1}{2}$ ft.. Acres Plowed in 10-hr. day: 10.
Motor: Waukesha; $4\frac{1}{2}$ x $5\frac{3}{4}$; vertical L-head, 4 cylinders, cast in pairs.
Lubrication: Constant level splash.
Carburetor: Kingston.
Ignition System: Kingston high tension.
Cooling System: Perfex radiator.
Bearings: Hyatt roller and Gurney ball in transmission.
Transmission: Selective gears; 2.43 to 3.74 m.p h. forward; 1.88 m.p.h. reverse.
Final Drive: Bull gear and pinion on each side.
Belt Pulley: 13 x 7; 900 r.p.m. and 3063 feet per minute at normal engine speed.

ILLINOIS SILO & TRACTOR CO.
Bloomington, Illinois

Illinois 12-30

1918

ILLINOIS 12-30
Illinois Silo & Tractor Co., Bloomington, Ill.

Traction Wheels: Four wheels; two drive members, 56 x 9, in rear.
No. of Plows Recommended: Two to three 14-in.
Length: 120 in.; **Width:** 62 in.; **Height:** 70 in.; **Weight:** 3,700 lbs.; **Price:** $1200.
Turning Radius: 8 ft.
Motor: Waukesha; $4\frac{1}{2}$ x $5\frac{3}{4}$; L-head, 4 cylinders, cast en bloc.
Lubrication: Splash system.
Carburetor: Bennett.
Ignition System: Dixie high tension magneto.
Cooling System: Modine "Spirex" honeycomb radiator.
Bearings: SKF ball in transmission and Hyatt roller on drive axle.
Transmission: Friction, to 6 m.p.h. forward; 3 m.p.h. reverse.
Final Drive: Enclosed gears.
Belt Pulley: $11\frac{1}{2}$ x $7\frac{1}{2}$, 900 r.p.m.

Combining the Best Features of Tractor, Automobile and Motor Truck Engineering.

Two Sizes
2-3-Plow
13-30
3-4 Plow
15-30

PLOW MAN TRACTORS
ALL-STANDARD CONSTRUCTION

Reserve Power—Better Service

Farmers have learned that reserve power is a most important factor in the work of a tractor. We rate our tractors conservatively—there is plenty of excess power for hard pulls and difficult conditions. As a result Plow Man tractors have made a record success here and abroad. The new 15-30 carries the idea of reserve power still further and is a great forward step for improved service and long tractor life.

TO FARMERS

You want a practical tractor — one that has made good—and which offers all around satisfaction. You can't afford to risk your good money on theories or freak construction. Investigate the Plow Man, and learn for yourself its sound construction and easy operation. Furthermore, it offers you extra good value at a reasonable price.

TO DEALERS

You want a tractor with an established reputation. Read the list of All-Standard Units at the right—you know each is a recognized leader in its class and the best that can be produced. The high grade character of Plow Man distributors is further evidence that both the tractor and the company behind it are right.

To Exporters:

We have sufficient output to handle a reasonable amount of export business. Hundreds of our Tractors are used in Great Britain and other foreign countries.

Send for catalog and latest prices, state which size Plow Man you want to know about.

> ### All Standard Units
> Plow Man Buda 4-cylinder Motor.
> 30 H. P. at the belt.
> Draw Bar Pull, up to 3600 lbs.
> Bennett Kerosene Carburetor.
> High Tension Magneto with impulse starter.
> Interstate Enclosed Fly-Ball Governor.
> Foote Standard Transmission, 2 speeds forward, 1 reverse.
> Hyatt Roller Bearings.
> Perfex Radiator, extra size.
> New Worm Gear Steering.
> New Foot Control Clutch.
> Pinion-Master Gear Drive.
> French & Hecht Wheels.
> Tractor dimensions: Length, 12 ft.; width, 5 ft.; height, 6 ft.
> Weight, 4400 to 4800 lbs.

Interstate Tractor Co., Waterloo, Iowa

INTERNATIONAL HARVESTER CO.
Chicago, Illinois

International 15-30

1918-1922

INTERNATIONAL 15-30
International Harvester Co., Chicago, Ill.

Traction Wheels: Four wheels, two traction members in rear, 66 x 14.
No. of Plows Recommended: Four 14-in.
Length: 160 in.; **Width:** 80 in.; **Height:** 118 in.; **Weight:** 8700 lbs; **Price** $2000.
Turning Radius: 38 ft.; **Acres Plowed in 10-hr. Day:** $13\frac{1}{2}$.
Motor: Own; $5\frac{1}{4}$ x 8; horizontal, 4 cylinders, cast in pairs.
Lubrication: Force feed system.
Carburetor: Own.
Ignition System: K-W high tension magneto.
Starting and Lighting Equipment: Own.
Cooling System: Radiator fan and thermo-syphon.
Transmission: Sliding gear; 1.8 to 2.4 m.p.h. forward; 1.8 m.p.h. reverse.
Final Drive: Chains.
Belt Pulley: 18 x 9; 575 r.p.m. and 2000 feet per minute at normal engine speed.

INTERSTATE TRACTOR CO.
Waterloo, Iowa

Plow Man 15-30

1918-1919

PLOW MAN 15-30
Interstate Tractor Co., Waterloo, Ia.

Traction Wheels: Four wheels, driven by two in rear, 60 x 10.
No. of Plows Recommended: Three or four 14-in.
Length: 156 in.; **Width:** 66 in.; **Height:** 69 in.; **Weight:** 4800 lbs.; **Price** $1795.
Turning Radius: 15 ft.
Motor: Buda; $4\frac{1}{2}$ x 6; vertical, 4 cylinders, cast en bloc.
Lubrication: Force feed.
Carburetor: Bennett.
Ignition System: Dixie high tension magneto with impulse starter.
Cooling System: Perfex radiator.
Bearings: Hyatt roller throughout.
Transmission: Sliding gear; 2 to 3 m.p.h. forward.
Final Drive: Internal gear.
Belt Pulley: 14 x 8; 590 r.p.m. and 2150 feet per minute at normal engine speed.

JOLIET OIL TRACTOR CO.
Joliet, Illinois

Bates Steel Mule, Model D, 12-20

1918

BATES STEEL MULE, MODEL D, 12-20
Joliet Oil Tractor Co., Joliet, Ill.

Traction Wheels: One crawler on each side, 52 x 10.
No. of Plows Recommended: Three and four 14-in.
Length: 105 in.; Width: 62 in.; Height: 58 in.; Weight: 4300 lbs.
Turning Radius: 7½ ft.; Acres Plowed in 10-hr. Day: 10.
Motor: Erd; 4 x 6, valve-in-head, 4 cylinders, cast en bloc.
Lubrication: Force feed system.
Carburetor: Bennett.
Ignition System: Eisemann high tension magneto.
Cooling System: Modine radiator and gear driven pump circulation.
Bearings: Timken bearings throughout.
Transmission: Sliding gear, 2¼ to 4 m.p.h. forward; 2 m.p.h. reverse.
Final Drive: Enclosed gears running in oil.
Belt Pulley: 12 x 8½; 725 r.p.m. and 2300 feet per minute at normal engine speed.

J. T. TRACTOR CO.
Cleveland, Ohio

J. T. 16-30

1918-1919

Traction Wheels: One "Planking Tread" crawler on each side, 57 x 10.
No. of Plows Recommended: Three and four 14-in.
Length: 104 in.; Width: 60 in.; Height: 58 in.; Weight: 4400 lbs.; Price: $1950.
Turning Radius: 5 ft.; Acres Plowed in 10-hr. Day: 10 to 12.
Motor: Erd; 4 x 6, vertical valve-in-head, 4 cylinders, cast en bloc.
Lubrication: Force feed and splash system.
Carburetor: "J. T." special kerosene.
Ignition System: Kingston high tension magneto with impulse starter.
Cooling System: Water, Perfex radiator, fan and centrifugal pump.
Bearings: Detroit radial ball in transmission and Bock roller on drive axle.
Transmission: Selective gears, 1¼ to 5 m.p.h. forward; 1¼ m.p.h. reverse.
Final Drive: Enclosed internal gears.
Belt Pulley: 10 x 8; 800 r.p.m. and 2600 feet per minute at normal engine speed.

J. T. 16-30
J. T. Tractor Co., Cleveland, O.

1918

165

KANSAS CITY HAY PRESS CO.

Kansas City, Missouri

Prairie Dog, Model L, 9-18

PRAIRIE DOG, MODEL L, 9-18
Kansas City Hay Press Co., Kansas City, Mo.

1918-1921

Traction Wheels: Driven by one rear wheel, 48 x 20, with two non-drive wheels in front.
No. of Plows Recommended: Two 14-in.
Length: 156 in.; **Width:** 74½ in.; **Height:** 65 in.; **Weight:** 3000 lbs.; **Price:** $1150.
Turning Radius: 13 ft.; **Acres Plowed in 10-hr. Day:** 10.
Motor: Waukesha; 3¾ x 5¼, 4 cylinders, cast en bloc.
Lubrication: Splash system.
Carburetor: Bennett.
Ignition System: Dixie high tension magneto.
Cooling System: Perfex radiator.
Bearings: Hyatt roller throughout.
Transmission: Gears, 2¾ to 6 m.p.h. forward; 2½ m.p.h. reverse.
Final Drive: Gear.
Belt Pulley: 10 x 8, 950 r.p.m. and 2600 feet per minute at normal engine speed.

KECK-GONNERMAN CO.

Mt. Vernon, Indiana

Keck-Gonnerman, 12-24

1918-1919

Traction Wheels: Four wheels, with two traction members, 61 x 12, in rear.
No. of Plows Recommended: Three 14-in.
Length: 150 in.; **Width:** 78 in.; **Height:** 96 in.; **Weight:** 6500 lbs.; **Price:** $1250.
Turning Radius: 30 ft.; **Acres Plowed in 10-hr. Day:** 10.
Motor: Own; 6½ x 8, horizontal, 2 cylinders, cast en bloc.
Lubrication: Pump and splash system.
Carburetor: Schebler.
Ignition System: K-W high tension magneto.
Cooling System: Radiator with pump and fan.
Bearings: Cast iron in transmission and cast iron and babbitt on drive axle.
Transmission: Sliding gears, 2 to 4 m.p.h. forward; 1 m.p.h. reverse.
Final Drive: Spur gears.
Belt Pulley: 12 x 8; 650 r.p.m.

KECK-GONNERMAN, 12-24
Keck-Gonnerman Co., Mt. Vernon, Ind.

PERFEX

THE PERFECT RADIATOR

The Biggest Thing to Look for on a Tractor

Front rank Tractor makers acknowledge **Perfex** superiority by choosing this radiator to protect their motors.

Perfex efficiency lies in the core construction. Cools under severest conditions due to extra wide water channels. No clogging! Every inch of surface cools.

Damage to core from freezing is eliminated by our exclusive "expansion slit"—the most important development in the history of radiator construction.

Perfex bonded joints are strongest—easily stand jolts and jars of heavy farm service.

For long trouble-free engine service demand the Perfex.

Write for book on "Engine Cooling" service.

Perfex Radiator Co.
592 Flett Ave.   RACINE, WIS.

For Tractors, Trucks and Commercial Cars

KINNARD & SONS MANUFACTURING CO.

Minneapolis, Minnesota

Flour City Junior 12-20   1918
Kinnard 15-25   1918
Flour City 20-35   1918-1927

Traction Wheels: Four wheels, traction through two in rear.
No. of Plows Recommended: Three 14-in.
Length: 142 in.; **Width:** 84 in.; **Weight:** 6500 lbs.
Motor: Own; $6\frac{1}{2}$ x 7, vertical valve-in-head, 2 cylinders, cast in pairs.
Lubrication: Splash system with pump feed to crank case.
Carburetor: Schebler.
Ignition System: K-W high tension magneto.
Cooling System: Modine radiator.
Transmission: Bevel gears, 2 to 7 m.p.h. forward; 2 m.p.h. reverse.
Final Drive: Gears.
Belt Pulley: 24 x $6\frac{1}{2}$; 280 r.p.m.

FLOUR CITY JUNIOR 12-20
Kinnard & Sons Mfg. Co., Minneapolis, Minn.

Traction Wheels: Four wheels, two in rear providing traction.
No. of Plows Recommended: Four 14-in.
Weight: 7900 lbs.
Motor: Own; 5 x 5, vertical valve-in-head, 4 cylinders, cast in pairs.
Lubrication: Splash system with pump feed to crank case.
Carburetor: Schebler.
Ignition System: K-W high tension magneto.
Cooling System: Perfex radiator, pump and fan.
Transmission: Selective type, $2\frac{1}{2}$ to 4 m.p.h. forward; $2\frac{1}{2}$ m.p.h. reverse.
Final Drive: Gears.
Belt Pulley: 14 x 8; 650 r.p.m.

KINNARD 15-25
Kinnard & Sons Mfg. Co., Minneapolis, Minn.

FLOUR CITY 20-35
Kinnard & Sons Mfg. Co., Minneapolis, Minn.

Traction Wheels: Four wheels, two in rear providing traction.
No. of Plows Recommended: Five or six 14-in.
Motor: Own; $5\frac{1}{4}$ x 6, vertical valve-in-head, 4 cylinders, cast in pairs.
Lubrication: Splash system with pump feed to crankshaft.
Carburetor: Schebler.
Ignition System: K-W high tension magneto.
Cooling System: Perfex radiator, pump and fan.
Transmission: Bevel gears, $2\frac{1}{4}$ to $2\frac{1}{2}$ m.p.h. forward; $2\frac{1}{4}$ m.p.h. reverse.
Final Drive: Gears.
Belt Pulley: 26 x 8; 350 r.p.m.

LEADER TRACTOR MANUFACTURING CO.
Des Moines, Iowa

Rex 12-25

1918-1921

REX 12-25
Leader Tractor Mfg. Co., Des Moines, Ia.

Traction Wheels: Four wheels, two drive wheels in rear, 64 x 10.
No. of Plows Recommended: Three 14-in.
Weight: 5000 lbs.
Turning Radius: 12 ft.
Motor: Waukesha; $4\frac{1}{4}$ x $5\frac{1}{2}$, vertical, 4 cylinders, cast en bloc.
Lubrication: Splash system.
Carburetor: Kingston dual.
Ignition System: Eisemann high tension magneto.
Cooling System: Perfex radiator.
Bearings: SKF ball in transmission and own on drive axle.
Transmission: Enclosed gears, $2\frac{1}{2}$ to 4 m.p.h. forward.
Final Drive: Enclosed gears.
Belt Pulley: $13\frac{1}{2}$ x 7; 900 r.p.m.

LENOX MOTOR CAR CO.
Boston, Massachusetts

Lenox American, Model 20, 22-30

1918-1919

Traction Wheels: Drives on all four wheels, 50 x 12.
No. of Plows Recommended: Four and five 14-in.
Length: 132 in.; **Width:** 76 in.; **Height:** 86 in.; **Weight:** 6500 lbs.; **Price:** $2500.
Turning Radius: 13 ft.; **Acres Plowed in 10-hr. Day:** 12 to 15.
Motor: Wisconsin; $4\frac{3}{4}$ x $5\frac{1}{2}$, T-head vertical, 4 cylinders, cast in pairs.
Lubrication: Force feed through hollow crank and copper tube to all cylinders.
Carburetor: Carter or optional.
Ignition System: Dixie high tension, with impulse starter.
Starting and Lighting Equipment: Special equipment.
Cooling System: Centrifugal pump, special radiator and gear-driven fan.
Bearings: Hyatt on drive axle and die cast in transmission.
Transmission: Three-speed selective, $\frac{5}{8}$ to 6 m.p.h. forward; $2\frac{3}{4}$ m.p.h. reverse.
Final Drive: Patented adjustable drop-forged chain, semi-enclosed.
Belt Pulley: 24 x 8; 325 r.p.m. and 2000 feet per minute at normal engine speed.

LENOX AMERICAN, MODEL 20, 22-30
Lenox Motor Car Co., Boston, Mass.

LEONARD TRACTOR CO.
Jackson, Michigan

Leonard Four Wheel Drive 12-35

1918-1921

Traction Wheels: Drives on four wheels, front, 30 x 9½, and rear, 50 x 12.
No. of Plows Recommended: Three and four 14-in.
Length: 140 in.; **Width:** 70 in.; **Height:** 68 in.; **Weight:** 4200 lbs.
Turning Radius: 18⅓ ft.; **Acres Plowed in 10-hr. Day:** 10.
Motor: Beaver; 4½ x 6, 4-cycle, 4 cylinders, cast en bloc.
Lubrication: Force feed and splash system.
Carburetor: Zenith.
Ignition System: Dixie high tension magneto.
Starting and Lighting Equipment: Optional.
Cooling System: Modine radiator and fan.
Bearings: SKF in transmission and Bower on drive axle.
Transmission: Sliding gear, 2.6 to 4 m.p.h. forward; 2 m.p.h. reverse.
Final Drive: Internal gear, running in thin oil.
Belt Pulley: 16 x 9; 560 r.p m. and 2340 feet per minute at normal engine speed.

LEONARD FOUR WHEEL DRIVE 12-35
Leonard Tractor Co., Jackson, Mich.

LIBERTY TRACTOR CO.
Minneapolis, Minnesota

Liberty 15-30

LIBERTY 15-30
Liberty Tractor Co., Minneapolis, Minn.

1918

Traction Wheels: Four wheel tractor with two traction wheels in rear.
No. of Plows Recommended: Four 14-inch.
Length: 144 in.; **Width:** 68 in.; **Height:** 60 in.; ..**Weight:**.. 5,500 lbs.; **Price** $1.800.
Turning Radius: 20 ft.; **Acres plowed in 10-hour day:** 15.
Motor: Climax, 5 x 6½.; Vertical, 4 cylinders, cast in pairs.
Lubrication: Pump and splash system.
Carburetor:.. Stromberg.
Ignition Syystem': Dixie high tension magneto.
Cooling Syystem: Shotwell-Hobart-Johnson honeycomb radiator.
Bearings: Hyatt roller in transmission and roller on drive axle.
Transmission: Enclosed gears, 2½ to 4½ m. p. h. forward; 2½ m. p. h. reverse.
Final Drive: Spur gear.
Belt Pulley: 12 x 8: 1,200 r. p. m. and 2,600 feet per minute at normal engine speed.

LYONS ATLAS CO.
Indianapolis, Indiana

Atlas 16-26

Traction Wheels: Three wheel tractor with two rear wheels providing traction, 66 x 12.

No. of Plows Recommended: Three 14-inch.

Length: 125 in.; **Width:** 67 in.; **Height:** 69 in.; **Weight:** 5,000 lbs.; **Price:** $1,565.

Turning Radius: 9 ft.; **Acres Plowed in 10-hour day,** 12.

Motor: Waukesha, $4\frac{1}{4}$ x $5\frac{3}{4}$; 4 cylinders, cast in pairs.

Lubrication: Force feed system.

Carburetor: Kingston.

Ignition System: Dixie high tension magneto.

Starting and Lighting Equipment: Optional.

Cooling System: Water pump circulation.

Bearings: Hyatt roller in transmission and own plain on drive axle.

Transmission: Gears 2 to 3 m.p.h. forward; 2 to 3 m. p. h. reverse.

Final Drive: Spur gear.

Belt Pulley: 10 x 8; 875 r.p.m. and 2,300 feet per minute at normal engine speed.

1918

ATLAS 16-26
Lyons Atlas Company, Indianapolis, Ind.

MINNEAPOLIS THRESHING MACHINE CO.
Hopkins, Minnesota

Minneapolis 20-40
Minneapolis 40-80

1918-1919
1918-1919

Traction Wheels: Four wheels with two in rear, 66 x 20, providing traction.

No. of Plows Recommended: Four to six 14-inch.

Length: 167 in.; **Width:** 96 in.; **Height:** 110 in.; **Weight:** 12,000 lbs.

Motor: Own, $5\frac{3}{4}$ x 7, horizontal L-head, 4 cylinders, cast separately.

Lubrication: Mechanical oil pump and splash.

Carburetor: Kingston kerosene burner.

Ignition System: K-W. high tension magneto.

Cooling System: Water, radiator, fan and water pump.

Bearings: Own make throughout.

Transmission: 2 to $2\frac{1}{2}$ m. p. h. forward.

Belt Pulley: 20 x 10, 700 r. p. m.

MINNEAPOLIS 20-40
Minneapolis Threshing Machine Co., Hopkins, Minn.

Just as easy as filling the Radiator

One-fourth the time of the old way

IF YOU BELIEVE IN-

Economy
Efficiency

Cleanliness
Convenience

Then You Will Believe In And Use
THE SHIELDS GREASE INJECTOR

Slip a Cartridge in the Injector and it's ready for use

For Tractors and Motor Cars

The New Way

The dirty, back-breaking old way of greasing your motor car or tractor with a bucket of grease and a paddle has been displaced by the "Shields Way." The new way saves many dollars in garage bills caused by neglect in lubricating, for it is so simple the lubrication is never neglected. It's really a safety device.

Mutual Transmission Grease packed in the Shields cartridges costs less than grease packed in cans. When the cartridge is emptied, simply insert a new one in the injector and you're ready to take care of your tractor or car at any time.

The injector works equally well wtih grease of a light or heavy consistency.

Shields
GREASE & OIL
INJECTOR
CARTRIDGE

Packed with 1½ lbs.
Mutual SERVICE

TRANSMISSION GREASE

FOR SALE BY
MUTUAL OIL CO
GENERAL OFFICES
KANSAS CITY, MO.

BRANCHES
GREAT FALLS ...... MONT
MISSOULA .... MONT
DENVER ... . COLO
FREMONT........NEBR
SUPERIOR... ... NEBR
AND
ALL WIDE AWAKE DEALERS.

Mutual SERVICE **OIL CO.**
Kansas City, Mo.
BRANCHES
Denver, Colo. Superior, Nebr.
Fremont, Nebr. Missoula, Mont.
Great Falls, Mont.

HELP WIN THE WAR BY
USING GREASE PACKED
IN FIBER HOLDERS
UNCLE SAM NEEDS THE TIN

Sole Distributors in this Territory!

172

1918

Traction Wheels: Four wheel type with two rear wheels, 85 x 30, providing traction.
No. of Plows Recommended: Six to ten 14-inch.
Length: 206 in,; **Width:** 108 in.; **Height:** 136 in.; **Weight:** 22,500 lbs.
Motor: Own, 7¼ x 9, horizontal 4 cylinders, cast in pairs.
Lubrication: Mechanical oil pump and splash.
Carburetor: Kingston kerosene burner.
Ignition System: K-W. high tension and batteries.
Cooling System: Water, radiator, fan and water pump.
Bearings: Own make throughout.
Transmission: 2 to 2½ m. p. h. forward.
Belt Pulley: 24 x 10¼; 500 r.p.m.

MINNEAPOLIS 40-80
Minneapolis Threshing Machine Co., Hopkins, Minn.

MINNESOTA TRACTOR CO.

Minneapolis, Minnesota

Minnesota 18-36

1918-1919

Traction Wheels: Four wheels, driven by two in rear, 61 x 16.
No. of Plows Recommended: Four 14-in.
Length: 144 in.; **Width:** 68 in.; **Height:** 66 in.; **Weight:** 8,000 lbs.
Motor: Own, 7½ x 8, vertical, 2 cylinders, cast separately.
Lubrication: Detroit force feed lubricator.
Carburetor: Kingston.
Ignition System: Dixie high tension magneto.
Cooling System: Perfex radiator.
Bearings: Babbitt in transmission and plain on drive axles.
Transmission: Friction, 2½ to 7 m. p. h. forward.
Final Drive: Gears and friction clutch.
Belt Pulley: 16 x 10; 500 r. p. m.

MINNESOTA 18-36
Minnesota Tractor Co., Minneapolis, Minn.

MONARCH TRACTOR CO.
Watertown, Wisconsin

Lightfoot 6-10

LIGHTFOOT 6-10
Monarch Tractor Co., Watertown, Wis.

1918-1919

Traction Wheels: Two crawlers, 39 x 6.
No. of Plows Recommended: Two 14-in.
Length: 94 in.; **Width:** 42 in.; **Height:** 55 in.; **Weight:** 3,000 lbs.; **Price:** $950.
Turning Radius: 6 ft.
Motor: Kermath, $3\frac{3}{4}$ x 4, L-head, 4 cylinders, cast en bioc.
Lubrication: Combination splash and pump system.
Carburetor: Kingston.
Ignition System: K-W, high tension magneto.
Lighting Equipment: Supplied to order.
Cooling System Circulating water pump to radiator.
Bearings: Bronze in speed change gears.
Transmission: Enclosed, $1\frac{7}{8}$ m.p.h. forward, $1\frac{7}{8}$ m.p.h. reverse.
Final Drive: Roller chain.
Belt Pulley: 9 x 7; 800 r.p.m.

NATIONAL TRACTOR CO.
Chicago, Illinois

National, Model E, 9-16
National, Model F, 12-22

Traction Wheels: Four wheels, two driving wheels in rear, 46 x 10.
No. of Plows Recommended: Two 14-in.
Length: 120 in.; **Width:** 57 in.; **Height:** 60 in.; **Weight:** 3,800 lbs.
Turning Radius: 13 ft.: **Acres Plowed in 10-hour day:** 10 to 12.
Motor: Waukesha, $3\frac{1}{2}$ x $5\frac{1}{2}$, vertical L-head, 4 cylinders, cast en bloc.
Lubrication: Force feed and splash system.
Carburetor: Bennett kerosene.
Ignition System: Dixie high tension magneto.
Cooling and Lighting System: Perfex cellulor radiator, pump and fan.
Bearings: SKF ball in speed change gears and plain on drive axle.
Transmission: Friction, 2 to $3\frac{1}{2}$ m.p.h. forward; 2 to $3\frac{1}{2}$ m.p.h. reverse.
Final Drive: Enclosed gears.
Belt Pulley: 10 x 6; 600 to 1,000 r.p.m.

1918
1918

NATIONAL, MODEL E, 9-16
National Tractor Co., Chicago, Ill.

Traction Wheels: Four wheels, two drive
  wheels in rear, 46 x 10.
No. of Plows Recommended: Three 14-in.
Length: 120 in.; Width: 61 in.; Height;
  60 in.; Weight: 4,200 lbs.
Turning Radius: 13 ft. Acres Plowed in
  10-hour day: 10 to 12.
Motor: Waukesha, $4\frac{1}{4}$ x $5\frac{3}{4}$, vertical L-
  head, 4 cylinders, cast in pairs.
Lubrication: Force feed and splash sys-
  tem.
Carburetor: Kingston kerosene.
Ignition System: Dixie high tension
  magneto with impulse starter.
Starting and Lighting Equipment: Spe-
  cial.
Cooling System: Perfex cellular radiator
  pump and fan.
Bearings: SKF ball on speed change
  gears and plain on drive axle.
Transmission: Friction 2 to $3\frac{1}{2}$ m. p. h.
  forward; 2 to $3\frac{1}{2}$ m. p. h. reverse.
Final Drive: Enclosed gears.
Belt Pulley: 10 x 6; 600-1000 r. p. m.

NATIONAL, MODEL F, 12-22
National Tractor Co., Chicago, Ill.

NEW AGE TRACTOR CO.
Minneapolis, Minnesota

New Age 16-28

NEW AGE 16-28
New Age Tractor Co., Minneapolis, Minn.

1918-1919

Traction Wheels: Three wheels; two
  drive wheels, 60 x 10, in front.
No. of Plows Recommended: Three 14-
  inch.
Length: 120 in;; width: 76 in; Height:
  68 in.; Weight: 4350 lbs; Price:
  $1450.
Turning Radius: 11 ft.; Acres Plowed
  in 10-hr. day: 10.
Motor: Beaver, $4\frac{1}{2}$ x 6, vertical, 4
  cylinders, cast en bloc.
Lubrication: Splash and pump systems.
Carburetor: Kingston.
Ignition System: Dixie high tension magneto.
Cooling System: S-H-J radiator, pump
  and fan.
Transmission: Sliding gears, 2 to $3\frac{3}{4}$
  m. p. h. forward; 2 m. p. h. reverse.
Final Drive: Spur gears on internal
  drive.
Belt Pulley: 13 x $7\frac{1}{2}$; 650 r. p. m. and
  2350 feet per minute at normal en-
  gine speed.

THE first duty of a tractor is **traction**. Most tractors obtain traction by weight. The Nilson obtains traction by the lever and fulcrum principle through its famous Lever Hitch.

Instead of employing a straight line drag from the engine to the plows, the Lever Hitch carries the pull **up over** the drive wheels and then **down** to the plows. Thus the Nilson obtains its traction by the pull of the plows, rather than by dead weight.

This gives the Nilson the four big features you need in your tractor: Traction, Economy, Light Weight and Speed.

Study the condensed specifications of the Nilson Senior and the Nilson Junior on the opposite page. The Nilson Junior has plowed 1,500 acres of Montana soil without stopping except for fuel and oil. The Nilson Senior has plowed and dragged 400 acres at the rate of 16 acres a day, on an average of 1½ gallons of gasoline an acre.

The Nilson is the only Lever Hitch Tractor. Write today for new booklet explaining the Lever Hitch Traction Principle.

The Nilson Tractor Co.

2628 University Ave. S. E.
MINNEAPOLIS, MINN.

THE TRACTOR WITH THE FAMOUS LEVER HITCH

176

1918

NILSON TRACTOR CO.
Minneapolis, Minnesota

Nilson Senior 24-36
Nilson Junior 16-27

1918-1919
1918-1919

Traction Wheels: Five wheel tractor with drive wheels, 52 x 20.
No. of Plows Recommended: Four or five 14-inch.
Length: 165 in.; **Width:** 90 in.; **Height:** 67 in.; **Weight:** 5900 lbs
Turning Radius: 17 ft.; **Acres Plowed in 10-hr. Day:** 15 to 20.
Motor: Waukesha, $4\frac{3}{4}$ x $6\frac{3}{4}$, vertical, 4 cylinders, cast in pairs.
Lubrication: Constant level splash system.
Carburetor: Kingston.
Ignition System: K-W high tension magneto with impulse starter.
Starting and Lighting Equipment: As extra equipment.
Cooling System: Radiator and fan.
Bearings: Hyatt roller throughout.
Transmission: Nilson special, $2\frac{1}{2}$ to $5\frac{1}{2}$ m. p. h. forward; $2\frac{1}{2}$ m. p. h. reverse.
Final Drive: Double roller chain.
Belt Pulley: 24 x 8, 360 r. p. m. and 2160 ft. per minute at normal engine speed.

NILSON SENIOR 24-36
Nilson Tractor Co., Minneapolis, Minn.

Traction Wheels: Five wheel tractor with three rear drive wheels, 50 x 16.
No. of Plows Recommended: Three and four, 14-in.
Length: 147 in.; **Width:** 82 in.; **Height:** 62 in.; **Weight:** 4300 lbs.
Turning Radius: 16 ft.; **Acres Plowed in 10 hr. day:** 11 to 16.
Motor: Waukesha, $4\frac{1}{4}$ x $5\frac{3}{4}$; vertical, 4 cylinders, cast in pairs.
Lubrication: Constant level splash system.
Carburetor: Kingston.
Ignition System: K-W high tension magneto with impulse starter.
Starting and Lighting Equipment: As extra equipment.
Cooling System: Radiator and fan.
Bearings: Hyatt roller throughout.
Transmission: Nilson special, $2\frac{1}{2}$ to $5\frac{1}{2}$ m. p. h. forward; $2\frac{1}{2}$ m. p. h. reverse.
Final Drive: Double roller chain.
Belt Pulley: 20 x 6, 400 r.p.m. and 1992 feet per minute at normal engine speed.

NILSON JUNIOR 16-27
Nilson Tractor Co., Minneapolis, Minn.

OHIO MANUFACTURING CO.
Upper Sandusky, Ohio

Whitney 9-18

1918-1919

WHITNEY 9-18
Ohio Mfg. Co., Upper Sandusky, O.

Traction Wheels: Four wheels, driving from two rear wheels, 48 x 10.
No. of Plows Recommended: Two 14- in.
Length: 123 in.; **Width:** 56 in.; **Height:** 58½ in.; **Weight:** 3000 lbs:; **Price:** $1075.
Turning Radius: 11 ft.; **Acres Plowed in 10-hr. Day:** 5 to 6.
Motor: Gile, 5½ x 6½.; opposed, two cylinders, cast separately.
Lubrication: Madison-Kipp force feed system.
Carburetor: Bennett.
Ignition System: Dixie high tension magneto.
Cooling System: Circulating pump and radiator.
Bearings: Timken roller in speed change gears and own roller on drive axle.
Transmission: Selective, 1½ to 4 m. p. h. forward; 3 m. p. h. reverse.
Final Drive: Chain.
Belt Pulley: 11 x 6¾; 750-900 r. p. m. and 2100 ft. per minute at normal engine speed.

PAN MOTOR CO.
St. Cloud, Minnesota

Pan Tank-Tread 12-24

1918

PAN TANK-TREAD 12-24
Pan Motor Co., St. Cloud, Minn.

Traction Wheels: Two crawlers, 39 x 12.
No. of Plows Recommended: Two and three, 14-inch.
Length: 84 in.; **Width:** 60 in.; **Height:** 60 in.; **Weight:** 4500 lbs.; **Price:** $1495.
Turning Radius: 5 ft.; **Acres Plowed In 10 hr. Day:** 8 to 10.
Motor: Buda, 4¼ x 5½; vertical, 4 cylinder, cast en bloc.
Lubrication: Force feed through hollow crank shaft.
Carburetor: Kingston.
Ignition System: Dixie high tension magneto.
Starting and Lighting Equipment: Bijur
Cooling System: Honey comb radiator, pump and fan.
Bearings: Timken and Hyatt roller in transmission and Hyatt on drive axle.
Transmission: Spur gears; 1½ to 4¼ m.p.h. forward; 1½ m.p.h. reverse.
Final Drive: Internal gear.
Belt Pulley: 14 x 8; 900 r.p.m. and 3375 feet per minute at normal engine speed.

PIONEER TRACTOR MANUFACTURING CO.
Winona, Minnesota

Pioneer Special 15-30
Pioneer 30, 30-60

1918
1918-1927

Traction Wheels; Four wheels, two drive members in rear, 60 x 18.
No. of Plows Recommended: Four 14-in.
Length: 168 in.; **Width:** 76 in.; **Height:** 66 in.; **Weight:** 8500 lbs
Turning Radius: 15 ft.; **Acres Plowed in 10-hr. day,** 14.
Motor: Own, $5\frac{1}{2}$ x 6; horizontal, 4 cylinders, cast in pairs.
Lubrication: Opposed force feed through drilled crank shaft for journal and connecting rods.
Carburetor: Kingston.
Ignition System: K-W high tension with impulse starter.
Starting and Lighting Equipment: K-W generator for lighting, extra.
Cooling System: Forced water circulation by centrifugal pump and S-H-J radiator.
Bearings: Own make, plain bearings throughout.
Transmission: Sliding spur, $1\frac{3}{4}$ to 4 m. p. h. forward; $2\frac{1}{2}$ m. p. h. reverse.
Final Drive: Roller chain, enclosed.
Belt Pulley: 14 x 8; 700 r p.m. and 2565 feet per minute at normal engine speed.

PIONEER SPECIAL 15-30
Pioneer Tractor Mfg. Co., Winona, Minn.

PIONEER 30, 30-60
Pioneer Tractor Mfg. Co., Winona, Minn.

Traction Wheels: Four wheel tractor with two drive members, 96 x 24, in rear.
No. of Plows Recommended: Eight to ten, 14-in.
Length: 237 in.; **Width:** 120 in.; **Height:** 144 in.; **Weight:** 2300 lbs.
Turning Radius: 25 ft.; **Acres Plowed in 10-hr. Day:** 25 to 32.
Motor: Own, 7 x 8; horizontal opposed, 4 cylinders, cost in pairs.
Lubrication: Force feed to cylinders and bearings.
Carburetor: Kingston, $2\frac{1}{2}$-inch.
Ignition System: K-W high tension magnegto with impulse starter.
Starting and Lighting Equipment: Electric generator and headlight furnished; starter special.
Cooling System: Radiator, fan and pump.
Bearings: Own make, plain throughout.
Transmission: Spur gear; $1\frac{3}{4}$ to 4 m.p.h. forward; $2\frac{1}{4}$ m.p.h. reverse.
Final Drive: Gear and pinion.
Belt Pulley: 18 x 15; 650 r.p.m. and 2827 ft. per minute at normal engine speed.

New Direct Axle Drive Transmission

Our new Live Axle Drive Transmission is now in production and we are prepared to quote price and make delivery. This Transmission represents the very best type of construction throughout and the highest efficiency is obtained. A pair of change gears outside of case makes it possible to get 4 speeds.

Our spring cushion drive on the rim of the wheel eliminates all shocks on axle and transmission, giving greater durability and maximum power at the drawbar. Write us for complete details.

Built in 3 to 4 and 4 to 6 plow sizes.

Our Model "D" transmission same as the D-U, excepting Bull Pinion drive type are now ready for the market.

The Foote-IXL Standard Transmission

Built For Enduring Service

The first complete transmission with power service shaft on the market. It Is the Penalty of Success to Be Copied, but why buy an experiment when you can get the Foote-IXL, which has been adopted by leading tractor manufacturers, and highly recommended by farmers.

Model "B"   The PIONEER Tractor Transmission

We Make All Kinds of Gears Up to 12 Feet Diameter.

Send Blue Prints For Estimates.

Foote Bros. Gear & Mach. Co.

213 North Curtis Street   **CHICAGO, ILLINOIS**

PEORIA TRACTOR CORP.

Peoria, Illinois

Peoria 12-25

1918-1921

Traction Wheels: Three, two drive members in rear, 56x12.
No. of Plows Recommended: Three 14-in.
Length: 152 in.; Width: 69 in.; Height: 68 in.; Weight 4750 lbs.; Price: $1585.
Turning Radius: 9 ft.; Acres plowed in 10-hr. day: 10-12.
Motor: Climax; 5 x 6½, vertical, 4 cylinders, cast in pairs.
Lubrication: Force feed through drilled crank shaft.
Carburetor: K.M.C.
Ignition System: Eisemann high tension.
Cooling System: Enclosed Eureka honeycomb radiator.
Bearings: Hyatt roller in transmission and plain on drive axle.
Transmission: Spur gear, 2½ to 4 m.p.h. forward; 2 m.p.h. reverse.
Final Drive: Internal spur gear.
Belt Pulley: 14 x 6; 650-800 r.p.m. and 2,450 feet per minute at normal engine speed.

PEORIA 12-25
Peoria Tractor Corporation, Peoria, Ill.

PLANO TRACTOR CO.

Plano, Illinois

Motox

MOTOX
Plano Tractor Co., Plano, Ill.

1918

Traction Wheels: Four wheel type, with rear wheels, 42 x 12, furnishing traction.
No. of Plows Recommended: Three 14-in.
Length: 125 in.; Width: 62¼ in ; Height: 47 in.; Weight: 4300 lbs.; Price, $1850.
Turning Radius: 13 ft.; Acres Plowed in 10-hr. Day: 10 to 12.
Motor: Buda, 4¼ x 5½, L-head, 4 cylinders, cast en bloc.
Lubrication: Forced feed to tractor bearings from motor, splash in motor.
Carburetor: Special.
Ignition System: Kingston high tension magneto with impulse starter.
Starting and Lighting Equipment: Remy electric.
Cooling System: Centrifugal pump and air washer.
Bearings: Hyatt in speed change gears and babbitt on drive axle.
Transmission: Spur gear selective in oil, 2½ to 3 m. p. h. forward; 2 m. p. h. reverse.
Final Drive: Manganese steel gears and pinions.
Belt Pulley: 10 x 8; 980 r. p. m. and 2565 ft. per minute at normal engine speed.

PORT HURON ENGINE & THRESHER CO.

Port Huron, Michigan

Port Huron 12-25

Traction Wheels: Four wheels, two drive wheels in rear, 56 x 10.

No. of Plows Recommended: Three 14-in.

Length: 156 in.; **Width:** 75 in.; **Height:** 105 in.; **Weight:** 5700 lbs.

Turning Radius: 6 ft.

Motor: Erd, 4 x 6, vert'cal, 4 cylinders, cast en bloc.

Lubrication: Constant level splash system.

Carburetor: Kingston single bowl.

Ignition System: Kingston high tension magneto with impulse starter.

Cooling System: Perfex radiator with forced circulation .

Bearings: SKF ball in transmission and own babbitt on drive axle.

Transmission: Spur gear with friction drive, 1⅞ to 4 m.p.h. forward; 1⅞ to 4 m.p.h. reverse.

Final Drive: Enclosed spur gears running in oil.

Belt Pulley: 14 x 8; 650 to 1,050 r.p.m. and 2,380 to 3,900 feet per minute at normal engine speed.

PORT HURON 12-25

Port Huron Engine & Thresher Co., Port Huron, Mich.

R. & P. TRACTOR CO.

Alma, Michigan

R & P 12-20

R & P 12-20

R. & P. Tractor Co., Alma, Mich.

Traction Wheels: Four wheel tractor with two rear "patent tread" drive wheels, 40 x 12.

No. of Plows Recommenled: Two 14-in.

Length: 120 in.; **Width:** 65½ in.; **Height:** 65 in.; **Weight:** 3500 lbs.; **Price,** $1365.

Turning Radius: 12½ ft.

Motor: Waukesha, 3¾ x 5½, 4-cycle; 4 cylinders, cast en bloc.

Lubrication: Forced feed system.

Carburetor: Kingston.

Ignition System: Eisemann high tension magneto.

Cooling System: Pump drive with radiator and fan.

Transmission: Selective gear, 1⅓ to 5 m. p. h. forward; 1 m. p. h. reverse.

Final Drive: R-P special internal gear axle.

Belt Pulley: 8 x 7; 550 r. p. m.

THE OLD RELIABLE RUSSELL LINE

Large Outfits

The Russell Giant Tractor 30/60 H. P. will handle the LARGEST NEW RUSSELL Thresher, with all modern attachments, pull 8 to 12 Plows and perform other heavy duties.

The "Big Boss"---20/40 H. P. is designed for all medium power propositions.

The Famous Russell Steam Traction Engines need no further word--- all sizes.

Portable Saw Mills.

Engines and Boilers.

Road Rollers.

Supplies.

Send for Catalogues

Small Outfits

THE RUSSELL JUNIOR TRACTOR and THE RUSSELL JUNIOR THRESHER, with all modern refinements makes the most complete and efficient small individual or community outfit on the market.

Get information about this really wonderful little rig---It is the very last word in economy, durability and efficiency.

AGENTS
WANTED.

Threshers for Grain Rice, Beans, Peas, Etc., Etc.

1842

1918

THE OLD RELIABLE RUSSELL LINE

Russell Junior, 10/20 H. P.

The "Little Boss", 15/30 H. P.

The "Big Boss," 20/40 H. P.

The Russell "Giant", 30/60 H. P.

RUSSELL KEROSENE TRACTORS

SCIENTIFICALLY DESIGNED AND BUILT!

1842 THE OLD RELIABLE RUSSELL LINE 1918

The Russell & Company, Massillon, Ohio, U.S.A.
Agents and Branches Everywhere

1918

THE RUSSELL & CO.

Massillon, Ohio

Russell 15-30

Traction Wheels: Four wheels with two traction members, 53 x 10, in rear.
No. of Plows Recommended: Three to four 14-in.
Length: 148 in.; **Width:** 67 in.; **Height:** 96 in.; **Weight:** 6900 lbs.
Turning Radius: 14 ft.
Motor: Waukesha, $4\frac{1}{2}$ x $6\frac{3}{4}$; vertical, 4 cylinders, cast in pairs.
Lubrication: Splash.
Carburetor: Kingston.
Ignition System: Dixie magneto.
Cooling System: Perfex honeycomb radiator.
Bearings: Ball and roller in transmission and plain on drive axle.
Transmission: Gearing, $1\frac{1}{2}$ to $3\frac{3}{4}$ m. p. h. forward; $1\frac{1}{4}$ m. p. h. reverse.
Final Drive: Gearing through rear wheels.
Belt Pulley: $12\frac{1}{2}$ x 7; 870 r. p. m.

1918-1919

RUSSELL 15-30
The Russell & Co., Massillon, O.

SAWYER-MASSEY CO., LTD.

Hamilton, Ontario, Canada

Sawyer-Massey 11-22	1918
Sawyer-Massey 17-34	1918
Sawyer-Massey 20-40	1918
Sawyer-Massey 27-50	1918

SAWYER-MASSEY 11-22
Sawyer-Massey Co., Ltd., Hamilton, Ont.

Traction Wheels: Four wheels, traction through two in rear, 54 x 14 inches.
No. of Plows Recommended: Three 14-in.
Length: 133 in.; **Width:** 61 in.; **Height:** 66 in.; **Weight:** 5400 lbs.; **Price,** $1750.
Turning Radius: 22 ft.
Motor: Erd, 4 x 6; valve-in-head; 4 cylinders, cast en bloc.
Lubrication: Splash system.
Carburetor: Kingston.
Ignition System: Kingston magneto.
Cooling System: Tubular radiator.
Bearings: Plain and babbitt throughout.
Transmission: 1.9 to 3 r.p.m. forward; 1.9 to 3 m. p. h. reverse.
Final Drive: Spur gearing in rear wheels.
Belt Pulley: 21 x 8; 440 r. p. m. and 2419 ft. per minute at normal engine speed.

Traction Wheels: Four wheel tractor, with two rear wheels, 62 x 20, affording traction.
No. of Plows Recommended: Four and five 14-in.
Length: 173 in.; **Width:** 81 in.: **Height:** 112 in.; **Weight:** 11500 lbs.; **Price,** $2900.
Motor: Twin City, $5\frac{1}{2}$ x $7\frac{1}{2}$; L-head, 4 cylinders, cast en bloc.
Lubrication: Detroit force feed and splash.
Carburetor: Bennett.
Ignition System: K-W.
Cooling System: Tubular radiator.
Bearings: Plain and babbitt throughout.
Transmission: 1.9 to 3 m.p.h. forward; 1.9 to 3 m.p.h. reverse.
Final Drive: Spur gear in rear wheel.
Belt Pulley: 27 x 9; 340 r. p. m. and 2403 ft. per minute at normal engine speed.

SAWYER-MASSEY 17-34

Sawyer-Massey Co., Ltd., Hamilton, Ont.

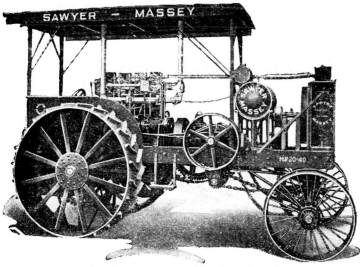

SAWYER-MASSEY 20-40

Sawyer-Massey Co., Ltd., Hamilton, Ont.

Traction Wheels: Four-wheel type, with two rear wheels, 62 x 20, affording traction.
No. of Plows Recommended: Four to six 14-in.
Length: 173 in.; **Width:** 81 in.; **Height:** 112 in.; **Weight:** 11500 lbs.; **Price** $3750.
Acres Plowed in 10-hr. Day: 10 to 15.
Motor: Own, $5\frac{5}{8}$ x 7; valve-in-head, 4 cylinders, cast singly.
Lubrication. Detroit force feed and splash system.
Carburetor: Bennett.
Ignition System: Kingston high tension magneto.
Cooling System: Tubular radiator.
Bearings: Plain and babbitt throughout.
Transmission: 1.9 to 3 m. p. h. forward; 1.9 to 3 m. p. h. reverse.
Final Drive: Spur gear.
Belt Pulley: 27 x 9; 340 r. p. m. and 2403 ft. per minute at normal engine speed.

Traction Wheels: Four-wheel tractor, with traction furnished by two rear wheels, 68 x 30.
No. of Plows Recommended: Six to eight 14-in.
Length: 190 in.; **Width:** 108 in.; **Height:** 124 in.; **Weight:** 17500 lbs.; **Price,** $4000.
Acres Plowed in 10-hr. Day: 14 to 20.
Motor: Own, $6\frac{1}{4}$ x 8; valve-in-head, 4 cylinders, cast singly.
Lubrication: Detroit force feed and splash.
Carburetor: Bennett.
Ignition System: Kingston high tension magneto.
Cooling System: Own, tubular radiator.
Bearings: Plain and babbitt throughout.
Transmission: 2 to $3\frac{1}{2}$ m. p. h. forward; 2 to $3\frac{1}{2}$ m. p. h. reverse.
Final Drive: Spur gear.
Belt Pulley: 32 x 10; 290 r. p. m. and 2429 ft. per minute at normal engine speed.

SAWYER-MASSEY 27-50

Sawyer-Massey Co., Ltd., Hamilton, Ont.

SQUARE TURN

NO CLUTCH TO SLIP — NO GEARS TO STRIP

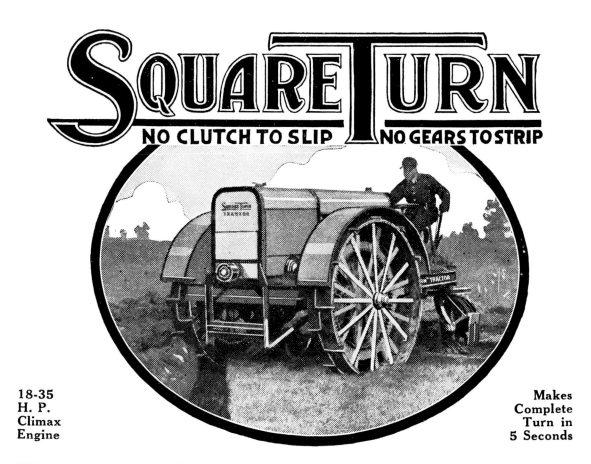

18-35
H. P.
Climax
Engine

Makes
Complete
Turn in
5 Seconds

The Most Completely Power Controlled Tractor on the Market

Drives Like Your Team—"The Levers Are the Lines"

Two handy driving levers (one for each hand) are all you use to stop, start, turn or back the Square Turn Tractor. It's just as easy as handling the reins of your team and much quicker. You have no foot work to do—no clutch to throw in or out—no steering wheel to spin—just shift the two levers and the tractor itself does everything by power. No other tractor is so completely power controlled. No other tractor will turn so short and quickly.

The Square Turn Tractor also operates equally well in either direction. All you need to do is to swing the driving seat around to face the direction you want to go and you drive with the same two handy levers and in the same manner as you would drive a team.

Plows are Underslung and Lifted by Power

Easy for One Man to Watch and Operate

Your work is always in plain sight. No twisting of the neck to watch the plows—no need for the help of an extra man—no getting off to clear trash from your plows nor to make adjustments. The adjusting levers for your plows are right at your side and you can instantly stop, lift your plows by power, back to clear trash, set plows any depth you wish and go ahead—all without leaving the driver's seat.

Our free catalog tells all about the patented "Giant Grip Drive"—the remarkable invention which does away with transmission gears, differential gears and clutch; reduces all possible tractor troubles more than half; does away with costly repairs and enables you to do things and go places where you cannot go with any other tractor. Write for free catalog today.

SQUARE TURN TRACTOR CO.

Factory—Norfolk, Neb.   1429 LYTTON BLDG., CHICAGO

SEXTON TRACTOR CORP.
Asbury Park, New Jersey

Sexton 12-25

SEXTON 12-25
Sexton Tractor Corporation, Asbury Park, N. J.

1918-1919

Traction Wheels: Drives on two rear wheels, 48 x 12; two wheels in front.
No. of Plows Recommended: Three to four 14-in.
Length: 144 in.; **Width:** 72 in.; **Height:** 62 in.; **Weight:** 4800 lbs.
Turning Radius: 17 ft.; **Acres Plowed In 10-hr. Day:** 9.
Motor: Erd, 4 x 6; vertical, valve-in-head, 4 cylinders, cast en bloc.
Lubrication: Force feed and splash system.
Carburetor: Bennett multiple jet kerosene.
Ignition System: Dixie high tension magneto with Sumter coupling.
Starting and Lighting Equipment: Westinghouse as an extra equipment.
Cooling System: Perfex enclosed radiator with centrifugal pump.
Bearings: Timken roller in transmission and on drive axle.
Transmission: Selective gears, 2½ to 4 m. p. h. forward; 1¾ m. p. h. reverse.
Final Drive: Live axle with spur gears, enclosed in oil.
Belt Pulley, 14 x 6; 475 r. p. m. and 2600 ft. per minute at normal engine speed.

SQUARE TURN TRACTOR CO.
Chicago, Illinois

Square Turn 18-35

Traction Wheels: Two drive wheels, 61 x 12, in front; one non-driver in rear.
No. of Plows Recommended: Three 14-in.
Length: 199 in.; **Width:** 98 in.; **Height:** 81 in.; **Weight:** 7800 lbs.; **Price,** $1875.
Acres Plowed in 10-hr. Day: 10.
Motor: Climax, 5 x 6½; vertical, 4 cylinder, cast in pairs.
Lubrication: Force feed through vane pump.
Carburetor: Stromberg.
Ignition System: Dixie magneto.
Cooling System: Water pump circulation with radiator and fan.
Bearings: Timken roller in transmission and on drive axle
Transmission: Giant grip friction, 2 to 2⅓ m.p.h. forward; 2⅓ m.p.h. reverse.
Final Drive: Bull gear and pinion.
Belt Pulley: 12 x 10; 850 r.p.m and 1838 feet per minute at normal engine speed.

1918-1921

SQUARE TURN 18-35
Square Turn Tractor Co., Chicago, Ill.

STINSON TRACTOR CO.
Minneapolis, Minnesota

Stinson 18-36

1918-1920

Traction Wheels: Three-wheel tractor; two drive wheels in rear, 60 x 12.
No. of Plows Recommended: Four 14-in.
Length: 176 in.; **Width:** 84 in.; **Height:** 82 in.; **Weight:** 6300 lbs.; **Price,** $2000.
Motor: Beaver, 4¾ x 6; vertical, 4 cylinders, cast en bloc.
Lubrication: Submerged pump and splash system.
Carburetor: Kingston.
Ignition System: Dixie high tension magneto.
Cooling System: Todd radiator, pump and fan.
Bearings: Hyatt roller in transmission.
Transmission: Spur gear, 2 to 3½ m. p. h. forward; 2 m. p. h. reverse.
Final Drive: Spur gear.
Belt Pulley: 12 x 8½; 1100 r. p. m.

STINSON 18-36
Stinson Tractor Co., Minneapolis, Minn.

STRITE TRACTOR CO.
New York, New York

Strite 12-25

1918-1919

Traction Wheels: Four wheels; two drive wheels in rear, 54 x 12.
No. of Plows Recommended: Three or four 14-in.
Length: 128 in.; **Width:** 64 in.; **Height:** 60 in.; **Weight:** 4800 lbs.; **Price** $1395.
Turning Radius: 12 ft.; **Acres Plowed in 10-hr. Day:** 8 to 10.
Motor: Waukesha; 4¼ x 5¾, L-head, 4 cylinders, cast in pairs.
Lubrication: Splash system.
Carburetor: Kingston or Bennett.
Ignition System: Dixie high tension magneto.
Starting and Lighting Equipment: Special.
Cooling System: Perfex auto type radiator, pump and fan.
Bearings: Hyatt roller in transmission.
Transmission: Foote-Strite sliding gears. 2½ to 4 m.p.h. forward.
Final Drive: Open gears.
Belt Pulley: 18 x 7; 500 to 550 r.p.m.

STRITE 12-25
Strite Tractor Co., New York, N. Y.

188

1918

A Record Worthy of the Name

IN ITS years of successful service in all parts of the United States and abroad, the Allis-Chalmers 10-18 H. P. Farm Tractor has established a record worthy of the Allis-Chalmers Manufacturing Co.

ALLIS-CHALMERS 10-18 H.P. FARM TRACTOR

It is just the sort of a tractor you would expect Allis-Chalmers to build—right in design, right in construction and right in **performance.** Uses kerosene or gasoline with remarkable economy and efficiency.

Write for complete illustrated details of construction and operation. Dealers in unallotted territory will find our proposition interesting.

Allis - Chalmers Manufacturing Co.

Milwaukee, Wisconsin, U. S. A.

TOPP-STEWART TRACTOR CO.
Clintonville, Wisconsin

Topp-Stewart Tractor

1918

TOPP-STEWART TRACTOR
Topp-Stewart Tractor Co., Clintonville, Wis.

Traction Wheels: Drives on all four wheels, 42 x 12.
No. of Plows Recommended: Four to six 14-in.
Length: 138 in ; Width: 78 in.; Height: 64 in.; Weight: 6000 lbs.; Price, $2650.
Turning Radius: 11 ft.
Motor: Waukesha, $4\frac{3}{4} \times 6\frac{3}{4}$; vertical. 4 cylinders.
Lubrication: Automatic splash system.
Carburetor: Kingston.
Ignition System: Eisemann high tension magneto.
Cooling System: Centrifugal water pump.
Transmission; Sliding gear, to 5 m. p. h. forward; $1\frac{1}{2}$ m. p. h. reverse.
Belt Pulley: 14 x 8.

TRENAM TRACTOR CO.
Stevens Point, Wisconsin

Trenam 12-24

1918-1920

Traction Wheels: Three wheels with two drive wheels in front.
No. of Plows Recommended: Three 14-in.
Length: 138 in.; Width: 79 in.; Height: 66 in ; Weight: 4200 lbs.
Motor: Erd, 4 x 6; L-head, 4 cylinders, cast en bloc.
Carburetor: Holley or Kingston.
Ignition System: Dixie high tension magneto.
Cooling System: Modine radiator, pump and fan.
Bearings: Hess-Bright roller opposite drive axle.
Transmission: Selective gears.
Final Drive: Open chain.
Belt Pulley: $20 \times 7\frac{1}{4}$; 900 r. p. m.

TRENAM 12-24
Trenam Tractor Co., Stevens Point, Wis.

TURNER MANUFACTURING CO.
Port Washington, Wisconsin

Turner Simplicity 12-20

TURNER SIMPLICITY 12-20
Turner Mfg. Co., Port Washington, Wis.

1918-1919

Traction Wheels: Four wheels, with two, 54 x 10, in rear, giving traction.
No. of Plows Recommended: Two and three 14-in.
Length: 128 in.: **Width:** 68 in.; **Height:** 60 in.; **Weight:** 4200 lbs.; **Price,** $1350.
Turning Radius: 12 ft.; **Acres Plowed in 10-hr. Day:** 10.
Motor: Waukesha, $3\frac{3}{4}$ x $5\frac{1}{4}$; 4-cycle, 4 cylinders, cast en bloc.
Lubrication: Constant level splash system.
Carburetor: Kingston.
Ignition System: Dixie high tension magneto and impulse starter.
Cooling System: Perfex radiator, pump and fan.
Bearings: Hyatt roller in transmission and own roller on drive axle.
Transmission: Selective gears, $1\frac{3}{4}$ to $3\frac{1}{2}$ m. p. h. forward; $1\frac{3}{4}$ m. p. h. reverse.
Final Drive: Sprocket and roller pinion.
Belt Pulley: 14 x 8; 600 r. p. m. and 2100 ft. per minute at normal engine speed.

U. S. TRACTOR & MACHINERY CO.
Chicago, Illinois

Uncle Sam 20-30

Traction Wheels: Four wheels; two drive wheels, 50 x 12, in rear.
No. of Plows Recommended: Three to four 14-in.
Length: 128 in.; **Width:** 72 in.; **Height:** 59 in.; **Weight:** 3500 lbs.; **Price:,** $1850.
Turning Radius: 9 ft.
Motor: Beaver, $4\frac{1}{2}$ x 6; valve-in-head, 4 cylinders, cast en bloc.
Lubrication: Force feed system.
Carburetor: Bennett.
Ignition System: Dixie high tension magneto.
Starting and Lighting Equipment: As specified.
Cooling System: Modine Spirex radiator with centrifugal pump.
Transmission Enclosed spur gears, $2\frac{1}{2}$ to $3\frac{3}{4}$ m. p. h. forward; $1\frac{3}{4}$ m. p. h. reverse.
Final Drive: Enclosed spur gear.
Belt Pulley 11 x $7\frac{1}{2}$; 900 r. p. m. and 2600 ft. per minute at normal engine speed.

1918-1921

UNCLE SAM 20-30
U. S. Tractor & Machinery Co., Chicago, Ill.

VELIE MOTORS CORP.

Moline, Illinois

Velie Biltwell 12-24

VELIE BILTWEL 12-24
Velie Motors Corporation, Moline, Ill.

1918-1921

Traction Wheels: Four wheels with two in rear, 50 x 10, as traction members.
No. of Plows Recommended: Three 14-in.
Length: 138 in.; **Width:** 62 in.; **Height:** 66 in.; **Weight:** 4300 lbs.
Turning Radius: 9 ft.; **Acres Plowed in 10-hr. Day:** 10.
Motor: Own, 4 x 5½; poppet valve, 4 cylinders, cast en bloc.
Lubrication: Gear pump force feed.
Carburetor: Kingston dual.
Ignition System: Magneto with impulse starter.
Cooling System: Fan, tubular radiator and pump.
Bearings: Hyatt and Timken in transmission and on drive axle.
Transmission: Own, 2 to 6 m. p. h. forward; 1¾ m. p. h. reverse.
Final Drive: Enclosed bull gear and pinion.
Belt Pulley: 13½ x 7½; 860 r. p. m. and 3000 ft. per minute at normal engine speed.

WALLIS TRACTOR CO.

Racine, Wisconsin

Wallis Cub Junior 13-25

Traction Wheels: Three wheel type with traction through two rear wheels, 48 x 12.
No. of Plows Recommended: Two and three 14-inch.
Length: 148 in.; **Width:** 61 in.; **Height:** 61½ in.; **Weight:** 3250 lbs.
Turning Radius: 10 ft.; **Acres Plowed in 10 hr. Day:** 10.
Motor: Own, 4¼ x 5¾; 4 cycle, 4 cylinders, cast enbloc with removable sleeves.
Lubrication: Positive pump and splash system.
Carburetor: Bennett, single bowl.
Ignition System: K-W high tension magneto.
Cooling System: Modine Spirex enclosed cellular type radiator.
Bearings: Hyatt roller throughout.
Transmission: Selective gears, 2½ to 3½ m. p. h. forward; 2½ m. p. h reverse.
Final Drive: Spur gear on two live rear axles.
Belt Pulley: 18 x 5; 430 r. p. m. and 2030 ft. per minute at normal engine speed.

1918

WALLIS CUB JUNIOR 13-25
Wallis Tractor Co., Racine, Wis.

WISCONSIN FARM TRACTOR CO.

Sauk City, Wisconsin

Wisconsin 16-32

1918-1919

Traction Wheels: Four wheels with two traction members, 52 x 12, in rear.

No. of Plows Recommended: Three or four 14 in.

Length: 130 in.; **Width:** 66 in.; **Height:** 65 in.; **Weight:** 4800 lbs.; **Price,** $1850.

Turning Radius: 11 ft.; **Acres Plowed in 10 hr. Day:** 10 to 15.

Motor: Climax, 5 x 6½; L-head, 4 cylinders, cast in pairs.

Lubrication: Force feed system.

Carburetor: Stromberg.

Ignition System: Kingston high tension magneto.

Cooling System: Water, Perfex radiator and fan.

Bearings: Hyatt roller in transmission and babbitt on drive axle.

Transmission: Enclosed 2⅓ to 4 m. p. h. forward; 2 m. p. h. reverse.

Final Drive: Spur gear.

Belt Pulley: 16 x 8; 630 r. p. m. and 2640 ft. per minute at normal engine speed.

WISCONSIN 16-32
Wisconsin Farm Tractor Co., Sauk City, Wis.

WORLD HARVESTER CORP.

New York, New York

Auto Tiller

1918-1920

Traction Wheels: Two wheels, each traction members, 36 x 5.

No. of Plows Recommended: One 14-in.

Length: 75 in.; **Width** 33¾ in; **Height:** 45 in.; **Weight:** 800 lbs.

Motor: Own, 5 x 7; L-head, 1 cylinder.

Lubrication: Splash; constant level and gravity.

Carburetor: Perrin-Ingram.

Ignition System: Atwater-Kent and Dixie magneto.

Cooling System: Water cooled.

Transmission: Worm gear, 2 to 2½ m. p. h. forward.

Final Drive: Worm.

AUTO TILLER
World Harvester Corporation, New York, N. Y.

YUBA MANUFACTURING CO.
Marysville, California

Yuba Ball Tread 40-70

1918-1920

Traction Wheels: Two rear crawlers; one front wheel.
No. of Plows Recommended: Twelve 14-in.
Length: 203 in.; **Width:** 92 in.; **Height:** 78 in. (without top); **Weight:** 21000 lbs.
Turning Radius: 12 ft.
Motor: Tractor Motor Co., $6\frac{1}{2}$ x $8\frac{1}{2}$; valve in head, 4 cylinders, cast separately.
Lubrication: Force feed system.
Carburetor: Stromberg.
Ignition System: Berling high tension magneto.
Starting and Lighting Equipment: K-W lighting system.
Cooling System: Own make of radiator.
Bearings: Hyatt roller in transmission.
Transmission: Sliding gear, $1\frac{1}{2}$ to 2.8 m. p. h. forward.
Final Drive: Bull pinion in track.
Belt Pulley: 18 x $10\frac{3}{4}$; 600 r. p. m.

YUBA BALL TREAD 40-70
Yuba Mfg Co., Marysville, Cal.

ZELLE TRACTOR CO.
St. Louis, Missouri

Zelle 12-25

1918-1921

ZELLE 12-25
Zelle Tractor Co., St. Louis, Mo.

Traction Wheels: Four wheel type with two drive members in rear, 54 x 12.
No. of Plows Recommended: Two to three 14-in.
Length: 137 in.; **Width:** 65 in.; **Height:** 71 in.; **Weight:** 3800 lbs.; **Price,** $1500.
Turning Radius: $8\frac{1}{2}$ ft.; **Acres Plowed in 10-hr. Day:** 6 to 9.
Motor: $4\frac{1}{4}$ x $5\frac{1}{2}$; vertical, 4 cylinders, cast in pairs.
Lubrication: Splash and force feed.
Carburetor: Carter.
Ignition System: Bosch high tension magneto.
Cooling System: Water with tubular radiator and pump.
Bearings: Roller bearings throughout.
Transmission: Selective gears, 1 to 5 m. p. h. forward; 1 to 5 m. p. h. reverse.
Final Drive: Pinion and bull gear.
Belt Pulley: 12 x 7; 600 r. p. m. and 1800 ft. per minute at normal engine speed.
Belt Pulley: 14 x 6; 650-800 r.p.m.

Champion
Dependable Spark Plugs

It's easy to make sure of the utmost spark plug efficiency in Tractor Motors.

Those taking ¾-inch sizes are best served by the Champion Two-Piece Heavy Stone Tractor Plug, Price $1.00.

Those taking ⅞-18 or ½-inch size need the Champion Tractor Plug, Price $1.00.

Dealers everywhere carry these standard Tractor Plugs in stock. See that "Champion" is on the porcelain as well as on the box. It is your guarantee of the utmost efficiency and dependability—a full day's work every day and no interruptions.

Champion Spark Plug Company

Toledo, Ohio

Champion Tractor $1.00

Champion Heavy Stone Tractor $1.00

—For— Tractors

1919

In 1919, 82 models of 64 makes not included in 1918 were added.

ADVANCE-RUMELY THRESHER CO.

La Porte, Indiana

Oil Pull 12-20	1919-1924
Oil Pull 16-30	1919-1924
Oil Pull 20-40	1919-1925

OIL PULL 12-20
Advance-Rumely Thresher Co., La Porte, Ind.

Traction Wheels: Four wheels with two rear drive wheels, 51x12.

No. of Plows Recommended: Three 14-in.

Length: 132 in.; **Width:** 64 in.; **Height:** 75 in.; **Weight:** 6430 lbs.

Turning Radius: 14 ft.; **Acres Plowed in 10-hrs. Day:** 7 to 8.

Motor: Own; 6x8, Horizontal, valve-in-head, 2 cylinders, cast en bloc.

Lubrication: Madison-Kipp force feed and splash.

Carburetor: Own Secor-Higgins.

Ignition System: Bosch high tension magneto.

Starting: Machanical starting device.

Cooling System: Circulating pump.

Bearings: Hyatt and bronze of own make.

Transmission: Spur gear, 2.1 to 3.26 m.p.h. forward; 2.62 m.p.h. reverse.

Final Drive: Spur gear, open.

Belt Pulley: 19x7; 560 r. p. m. and 2790 f. p. m. at normal engine speed.

RUMELY OilPull TRACTOR *Tractors*
LA PORTE IND.

FOR 1919 the famous Rumely OilPull tractor can be had in all sizes from 3 plow to 10 plow. Three sizes are illustrated—still another size is to come.

The reputation of the OilPull for power, dependability and economy is firmly established. Ten years of service on farms from one end of the country to the other have taken care of that, and back of the machine itself is a company that has been building farm machinery for eighty years—an organization with 26 branch offices and warehouses, insuring immediate machine and repair shipments, and expert assistance.

Don't Be Misled!

The success of the Rumely OilPull tractor has been so far-reaching that the name Oil-Pull has become almost a household word. So strong is its following that, like most good things, it has been imitated. "Oil-Pull" is registered and is our exclusive name and trademark—its use by other manufacturers as applied to their tractors is in violation of the law. For your own protection, whether as a dealer or as an owner, just remember that there is only one OilPull—Rumely, LaPorte.

Advance - Rumely Thresher Company
(*Incorporated*)

LaPorte   **Indiana**

BACKED BY WRITTEN GUARANTEE · ADVANCE · RUMELY ·

30-60 H. P.

20-40 H. P.

16-30 H. P.

1919   197

Traction Wheels: Four wheels, with two drive wheels, 56 x 18. in rear.
No. of Plows Recommended:.. Four 14 in.
Length: 155 in.; Width: 80¼ in.; Height: 99 in.
Turning Radius: 17 ft.; Acres Plowed In 10-hr. Day: 8 to 10.
Motor: Own; 7 x 8½, horizontal, 2 cylinders, cast en bloc.
Lubrication: Force feed and splash.
Carburetor: Secor-Higgins.
Ignition System: High tension magneto.
Starting Equipment: Mechanical.
Bearings: Hyatt roller in transmission and on drive axle.
Cooling System: Circulating pump.
Transmission: Spur gear enclosed, 2.1 to 3 m.p.h. forward; 2.65 m.p.h. reverse.
Final Drive: Open.
Belt Pulley: 23 x 8½; 530 r.p.m. and 3190 feet per minute at normal engine speed.

OIL PULL 16-30
Advance-Rumely Thresher Co., La Porte, Ind.

OIL PULL 20-40
Advance-Rumely Thresher Co., La Porte, Ind.

Traction Wheels: Four wheels, with two drive wheels in rear, 64x20.
No. of Plows Recommended: Five to six 14 in.
Length: 175 in.; Width: 89 in.; Height: 108 in.; Weight: 12880 lbs.
Turning Radius: 21 ft.; Acres Plowed In 10-hr. Day: 12 to 15.
Motor: Own, 8x10, horizontal, 2 cylinder, Cast singly.
Lubrication: Force feed and splash.
Carburetor: Secor-Higgins, 2¾ in.
Ignition System: High tension magneto.
Starting Equipment: Mechanical starting device.
Cooling System: Circulating pump.
Bearings: Hyatt roller and bronze of own make.
Transmission: Spur gear. 2 to 3.2 m. p. h. forward and 2.53 m. p. h. reverse.
Final Drive: Open spur gear.
Belt Pulley: 26x9; 450 r. p. m. and 3060 f. p. m. at normal engine speed.

ALLIS-CHALMERS MANUFACTURING CO.

Milwaukee, Wisconsin

General Purpose 6-12   1919-1925
Allis-Chalmers 18-30   1919-1923

Traction Wheels: Two drive wheels, 48x6.

No. of Plows Recommended: One 14-in.

Length: 156 in.; **Width:** 54 in.; **Height:** 72 in.; **Weight:** 2250 lbs. **Price:** $850.

Acres Plowed in 10-hr. Day: Four to five.

Motor: Le Roi, $3\frac{1}{8}$x$4\frac{1}{2}$, vertical, 4 cycle, 4 cylinders, cast en bloc.

Lubrication: Plunger pump and gravity pressure.

Carburetor: Kingston, $\frac{7}{8}$ in.

Ignition System: Eisemann or Dixie.

Cooling System: Thermo-syphon.

Bearings: Babbitt bushings.

Transmission: Selective gears, $1\frac{1}{2}$ to 2 4/5 m.p.h. forward and $1\frac{1}{2}$ to 2 4/5 m.p.h. reverse.

Final Drive: Bull pinion and segment.

Belt Pulley: 10 x $5\frac{1}{2}$; 2600 f.p.m. at normal engine speed.

GENERAL PURPOSE 6-12
Allis-Chalmers Mfg. Co., Milwaukee, Wis.

Traction Wheels: Four wheels, two in rear, 48x12, furnishing traction.

No. of Plows Recommended: Three to four 14-in.

Length: 96 in.; **Width:** 66 in.; **Height:** 68 in.; **Weight:** 5,300 lbs.

Acres Plowed n 10-hr. Day: 9 to 10.

Motor: Own; $4\frac{3}{4}$x$6\frac{1}{2}$, 4 cylinders, vertical, cast en bloc.

Lubrication: Force feed.

Carburetor: Kingston.

Ignition System: K-W.

Cooling System: Centrifugal pump and radiator.

Bearings: Roller and ball throughout.

Transmission: Selective sliding, 2 3/10 to 2 4/5 m.p.h. forward and 2 3/10 m.p.h. reverse.

Final Drive: Gear.

Belt Pulley: 15x$7\frac{1}{2}$: 2,600 f.p.m. at normal engine speed.

ALLIS-CHALMERS 18-30
Allis-Chalmers Mfg. Co., Milwaukee, Wis.

Allis-Chalmers Farm Tractors

For more than 65 years the Allis-Chalmers Mfg. Co. has been known as one of the largest leading manufacturers of high grade machinery in the world.

The 6-12 "General Purpose" Tractor

The Ideal "One-Man" Farm Tractor

THE ALLIS-CHALMERS 6-12

"General Purpose" Tractor solves the farm labor problem. Requires one man only—operator riding over implement or on implement seat. Has 1,000-lb. drawbar pull—26½-inch clearance for cultivating and pulls any standard 4-horse implement. Plows five acres per day at extremely low fuel, oil and maintenance costs. The ideal tractor for the small farm.

The 18-30

for large acreage

Here is the big tractor for big farms. Does 4-plow work at 3-plow costs. Plows 16 acres in 10 hours—pulls a 28-inch separator—develops 20 per cent surplus power over rated strength—3,000-lb. drawbar pull. Does all of the heaviest work on the farm and is an ideal machine for roadmaking. Use either gasoline or kerosene. All Allis-Chalmers tractors are built complete in the Allis-Chalmers plant—with the exception of magnetos and carburetors.

Write for details and specifications.

ALLIS-CHALMERS MFG. CO., Tractor Division

MILWAUKEE,   WISCONSIN

The 18-30

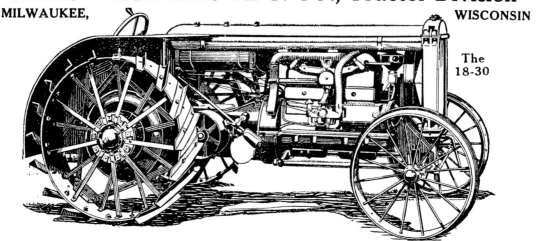

AMERICAN TRACTOR & FOUNDRY CO.
Charles City, Iowa

American 15-30   1919

AMERICAN 15-30
Amer. Tractor & Foundry Co., Charles City, Ia.

Traction Wheels: Four wheels, two rear traction, 52x12.

No. of Plows Recommended: Three to four 14-in.

Length: 140 in.; **Width:** 76 in.; **Height:** 60 in.; **Weight:** 5400 lbs.; **Price:** $1895.

Turning Radius: 10 ft.; **Acres Plowed in 10-hr. Day:** 10 to 12.

Motor: Beaver: 4¾ to 6, vertical, 4 cylinders, cast en bloc.

Lubrication: Force feed and splash.

Carburetor: Holley, 1½-in.

Ignition System: Bosch high tension magneto.

Cooling System: Shotwell-Johnson radiator and pump.

Bearings: Hyatt roller in transmission.

Transmission: Enclosed, 2 1/3 to 3 1/3 m.p.h. forward and 2 m.p.h. reverse.

Final Drive: Internal gear.

Belt Pulley: 18x8; 550 r.p.m. and 2600 f.p.m. at normal engine speed.

APPLETON MANUFACTURING CO.
Batavia, Illinois

Appleton 12-20   1919-1921

Traction Wheels: Four-wheel type, with two drive members in rear, 54 x 12.

No. of Plows Recommended: Three 14-in.

Length: 152 in.; **Width:** 67½ in.; **Height:** 61 in.; **Weight:** 4900 lbs.; **Price:** $1800.

Turning Radius: 10 ft.; **Acres Plowed in 10-hr. Day:** 8.

Motor: Buda; 4¼x5½, vertical, 4 cylinders, cast en bloc.

Lubrication: Force feed and splash.

Carburetor: Schebler, 1¼-in.

Ignition System: Bosch, with impulse starter.

Cooling System: Pump and cellular radiator.

Bearings: Hyatt roller throughout transmission and on drive axle.

Transmission: Enclosed gears in oil, 2¼ to 3½ m.p.h. forward and 2 m.p.h. reverse.

Final Drive: Spur gear and pinion.

Belt Pulley: 12 x 7½; 825 r.p.m. and 2600 feet per minute at normal engine speed.

APPLETON 12-20
Appleton Mfg. Co., Batavia, Ill.

AULSON TRACTOR CO.

Waukegan, Illinois

Aulson 12-25

1919

AULSON 12-25
Aulson Tractor Co., Waukegan, Ill.

Traction Wheels: Four wheel type; two, 48x18 drive wheels in rear.
No. of Plows Recommended: Three to four 14-in.
Length: 130 in.; **Width:** 75 in.; **Height:** 68 in.; **Weight:** 5400 lbs.
Turning Radius: 9 ft.
Motor: Climax, 4 cylinders, 5 x 6½, vertical, cast en bloc.
Lubrication: Force feed.
Carburetor: Stromberg, 1½ in.
Ignition System: Dixie high tension magneto.
Cooling System: Radiator, pump and fan.
Bearings: Ball and plain in transmission.
Transmission: Bevel and spur gear; 2½ to 4 m.p.h. forward.
Final Drive: Chain; open.
Belt Pulley: 16x7; 562 r.p.m at normal engine speed.

AULTMAN & TAYLOR MACHINERY CO.

Mansfield, Ohio

Aultman & Taylor 15-30
Aultman & Taylor 22-45

1919-1924
1919-1924

Traction Wheels: Four wheels, two traction in rear, 70 x 12.
No. of Plows Recommended: Four 14-in.
Length: 176 in.; **Width:** 80 in.; **Height:** 104 in.; **Weight:** 7800 lbs.
Turning Radius: 10 ft.; **Acres Plowed in 10-hr. Day:** 10 to 12.
Motor: Waukesha: 4¾ x 6¾, 4 cylinders, cast in pairs.
Lubrication: Detroit force feed pump.
Carburetor: Kingston, 1¼-in.
Ignition System: Eisemann.
Cooling System: Todd radiator and pump.
Bearings: Own babbitt on drive axle; Hyatt roller on clutch; counter and intermediate shafts.
Transmission: Enclosed, 2.21 to 2.49 m p.h. forward.
Final Drive: Spur gear.
Belt Pulley: 20 x 8; 450 r.p.m. and 2400 f.p.m. at normal engine speed.

AULTMAN & TAYLOR 15-30
Aultman & Taylor Mchy. Co., Mansfield, Ohio.

AULTMAN & TAYLOR 22-45
Aultman & Taylor Mchy. Co., Mansfield, Ohio.

Traction Wheels: Four wheels, two traction, 70 x 20, in rear.
No. of Plows Recommended: Four to six 14-in.
Length: 166 in.; **Width:** 89¾ in.; **Height:** 125 in.; **Weight:** 12800 lbs.
Turning Radius: 15 ft; **Acres Plowed in 10-hr. Day:** 15 to 18.
Motor: Own; 5½ x 8, vertical, valve-in-head, 4 cylinders, cast in pairs.
Lubrication: Detroit force feed.
Carburetor: Kingston, 2-in.
Ignition System: Eisemann dual.
Cooling System: Own, pump and radiator.
Bearings: Own babbitt.
Transmission: Open, 2.13 to 2.93 m.p.h. forward and 2.08 m.p.h. reverse.
Final Drive: Spur gear.
Belt Pulley: 20 x 10; 600 r.p.m. and 3150 f.p.m. at normal engine speed.

F. C. AUSTIN CO., INC.

Chicago, Illinois

Austin 12-20	1919
Austin 15-30	1919-1920
Multipedal 20-40	1919

Traction Wheels: Crawler type, one tracklayer on each side, 50x8.
No. of Plows Recommended: Two to three 14-in.
Length: 99 in.; **Width:** 54 in.; **Height:** 52 in.; **Weight:** 3400 lbs.
Motor: Buffalo, 4 cylinders, 4 x 5, cast in pairs.
Lubrication: Force feed system.
Carburetor: Special; gasoline or kerosene.
Ignition System: Bosch high tension magneto with impulse starter.
Cooling System: Modine radiator, fan and pump.
Bearings: Hyatt roller.
Transmission: Own make; 2½ to 3½ m. p.h. forward.
Final Drive: Internal gear.
Belt Pulley: 8x6; 1000 r.p.m. at normal engine speed.

AUSTIN 12-20
F. C. Austin Co., Inc., Chicago, Ill.

AUSTIN 15-30
F. C. Austin Co., Inc., Chicago, Ill.

Traction Wheels: Four wheels; driving from two in rear, 54 x 12.

Motor: Buffalo, 4 cylinders, $4\frac{3}{4}$x5, cast in pairs.

Lubrication: Detroit force feed.
Carburetor: Schebler.

Ignition System: K-W high tension magneto with impulse starter.

Cooling System: Modine radiator, fan and pump.

Transmission: Own make, $1\frac{3}{4}$ to $3\frac{1}{2}$ m. p.h. forward.

Belt Pulley: 10 x $6\frac{1}{2}$; 965 r.p.m at normal engine speed.

MECHANICAL
FAN BELTING

Keeps Tractor Motors Cool and Efficient
UNCONDITIONAL GUARANTEE----15000 MILES

Not Affected By Heat,

Water, Dirt, Oil or Grease

The simple method of disconnecting a link at any desired length makes the "Crowe" Belt instantly adjustable.

Easily Adjusted

"Crowe" Fan Belts Will

Not SLIP, STRETCH or

BREAK.

Steel and Wire Links produce **Strength** and **Durability** while the **Sole Leather Blocks** provide **Noiseless Friction.**

ATTRACTIVE PROPOSITION TO DEALERS
Write or Wire us for details of our 1919 Sales Cooperation Policy

MECHANICAL BELT CO.
2014 Frederic Ave.   **St. Joseph, Mo.**

OPERATOR ALWAYS ON VEHICLE OR IMPLEMENT

IT DRIVES LIKE A TEAM

The Automotive One-Man Tractor

The many new and advanced ideas embodied in the construction of the "Automotive" Tractor makes it an exceedingly attractive selling proposition.

It is practical, efficient, economical and adaptable to every kind of soil condition. Every operation is controlled by ordinary driving reins, and—

IT IS DRIVEN LIKE A TEAM

Every farmer knows the advantages of these features—operator always on vehicle or implement—90% of weight on drive wheels—short turning radius—power on both drive wheels at all times—all moving parts enclosed and operating in oil—adaptable to any horse-drawn or tractor implement or vehicle—highest grade materials and workmanship throughout.

A five-minute demonstration will sell it to any farmer. Write for full description and dealers' proposition. Address Dept. C. T.-4.

THE AUTOMOTIVE CORPORATION
"Members American Tractor Association"

Sixth Floor Shoaff Building   Fort Wayne, Indiana

The Bolts and Nuts on a Tractor are an Important Part of the Assembly

If a tractor assembly is to hold together under the terrific strain of service—through mud, ruts, furrows, over stones, hills and stumps—its bolts and nuts must have more than ordinary stamina.

Empire Bolts and Nuts give you the much needed assurance of surplus strength, perfect accuracy—ability to STAY ON THE JOB just as long as they are wanted.

Back of them are 74 years of concentrated manufacturing experience—the longest in the history of the bolt and nut industry.

BOLTS EMPIRE NUTS-RIVETS

RUSSELL, BURDSALL & WARD BOLT & NUT COMPANY

PEMBERWICK, CONN.   **PORT CHESTER, NEW YORK**   ROCK FALLS, ILLINOIS

Makers of Bolts Nuts and Rivets Since 1845

Western Office: 208 S. LaSalle St., Chicago, Ill.

Traction Members: Two crawlers, one on each side, 84 x 12.
No. of Plows Recommended: Four 14-in.
Length: 151 in.; **Width:** 73 in.; **Height:** 90 in.; **Weight:** 10250 lbs.
Turning Radius: 12 7-12 ft.
Motor: Automatic; $5\frac{1}{2}$ x 7, vertical, 4 cylinders, cast singly.
Lubrication: Detroit, force feed.
Carburetor: Bennett.
Ignition System: K-W high tension magneto.
Cooling System: Water pump and fan.
Bearings: Hyatt rollers in transmission.
Transmission: Gear, $1\frac{3}{4}$ to $3\frac{1}{2}$ m.p.h. forward; $1\frac{3}{4}$ m.p.h. reverse.
Final Drive: Chain.
Belt Pulley: 20 x 6; 140 to 420 r.p.m. and 700 to 2100 feet per minute at normal engine speed.

MULTIPEDAL 20-40

F. C. Austin Co., Inc., Chicago, Ill.

AUTOMOTIVE CORP.

Fort Wayne, Indiana

Automotive 12-24   1919

Traction Wheels: Four wheels, with two traction, 42 x 12, in rear.
No. of Plows Recommended: Two 14-in.
Length: 108 in.; **Width:** 63 in.; **Height:** 69 in.; **Weight:** 3200 lbs.; **Price:** $1450.
Turning Radius: 7 ft.; **Acres Plowed In 10-hr. Day:** 7.
Motor: Hercules, $3\frac{3}{4}$ x $5\frac{1}{8}$; 4-cycle, 4 cylinders, cast en bloc.
Lubrication: Force feed throughout.
Carburetor: Kingston, $1\frac{1}{8}$-in.
Ignition System: Eisemann.
Cooling System: Pump, radiator and fan.
Bearings: Hyatt and Timken roller throughout.
Transmission: Own; $2\frac{5}{8}$ to $5\frac{1}{4}$ m.p.h. forward and $2\frac{5}{8}$ m.p.h. reverse.
Final Drive: Internal gear.
Belt Pulley: 8 x $6\frac{1}{2}$; 1000 r.p.m. and 2600 f.p.m. at normal engine speed.

AUTOMOTIVE 12-24

Automotive Corp., Fort Wayne, Ind.

AVERY CO.
Peoria, Illinois

Avery Model B 5-10   1919

AVERY MODEL B 5-10
Avery Co., Peoria, Ill.

Traction Wheels: Four wheels, driving from two rear wheels, 38x10.
No. of Plows Recommended: Two 12-in.
Length: 135 in.; **Width:** 50 in.; **Height:** $54\frac{3}{4}$ in.; **Weight:** 2600 lbs.
Turning Radius: $10\frac{1}{2}$ ft.
Motor: Own, 3 x 4; vertical, 4 cylinders cast en bloc.
Lubrication: Circulating splash, gravity to gearing.
Carburetor: Kingston, $\frac{3}{4}$-in.
Ignition System: K-W high tension magneto.
Cooling System: Thermo syphon.
Transmission: Sliding gear, $1\frac{1}{2}$ to $4\frac{1}{8}$ m.p.h. forward, $1\frac{1}{2}$ m.p.h. reverse.
Final Drive: Double spur gear.
Belt Pulley: $12x5\frac{1}{4}$; 780 r.p.m. and 2450 f.p.m. at normal engine speed.

BAILOR PLOW MANUFACTURING CO.
Atchison, Kansas

Bailor, One-Row Motor Cultivator   1919-1929
Bailor, Two-Row Motor Cultivator   1919-1929

BAILOR, ONE-ROW MOTOR CULTIVATOR
Bailor Plow Mfg. Co., Atchison, Kan.

Traction Wheels: Four wheels; two traction members in rear, 40 x 4.
Turning Radius: 6 ft.
Motor: Cushman; 2 cylinders, 4x4, cast en bloc.
Lubrication: Gravity and splash.
Carburetor: Schebler.
Ignition System: Dixie single unit magneto.
Cooling System: Perfex radiator, centrifugal pump and fan.
Bearings: Hyatt roller in transmission.
Transmission: Sliding gear; $1\frac{1}{4}$ to 3 m.p.h. forward.
Final Drive: Open, chain.

Light, Durable And Flexible

Note the Flexibility.

Does Not Pack the Ground.

Steers Itself When Plowing.

Does Belt Work, Too.

The Model D Bates Steel Mule is a light-weight tractor which does the work cheaper than heavier machines of like rating do. Does it on account of its Crawler tread. The Bates Steel Mule is a high-grade tractor—powerful, sturdy, flexible and durable—everything that a farm tractor *must* be.

The Bates Steel Mule

Fully Covered by Patents.

The Model D has a double-crawler drive that grips the ground firmly under any and all conditions. There's no slip—no waste of power—but a strong, steady pull.

Has heavy-duty, four-cylinder, valve-in-head motor. Pulls three plows at a speed of 2¼ to 3½ miles per hour. Burns kerosene, distillate or other low-grade fuel.

Nickel-steel roller bearings are used throughout. Gears and all moving parts run in oil, enclosed against dust.
Does heavy belt work easily and economically. All in all, the Model D is the one light tractor that every farmer can use all the year 'round·

Reserve Your Territory Now

Twenty-four hours every day our modern ten-acre plant is turning out the Model D for dealers who are fortunate to have our contract. We advise live dealers to keep in touch with us, as we put on new agents as fast as we increase our production.

BATES MACHINE & TRACTOR CO.

477 Jackson Street   **Joliet, Illinois**

Traction Wheels: Three or four wheels; two, 44x6, in rear giving traction.

Turning Radius: 8½ ft.

Motor: Le Roi, 4 cylinders, 3⅛x4½, cast en bloc.

Lubrication: Force feed and splash.

Carburetor: Kingston.

Ignition System: Dixie single unit magneto.

Cooling System: Thermo-syphon; Perfex radiator.

Bearings: Hyatt roller in transmission.

Transmission: Sliding gear; 1¼ to 3 m. p.h. forward

Final Drive: Chain, open.

BAILOR, TWO-ROW MOTOR CULTIVATOR
Bailor Plow Mfg. Co., Atchison, Kan.

BATES MACHINE & TRACTOR CO.

Joliet, Illinois

Bates Steel Mule, Model D, 15-22   1919-1920

Traction Wheels: One crawler on each side, 52 x 10.

No. of Plows Recommended: Three and four 14-in.

Length: 105 in.; Width: 62 in.; Height: 58 in.; Weight: 4300 lbs.

Turning Radius: 7½ ft.; Acres Plowed in 10-hr. Day: 10.

Motor: Erd; 4 x 6, valve-in-head, 4 cylinders, cast en bloc.

Lubrication: Force feed system.

Carburetor: Bennett.

Ignition System: Eisemann high tension magneto.

Cooling System: Modine radiator and gear driven pump circulation.

Bearings: Timken bearings throughout.

Transmission: Sliding gear, 2¼ to 4 m.p.h. forward; 2 m.p.h. reverse.

Final Drive: Enclosed gears running in oil.

Belt Pulley: 12 x 8½; 725 r p.m. and 2300 feet per minute at normal engine speed.

BATES STEEL MULE, MODEL D, 15-22
Bates Machine & Tractor Co., Joliet, Ill·

BATES TRACTOR CO.

Lansing, Michigan

Bates All-Steel Oil 15-25

1919-1921

BATES ALL-STEEL OIL 15-25
Bates Tractor Co., Lansing, Mich.

Traction Wheels: Four wheel type; two in rear giving traction, 50x14.

No. of Plows Recommended: Two to three 14-in.

Length: 144 in.; Width: 72 in.; Height: 56 in.; Weight: 4000 lbs.

Turning Radius: 12 ft.

Motor: Bates, 4 cylinders; vertical; $4\frac{1}{2}$ x $5\frac{3}{4}$; cast en bloc.

Lubrication: Force feed system.

Carburetor: Bates, $1\frac{1}{2}$ in.

Ignition System: Dixie high tension magneto.

Cooling System: Fan, pump and radiator.

Transmission: Own make, sliding gear; 5 m.p.h. forward and $2\frac{1}{2}$ m.p.h. reverse.

Final Drive: Spur gear, enclosed.

Belt Pulley: 12x7; 800 r.p.m. at normal engine speed.

C. L. BEST GAS TRACTION CO.

San Leandro, California

Tracklayer, Model 25

1919-1920

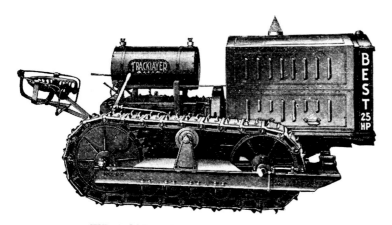

TRACKLAYER, MODEL 25
C. L. Best Gas Traction Co., San Leandro, Cal.

Traction Wheels: Two crawlers, each 66 x 26.

No. of Plows Recommended: Three to four 14-in.

Length: 125 in.; Width: 51 in.; Height: 55 in.; Weight: 5200 lbs.; Price: $2450.

Turning Radius: 13 ft.; Acres Plowed In 10-hr. Day: 10.

Motor: Own; $4\frac{5}{8}$ x $5\frac{1}{4}$, 4-cycle, 4 cylinders, cast separately.

Lubrication: Splash system throughout.

Carburetor: Ensign.

Ignition System: Dixie magneto with impulse starter.

Cooling System: Water pump, fan and radiator.

Bearings: Hyatt and Timken anti-friction; 35 in all.

Transmission: Selective gears, 2 to 3 m. p. h. forward; $1\frac{1}{4}$ m. p. h. reverse.

Final Drive: Internal gear.

Belt Pulley: 12 x 8; 750 r. p. m. and 2700 feet per minute at normal engine speed.

BETHLEHEM MOTORS CORP.

Allentown, Pennsylvania

Bethlehem 18-36　　　　　　　　　　　　1919

Traction Wheels: Four wheels, driving from two rear wheels, 54 x 12.

No. of Plows Recommended: Four.

Length: 144 in.; Width: 73 in.; Height: 67 in.; Weight: 6200 lbs.

Turning Radius: 15 ft.; Acres Plowed in 10-hr. Day: 10.

Motor: Beaver, $4\frac{3}{4}$ x 6; valve-in-head, 4 cylinders, cast en bloc.

Lubrication: Beaver splash system.

Carburetor: Stromberg, $1\frac{3}{8}$.

Ignition System: Bosch high tension magneto.

Cooling System: Pump, radiator and fan.

Bearings: Hyatt roller in transmission.

Transmission: Selective spur gear, 3.3 m.p.h. forward and 1.8 m.p.h reverse.

Final Drive: Spur gear.

Belt Pulley: 10 x $7\frac{1}{2}$; 1278 r.p.m. and 3345 f.p.m. at normal engine speed.

BETHLEHEM 18-36
Bethlehem Motors Corp., Allentown, Pa.

BULLOCK TRACTOR CO.

Chicago, Illinois

Creeping Grip 18-30　　　　　　　　　　1919-1920

Traction Wheels: Driven by crawler on each side.

No. of Plows Recommended: Four 14-in.

Length: 114 in.; Width: 81 in.; Height: 72 in.; Weight: 7200 lbs.; Price: $2250.

Turning Radius: 10 ft.; Acres Plowed in 10-hr. Day: 8 to 12.

Motor: Waukesha; $4\frac{3}{4}$ x $6\frac{3}{4}$, vertical, 4 cylinders, cast in pairs.

Lubrication: Splash system.

Carburetor: Bennett, with Bennett air cleaner.

Ignition System: High tension magneto.

Cooling System: Modine radiator, pump and fan.

Bearings: Standard ball bearings throughout.

Transmission: Own, 1 speed forward and 1 reverse.

Final Drive: Chain.

Belt Pulley: 12 x 8; 600 r.p.m. and 2250 f.p.m. at normal engine speed.

CREEPING GRIP 18-30
Bullock Tractor Co., Chicago, Ill.

J. I. CASE THRESHING MACHINE CO.
Racine, Wisconsin

Case 10-18
Case 15-27

1919-1921
1919-1924

Traction Wheels: Four wheels, two drive wheels in rear, 42 x 9.

No. of Plows Recommended: Two 14-in.

Length: 108 in.; **Width:** 52 in.; **Height:** 58 in.; **Weight:** 3500 lbs.; **Price:** $1200.

Turning Radius: 11 ft.; **Acres Plowed in 10-hr. Day:** 6 to 9.

Motor: Own; $3\frac{7}{8}$ x 5, vertical valve-in-head, 4 cylinders, cast en bloc.

Lubrication: Circulating splash system.

Carburetor: Kingston.

Ignition System: Kingston high tension magneto, impulse starter.

Cooling System: Pump, fan and radiator.

Bearings: Hyatt roller on drive axle.

Transmission: Sliding gear. $2\frac{1}{4}$ to $3\frac{1}{2}$ m.p.h forward, and $2\frac{1}{4}$ m.p.h. reverse.

Final Drive: Enclosed spur gears.

Belt Pulley: $14\frac{1}{4}$ x $5\frac{1}{4}$, and 3916 f.p.m. at normal engine speed.

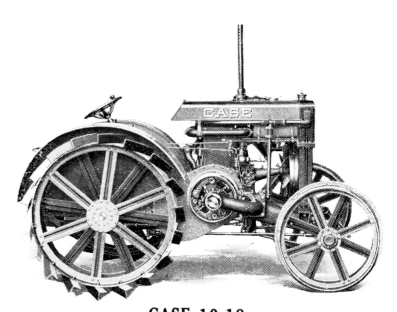

CASE 10-18
J. I. Case Threshing Machine Co., Racine, Wis.

Traction Wheels: Four wheels, with two drive wheels, 52 x 12, in rear.

No. of Plows Recommended: Three to four 14-in.

Length: 127 in.; **Width:** 72 in.; **Height:** 78 in.; **Weight:** 5700 lbs.; **Price:** $1600.

Turning Radius: $13\frac{1}{2}$ ft.; **Acres Plowed in 10-hr. Day:** 10 to 14.

Motor: Case; $4\frac{1}{2}$ x 6, 4 cylinders, cast en bloc.

Lubrication: Circulating and splash.

Carburetor: Kingston, $1\frac{3}{8}$.

Ignition System: Kingston high tension magneto.

Cooling System: Pump, radiator and fan.

Bearings: Hyatt roller, Fafnir ball and plain.

Transmission: Selective sliding gear, $2\frac{1}{4}$ to $3\frac{1}{2}$ m. p. h. forward; $2\frac{1}{4}$ m. p. h. reverse.

Final Drive: Spur gear, enclosed.

Belt Pulley: 16 x $6\frac{1}{2}$; 900 r.p.m. and 3762 feet per minute at normal engine speed.

CASE 15-27
J. I. Case Threshing Machine Co., Racine, Wis.

COLEMAN
WORM DRIVE TRACTOR

An Ideal Combination for the Dealer

A tractor that sells readily, because it is built to fill every requirement of the average farmer. Simple, durable and economical in its operation. The sort of a tractor you can build substantial and lasting business on.

A company behind that tractor that understands the sort of help a dealer needs, and gives it to him every day in the year. Sales helps that not only assist in making sales, but create a real business for the dealer, a business that will grow consistently year after year. Our dealers' proposition means money to you. Send for it today.

Coleman Tractor Corporation
Kansas City, Mo.

CHAMPION TRACTOR CO.
Argo, Illinois

Champion 15-30

1919-1920

CHAMPION 15-30
Champion Tractor Co., Argo, Ill.

Traction Wheels: Four wheels, two 48 x 12 in rear, furnishing traction.
No. of Plows Recommended: Three 14-in.
Width: 70 in.; **Weight:** 3190 lbs.; **Price:** $1465.
Motor: Buda; vertical, 4 cylinders, $4\frac{1}{4}$ x $5\frac{1}{2}$, cast en bloc.
Lubrication: Force feed.
Carburetor: Carter U. S. A., $1\frac{1}{4}$-in.
Ignition System: Dixie high tension magneto.
Cooling System: Radiator, pump and fan.
Bearings: Annular ball in transmission.
Transmission: Sliding gear.
Final Drive: Enclosed worm gear.
Belt Pulley: 12 x 6; 850 r.p.m. and 2600 f.p.m. at normal engine speed.

COLEMAN TRACTOR CORP.
Kansas City, Missouri

Coleman 16-30

1919-1921

COLEMAN 16-30
Coleman Tractor Corp., Kansas City, Mo.

Traction Wheels: Four wheels; two drive wheels, 42 x 10, in rear.
No. of Plows Recommended: Three 14-in.
Length: 106 in.; **Width:** 66 in.; **Height:** 66 in.; **Weight:** 5100 lbs.; **Price:** $1750.
Turning Radius: 10 ft. 6 in.; **Acres Plowed in 10-hr. Day:** 10 to 12.
Motor: Climax; 5 x $6\frac{1}{2}$, L-head, 4 cylinders, cast in pairs.
Lubrication: Force feed.
Carburetor: Stromberg.
Ignition System: Dixie high tension magneto with impulse starter.
Cooling System: Simplex radiator, pump and fan.
Bearings: Hyatt, Timken and own roller.
Transmission: Worm drive, $2\frac{3}{4}$ m.p.h. forward; $1\frac{1}{2}$ m.p.h reverse.
Final Drive: Worm gear enclosed.
Belt Pulley: 14 x 7; 800 r.p.m. and 2300 f.p.m. at normal engine speed.

CLARK TRUCTRACTOR CO.
Chicago, Illinois

Clark Tructractor   1919

CLARK TRUCTRACTOR
Clark Tructractor Co., Chicago, Ill.

Traction Wheels: Three wheels, two interchangeable tractor type and rubber tired in rear.
Length: 125 in.; **Width:** 45 in.; **Height:** 56 in.; **Weight:** 2050 lbs.; **Price:** $1135.
Turning Radius: 6 ft.
Motor: Le Roi, $3\frac{1}{8}$x$4\frac{1}{4}$, 4 cylinders, cast en bloc.
Lubrication: Force feed.
Carburetor: Zenith.
Ignition System: Berling magneto.
Cooling System: Thermo-syphon.
Bearings: Hyatt and New Departure.
Transmission: Selective gear; $\frac{1}{4}$ to 15 m.p.h. forward and 3 m.p.h. reverse.
Final Drive: Internal gear.

CRAIG TRACTOR CO.
Cleveland, Ohio

Craig 15-25   1919-1921

CRAIG 15-25
Craig Tractor Co., Cleveland, Ohio.

Traction Wheels: Four wheels, two 44 x 12 traction in rear.
No. of Plows Recommended: Three 14-in.
Length: 148 in.; **Width:** 74 in.; **Height:** 67 in.; **Weight:** 5500 lbs.; **Price:** $2385.
Motor: Craig-Beaver; $4\frac{3}{4}$ x 6, overhead, 4 cylinders, cast en bloc.
Lubrication: Pressure.
Carburetor: Stromberg, $1\frac{1}{2}$-in.
Ignition System: Berling magneto.
Cooling System: Modine radiator, 22-in. fan, centrifugal pump.
Bearings: Bronze backed babbitt in engine and Timken.
Transmission: Spur gear; 2.4 to 3.85 m.p.h. forward and 1.5 m.p.h. reverse.
Final Drive: Enclosed spur gears.
Belt Pulley: 12 x 8; 830 r.p.m. and 2610 f.p.m. at normal engine speed.

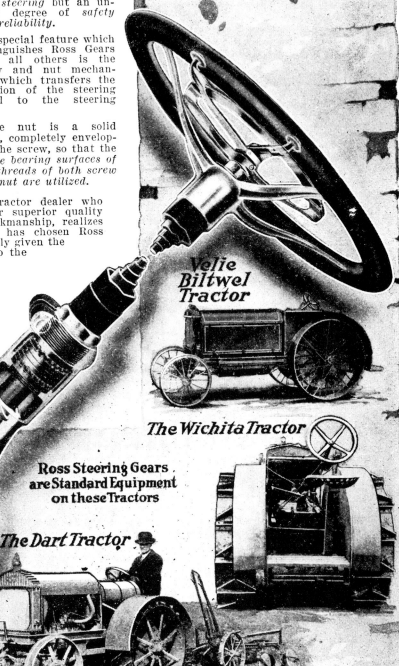

DART TRUCK & TRACTOR CO.
Waterloo, Iowa

Dart "Blue J" 15-30   1919

Traction Wheels: Four wheels, two rear drive wheels, 40 x 12.

No. of Plows Recommended: Three 14-in.

Length: 125 in.; Width: 56 in.; Height: 65 in.; Weight: 4500 lbs.; Price: $1750.

Turning Radius: 10 ft.; Acres Plowed in 10-hr. Day: 10.

Motor: Buda; vertical, 4 cylinders, $4\frac{1}{2}$ x $5\frac{1}{2}$, cast en bloc.

Lubrication: Force feed.

Carburetor: Kingston, $1\frac{1}{4}$-in.

Ignition System: Eisemann magneto.

Starting and Lighting Equipment: Special, optional.

Cooling System: Fan, radiator and centrifugal pump.

Bearings: 37 roller and ball.

Transmission: Own, selective gear; $1\frac{1}{4}$ to 6 m.p.h. forward and $1\frac{1}{4}$ m.p.h. reverse.

Final Drive: Double reduction worm and enclosed bull gear.

Belt Pulley: 12 x 6; 800 r.p.m. and 2400 f.p.m. at normal engine speed.

DART "BLUE J" 15-30
Dart Truck and Tractor Co., Waterloo, Ia.

DAYTON-DOWD CO.
Quincy, Illinois

Leader, Model B, 12-18   1919-1921
Leader, Model C, 25-40   1919

Traction Wheels: Four-wheel type, with two drive wheels, 48 x 12.

No. of Plows Recommended: Two or three 14-in.

Length: 129 in.; Width: 60 in.; Height: 66 in.; Weight: 4800 lbs.; Price: $1000.

Turning Radius: 16 ft.; Acres Plowed in 10-hr. Day: 8 to 10.

Motor: Own; $6\frac{1}{4}$ x 6, opposed L-head, 2 cylinders, cast separately.

Lubrication: Force and splash system.

Carburetor: Kingston.

Ignition System: High tension magneto with impulse starter.

Cooling System: Perfex radiator, fan and pump.

Bearings: Modern die cast babbitt in transmission and plain on drive axle.

Transmission: Selective spur gear, 1.8 to 2.5 m.p.h. forward; 2 m.p.h. reverse.

Final Drive: Gear.

Belt Pulley: 14 x 7; 750 r.p.m. and 2700 feet per minute at normal engine speed.

LEADER, MODEL B, 12-18
Dayton-Dowd Co., Quincy, Ill.

LEADER, MODEL C, 25-40
Dayton-Dowd Co., Quincy, Ill.

Traction Wheels: Two crawlers, 44 x 15.

No. of Plows Recommended: Four to six 14-in.

Length: 153 in.; Width: 64 in.; Height: 96 in.; Weight: 6500 lbs.; Price: $2250.

Turning Radius: 26 ft.; Acres Plowed in 10-hr. Day: 12 to 18.

Motor: Twin City; 5 x 7½, L-head, 4 cylinders, cast en bloc.

Lubrication: Force and splash system.

Carburetor: Kingston.

Ignition System: High tension magneto with impulse starter.

Cooling System: Perfex radiator, fan and pump.

Bearings: Hyatt roller on drive axle and Modern die cast babbitts in transmission.

Transmission: Selective gears, 1.89 to 2.6 m.p.h. forward; 1.44 m.p.h. reverse.

Final Drive: Double chain.

Belt Pulley: 14 x 8; 750 r.p.m. and 2750 feet per minute at normal engine speed.

DEPUE BROS. MANUFACTURING CO.

Clinton, Iowa

Depue 20-32   1919-1921

Traction Wheels: Four-wheel tractor, driven by all four wheels, each 40 x 10.

No. of Plows Recommended: Four 14-in.

Length: 99 in.; Width: 56 in.; Height: 80 in.; Weight: 6500 lbs.; Price, $2500.

Turning Radius: 16 ft.; Acres Plowed in 10-hr. Day: 15.

Motor: Buda; 4½ x 6, vertical, 4-cylinders, cast en bloc.

Lubrication: Geared pump.

Carburetor: Stromberg, 1½ in.

Ignition System: Bosch high tension magneto, with impulse starter.

Cooling System: Perfex radiator, pump and fan.

Bearings: Timken roller in transmission and on drive axle.

Transmission: Sliding gear, 1½ to 5 m. p. h. forward; 1 m. p. h. reverse.

Final Drive: Bevel gears.

Belt Pulley: 12 x 8; 800 r. p. m. and 2513 feet per minute at normal engine speed.

DEPUE 20-32
Depue Bros. Mfg. Co., Clinton, Ia.

Why Farmers Like The Waterloo Boy

Farmers buy the Waterloo Boy for downright tractor dependability—and get it.

They find to their satisfaction that they can rely on getting the full rated 12-25 horse power continuously, evenly, with no motor vibration and with plenty of reserve power for emergencies.

They find that the Waterloo Boy's perfect combustion and conservation of kerosene saves many dollars in fuel cost and prevents trouble from carbonized cylinders or foul spark plugs.

They find that the simple, correctly-designed construction and the ready accessibility to all parts enable them to take care of the tractor with much the same ease with which they take care of other standard farm machinery.

When a dealer sells one Waterloo Boy it helps him sell others. Its owner likes it. So do his neighbors. When they get ready to buy, they are favorably inclined toward the Waterloo Boy.

Write us today for full information regarding the Waterloo Boy—the tractor with five years of success behind it. It offers an opportunity to you.

JOHN DEERE, MOLINE, ILLINOIS

DEERE & CO.
Moline, Illinois

Waterloo Boy, Model N, 12-25   1919-1925

Traction Wheels: Four wheels with two traction members, 52 x 12, in rear.
No. of Plows Recommended: Three 14 in.
Length: 136 in.; **Width:** 72 in.; **Height:** 66 in.; **Weight:** 6000 lbs.
Turning Radius: 12 ft.; **Acres Plowed in 10-hr. Day:** 10.
Motor: Own, $6\frac{1}{2}$ x 7; twin horizontal, 2 cylinders, cast en bloc.
Lubrication: Pump system.
Carburetor: Schebler, $1\frac{1}{2}$-in.
Ignition System: Dixie high tension magneto.
Cooling System: Circulating pump, Modine radiator and fan.
Bearings: Hyatt roller in transmission and on drive axle.
Transmission: Sliding gear, $2\frac{1}{4}$ to 3 m.p.h. forward; $2\frac{1}{4}$ m.p.h. reverse.
Final Drive: Internal gears in drive wheels.
Belt Pulley: 14 x 8; 750 r. p. m. and 2750 ft. per minute at normal engine speed.

WATERLOO BOY, MODEL N, 12-25
Deere & Co., Moline, Ill.

G. I. DILL TRACTOR MANUFACTURING CO.
Harrisburg, Arkansas

Dill 20-40   1919-1921

DILL 20-40
G. I. Dill Tractor Mfg. Co., Harrisburg, Ark.

Traction Wheels: Four wheels, driven by two in rear, 42 x 36.
No. of Plows Recommended: Three 14-in.
Length: 207 in.; **Width:** 105 in.; **Height:** 70 in.; **Weight:** 5000 lbs.; **Price:** $2480.
Turning Radius: 30 ft.
Motor: Continental; $4\frac{1}{2}$ x $5\frac{1}{2}$, vertical, 4 cylinders, cast in pairs.
Lubrication: Splash and pressure.
Carburetor: Byrne-Kingston.
Ignition System: Bosch high tension dual magneto.
Cooling System: Eureka radiator, fan and pump.
Bearings: Hyatt roller on drive axle.
Transmission: Individual clutch, $1\frac{1}{2}$ to 5 m.p.h. forward; 1 to $1\frac{1}{2}$ m.p.h. reverse.
Final Drive: Chain.

ELDERFIELDS MECHANICS CO.

Port Washington, Long Island, New York

Universal 1-4.9   1919-1920

UNIVERSAL 1-4.9
Elderfields Mechanics Co., Port Washington, L. I., N. Y.

Traction Wheels: Three-wheel type; two 36 x 5 traction wheels in front.

No. of Plows Recommended: One 9-in.

Length: 84 in.; **Width:** 33½ in. **Height:** 42 in.; **Weight:** 750 lbs.; **Price:** $425.

Turning Radius: 2 ft.

Motor: Own, 3½ x 5, L-head, 4-cycle, 1 cylinder.

Lubrication: Splash.

Carburetor: Zenith, ⅝-in.

Ignition System: Atwater-Kent battery.

Cooling System: Thermo-syphon.

Bearings: Die cast in motor, ball thrust on drive.

Transmission: Single speed.

Final Drive: Worm gear.

Belt Pulley: 5¼ x 2; 500 to 1000 r.p.m.

ELGIN TRACTOR CORP.

Piqua, Ohio

New Elgin 12-25   1919

Traction Wheels: Four wheels, two traction wheels in rear, 42 x 10.

No. of Plows Recommended: Two to three 14-in.

Length: 123 in.; **Width:** 60 in.; **Height:** 58 in.; **Weight:** 3400 lbs.

Turning Radius: 11 ft.; **Acres Plowed in 10-hr. Day:** 7 to 10.

Motor: Erd; 4 x 6, vertical, 4 cylinders, cast en bloc.

Lubrication: Pump and splash.

Carburetor: Kingston, 1¼ in.

Ignition System: Dixie high tension magneto with impulse starter.

Cooling System: Modine radiator, fan, water and pump.

Bearings: Hyatt roller in transmission and Timken roller on drive axle.

Transmission: Friction, ¼ to 6 m.p.h. forward and 1 m.p.h. reverse.

Final Drive: Double chain.

Belt Pulley: 9 x 8; 900 r.p.m.

NEW ELGIN 12-25
Elgin Tractor Corporation, Piqua, O.

EMERSON-BRANTINGHAM IMPLEMENT CO.

Rockford, Illinois

E-B, Model AA, 12-20   1919-1928
E-B, Reeves, 40-65   1919-1920

Traction Wheels: Four wheels, with two drive wheels, 54 x 12, in rear.

No. of Plows Recommended: Three 14-in.

Length: 132 in.; **Width:** 61 in.; **Height:** 75¼ in.; **Weight:** 4755 lbs.

Turning Radius: 12½ ft.

Motor: Own; vertical, 4 cylinders, 4¾ x 5.

Lubrication: Circulating splash.

Carburetor: Bennett, 1½-in.

Ignition System: K-W high tension magneto.

Starting Equipment: Impulse starter.

Cooling System: Radiator and pump.

Bearings: Hyatt rollers.

Transmission: Gear; 1.81 to 2.33 m.p.h. forward and 1.81 m.p.h. reverse.

Final Drive: Enclosed gear.

Belt Pulley: 12 x 6⅜; 900 r.p.m.

E.-B., MODEL AA, 12-20
Emerson-Brantingham Implement Co., Rockford, Ill.

Traction Wheels: Four-wheel tractor, with two drive members in rear, 90 x 24.

No. of Plows Recommended: Eight to ten 14-in.

Length: 192 in.; **Width:** 111 in.; **Height:** 126 in.; **Weight:** 23000 lbs.; **Price:** $3680.

Turning Radius: 23½ ft.; **Acres Plowed in 10-hr. Day:** 20 to 30.

Motor: Special; 7¼ x 9, vertical, 4 cylinders cast separately.

Lubrication: Force feed and splash system.

Carburetor: Bennett.

Ignition System: K-W high tension magneto.

Lighting Equipment: K-W.

Cooling System: Perfex radiator.

Bearings: Own; plain in transmission.

Transmission: Sliding gear, 2 m.p.h. forward; 2 m.p.h. reverse.

Final Drive: Spur gear.

Belt Pulley: 22 x 10; 500 r.p.m. and 2880 feet per minute at normal engine speed.

E-B, REEVES, 40-65
Emerson-Brantingham Implement Co., Rockford, Ill.

1919   223

EVANS MANUFACTURING CO.
Hudson, Ohio

Hudson, Model K, 20-35   1919

Traction Wheels: Four wheels, two 60 x 12 driving in rear.

No. of Plows Recommended: Three to four 14-in.

Length: 160 in.; **Width:** 56 in.; **Height:** 60 in.; **Weight:** 5300 lbs.

Turning Radius: 10 ft.; **Acres Plowed in 10-hr. Day:** 12.

Motor: Buda; $4\frac{1}{2}$ x 6, vertical 4 cylinders, cast en bloc.

Lubrication: Force Feed.

Carburetor: Rayfield, $1\frac{1}{4}$.

Ignition System: Dixie high tension magneto.

Starting and Lighting Equipment: Optional.

Cooling System: Fan, pump and radiator.

Bearings: Timken roller throughout.

Transmission: Enclosed spur gear; $2\frac{1}{2}$ to 4 m.p.h. forward and $2\frac{1}{2}$ m.p.h. reverse.

Final Drive: Internal gears.

Belt Pulley: 15 x 8; 660 r.p.m. and 26 f.p.m. at normal engine speed.

HUDSON, MODEL K, 20-35
Evans Mfg. Co., Hudson, O.

A. B. FARQUHAR CO., LTD.
York, Pennsylvania

Farquhar 15-25   1919-1923
Farquhar 25-50   1919-1923

Traction Wheels: Four wheel type; two traction members in rear, 54x14.

No. of Plows Recommended: Three to four 14-in.

Length: 161 in.; **Width:** 74 in.; **Height:** 68 in.; **Weight:** 6000 lbs.

Turning Radius: $11\frac{1}{2}$ ft.

Motor: Buda, 4 cylinders. L head, vertical, $4\frac{1}{2}$x6.

Lubrication: Force feed.

Carburetor: Kingston, $1\frac{1}{2}$ in.

Ignition System: K-W high tension magneto with impulse starter.

Cooling System: Perfex radiator, pump and fan.

Bearings: Hyatt roller in transmission.

Transmission: Worm gear; 1 to 4 m.p.h. forward and $2\frac{1}{4}$ m.p.h. reverse.

Final Drive: Enclosed spur gear.

Belt Pulley: 14x7; 800 r.p.m. and 2900 f.p.m. at normal engine speed.

FARQUHAR 15-25
A. B. Farquhar Co., Ltd., York, Pa.

FARQUHAR 25-50
A. B. Farquhar Co., Ltd., York, Pa.

Traction Wheels: Four wheels; two, 84x 20, in rear giving traction.
No. of Plows Recommended: Six to seven 14-in.
Length: 216 in.; **Width:** 106 in.; **Height:** 118 in.; **Weight:** 19000 lbs.
Motor: Own make, 4 cylinders, vertical, 7x8, cast in pairs.
Lubrication: Detroit force feed.
Carburetor: Kingston, 2-in.
Ignition System: K-W high tension magneto.
Cooling System: Own make of radiator, fan and pump.
Bearings: Own make, plain, in transmission.
Transmission: 1 to 2.3 m.p.h. forward.
Final Drive: Open spur gear.
Belt Pulley: 32x9; 275 r.p.m. at normal engine speed.

FOUR DRIVE TRACTOR CO.

Big Rapids, Michigan

Fitch Four Drive 20-36   1919-1930

Traction Wheels: Drives on all four wheels, front, 36 x 12, and rear, 42 x 12.
No. of Plows Recommended: Four 14-in.
Length: 120 in.; **Width:** 69 in.; **Height:** 73 in.; **Weight:** 5100 lbs.; **Price:** $2500.
Turning Radius: 4¾ ft.; **Acres Plowed in 10-hr. Day:** 12.
Motor: Climax; 5 x 6½, R-U-4-R, 4 cylinders, cast in pairs.
Lubrication: Automatic system.
Carburetor: Kingston.
Ignition System: Dixie high tension magneto.
Cooling System: Circulating pump, Modine radiator and Oakes fan.
Bearings: Timken roller throughout.
Transmission: Cotta sliding gear up to 4 m.p.h. forward; 1 m.p.h. reverse.
Transmission: Selective sliding gear up to 4 m.p.h. forward; 1 m.p.h. reverse.
Final Drive: Worm on rear axle, bevel gears in front.
Belt Pulley: 12 x 10; 856 r.p.m. and 2690 feet per minute at normal engine speed.

FITCH FOUR DRIVE 20-36
Four Drive Tractor Co., Big Rapids, Mich.

GEHL BROS. MANUFACTURING CO.

West Bend, Wisconsin

Gehl 15-30   1919

Traction Wheels: Three wheels, one drum drive in rear, 48 x 42.
No. of Plows Recommended: Three 14-in.
Length: 162 in.; Width: 86 in.; Height: 59 in.; Weight: 4600 lbs.; Price: $1450.
Turning Radius: 18 ft.
Motor: Waukesha, 4½ x 6¾; vertical, 4 cylinders, cast in pairs.
Lubrication: Circulating splash system.
Carburetor: Bennett.
Ignition System: Kingston high tension independent magneto.
Cooling System: Cellular radiator, pump and fan.
Bearings: Hyatt roller in transmission and on drive axle.
Transmission: Sliding gear.
Final Drive: Spur gears.
Belt Pulley: 14 x 8.

GEHL 15-30
Gehl Bros. Mfg. Co., West Bend, Wis.

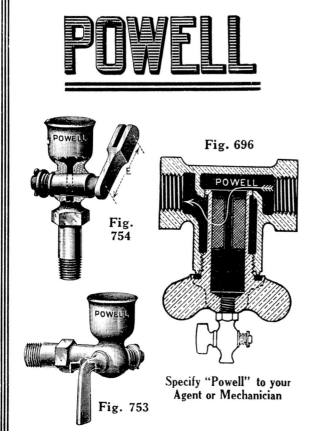

GRAIN BELT MANUFACTURING CO.

Fargo, North Dakota

Grain Belt 15-30

1919

Traction Wheels: Four wheels, with two drive wheels in rear, 60 x 14.
No. of Plows Recommended: Four 14-in.
Length: 144 in.; **Width:** 90 in.; **Height:** 60 in.; **Weight:** 7200 lbs.; **Price:** $2250.
Turning Radius: 12 ft.; **Acres Plowed in 10-hr. Day:** 12.
Motor: Waukesha; 4¾ x 6¾; T-head, 4 cylinders, cast in pairs.
Lubrication: Pump and splash system.
Carburetor: Bennett.
Ignition System: K-W.
Starting Equipment: Impulse starter.
Cooling System: Pump and syphon.
Bearings: Hyatt roller in speed change gears.
Transmission: Direct drive to 2½ m.p.h. forward; 2½ m.p.h. reverse.
Final Drive: Spur gears.
Belt Pulley: 18 x 10; 850 r.p.m. and 4250 feet per minute at normal engine speed.

GRAIN BELT 15-30
Grain Belt Mfg. Co., Fargo, N. D.

GREAT WESTERN TRACTOR CORP.

Omaha, Nebraska

Great Western, St. 20-35

1919-1921

Traction Wheels: Two front steering wheels and two 60 x 12 drive wheels in rear.
No. of Plows Recommended: Four 14-in.
Length: 148 in.; **Width:** 72 in.; **Height:** 65 in.; **Weight:** 4900 lbs.; **Price:** $1750.
Turning Radius: 12 ft.
Motor: Beaver; 4 cylinders, cast in pairs.
Lubrication: Force feed and splash.
Carburetor: Kingston.
Ignition System: Dixie high tension magneto with impulse starter.
Cooling System: Fan, radiator and pump.
Bearings: Hyatt roller throughout.
Transmission: Own special gear, 3 to 5 m.p.h. forward.
Final Drive: Enclosed gear and pinion.
Belt Pulley: 10 x 18; 2624 f.p.m. at normal engine speed.

GREAT WESTERN, SR. 20-35
Great Western Tractor Corp., Omaha, Neb.

Great Western Kerosene Farm Tractors

The strongest Tractor made with the least number of gears possible, denoting the highest efficiency obtainable and with all bearings self-aligning and all gears enclosed and running in oil and dust-proof thruout.

This is the dealers' opportunity to get the best tractor made.

The Tractor Without a Fault

GREAT WESTERN TRACTOR CORP.
Omaha, Nebraska

HESSION TILLER & TRACTOR CORP.
Buffalo, New York

Wheat Tractor 12-24   1919

WHEAT TRACTOR 12-24
Hession Tiller & Tractor Corp., Buffalo, N. Y.

Traction Wheels: Two, 48 x 12, rear traction wheels and two front.
No. of Plows Recommended: Three 14-in.
Length: 132 in.; **Width:** 58 in.; **Height:** 58 in.; **Weight:** 4250 lbs.; **Price:** $1695.
Turning Radius: 9½ ft.; **Acres Plowed In 10-hr. Day:** 10.
Motor: Erd; 4 x 6, valve-in-head, 4 cylinders, cast en bloc.
Lubrication: Force feed and splash.
Carburetor: Kingston, 1¾-in.
Ignition System: Dixie high tension magneto.
Cooling System: Fan, pump and radiator.
Bearings: Timken and Hyatt roller and New Departure ball.
Transmission: Foote sliding gear; 2½ to 4 m.p.h. forward and 2 7/10 m.p.h. reverse.
Final Drive: Internal spur gear.
Belt Pulley: 18 x 7; 600 r.p.m. and 2800 f.p.m. at normal engine speed.

HOLT MANUFACTURING CO.
Peoria, Illinois

Caterpillar 25-40   1919
Caterpillar 40-60   1919

Tractor Wheels: Two caterpillar tracks, 84 in. long and 11 in. face.
No. of Plows Recommended: Four 14-in.
Turning Radius: 4 ft.
Motor: Own make, 4¾x6, vertical, 4 cylinders, cast in pairs.
Lubrication: Force feed system.
Carburetor: Schebler.
Ignition System: Eisemann high tension magneto.
Cooling System: Modine radiator, pump and fan.
Bearings: 17 Hyatt roller in transmission.
Transmission: Own make, selective gear, 1.3 to 4.9 m.p.h. forward.
Final Drive: Enclosed spur gear.
Belt Pulley: 12x8½; 865 r.p.m. and 2700 f.p.m. at normal engine speed.

CATERPILLAR 25-40
Holt Mfg. Co., Peoria, Ill.

THE TRACTOR THAT TOPS THEM ALL

The Illinois Super-Drive Tractor is the best designed, best engineered, most powerful for its weight and the most economical in performance of any of the farm tractors now in use.

It is the **New Idea** tractor—with the Live-Axle, Spring Cushion Drive—and a score of absolutely new and superior features which mean efficiency.

It has a unit Frame—with a much needed roomy platform on the rear.

It has a Live-Axle which delivers the power to the rims of the wheels—not to the hubs and spokes.

It has Cushion Springs which relieve backlash and shock on the gears when the machine is running over rough ground.

It has a powerful, slow-speed, Kerosene-burning motor.

It has a driving principle, which delivers more engine power to the drawbar than any other driving principle in tractor use.

It meets the accepted standard of performance—3 to 4 plows—and the accepted standard of weight—4,800 pounds.

The Illinois Super-Drive represents the best in tractor making that has yet been brought out in this country. It is far ahead of its time—and is the tractor that farmer and dealer have been waiting for. Write for complete information.

ILLINOIS TRACTOR CO., Bloomington, Ill., U. S. A.

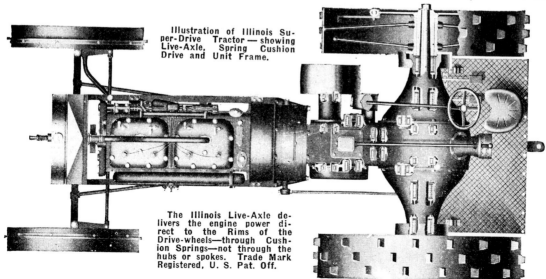

Illustration of Illinois Super-Drive Tractor — showing Live-Axle, Spring Cushion Drive and Unit Frame.

The Illinois Live-Axle delivers the engine power direct to the Rims of the Drive-wheels—through Cushion Springs—not through the hubs or spokes. Trade Mark Registered, U. S. Pat. Off.

1919

229

Traction Wheels: One caterpillar track on each side giving 1440 sq. in. of traction surface.

No. of Plows Recommended: Six 14-in.

Turning Radius: 5 1-6 ft.

Motor: Own; vertical, 6½x7, 4 cylinders, cast singly.

Lubrication: Force feed.

Carburetor: Kingston.

Ignition System: K-W high tension magneto.

Cooling System: Radiator, fan and centrifugal pump.

Bearings: Hyatt and Gurney throughout.

Transmission: Selective gear; 1.35 to 3.88 m.p.h. forward.

Final Drive: Enclosed spur gear.

Belt Pulley: 14x10½; 710 r.p.m. and 2600 f.p.m. at normal engine speed.

CATERPILLAR 40-60
Holt Mfg. Co., Peoria, Ill.

ILLINOIS TRACTOR CO.

Bloomington, Illinois

Illinois Super-Drive 16-36   1919-1921

Traction Wheels: Four wheels; two drive members, 54 x 10, in rear.

No. of Plows Recommended: Four 14-in.

Length: 142 in.; **Width:** 72 in.; **Height:** 60 in.; **Weight:** 5200 lbs.; **Price:** $2250.

Turning Radius: 11 ft.; **Acres Plowed In 10-hr. Day:** 12.

Motor: Climax; 5 x 6½, L-head, 4 cylinders, cast in pairs.

Lubrication: Pressure system.

Carburetor: Stromberg, 1½-in.

Ignition System: Dixie high tension magneto.

Cooling System: Modine "Spirex" radiator, pump and fan.

Bearings: Hyatt roller in transmission and on drive axle.

Transmission: Enclosed spur gear, 2½ to 3½ m.p.h. forward; 2½ m.p.h. reverse.

Final Drive: Enclosed gears.

Belt Pulley: 14 x 8½; 600 r.p.m. and 2250 f.p.m. at normal engine speed.

ILLINOIS SUPER-DRIVE 16-36
Illinois Tractor Co., Bloomington, Ill.

SELL THE FARMER WHAT HE NEEDS

What a man **needs** he is paying for, whether he has it or not. Above all things the farmer needs cheap, dependable power. He is already sold on that proposition. Anything

will of an organization that for nearly a century has studied farm needs and worked for farm efficiency and economy.

These things count big from a

less means for him a narrower margin between income and outgo.

The dealer selling **International** and **Titan kerosene tractors** sells simple, durable machines operating on low-cost fuels designed and built for the one purpose of supplying cheap dependable power for farm work.

Behind the dealer selling Internationals is all the prestige and good

sales standpoint. Farmers know the International standard of quality and service and know that the same standard applies to every International and Titan kerosene tractor.

This is your opportunity. A contract to sell something that has a market already waiting is certainly a valuable contract. Speak to the blockman about it the next time you see him, or write us.

International Harvester Company
of America

CHICAGO   **U S A**

INDIANA SILO CO.
Anderson, Indiana

Indiana 5-10　　　　　　　　　　　　　　　　1919-1924

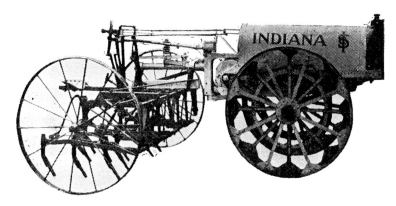

INDIANA 5-10
Indiana Silo Co., Anderson, Ind.

Traction Wheels: Four Wheels; two drive members in front, 50x12.
No. of Plows Recommended: One 16-in.
Length: 108 in.; **Width:** 54 in.; **Height:** 62 in.; **Weight:** 2000 lbs.
Turning Radius: 7 ft.; **Acres Plowed in 10-hr. Day:** 4.
Motor: Le Roi, 4 cylinders, $3\frac{1}{8}x4\frac{1}{2}$, vertical, cast en bloc.
Lubrication: Force feed and splash.
Carburetor: Kingston, $\frac{7}{8}$-in.
Ignition System: Atwater-Kent high tension.
Cooling System: Chandler radiator and fan.
Bearings: Ball bearings in transmission and plain in rear axle.
Transmission: Selective; $1\frac{1}{2}$ to 4 m.p.h. forward and $1\frac{1}{2}$ to 4 m.p.h reverse.
Final Drive: Chain, open.
Belt Pulley: $7x6\frac{1}{2}$; 1200 r.p.m. and 2600 f.p.m. at normal engine speed.

INTERNATIONAL HARVESTER CO.
Chicago, Illinois

International 8-16　　　　　　　　　　　　　　1919-1922

Traction Wheels: Four wheels; two, 40x10, drive wheels in rear.
No. of Plows Recommended: Two 14-in.
Length: 132 in.; **Width:** 54 in.; **Height:** 65 in.; **Weight:** 3300 lbs.
Turning Radius: 27 ft.
Motor: Own make; 4 cylinders, 4x5, vertical.
Lubrication: Splash system.
Carburetor: Ensign, kerosene.
Ignition System: Dixie high tension magneto.
Cooling System: Radiator and fan.
Bearings: Own make, roller in rear axle.
Transmission: Sliding gear; $1\frac{3}{4}$ to 4 m.p.h. forward.
Final Drive: Open, chain.
Belt Pulley: $12\frac{1}{4}x8\frac{1}{2}$; 635 r.p.m. and 2060 f.p.m. at normal engine speed.

INTERNATIONAL 8-16
International Harvester Co., Chicago, Ill.

FLOUR CITY TRACTORS

Made In

Four Practical Sizes.

14-24 H. P.   20-35 H. P.
30-50 H. P.   40-70 H. P.

The only complete line of Kerosene burning tractors in which the same mechanical principles are followed out in all sizes.

You can conscientiously recommend Flour City Tractors. They are the result of nineteen years' successful tractor making experience. With this complete line you are never compelled to recommend a tractor too large or too small for the work, but can sell your trade a size tractor that is exactly suited to the conditions.

Catalog on Request

Kinnard & Sons Mfg .Co.

823 44th Ave. North,   Minneapolis, Minn.

C. O. D. Kerosene Tractor

13-25 Horse Power

The C. O. D. Kerosene Tractor meets every power demand on the farm, drawbar and belt. Reliable, easy to operate. Practical four wheel design, strongly built. Plows an acre per hour on cheap **Kerosene.** Backed by positive guarantee from responsible manufacturer. Sells at a low price.

Investigate the RELIABLE C. O. D. before you buy. Hundreds of farmers are now using C. O. D. Tractors with complete success and satisfaction. Write us today for illustrated circular and further information.

C. O. D. TRACTOR CO.

Minneapolis, Minn.

"The Master of All Farm Jobs."

KINNARD & SONS MANUFACTURING CO.

Minneapolis, Minnesota

Flour City Jr. 14-24	1919-1927
Flour City 30-50	1919-1927
Flour City 40-70	1919-1927

Traction Wheels: Four wheel type with two traction members in rear 60x12.

No. of Plows Recommended: Three 14-in.

Weight: 6700 lbs.

Motor: Own, 5x5, vertical, 4 cylinders, cast in pairs.

Lubrication: Splash with force feed to crank shaft.

Carburetor: Schebler, $1\frac{1}{2}$-in.

Ignition System: Atwater-Kent high tension magneto with impulse starter.

Cooling System: Modine radiator, fan and pump circulation.

Transmission: Own; 2.2 to 3.25 m.p.h. forward.

Final Drive: Gear, own make.

Belt Pulley: $26x7\frac{1}{2}$; 320 r.p.m at normal engine speed.

FLOUR CITY JR. 14-24
Kinnard & Sons Mfg. Co., Minneapolis, Minn.

INLET AND EXHAUST
VALVES

Hardened and Ground Shackle Bolts, King Bolts, Pins and Screw Machine Products of this Character

We have a modern and complete equipment for the manufacturing of these parts and solicit inquiries covering production requirements of the automotive industries, together with the specifications placed for the maintaining of service department stocks.

A DEPENDABLE SOURCE OF SUPPLY ON VALVES AND BOLTS.

The FORD-CLARK CO.

3125 Perkins Avenue
Cleveland, O.

Traction Wheels: Four wheels; two traction in rear, 84x24.

No. of Plows Recommended: Six to eight 14-in.

Weight: 14000 lbs.

Motor: Own make; 6¼x7, vertical, 4 cylinders, cast in pairs.

Lubrication: Splash with force feed to crank case.

Carburetor: Schebler, 2-in.

Ignition System: High tension magneto with impulse starter.

Cooling System: Water, radiator and fan.

Transmission: Own make; 2 to 2½ m.p.h. forward and 2 to 2½ m.p.h. reverse.

Final Drive: Gear.

Belt Pulley: 32x9; 275 r.p.m. at normal engine speed.

FLOUR CITY 30-50
Kinnard & Sons Mfg. Co., Minneapolis, Minn.

Traction Wheels: Four wheels, two, 96x 24, in rear furnishing traction.

No. of Plows Recommended: Eight to ten 14-in.

Motor: Own make; 7½x9, vertical, 4 cylinders, cast in pairs.

Lubrication: Splash with force feed to crank case.

Carburetor: Schebler, 2-in.

Ignition System: High tension magneto with impulse starter.

Cooling System: Pump, radiator and fan.

Transmission: Own make; 2 to 2½ m.p.h. forward and 2 to 2½ m.p.h. reverse.

Final Drive: Gear.

Belt Pulley: 34x10; 275 r.p.m at normal engine speed.

FLOUR CITY 40-70
Kinnard & Sons Mfg. Co., Minneapolis, Minn.

HOMER LAUGHLIN ENGINEERS CORP.

Los Angeles, California

Laughlin 8-20

Traction Wheels: Two creeper tracks giving 1200 sq. in. traction surface.

No. of Plows Recommended: Two 14-in.

Length: 106 in.; **Width:** 56⅛ in.; **Height:** 49 in.; **Weight:** 6000 lbs.; **Price:** $2,500.

Turning Radius: 9 ft.; **Acres Plowed in 10 Hour Day;** 8.

Motor: Own; 4⅜x5½, valve-in-head, 4 cylinders, cast in pairs.

Lubrication: Splash system.

Carburetor: Ensign, 1¼.

Ignition System: Dixie high tension magneto.

Cooling System: Radiator, fan and centrifugal pump.

Bearings: Hyatt roller.

Transmission: Sliding gear; 1¾ to 2¾ m.p.h. forward; 1¾ m.p.h. reverse.

Final Drive: Enclosed, external spur gears.

Belt Pulley: 10x6; 700 r.p.m. at normal engine speed.

1919

LAUGHLIN 8-20
Homer Laughlin Engineers Corp., Los Angeles, Cal.

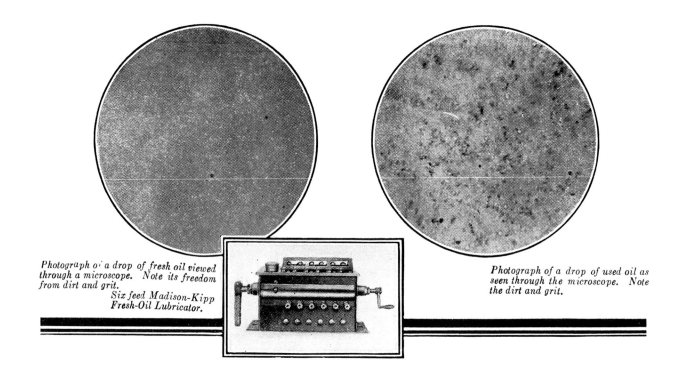

Photograph of a drop of fresh oil viewed through a microscope. Note its freedom from dirt and grit.

Six feed Madison-Kipp Fresh-Oil Lubricator.

Photograph of a drop of used oil as seen through the microscope. Note the dirt and grit.

Fresh Oil vs. Used Oil in Tractors

There is a good deal of confusion right now in the names used to describe tractor lubricating systems.

There are only two kinds of lubricating systems: those using oil over again and those which use fresh oil only.

The first kind is described by many names—such as circulating, force-pump, splash, crank-case system and the like—but they all mean that the oil is used over and over.

The fresh-oil kind is generally described in specifications by naming the lubricator used and the great majority of tractors now built specify Madison-Kipp Lubricators.

Why Fresh Oil is Better

The experienced tractor manufacturers use Madison-Kipp Lubricators because their fresh oil keeps down repair costs and betters the working of the motor.

This holds for both two and four cylinder motors using kerosene or low grade gasoline.

Fresh oil is the only kind of oil that really lubricates—and that really protects the working parts and bearings from undue wear.

Used oil, on the contrary, is so full of grit and sediment that it grinds down the parts it is supposed to protect.

What the Microscope Tells

The photographs at the top of this page show the difference between fresh oil and the used oil from a tractor's crank case.

These photographs are taken through a microscope. Note how smooth and clear the fresh oil is.

Note the sharp sediment and grit in the used oil.

Your motor doesn't need a

microscope to detect this grinding grit any more than a gear box needs help in detecting a handful of sand thrown into it.

Protect Yourself

Before you buy a tractor study the lubrication specifications.

Remember that there are only two kinds of systems although many names are used to describe the less scientific kind.

Note that generally the manufacturers who have made good tractors for a term of years use Madison-Kipp Lubricators although these cost them more than other systems.

And that Kipp-Equipt tractors cost you no more and are worth much more.

The Madison-Kipp Lubricator Company,
Madison, Wis.

Madison-Kipp Lubricators

FRESH OIL SYSTEMS

LIBERTY TRACTOR CO.
Minneapolis, Minnesota

Liberty 20-36   1919

Traction Wheels: Four wheel tractor with two traction wheels in rear.
No. of Plows Recommended: Four 14-inch.
Length: 144 in.; **Width:** 68 in.; **Height:** 60 in.; **Weight:** 5,500 lbs.
Turning Radius: 48 ft.; **Acres Plowed in 10-hour day:** 15.
Motor: Climax, 5 x 6½.; Vertical, 4 cylinders, cast in pairs.
Lubrication: Pump and splash system.
Carburetor: Stromberg, 1½ in.
Ignition Syystem': Dixie high tension magneto.
Cooling System: Shotwell-Johnson honeycomb radiator.
Bearings: Hyatt roller in transmission.
Transmission: Enclosed gears, 2½ to 4½ m. p. h. forward; 2½ m. p. h. reverse.
Final Drive: Spur gear.
Belt Pulley: 12 x 8; 1100 r. p. m. and 2,600 feet per minute at normal engine speed.

LIBERTY 20-36
Liberty Tractor Co., Minneapolis, Minn.

LITTLE GIANT CO.
Mankato, Minnesota

Little Giant, Model B, 16-22   1919-1924
Little Giant, Model A, 26-35   1919-1923

LITTLE GIANT, MODEL B, 16-22
Little Giant Co., Mankato, Minn.

Traction Wheels: Four wheels with two drivers in rear, 54 x 14.
No. of Plows Recommended: Three or four 14-inch.
Length: 144 in.; **Width:** 52 in.; **Height:** 59 in.; **Weight:** 5,200 lbs.; **Price:** $1,650.
Turning Radius 11 ft.; **Acres Plowed in 10-hour day;** 10 to 15.
Motor: Own; 4½ x 5, L-head, 4 cylinders, cast in pairs.
Lubrication: Force feed and splash combined.
Carburetor: Kingston.
Ignition System: K-W. high tension magneto.
Cooling System: Water and pump system.
Bearings: Hyatt roller throughout.
Transmission: Sliding gear, 1½, 3 and 6 m. p. h. forward; 1½ m. p. h. reverse.
Final Drive: Direct gear drive.
Belt Pulley: 9 x 7; 900 r. p. m. and 2,120 feet per minute at normal engine speed.

Traction Wheels: Four wheels with two drivers in rear, 66 x 20.

No. of Plows Recommended: Four to six 14-inch.

Length: 168 in.; Width: 75 in.; Height 73 in.; Weight: 8,700 lbs.; Price: $2,500.

Turning Radius: 15 ft.; Acres Plowed in 10-hour day: 15 to 25.

Motor: Own; 5½ x 6, L-head, 4 cylinders, cast in pairs.

Lubrication: Force feed and splash combined.

Carburetor: Kingston.

Ignition System: K-W. high tension magneto.

Cooling System: Water and pump system.

Bearings: Hyatt roller throughout.

Transmission: Sliding gear, 1½, 3 and 6 m. p. h. forward, 1½ m. p. h. reverse.

Final Drive: Direct gear drive.

Belt Pulley: 13 x 9; 750 r. p. m. and 2,520 feet per minute at normal engine speed.

LITTLE GIANT, MODEL A, 26-35
Little Giant Co., Mankato, Minn.

LOMBARD AUTO TRACTOR-TRUCK CORP.

New York, New York

Lombard Auto Tractor-Truck   1919-1921

Traction Wheels: Two front wheels and two crawlers in rear, 120x12.

No. of Plows Recommended: Six to twelve 14-in.

Length: 144 in.; Width: 78 in.; Height: 72 in.; Weight: 1800 lbs.

Turning Radius: 48 ft.

Motor: Special, 6 cylinders, 5¾x7, cast in pairs.

Lubrication: Force feed.

Ignition System: Dixie high tension magneto.

Cooling System: Radiator, fan and pump.

Transmission: Special, selective gear; 2 to 6 m.p.h forward.

Final Drive: Enclosed worm gear.

LOMBARD AUTO TRACTOR-TRUCK
Lombard Auto Tractor-Truck Corp., New York, N. Y.

MAXIM CORP.
New York, New York

Maxim Model A, 12-24   1919
Maxim-Dart "Blue J." 13-30   1919

MAXIM MODEL A, 12-24
Maxim Corporation, New York, N. Y.

No. of Plows Recommended: Three 14-in.
Length: 118 in.; **Width:** 63 in.; **Height:** 54 in.; **Weight:** 3865 lbs.; **Price:** $1685.
Turning Radius: $10\frac{1}{2}$ ft.; **Acres Plowed In 10-hr. Day:** 9 to 10.
Motor: Own make, $4\frac{1}{2}$x$5\frac{1}{2}$, vertical, 4 cylinders, cast en bloc.
Lubrication: Force feed.
Carburetor: Holley.
Ignition System: Dixie magneto.
Cooling System: Water circulated by pump.
Bearings: Hyatt and Timken.
Transmission: Selective gear; $1\frac{1}{2}$ to 6 m. p.h. forward and $1\frac{1}{2}$ m.p.h. reverse.
Final Drive: Worm gear.
Belt Pulley: 8x8; 950 r.p.m and 2400 f.p.m. at normal engine speed.

No. of Plows Recommended: Three 14-in.
Length: 125 in.; **Width:** 56 in.; **Height:** 65 in.; **Weight:** 4500 lbs.; **Price:** $1750.
Turning Radius: $10\frac{1}{2}$ ft.; **Acres Plowed in 10-hr. Day:** 10.
Motor: Buda, $4\frac{1}{4}$x$5\frac{1}{2}$, cast en bloc.
Lubrication: Force feed.
Carburetor: Kingston, $1\frac{1}{4}$-in.
Ignition System: Eisemann magneto.
Cooling System: Water.
Bearings: Timken.
Transmission: Selective gear; $1\frac{1}{2}$ to 6 m. p.h. forward and $1\frac{1}{2}$ m.p.h. reverse.
Final Drive: Combined worm and internal gears.
Belt Pulley: 12x6; 950 r.p.m and 2980 f.p.m. at normal engine speed.

MAXIM-DART "BLUE J." 13-30
Maxim Corporation, New York, N. Y.

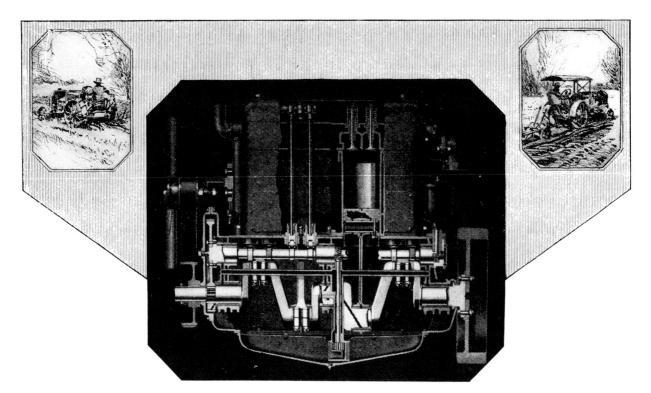

Why Chief Motors Need No Introduction

About a year ago, John G. Erd watched the first test of the first completed "Chief" Motor and gave the results of the test his approval.

At that time there were a hundred odd types of tractor motors in use—each fighting for supremacy—each blazoning its merits thru the pages of hundreds of periodicals.

Yet, without a single line of advertising, word crept thru the industry that Mr. Erd's new motor was ready. Orders came—came even before the motor's merits were exposed.

John G. Erd's twenty years of successful invention, development and production of gasoline and kerosene motors had taught the engineers of the country that what he produced was **right**.

A Kerosene Burning Valve-in-Head Motor—Backed by Written Guarantee.

When Mr. Erd began designing the "Chief" Motor he kept kerosene as fuel constantly in mind. He knew that the need of the industry was a kerosene motor that would actually develop more power with less consumption of fuel per horsepower hour.

---**The Guarantee**---

We unconditionally guarantee Chief Motors to operate successfully at all loads, under all conditions, not only on all grades of kerosene but on distillate. We guarantee this successful operation for the life of the motor.
CHIEF MOTOR CORP.

Not only did Mr. Erd produce a kerosene burning motor, but he produced with it a **written guarantee** backing it—a positive proof of his faith in the motor's ability.

Read the guarantee. Note that it says "Chief" Motors are guaranteed to operate on **all** grades of kerosene, at **all** loads, under **all** conditions. No strings to that. Just an above-board, written, s i g n e d statement, guaranteeing the performance of "Chief" Motors. You get it with every tractor that is operated by a "Chief."

Remember that **if** a motor will burn kerosene successfully, it **can** be guaranteed, **in writing**. Ask for a written guarantee with **your** motor. You are entitled to it.

A Size for Every Tractor

One standard design in three sizes—a type for every size tractor.

Write for Catalog.

Chief Motors Corporation

Port Huron   Michigan

MINNEAPOLIS THRESHING MACHINE CO.

Hopkins, Minnesota

Minneapolis, All Purpose, 15-30   1919

Traction Wheels: Four wheels with two drive wheels, 56 x 12, in rear.

No. of Plows Recommended: Two to four 14-inch.

Length: 166 in.; **Width:** 81 in.; **Height:** 70 in.; **Weight:** 6,600 lbs.

Motor: Own, $4\frac{1}{2}$ x 7, vertical L-head, 4 cylinders, cast en bloc.

Lubrication: Mechanical oil pump and splash.

Carburetor: Kingston kerosene burner.

Ignition System: K-W. high tension magneto.

Cooling System: Water, radiator, fan and water pump.

Bearings: Own make throughout.

Transmission: $2\frac{1}{2}$ to 3 m. p. h. forward.

Belt Pulley: 15 x $6\frac{1}{2}$, 750 r. p. m.

MINNEAPOLIS, ALL PURPOSE, 15-30
Minneapolis Threshing Machine Co., Hopkins, Minn.

NICHOLS & SHEPARD CO.

Battle Creek, Michigan

Nichols & Shepard 25-50   1919-1928
Nichols & Shepard 35-70   1919-1920

Traction Wheels: Four wheel type; two drive members, 69x28, in rear.

No. of Plows Recommended: Four to five 14-in.

Length: 199 in.; **Width:** 116 in.; **Height:** 113 in.; **Weight:** 19000 lbs.

Motor: Own, 2 cylinders, 9x12, cast singly.

Lubrication: Force feed system.

Carburetor: Kingston.

Ignition System: Magneto.

Cooling System: Radiator, pump and fan.

Bearings: Own make, plain.

Final Drive: Bevel gear.

Belt Pulley: 24x9; 425 r.p.m. at normal engine speed.

NICHOLS & SHEPARD 25-50
Nichols & Shepard Co., Battle Creek, Mich.

1919   241

NICHOLS & SHEPARD 35-70
Nichols & Shepard Co., Battle Creek, Mich.

Traction Wheels: Four wheels; two, 73x 32, in rear giving traction.
No. of Plows Recommended: Eight to ten 14-in.
Length: 222 in.; Width: 134 in.; Height: 124 in.; Weight: 30000 lbs.
Motor: Own make; 2 cylinders, $10\frac{1}{2}$x14, horizontal, cast singly.
Lubrication: Force feed.
Carburetor: Kingston.
Ignition System: High tension magneto.
Cooling System: Own make radiator, centrifugal pump and fan.
Bearings: Plain, own make.
Final Drive: Bevel gear.
Belt Pulley: 30x12; 375 r.p.m. at normal engine speed.

OLIVER TRACTOR CO.

Knoxville, Tennessee

Oliver "A" 15-30   1919-1920

OLIVER "A" 15-30
Oliver Tractor Co., Knoxville, Tenn.

Traction Wheels: Track type; two tracks, extending full length of machine, 11 x 60 on ground.
No. of Plows Recommended: Three to four 14-in.
Length: 135 in.; Width: 52 in.; Height: 53 in.; Weight: 6500 lbs.
Turning Radius: $5\frac{1}{2}$ ft.; Acres Plowed in 10-hr. Day: 10 to 13.
Motor: Beaver; $4\frac{1}{2}$ x 6, valve-in-head, 4 cylinders, cast en bloc.
Lubrication: Force feed and splash.
Carburetor: Bennett, $1\frac{1}{2}$-in.
Ignition System: Dixie high tension magneto, with impulse starter.
Lighting Equipment: Remy generator.
Cooling System: Water circulated by centrifugal pump.
Bearings: Hyatt roller in transmission.
Transmission: Selective gear; $1\frac{3}{4}$ to 2 1/3 m.p.h. forward and $1\frac{1}{4}$ m.p.h. reverse.
Final Drive: Spur gear to live axle.
Belt Pulley: 24 x $7\frac{1}{2}$; 450 r.p.m. and 2800 f.p.m. at normal engine speed.

"See How Simply It's Built"

Dealers are proud to show the simple, dependable, economical construction of the Parrett tractor—a tractor short on extra service-demands and long on profits. The power of its strong, sturdy motor is delivered by direct drive to the belt pulley and with simple spur gears to the wheels whether the tractor is running on high or low gear.

This elimination of power-consuming parts spells "ECONOMY" in big letters. The maximum power of the engine is delivered to draw-bar or belt with the minimum consumption of fuel.

Furthermore, this simple gearing in the Parrett Tractor is made of heat-treated hardened, cut steel with shafts mounted on high-grade, anti-friction bearings. This still further reduces the friction loss of power. But the cost is even further reduced by the use of a sensitive governor which makes it impossible to use more than enough fuel to accomplish the work in hand.

No wonder that for six years the Parrett has proved such a decided success with farm owners in all parts of the country.

The Parrett 12-25 tractor pulls three plows under ordinary conditions and will accomplish belt work equal to running a 20-in. to 24-in. separator. There may be a Parrett agency open in your territory. Write or wire today.

Parrett Tractor Co., 493 Fisher Bldg., Chicago, Ill.

PARRETT
12-25 TRACTOR
PARRETT QUALITY SPEAKS FOR ITSELF
ONE MAN · ALL PURPOSE

1919

243

PARRETT TRACTOR CO.
Chicago, Illinois

Parrett, Model E, 12-25
Parrett, Model H, 12-25

1919-1920
1919-1920

Traction Wheels: Four wheel tractor with two rear drive wheels, 60 x 10.

No. of Plows Recommended: Three 14-in.

Length: 146 in.; **Width:** 72 in.; **Height:** 67 in.; **Weight:** 5200 lbs.; **Price,** $1450.

Turning Radius: 15 ft.; **Acres Plowed in 10-hr. day:** 8 to 10.

Motor: Buda, $4\frac{1}{4}$ x $5\frac{1}{2}$; 4 cylinder, cast en bloc.

Lubrication: Circulating force feed system.

Carburetor: Kingston.

Ignition System: High tension magneto.

Cooling System: Pump and radiator with fan.

Bearings: SKF ball and Hyatt roller in transmission and plain on drive axle.

Transmission: Gears; $2\frac{3}{8}$ to $3\frac{3}{4}$ m.p.h. forward; 1.8 m.p.h. reverse.

Final Drive: Spur gears.

Belt Pulley: 12 x 7; 975 r.p.m. and 3100 feet per minute at normal engine speed.

PARRETT, MODEL E, 12-25
Parrett Tractor Co., Chicago, Ill.

Traction Wheels: Four wheel type with two traction wheels in rear, 60x10.

No. of Plows Recommended: Three 14-in.

Length: 146 in.; **Width:** 72 in.; **Height:** 67 in.; **Weight:** 5200 lbs.

Turning Radius: 11 11-12 ft.

Motor: Buda, 4 cylinders, vertical, $4\frac{1}{4}$x $5\frac{1}{2}$, cast en bloc.

Lubrication: Force feed system.

Carburetor: Kingston, $1\frac{1}{4}$-in.

Ignition System: Eisemann high tension magneto.

Cooling System: Modine radiator, fan and centrifugal pump.

Bearings: Hyatt and SKF in transmission.

Transmission: Sliding gear.

Final Drive: Enclosed gear.

Belt Pulley: 12x7½; 1000 r.p.m. and 3141.6 f.p.m at normal engine speed.

PARRETT MODEL H, 12-25
Parrett Tractor Co., Chicago, Ill.

AS SIMPLE AS A WATER WHEEL

Model HK Magneto with Impulse Starter

THE simplest form of power generation is the water wheel, which consists of a series of paddles mounted on a shaft, running in simple bearings, and requiring only an occasional oiling.

Like the water wheel, the K-W Magneto owes its reliability to this same simple construction. The windings (A) are stationary, while the paddle-like rotor (BB) revolves in ball bearings (CC) and generates the current. Like the water wheel, the internal parts of K-W Magnetos need absolutely no attention, except for an occasional oiling.

There are no moving wires, revolving windings, troublesome commutators and brushes, current collector rings, etc., in this patented K-W construction. We thereby eliminate all internal sparking and trouble, due to sliding contacts and poor connections. In K-W construction all internal connections are permanent.

Don't put up with inefficient, troublesome ignition. Insist upon

MAGNETOS fire any kind of FUEL

which require no more attention than a water wheel —magnetos that are as efficient as they are reliable. There is a type for every tractor.

Forty of America's leading tractor manufacturers use K-W Magnetos as standard. These manufacturers know that K-W "Inductor" design gives the tractor user the utmost in reliability and efficiency. These manufac-

turers know the unvarying quality of K-W and the service built into K-W Magnetos.

See that the tractor you sell is K-W equipped. K-W equipped tractors sell easier, because tractor buyers everywhere know that a K-W Magneto needs no more attention than a water wheel.

Write for a list of K-W equipped tractors.

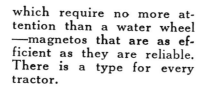

THE K-W IGNITION Co.

2845 Chester Ave. CLEVELAND, OHIO. U.S.A.

1919

245

PIONEER TRACTOR MANUFACTURING CO.
Winona, Minnesota

Pioneer 18-36

1919-1927

Traction Wheels; Four wheels, two drive members in rear, 60 x 18.

No. of Plows Recommended: Four 14-in.

Length: 168 in.; Width: 76 in.; Height: 66 in.; Weight: 6000 lbs.

Turning Radius: 13 ft.; Acres Plowed in 10-hr. day, 14.

Motor: Own, $5\frac{1}{2}$ x 6; horizontal, 4 cylinders, cast in pairs.

Lubrication: Force feed through drilled crank shaft for journal and connecting rods.

Carburetor: Kingston.

Ignition System: K-W high tension with impulse starter.

Cooling System: Forced water circulation by centrifugal pump and S-J radiator.

Bearings: Timken roller bearings throughout.

Transmission: Sliding spur, $1\frac{3}{4}$ to $4\frac{1}{2}$ m. p. h. forward; $2\frac{1}{2}$ m. p. h. reverse.

Final Drive: Spur gear, enclosed.

Belt Pulley: 14 x 7; 750 r.p.m. and 2565 feet per minute at normal engine speed.

PIONEER 18-36
Pioneer Tractor Mfg. Co., Winona, Minn.

POST TRACTOR CO.
Cleveland, Ohio

Post, Model C, 12-20

1919-1921

Traction Wheels: Four wheels, one drive wheel in front and one in rear, 28 × 12.

No. of Plows Recommended: Two 14-in.

Length: 118 in.; Width: 64 in.; Height: 60 in.; Weight: 3950 lbs.; Price: $1250.

Turning Radius: 7 ft.; Acres Plowed in 10-hr. Day: 8.

Motor: G. B. & S.; $3\frac{3}{4}$ x $4\frac{1}{4}$, vertical, 4 cylinders, cast en bloc.

Lubrication: Circulating splash.

Carburetor: Schebler, 1-in.

Ignition System: Dixie high tension magneto, with impulse starter.

Cooling System: Thermo-syphon.

Bearings: Timken throughout.

Transmission: Sliding gear; $1\frac{3}{4}$ to 5 m.p.h. forward and $1\frac{3}{4}$ m.p.h. reverse.

Final Drive: Bull gear.

Belt Pulley: 9 x $6\frac{1}{2}$; 1000 r.p.m. and 2827 f.p.m. at normal engine speed.

POST, MODEL C, 12-20
Post Tractor Co., Cleveland, O.

POWER TRUCK & TRACTOR CO.
Detroit, Michigan

Power 15-30   1919

Traction Wheels: Four wheel type; two traction wheels in rear, 60x10.

No. of Plows Recommended: Three 14-in.

Length: 148 in.; **Width:** 53 in.; **Height:** 68 in.; **Weight:** 4250 lbs.; **Price:** $1485.

Turning Radius: 8 ft.; **Acres Plowed in 10-hr. Day:** 9.

Motor: Own, 9x12, horizontal, one cylinder.

Lubrication: Force feed system.

Carburetor: Own, 2-in.

Ignition System: Kingston high tension battery.

Cooling System: Hopper.

Bearings: Bronze throughout.

Transmission: Selective gear; 3 m.p.h. forward and 1 m.p.h. reverse.

Final Drive: Internal gear.

Belt Pulley: 20x9; 500 r.p.m and 2500 f.p.m. at normal engine speed.

POWER 15-30
Power Truck & Tractor Co., Detroit, Mich.

ROYER TRACTOR CO.
Wichita, Kansas

Royer 12-25   1919-1920

Traction Wheels: Four wheel type; two traction wheels in rear, 54x12.

No. of Plows Recommended: Three 14-in.

Length: 132 in.; **Width:** 80 in.; **Height:** 96 in.; **Weight:** 4500 lbs.; **Price:** $1650.

Turning Radius: 15 ft.; **Acres Plowed in 10-hr. Day:** 10.

Motor: Erd, 4 cylinder, vertical, 4x6, cast en bloc.

Lubrication: Force feed and splash.

Carburetor: Kingston, $1\frac{1}{4}$ in.

Ignition System: Dixie high tension.

Cooling System: Perfex radiator, pump and fan.

Bearings: Babbitt and bronze.

Transmission: Friction, spur and chain, 1 to 4 m.p.h. forward and 1 to 4 m.p.h. reverse.

Final Drive: Chain.

Belt Pulley: 18x8; 600 r.p.m. and 2500 f.p.m. at normal engine speed.

ROYER 12-25
Royer Tractor Co., Wichita, Kan.

STANDARD PARTS

BOCK TAPER ROLLER BEARINGS

Well adapted to every tractor duty

THE REASON:

END THRUST OF THE ROLLER IS TAKEN BY THE BALL END WHICH ACTUALLY ROLLS WITHOUT SCRAPING

ALSO

Axles, Springs, Forgings, Brake Rods, Tubing, Tubular Parts, Gear Ring Blanks, Bands for Built-up Wheels

TWELVE PLANTS

Cleveland, Toledo, Cincinnati, Canton, St. Louis, Connersville, Pontiac, Flint, Wheeling.

THE STANDARD PARTS COMPANY

GENERAL OFFICES   CLEVELAND, OHIO

SHELBY TRACTOR & TRUCK CO.
Shelby, Ohio

Shelby 9-18

1919

SHELBY 9-18
Shelby Tractor & Truck Co., Shelby, Ohio.

Traction Wheels: Four-wheel type; two 42 x 12 traction wheels in rear.

No. of Plows Recommended: Two 14-in.

Length: 109 in.; **Width:** 66 in.; **Height:** 54 in.; **Weight:** 3600 lbs.

Turning Radius: 8 ft.; **Acres Plowed in 10-hr. Day:** 7.

Motor: Waukesha; $3\frac{3}{4}$ x $5\frac{1}{2}$, L-head, 4 cylinders, cast en bloc.

Lubrication: Force feed and splash.

Carburetor: Kingston, 1-in.

Ignition System: Dixie magneto.

Cooling System: Perfex radiator and fan.

Bearings: Timken throughout.

Transmission: Sliding gear; $1\frac{3}{4}$ to $4\frac{3}{4}$ m.p.h. forward and $1\frac{3}{4}$ m.p.h. reverse.

Final Drive: Enclosed gear.

Belt Pulley: 10 x 7; 900 r.p.m. and 2600 f.p.m. at normal engine speed.

TOPP-STEWART TRACTOR CO.
Clintonville, Wisconsin

Topp-Stewart 20-35

1919

TOPP-STEWART 20-35
Topp-Stewart Tractor Co., Clintonville, Wis.

Traction Wheels: Drives on all four wheels, 42 x 12.

No. of Plows Recommended: Four 14-in.

Length: 167 in.; **Width:** 80 in.; **Height:** 77 in.; **Weight:** 7000 lbs.; **Price:** $3000.

Turning Radius: 11 ft.

Motor: Waukesha, $4\frac{3}{4}$ x $6\frac{3}{4}$; vertical, 4 cylinders, cast in pairs.

Lubrication: Automatic splash system.

Carburetor: Kingston, $1\frac{1}{4}$-in.

Ignition System: Eisemann high tension magneto.

Cooling System: Centrifugal water pump.

Transmission: Sliding gear, $1\frac{1}{4}$ to 4 m.p.h. forward; $1\frac{3}{4}$ m.p.h. reverse.

Drive: Internal gear, four-wheel.

Belt Pulley: 14 x 8; 615 r.p.m. and 2700 f.p.m. at normal engine speed.

TORO MOTOR CO.
Minneapolis, Minnesota

Toro Motor Cultivator   1919-1927

Traction Wheels: Three wheels; two traction members in front, 42x6.
Weight: 2400 lbs.; **Price:** $875.
Motor: Le Roi, 4 cylinders, $3\frac{1}{8}$x$4\frac{1}{2}$, vertical, cast en bloc.
Carburetor: Kingston.
Ignition System: Dixie high tension magneto.
Cooling System: Shotwell radiator, pump and fan.
Transmission: Own make, selective gear; two speeds forward and one reverse.
Final Drive: Enclosed, own make.

TORO MOTOR CULTIVATOR
Toro Motor Co., Minneapolis, Minn.

TOWNSEND MANUFACTURING CO.
Janesville, Wisconsin

Townsend 15-30   1919-1924

TOWNSEND 15-30
Townsend Mfg. Co., Janesville, Wis.

Traction Wheels: Two steering wheels in front and two 56 x 18 traction wheels in rear.
No. of Plows Recommended: Three to four 14-in.
Length: 140 in.; **Width:** 78 in.; **Height:** 78 in.; **Weight:** 7000 lbs.
Turning Radius: 26 ft.
Motor: Own; low speed, 7 x 8, 2 cylinders, cast en bloc.
Lubrication: Force feed.
Carburetor: Own.
Ignition System: Dixie high tension magneto.
Cooling System: Pump and radiator.
Bearings: Own; plain babbitt throughout.
Transmission: Spur gear.
Final Drive: Spur gear.
Belt Pulley: 20 x 8; 500 r.p.m.

Tractors May Come and Tractors May Go, But–
Kerosene Tractors Are Here to Stay!

It always pays to sell well-known goods that have an established reputation—such as the old reliable Eagle Tractor. This tractor has long since passed the experimental stage—the Eagle Manufacturing Co. was incorporated 31 years ago and has been making gas engines successfully ever since—and tractors since 1910.

Eagle Tractors Are Equally Good For Belt and Traction Work

Two sizes—12-22 and 16-30—built to deliver the most dependable power in the most economical manner. Powerful motor, large and wide belt pulleys, plenty of belt clearance and a 100 point perfection friction clutch. Any man can run the Eagle and keep it in repair without help.

WRITE FOR CATALOG, prices and full particulars of our proposition to dealers.

EAGLE MFG. CO.
ESTABLISHED 1888

Appleton,   **Wisconsin**

TRACTION ENGINE CO.
Boyne City, Michigan

Heinze Four Wheel Drive

1919

Traction Wheels: Four-wheel drive, two in front and two at rear.

No. of Plows Recommended: Three to four 14-in.

Length: 126 in.; **Width:** 72 in.; **Height:** 62 in.; **Weight:** 4000 lbs.; **Price:** $2000.

Turning Radius: 6 ft.

Motor: Own; $4\frac{1}{4}$ x 6, vertical 4 cylinders, cast separately.

Lubrication: Pump and splash.

Ignition System: High tension magneto.

Starting and Lighting Equipment: Optional.

Cooling System: Cellular radiator and pump.

Transmission: Selective gear; 3 m.p.h. forward and 1 m.p.h. reverse.

Final Drive: Worm and chain.

Belt Pulley: 8 x 8; 1200 r.p.m. and 2600 f.p.m. at normal engine speed.

HEINZE FOUR WHEEL DRIVE
Traction Engine Co., Boyne City, Mich.

TURNER MANUFACTURING CO.
Port Washington, Wisconsin

Turner Simplicity 14-25

1919-1921

TURNER SIMPLICITY 14-25
Turner Manufacturing Co., Port Washington, Wis.

Traction Wheels: Two traction wheels in rear, 54x12, and two steering wheels in front.

No. of Plows Recommended: Three 14-in.

Length: 128 in.; **Width:** 68 in.; **Height:** 60 in.; **Weight:** 4300 lbs.; **Price:** $1675.

Turning Radius: 12 ft.; **Acres Plowed in 10-hr. Day:** 10.

Motor: Buda, $4\frac{1}{4}$x$5\frac{1}{2}$, L head, 4 cylinders, cast en bloc.

Lubrication: Geared pump force feed system.

Carburetor: Kingston, $1\frac{1}{4}$-in.

Ignition System: Dixie magneto.

Cooling System: Perfex radiator, fan and pump circulation.

Bearings: Hyatt roller in transmission.

Transmission: Selective gear; $1\frac{3}{4}$ to $2\frac{1}{2}$ m.p.h. forward and $1\frac{3}{4}$ m.p.h. reverse.

Final Drive: Roller.

Belt Pulley: 14x8; 600 r.p.m. and 2200 f.p.m. at normal engine speed.

252

1919

UNITED TRACTORS CO., INC.
New York, New York

Cultitractor 7-12   1919-1920

Traction Wheels: Two-wheel type; both traction, located in front, 40 x 8.

No. of Plows Recommended: One 14-in.

Length: 120 in.; **Width:** 56 in.; **Height:** 56 in.; **Weight:** 2350 lbs.; **Price:** $785.

Turning Radius: 4 ft.

Motor: Light "H;" $3\frac{1}{4}$ x $4\frac{1}{2}$, 4 cylinders, cast en bloc.

Lubrication: Pump system.

Carburetor: Kingston, $\frac{7}{8}$-in.

Ignition System: Simms magneto.

Cooling System: Rex radiator and fan.

Bearings: Timken throughout.

Final Drive: Enclosed spur gear.

Belt Pulley: 8 x 4; 600 r.p.m.

CULTITRACTOR 7-12
United Tractors Co., Inc., New York, N. Y.

VICTORY TRACTOR CO.
Greensburg, Indiana

Victory 10-20   1919

Traction Wheels: Three wheels; two rear traction wheels, 48x12.

No. of Plows Recommended: Two, 14-in.

Length: 130 in.; **Width:** 70 in.; **Height:** 56 in.; **Weight:** 3200 lbs.; **Price:** $1385.

Turning Radius: 7 2-3 ft.; **Acres Plowed in 10-hr. Day:** 9.

Motor: Gray, $3\frac{1}{2}$x5, vertical, 4 cylinders, cast en bloc.

Lubrication: Force feed from crankcase pump.

Carburetor: Carter, 1-in.

Ignition System: Dixie magneto.

Starting and Lighting Equipment: Special.

Cooling System: Jamestown radiator; thermo-syphon, fan.

Bearings: Annular ball and Hyatt roller throughout.

Transmission: Sliding gear; $1\frac{3}{4}$ to $4\frac{1}{2}$ m. p.h. forward and 2 m.p.h. reverse.

Final Drive: Worm and spur gear, live axle; enclosed.

Belt Pulley: 10x6; 1070 r.p.m. and 3000 f.p.m. at normal engine speed.

VICTORY 10-20
Victory Tractor Co., Greensburg, Ind.

1919   253

H. A. WETMORE
Sioux City, Iowa

Wetmore 12-25 1919-1928

WETMORE 12-25
H. A. Wetmore, Sioux City, Ia.

Traction Wheels: Four wheels; two drive wheels at rear, 46x10.

No. of Plows Recommended: Two 14-in.

Weight: 2900 lbs.; **Price:** $1385.

Turning Radius: 20 ft.; **Acres Plowed In 10-hr. Day:** 8 to 10.

Motor: Rutenber, $4\frac{1}{8}x5\frac{1}{2}$, vertical, 4 cylinders, cast in pairs.

Lubrication: Pressure system.

Carburetor: Kingston, $1\frac{1}{4}$-in.

Ignition System: Dixie magneto.

Cooling System: Ideal radiator, fan and centrifugal pump.

Bearings: Timken roller in rear axle.

Transmission: Sliding gear; $4\frac{3}{4}$ m.p.h. forward.

Final Drive: Internal gear.

Belt Pulley: 12x7; 800 r.p.m. at normal engine speed.

WILSON TRACTOR CO.
Peoria, Illinois

Wilson 6-12 1919

WILSON 6-12
Wilson Tractor Co., Peoria, Ill.

Traction Wheels: Three wheels; two drive members, 44x6, in rear.

Length: 160 in.; **Width:** 104 in.; **Height:** 64 in.; **Weight:** 2800 lbs.

Turning Radius 7 2-3 ft.; **Acres Cultivated in 10-hr. Day:** 15 to 24.

Motor: Le Roi, $3\frac{1}{8}x4\frac{1}{2}$, vertical, 4 cylinders, cast en bloc.

Lubrication: Splash system.

Carburetor: Kingston, $\frac{7}{8}$-in.

Ignition System: Kingston magneto.

Cooling System: Thermo-syphon.

Bearings: Hyatt roller in rear axle.

Transmission: Sliding gear; 1.25 to 3.3 m.p.h. forward and 1 m.p.h. reverse.

Final Drive: Internal gear and pinion.

Belt Pulley: 6x5; 900 r.p.m at normal engine speed.

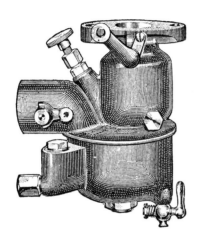
1919

1920

In 1920, 105 models of 82 makes not included in 1919 were added.

S. L. ALLEN & CO.
Philadelphia, Pennsylvania

Planet, Jr.

1920-1921

Traction Wheels: Two drive wheels, flanged. 44x7.
No. of Plows Recommended: One, 14 in.
Width: 53 in.; **Height:** 58 in.; **Weight,** 2,000 lbs.; **Price:** $1,000.
Turning Radius: 22 ft.
Motor: Le Roi, $3\frac{1}{8}x4\frac{1}{2}$, L-head, 4 cylinders, cast en bloc.
Lubrication: Splash.
Carburetor: Kingston, $\frac{7}{8}$-in.
Ignition System: Splitdorf magneto.
Cooling System: Thermo syphon.
Bearings: Babbitt.
Transmission: 2 to 3 m. p. h. forward.
Final Drive: Pinion and internal enclosed gears.
Belt Pulley: 10x4: 600 r. p. m.

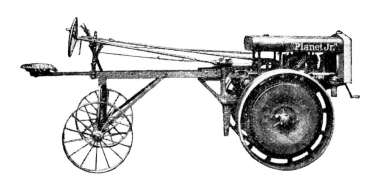

PLANET, JR.
S. L. Allen & Co., Inc., Philadelphia, Pa.

AMERICAN FARM MACHINERY CO.
Minneapolis, Minnesota

Kinkade Garden Tractor 3   1920-1921
Andrews-Kinkade 18-36   1920-1921

Traction Wheels: One wheel type; power unit circled by traction wheel, 20x5.

Length: 26 in.; **Width:** 8 in.; **Height:** 20 in.; **Weight:** 150 lbs.; **Price:** $175.

Motor: Own, 3x3 vertical, 1 cylinder.

Lubrication: Splash.

Carburetor: Optional, ¾-in.

Ignition System: Battery and coil; magneto extra.

Cooling System: Air.

Bearings: Plain special bronze.

Transmission: Gear, 1 to 2½ m.p.h. forward.

Final Drive: Internal gear.

Belt Pulley: 3½x3; 1,200 r.p.m. and 1200 feet per minute at normal engine speed.

KINKADE GARDEN TRACTOR 3
American Farm Machinery Co., Minneapolis, Minn.

ANDREWS-KINKADE 18-36
American Farm Machinery Co., Minneapolis, Minn.

Traction Wheels: Two traction wheels in rear, 54x14, and two non-drive in front, 36x6.

No. of Plows Recommended: Two to four 14-in.; **Weight:** 5000 lbs.; **Price:** $2300.

Turning Radius: 12½ ft.; **Acres Plowed in 10-Hour Day:** 10-12.

Motor: Climax, 5x6½, vertical, 4 cylinders, cast in pairs.

Lubrication: Force feed.

Carburetor: Stromberg, 1½-in.

Ignition System: Splitdorf magneto.

Cooling System: Perfex radiator, Oakes fan and centrifugal pump.

Bearings: Hyatt, Timken and plain.

Transmission: Progressive gear, 2½ to 3¼ m.p.h. forward; 2 m.p.h. reverse.

Final Drive: Enclosed internal gear.

Belt Pulley: 14x10; 800 r.p.m. and 2600 feet per minute at normal engine speed.

ATLANTIC MACHINE & MANUFACTURING CO.

Cleveland, Ohio

Merry Garden Auto Cultivator   1920-1923

MERRY GARDEN AUTO CULTIVATOR
Atlantic Machine & Manufacturing Co., Cleveland, O.

Traction Wheels: Two wheels, both traction, 20x3.
Weight: 250 lbs.; **Price:** $195.
Motor: Evinrude; 2⅝x2½, 2 cylinders.
Ignition System: Evinrude high tension magneto.
Cooling System: Thermo syphon.
Belt Pulley: 6x2; 200 r.p.m.

F. C. AUSTIN MACHINERY CO.

Chicago, Illinois

Austin 15-30   1920
Multipedal 15-30   1920
Multipedal 20-40   1920

AUSTIN 15-30
F. C. Austin Machinery Co., Chicago, Ill.

Traction Wheels: Four wheels; driving from two in rear, 54 x 12.
Motor: Buffalo, 4 cylinders, 4¾x5, cast in pairs.
Lubrication: Detroit force feed.
Carburetor: Schebler.
Ignition System: K-W high tension magneto with impulse starter.
Cooling System: Modine radiator, fan and pump.
Transmission: Own make, 1¾ to 3½ m. p.h. forward.
Belt Pulley: 10 x 6½; 965 r.p.m at normal engine speed.

Traction Wheels: Crawler type, one tracklayer on each side, 50x8.
No. of Plows Recommended: Three 14-in.
Length: 99 in.; Width: 54 in.; Height: 52 in.; Weight: 4500.
Motor: Buffalo; 4 cylinders, $4\frac{3}{4}$x5, cast in pairs.
Lubrication: Force feed system.
Carburetor: Schebler; gasoline or kerosene.
Ignition System: K-W high tension magneto with impulse starter.
Cooling System: Modine radiator, fan and pump.
Bearings: Hyatt roller.
Transmission: Own make; $2\frac{1}{2}$ to $3\frac{1}{2}$ m.p.h. forward.
Final Drive: Internal gear.
Belt Pulley: 8x6; 1000 r.p.m. at normal engine speed.

MULTIPEDAL 15-30
F.C. Austin Machinery Co., Chicago, Ill.

Traction Members: Two crawlers, one on each side, 84 x 12.
No. of Plows Recommended: Four 14-in.
Length: 151 in.; Width: 73 in.; Height: 90 in.; Weight: 10250 lbs.
Turning Radius: 12 7-12 ft.
Motor: Automatic; $5\frac{1}{2}$ x 7, vertical, 4 cylinders, cast singly.
Lubrication: Detroit, force feed.
Carburetor: Bennett.
Ignition System: K-W high tension magneto.
Cooling System: Water pump and fan.
Bearings: Hyatt rollers in transmission.
Transmission: Gear, $1\frac{3}{4}$ to $3\frac{1}{2}$ m.p.h. forward; $1\frac{3}{4}$ m.p.h. reverse.
Final Drive: Chain.
Belt Pulley: 20 x 6; 140 to 420 r.p.m. and 700 to 2100 feet per minute at normal engine speed.

MULTIPEDAL 20-40
F. C. Austin Machinery Co., Chicago, Ill.

AUTOMOTIVE CORP.

Toledo, Ohio

Automotive 12-24

1920-1921

AUTOMOTIVE 12-24
Automotive Corporation, Toledo, O.

Traction Wheels: Four wheels, with two traction, 40x12, in front.
No. of Plows Recommended: Two 14-in.
Length: 123 in.; Width; 62 in.; Height: 66 in.; Weight: 3400 lbs.; Price: $1450.
Turning Radius: 7 ft.; Acres Plowed In 10-hr. Day: 6.
Motor: Hercules, 4x$5\frac{1}{8}$; 4-cycle, 4 cylinders, cast en bloc.
Lubrication: Force feed throughout.
Carburetor: Kingston, $1\frac{1}{4}$-in.
Ignition System: Eisemann.
Cooling System: Pump, radiator and fan.
Bearings: Gurney, Hyatt and Stromberg ball and roller.
Transmission: .Own; 2.29 to 3.94 m.p.h. forward and $2\frac{1}{2}$ m.p.h. reverse.
Final Drive: Internal gear.
Belt Pulley: 10x8; 1000 r.p.m. and 2600 f.p.m. at normal engine speed.

AVERY CO.

Peoria, Illinois

Traction Wheels: Two front, 28x5; two traction in rear, 38x10.

Length: 136 in.; **Width:** 50 in.; **Weight:** 3150 lbs.

Turning Radius: 11 ft.

Motor: Own, 3x4, vertical, 6 cylinders, cast en bloc.

Lubrication: Circulating splash.

Carburetor: Kingston, ¾-in.

Ignition System: K-W high tension.

Starting Equipment: K-W impulse starter.

Cooling System: Thermo syphon.

Bearings: Hyatt roller.

Transmission: Sliding gear, 1½ to 4¼ m.p.h. forward; 1½ m.p.h. reverse.

Final Drive: Double spur gear, open.

Belt Pulley: 12x5¼; 780 r.p.m.

AVERY 6-CYLINDER
Avery Co., Peoria, Ill.

AVERY 14-28
Avery Co., Peoria, Ill.

Traction Wheels: Four wheels, driving from two rear wheels, 60x16.

No. of Plows Recommended: Three to four 14-in.

Length: 152 in.; **Width:** 68 in.; **Height:** 104 in.; **Weight:** 6800 lbs.

Turning Radius: 12 ft.

Motor: Own; 4⅝ x 7, horizontal opposed, valve in head, 4 cylinders, cast en bloc.

Lubrication: Circulating splash, gravity to gearing.

Carburetor: Kingston double, 1¼-in.

Ignition System: K-W high tension magneto.

Starting System: Impulse starter.

Cooling System: Thermo-syphon.

Bearings: Hyatt roller in differential.

Transmission: Spur gear; 2 1-3 to 3½ m.p.h. forward and 2 1-3 m.p.h. reverse.

Final Drive: Double spur gear.

Belt Pulley: 16x7; 700 r.p.m. at normal engine speed.

AVERY MOTOR PLANTER "C"
Avery Co., Peoria, Ill.

Traction Wheels: Three wheels, driving from two rear wheels, 42 x 6.
Length: 184 in.; Width: 112 in.; Height: 65 in.; Weight: 3920 lbs.
Acres Planted in 10-hr. Day: 16 to 18.
Turning Radius: 9 1-3 ft.
Motor: Own; 3 x 4, vertical, 6 cylinders, cast en bloc.
Lubrication: Circulating splash, gravity to gearing.
Carburetor: Kingston, ¾-in.
Ignition System: K-W high tension magneto.
Starting System: Impulse starter.
Cooling System: Thermo-syphon.
Bearings: Hyatt roller and Bantam ball in transmission.
Transmission: Own, enclosed and sliding gear; 1⅝ to 4 2-3 m.p.h. forward and 1⅝ m.p.h. reverse.
Final Drive: Double spur gear.
Belt Pulley: 10 x 5¼; 780 r.p.m.

Traction Wheels: Four wheels; two in rear, 42x4, giving traction.
Length: 118 in.; Width: 53 in.; Weight: 2650 lbs.
Motor: Own; vertical, 3x4, 6 cylinders, cast en bloc.
Lubrication: Circulating splash.
Carburetor: Kingston, ¾ in.
Ignition System: K-W high tension magneto.
Starting Equipment: K-W impulse starter.
Cooling System: Thermo syphon.
Bearings: Hyatt roller.
Transmission: Sliding gear, 1⅝ to 4 2-3 m.p.h. forward; 1⅝ m.p.h. reverse.
Final Drive: Double spur gear, open.

AVERY SINGLE-ROW MOTOR CULTIVATOR
Avery Co., Peoria, Ill.

AVERY MOTOR CULTIVATOR "C"
Avery Co., Peoria, Ill.

Traction Wheels: Three wheels, driving from two rear wheels, 42 x 6.
Length: 184 in.; Width: 112 in.; Height: 65 in.; Weight: 3450 lbs.
Turning Radius: 9 1-3 ft.
Acres Cultivated in 10-hr. Day: 16 to 18.
Motor: Own; 3x4, vertical, 6 cylinders, cast en bloc.
Lubrication: Circulating splash, gravity to gearing.
Carburetor: Kingston, ¾-in.
Ignition System: K-W high tension magneto.
Starting System: Impulse starter.
Cooling System: Thermo-syphon.
Bearings: Hyatt roller and Bantam ball in transmission.
Transmission: Own; enclosed sliding gear; 1⅝ to 4 2-3 m. p. h. forward and 1⅝ m. p. h. reverse.
Final Drive: Double spur gear.
Belt Pulley: 10 x 5¼; 780 r. p. m.

BACKUS TRACTOR CO.

Alton, Illinois

Baby Savidge 8-16   1920

Traction Wheels: Four wheel type; two traction in front, 68x10.

No. of Plows Recommended: Two 14-in.

Length: 156 in.; Width: 84 in.; Height: 78 in.; Weight: 3500 lbs.; Price: $1395.

Turning Radius: 7 ft.: Acres Plowed In 10-hr. Day: 8.

Motor: Victory, 3½x5. valve-in-head: 4 cylinders, cast en bloc.

Lubrication: Pump and splash system.

Carburetor: Kingston.

Ignition System: Splitdorf magneto.

Cooling System: McCord radiator and fan.

Bearings: Timken and S. K. F.

Transmission: Own. 3 m.p.h. forward: 3 m.p.h. reverse.

Final Drive: Bull gear and pinion.

Belt Pulley: 11x6; 675 r.p.m.

BABY SAVIDGE 8-16
Backus Tractor Co., Alton, Ill.

ROBERT BELL ENGINE & THRESHER CO., LTD.

Seaforth, Ontario, Canada

Imperial Superdrive 15-30   1920-1921

IMPERIAL SUPERDRIVE 15-30
Robert. Bell Engine & Thresher Co., Ltd.,
Seaforth, Ontario, Canada

Traction Wheels: Four wheels. two drive wheels in rear, 54x12.

No. of Plows Recommended: Three to four 14-in.

Length: 132 in.; Width: 72 in.; Height: 66 in.; Weight: 5,500 lbs.

Turning Radius: 11 ft.; Acres Plowed in 10-hr. Day: 10 to 12.

Motor: Own make, 5x6½, L-head. 4 cylinders, cast in pairs.

Lubrication: Force feed and splash system.

Carburetor: Stromberg. 1½-in.

Ignition System: Splitdorf high tension magneto with impulse starter.

Cooling System: Perfex cellular radiator. centrifugal pump with Oakes fan at 2,100 r.p.m.

Bearings: Hyatt roller in transmission; plain in rear axles.

Transmission: Spur gear, 2¼ to 3½ m.p.h. forward: 2 m.p.h. reverse.

Final Drive: Internal gear, enclosed.

Belt Pulley: 14x8, 600 r.p.m.

C. L. BEST GAS TRACTOR CO.
San Leandro, California

Best Tracklayer 35-60

1920-1921

Traction Wheels: Two crawlers, each 88x20.

No. of Plows Recommended: Nine 14-in.

Length: 140 in.; **Width:** 90 in.; **Height:** 76½ in.; **Weight:** 17500 lbs.; **Price:** $5,750.

Motor: Best, $6\frac{1}{2} \times 8\frac{1}{2}$, valve-in-head, 4 cylinders, cast singly.

Lubrication: Splash system.

Carburetor: Ensign.

Ignition System: Bosch.

Cooling System: Fan, pump and radiator.

Bearings: Anti-friction throughout.

Transmission: Sliding gear.

Final Drive: Internal gear.

Belt Pulley: 16x12; 650 r.p.m. and 2720 feet per minute at normal engine speed.

BEST TRACKLAYER 35-60
C. L. Best Gas Tractor Co., San Leandro, Calif.

BLEWETT TRACTOR CO.
Tacoma, Washington

Webfoot 53

1920-1921

WEBFOOT 53
Blewett Tractor Co., Tacoma, Wash.

Traction Wheels: One front wheel and two crawlers, 72x20, in rear.

No. of Plows Recommended: Six 14-in.

Length: 192 in.; **Width:** 88 in.; **Height:** 72 in.; **Weight:** 14650 lbs.; **Price:** $5,000.

Turning Radius: 12 ft.; **Acres Plowed in 10-hr. Day:** 27.

Motor: Wisconsin "M", 5¾x7, vertical, 4 cylinders, cast in pairs.

Lubrication: Force feed.

Carburetor: Schebler, model D, 1½-in.

Ignition System: K-W.

Starting & Lighting Equipment: Special.

Cooling System: Tubular radiator, circulating pump and fan.

Bearings: Hyatt roller in transmission, own babbitt in axles.

Transmission: Foote Bros., 1.69 to 3.27 m.p.h. forward; 1.37 m.p.h. reverse.

Final Drive: Enclosed internal gear.

Belt Pulley: 12x8; 800 r.p.m. and 2600 feet per minute at normal engine speed.

J. G. BOLTE & CO.
Davenport, Iowa

Bolte 20-40

1920

Tractor Wheels: Two drive wheels in rear, 54x12, with two non-drive in front, 30x5.

No. of Plows Recommended: Four 14-in.

Length: 134 in.; **Width:** 60 in.; **Height:** 100 in.; **Weight:** 5500 lbs.; **Price:** $3,000.

Turning Radius: 10 ft.; **Acres Plowed in 10-hr. Day:** 15.

Motor: Buffalo, 5½x7, L-head, 4 cylinders, cast in pairs.

Lubrication: Force feed and splash.

Carburetor: Kingston, 2-in.

Ignition System: K-W magneto with impulse starter.

Cooling System: Fan, pump and radiator.

Bearings: Hyatt roller in transmission and rear axle.

Transmission: Enclosed, 1¾ to 3½ m.p.h. forward; 1.9 to 2½ m.p.h. reverse.

Final Drive: Spur gear.

Belt Pulley: 20x10; 550 r.p.m. and 2900 feet per minute at normal engine speed.

BOLTE 20-40
J. G. Bolte & Co., Davenport, Ia.

BUCKEYE MANUFACTURING CO.
Anderson, Indiana

Trundaar 25-40

1920-1921

Traction Wheels: Crawler on each side, 66 x 15.

No. of Plows Recommended: Four 14-in.

Length: 120 in.; **Width:** 72 in.; **Height:** 58 in.; **Weight:** 8800 lbs.

Turning Radius: 12 ft.; **Acres Plowed in 10-hr. Day:** 14.

Motor: Waukesha; 5 x 6¼, vertical, 4 cylinders, cast in pairs.

Lubrication: Force feed.

Carburetor: Stromberg, 1½-in.

Ignition System: Bosch high tension magneto.

Cooling System: Radiator, pump and fan.

Bearings: Hyatt and Timken throughout.

Transmission: Sliding gear, 1½ to 2½ m.p.h. forward.

Final Drive: Spur gear.

Belt Pulley: 12x8; 900 r.p.m. and 2827 feet per minute at normal engine speed.

TRUNDAAR 25-40
Buckeye Mfg. Co., Anderson, Ind.

BULL DOG TRACTOR CO.
Oshkosh, Wisconsin

Bull Dog 30

1920

BULL DOG 30
Bull Dog Tractor Co., Oshkosh, Wis.

Traction Wheels: Four wheel drive, each wheel 42x12.
Length: 140 in.; **Width:** 77 in.; **Height:** 90 in.; **Weight:** 8,000 lbs.
Turning Radius: 13 ft.
Motor: Waukesha E. U., 5x6¼.
Carburetor: Kingston, 1½-in.
Ignition System: Eisemann high tension magneto with impulse starter.
Cooling System: Spirex radiator and centrifugal pump.
Transmission: Square-jawed clutches, 1⅛ to 5 m.p.h. forward.
Final Drive: Bull pinions.

J. I. CASE PLOW WORKS CO.
Racine, Wisconsin

Cub-Junior 15-25
Wallis 15-25

1920
1920-1922

Traction Wheels: Three wheel type with traction through two rear wheels, 48 x 12.
No. of Plows Recommended: Two and three 14-inch.
Length: 148 in.; **Width:** 61 in.; **Height:** 61½ in.; **Weight:** 3250 lbs.
Turning Radius: 10 ft.; **Acres Plowed in 10 hr. Day:** 10.
Motor: Own, 4¼ x 5¾; 4 cycle, 4 cylinders, cast enbloc with removable sleeves.
Lubrication: Positive pump and splash system.
Carburetor: Bennett, single bowl.
Ignition System: K-W high tension magneto.
Cooling System: Modine Spirex enclosed cellular type radiator.
Bearings: Hyatt roller throughout.
Transmission: Selective gears, 2½ to 3½ m. p. h. forward; 2½ m. p. h. reverse.
Final Drive: Spur gear on two live rear axles.
Belt Pulley: 18 x 5; 430 r p m. and 2030 ft. per minute at normal engine speed.

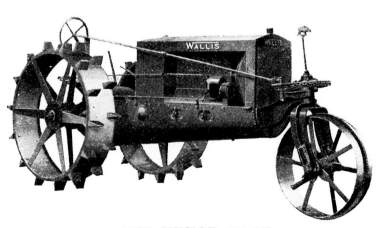

CUB-JUNIOR 15-25
J. I. Case Plow Works Co., Racine, Wis.

1920

265

Traction Wheels: Four wheels with two, built up, traction in rear, 48x12.

No. of Plows Recommended: Three 14-in.

Length: 132 in.; **Width:** 61 in.; **Height:** 65 in.; **Weight,** 2560 lbs.

Turning Radius: 10 ft.

Motor: Own, $4\frac{1}{4}$x$5\frac{3}{4}$, valve-in-head, 4 cylinders, cast en bloc.

Lubrication: Splash.

Carburetor: Bennett, $1\frac{1}{4}$-in.

Ignition System: Berling high tension magneto, with impulse starter.

Cooling System: Modine radiator, centrifugal pump and fan.

Bearings: Timken roller in rear axle.

Transmission: Selective gear, $2\frac{1}{2}$ to $3\frac{1}{2}$ m.p.h. forward; $2\frac{1}{2}$ m.p.h. reverse.

Final Drive: Spur gear.

Belt Pulley: 18x$6\frac{3}{4}$; 430 r.p.m. and 2020 feet per minute at normal engine speed.

WALLIS 15-25
J. I. Case Plow Works Co., Racine, Wis.

J. I. CASE THRESHING MACHINE CO.

Racine, Wisconsin

Case 22-40

1920-1924

CASE 22-40
J. I. Case Threshing Machine Co., Racine, Wis.

Traction Wheels: Four wheels with two drive wheels, 56 x 16, in rear.

No. of Plows Recommended: Four to five 14 in.

Length: 153 in.; **Width:** $82\frac{1}{2}$ in.; **Height:** $79\frac{1}{2}$ in.; **Weight:** 10200 lbs.; **Price:** $2700.

Turning Radius: $20\frac{1}{4}$ ft.;

Motor: Own, vertical, $5\frac{1}{2}$ x $6\frac{3}{4}$, 4 cylinders, cast in pairs.

Lubrication: Force Feed system.

Carburetor: Kingston, 2 in.

Ignition System: Bosch high tension magneto.

Cooling System: Pump, radiator and fan.

Bearing: Hyatt roller, Timken roller and New Departure ball.

Transmission: Selective sliding gear, 2.2 to 3.2 m. p. h. forward; 1.4 m. h. p. reverse.

Final Drive: Spur gear, enclosed.

Belt Pulley: $16\frac{1}{2}$ x $8\frac{1}{2}$; 850 r. p. m. and 3669 feet per minute at normal engine speed.

Leadership

CLIMAX

The "No Trouble" Engine
FOR FARM TRACTORS

—fought for and won its position in the tractor industry solely on its record of field performance.

It is now being used in **Eighteen Makes of Farm Tractors,** including four-wheel types, three-wheel types, four-drive and crawler types. If you are thinking of buying a tractor you can get the Climax Engine in the type of tractor best suited to your farm.

CLIMAX ENGINEERING CO.
Clinton, Iowa

CHASE TRACTOR CORP., LTD.
Toronto, Ontario, Canada

Chase 12-25   1920-1921

Traction Wheels. Three wheel type; two traction in rear, 48 x 12.

No. of Plows Recommended: Two to three 14-in.

Length: 144 in.; **Width:** 69 in.; **Height:** 60 in.; **Weight:** 5200 lbs.; **Price:** $1725

Turning Radius: 8 5-12 ft.

Motor: Buda, $4\frac{1}{4}$ x 5 $\frac{1}{2}$, vertical, 4 cylinders, cast en bloc.

Lubrication: Force feed.

Carburetor: Kingston, $1\frac{1}{4}$-in.

Ignition System: High tension magneto.

Cooling System: Fan, pump and radiator.

Bearings: Hyatt roller in transmission.

Transmission: Sliding gear, $1\frac{3}{4}$ to $2\frac{1}{2}$ m. p. h. forward; $1\frac{3}{4}$ m. p. h. reverse.

Final Drive: Internal bull gear.

Belt Pulley: 10 x 8; 1000 r. p. m. and 2600 ft. per minute at normal engine speed.

CHASE 12-25
Chase Tractor Corp., Ltd., Toronto, Ontario, Canada.

DART TRUCK & TRACTOR CORP.
Waterloo, Iowa

Dart "Blue J", Model TY   1920-1921

DART "BLUE J", MODEL TY
Dart Truck & Tractor Corp., Waterloo, Ia.

Traction Wheels: Four wheels, two rear drive wheel 46 x 12.

No. of Plows Recommended: Three 14-in.

Length: 125 in.; **Width:** $66\frac{1}{2}$ in.; **Height:** 65 in.; **Weight:** 4500 lbs.; **Price** $2000.

Turning Radius: 10 ft.; **Acres Plowed in 10-hr. Day:** 10.

Motor: Buda; vertical, 4 cylinders, $4\frac{1}{2}$ x 6, cast en bloc.

Lubrication: Force feed.

Carburetor: Kingston, $1\frac{1}{4}$-in.

Ignition System: Eisemann magneto.

Starting and Lighting Equipment: Special, optional.

Cooling System: Fan, radiator and centrifugal pump.

Bearings: 37 roller and ball.

Transmission: Own, selective gear; $1\frac{1}{4}$ to 6 m.p.h. forward and $1\frac{1}{4}$ m.p.h. reverse.

Final Drive: Double reduction worm and enclosed bull gear.

Belt Pulley: 12 x 6; 710 r.p.m. and 2230 f.p.m. at normal engine speed.

THE
TRACTOR OF THE FUTURE IS HERE
New Leader 16-32

A Tractor representing the greatest strides ever made in the Tractor field—combining the fundamentals proven best—avoiding the mistakes—improving the good.

Dealers have been waiting for the Leader 16-32.
Farmers are ready for it.
The factory can produce it in quantity.

Users of Tractors soon recognize superiority in construction and performance; dealers have a rare opportunity with the New Leader.

Hogs for Work — consume low-priced kerosene but give surplus power without waste. They wade in where there's work to do and **do it.**

Hogs for Work — deliver reliable power for farm work, all day, every day, year in and year out.

Over eight years of actual work on the farms of America taught the makers of the Leader to give their tractor these qualities: Overabundance of power; endurance; a cooling system that takes care of the temperature of the motor under the heaviest loads; small turning radius, meaning easier plowing; liberal use of ball and roller bearings; comfortable driving position.

All these features and many more of great interest of the tractor trade are described in our new Leader 16-32 booklet. Let us send you a copy. Write for it today.

We also make Crawler Types 18-24 and 25-40 that are recognized leaders—Crawler Tractors.

DAYTON-DOWD COMPANY
Builders of Four Wheel and Crawler
Tractors since 1911
342 YORK STREET
QUINCY, ILLINOIS, U. S. A.

RELIABLE POWER—ALL DAY—EVERY DAY

DAYTON-DOWD CO.

Quincy, Illinois

Leader, Model N, 16-32   1920-1925
Leader, Model C, 18-36   1920
Leader, Model D, 25-40   1920

LEADER, MODEL N, 16-32
Dayton-Dowd Co., Quincy, Ill.

Traction Wheels: Four wheel type, with two drive wheels, 54 x 12, in rear.
No. of Plows Recommended: Three 14-in.
Length: 134 in.; **Width:** 70 in.; **Height:** 72 in.; **Weight:** 5000 lbs.; **Price:** $1985.
Turning Radius: 15 ft.; **Acres Plowed in 10-hr. Day:** 10.
Motor: Climax, 5 x 6½, vertical, 4 cylinders, cast in pairs.
Lubrication: Force feed through drilled crankshaft.
Carburetor: Stromberg, 1½ in.
Ignition System: High tension magneto with impulse starter.
Lighting Equipment: Electric lighting equipment extra.
Cooling System: Cellular radiator, fan and pump.
Bearings: New departure in transmission; Hyatt in differential and rear axle.
Transmission: Selective; 2 ¼ to 3½ m.p.h. forward; 2½ m.p.h. reverse.
Final Drive: Forged Steel internal gear; cut teeth; inclosed in oil.
Belt Pulleys: 14 x 7; 800 r.p.m. and 2900 ft. per minute at normal engine speed.

Traction Wheels: Two crawlers, 44 x 15.
No. of Plows Recommended: Four to six 14 in.
Length: 153 in.; **Width:** 64 in.; **Height** 96 in.; **Weight:** 6500 lbs.; **Price** $2495.
Turning Radius: 26 ft.; **Acres Plowed In 10-hr. Day:** 12 to 18.
Motor: Twin City; 5 x 7½. L-Head. 4 cylinders, cast en bloc.
Lubrication: Force and splash system.
Carburetor: Holley.
Ignition System: High tension magneto with impulse starter.
Cooling System: Cellular radiator, fan and pump.
Bearings: Hyatt roller on drive axle and own die cast babbitts in transmission.
Transmission: Selective gears, 1.89 to 2.6 m.p.h. forward; 1.44 m.p.h. reverse.
Final Drive: Double Chain.
Belt Pulley: 14 x 8; 750 r.p.m. and 2750 ft. per minute at normal engine speed.

LEADER, MODEL C, 18-36
Dayton-Dowd Co., Quincy, Ill.

Traction Wheels: Two crawlers, 44 x 15.

No. of Plows Recommended: Five to Six 14-in.

Length: 153 in.; Width: 64 in.; Height: 96 in.; Weight: 6500 lbs.; Price: $2895.

Turning Radius: 26 ft.; Acres Plowed in 10-hr. Day; 18 to 20.

Motor: Doman; 6 x 7, T-head, 4 cylinders, cast singly.

Lubrication: Force.

Carburetor: Holley vaporizing.

Ignition System: High tension magneto with impulse starter.

Cooling System: Cellular radiator, fan and pump.

Bearings: Hyatt roller on drive axle and Own die cast babbitts in transmission.

Transmission: Selective gears, 1.89 to 2.6 m.p.h. forward; 1.44 m.p.h. reverse.

Final Drive: Double chain.

Belt Pulley: 14 x 8; 750 r.p.m. and 2750 feet per minute at normal engine speed.

LEADER, MODEL D, 25-40
Dayton-Dowd Co., Quincy, Ill.

DIXIELAND MOTOR TRUCK CO.

Texarkana, Texas

Dixieland, 12-25

1920-1921

Traction Wheels. Three-wheel type with two 52 x 8, in rear, giving traction.

No. of Plows Recommended: Two 14-in.

Length: 112 in.; Width, 94 in.; Height 66 in.; Weight: 2800 lbs.

Turning Radius 9 1-3 ft.; Acres Plowed in 10-hr. Day: 8.

Motor: Erd; 4 x 6, vertical, 4 cylinders, cast en bloc.

Lubrication: Force feed.

Carburetor: Stromberg, 1½ in.

Ignition System: Eisemann magneto.

Cooling System: Fan, pump and radiator.

Bearings: Roller throughout.

Transmission: Selective gear; ¾ to 5 m.p.h. forward; ¾ to 1½ m.p.h. reverse.

Final Drive: Internal gear.

Belt Pulley: 12 x 8; 900 r.p.m. and 2775 ft. per minute at normal engine speed.

DIXIELAND, 12-25
Dixieland Motor Truck Co., Texarkana, Texas.

120 H. P. LOMBARD AUTO TRACTOR-TRUCK

Speed — Six miles per hour with load of 30 tons.
Capacity as Truck—5 tons on own platform.
Capacity as Tractor — 40 to 60 tons on trailers or sleds.

LOMBARD AUTO TRACTOR-TRUCK CORP.,   480 Lexington Ave. NEW YORK CITY, N. Y.

EMERSON-BRANTINGHAM IMPLEMENT CO.
Rockford, Illinois

E-B Motor Cultivator   1920-1928

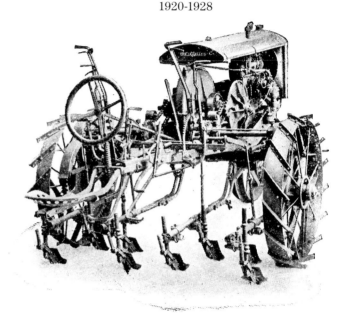

Traction Wheels: Two drive wheels, in rear, 42 in. in diameter.

Motor: LeRoi, $3\frac{1}{8}$ x $4\frac{1}{2}$, vertical, 4 cylinders, cast en bloc.

Ignition System: Splitdorf high tension magneto.

Cooling System: Thermo-Syphon.

Bearings: Hyatt roller in transmission and rear axle.

Transmission: Friction; 1 to $3\frac{1}{2}$ m.p.h. forward.

Belt Pulley: 995 to 1475 r.p.m.

E-B MOTOR CULTIVATOR
Emerson-Brantingham Implement Co., Rockford, Ill.

THE ESSEX TRACTOR CO., LTD.
Essex, Ontario, Canada

Essex 12-20   1920
Essex 15-30   1920

Traction Wheels: Four wheel type, two drive wheels in rear, 46 x 10.

No. of Plows Recommended: Two 14 in.

Turning Radius: 7 ft.

Motor: Waukesha, $3\frac{3}{4}$ x $5\frac{1}{4}$, vertical, 4 cylinders, cast en bloc.

Lubrication: Circulating and splash.

Carburetor: Kingston, $1\frac{1}{4}$-in.

Ignition System: Splitdorf high tension magneto.

Cooling System: Perfex radiator, fan and pump.

Bearings: Hyatt roller in transmission.

Transmission: 2 to 3 m.p.h. forward.

Final Drive: Open bull gear.

Belt Pulley: 10 x 7; 600 r.p.m.

ESSEX 12-20
The Essex Tractor Co., Ltd., Essex, Ontario, Canada.

ESSEX 15-30
The Essex Tractor Co., Ltd., Essex, Ontario, Canada.

Traction Wheels: Two drive wheels in rear, 52 x 10, with two non-drive in front, 34 x 6.
No. of Plows Recommended: Three 14-in.
Length: 133 in.; **Width:** 80 in.; **Height:** 68 in.; **Weight:** 5000 lbs.; **Price:** $1600.
Turning Radius: 11 ft.; **Acres Plowed in 10-hr. Day:** 8 to 11.
Motor: Waukesha, $4\frac{1}{2}$ x $6\frac{1}{4}$, vertical, 4 cylinders, cast in pairs.
Lubrication: Circulating and splash.
Carburetor: Kingston, $1\frac{1}{2}$-in.
Ignition System: Splitdorf high tension magneto.
Starting Epuipment: Impulse starter.
Cooling System: Radiator, pump and fan.
Bearings: Hyatt roller in transmission and rear axle.
Transmission: Sliding gear, 2 to 4 m.p.h. forward; $1\frac{1}{2}$ m.p.h. reverse.
Final Drive: Enclosed internal gear.
Belt Pulley: 14 x 8.

EVANS MANUFACTURING CO.

Hudson, Ohio

Evans, Model L, 18-30

1920-1921

Traction Wheels: Four wheels, two 60 x 12 driving in rear.
No. of Plows Recommended: Three to four 14-in.
Length: 160 in.; **Width:** 56 in.; **Height:** 60 in.; **Weight:** 5300 lbs.
Turning Radius: 10 ft.; **Acres Plowed in 10-hr. Day:** 12.
Motor: Buda; $4\frac{1}{2}$ x 6, vertical 4 cylinders, cast en bloc.
Lubrication: Force Feed.
Carburetor: Stromberg, $1\frac{1}{4}$.
Ignition System: Eisemann high tension magneto.
Starting and Lighting Equipment: Optional.
Cooling System: Fan, pump and radiator.
Bearings: Timken roller throughout.
Transmission: Enclosed spur gear; $2\frac{1}{2}$ to 4 m.p.h. forward and $2\frac{1}{2}$ m.p.h. reverse.
Final Drive: Internal gears.
Belt Pulley: 15 x 8; 660 r.p.m. and 26 f.p.m. at normal engine speed.

EVANS, MODEL L, 18-30
Evans Mfg. Co., Hudson, O.

FAGEOL MOTORS CO.
Oakland, California

Fageol 9-12

1920-1921

FAGEOL 9-12
Fageol Motors Co., Oakland, Cal.

Traction Wheels: Four-wheel tractor, with two driving wheels, 48 inches in diameter, in rear, with spokes extended.

No. of Plows Recommended: Two 12 or 14-in.

Length: 117 in.; **Width:** 53 in.; **Height:** 56 in.; **Weight:** 3500 lbs.; **Price:** $1525.

Turning Radius: 13½ ft.

Motor: Lycoming; 3½ x 5, vertical L-head, 4 cylinders, cast en bloc.

Lubrication: Impulse pump and splash.

Carburetor: Tillotson.

Ignition System: Splitdorf high tension magneto.

Cooling System: Ten-gal. cast radiator and centrifugal pump.

Bearings: Fafnir radial ball in transmission and Timken on drive axle.

Transmission: One speed, ¾ to 3 m.p.h. forward; same reverse.

Final Drive: Live axle and expanding clutch, 25 x 4 inches.

Belt Pulley: 8 x 6; 1250 r.p.m. and 2600 feet per minute at normal engine speed.

FARMERS TRACTOR CORP.
Oshkosh, Wisconsin

M. P.-4, 25-40

1920-1921

M. P.-4, 25-40
Farmers Tractor Corporation, Oshkosh, Wis.

Traction Wheels. Four wheels with two traction in rear, 50 x 20.

No. of Plows Recommended: Four 14-in.

Length: 140 in.; **Width,** 60 in.; **Height:** 58 in.; **Weight:** 6000 lbs.

Turning Radius: 10 ft.; **Acres Plowed in 10-hr. Day:** 12 to 18.

Motor: 5½ x 6, vertical, 4 cylinders, cast en bloc.

Lubrication: Madison-Kipp, force feed.

Carburetor: Stromberg.

Ignition System: Atwater-Kent.

Starting and Lighting Equipment: Westinghouse electric.

Cooling System: Thermo-Syphon, radiator and fan.

Bearings: SKF ball in transmission and Hyatt roller on rear axle.

Transmission: Spur gear, 2½ to 3½ m.p.h. forward; 2 1-3 m.p.h. reverse.

Final Drive: Internal, enclosed spur gear and sleeve.

Belt Pulley: 12 x 10; 800 r.p.m. and 2500 ft. per minute at normal engine speed.

FARM HORSE TRACTION WORKS
Guttenberg, Iowa

Farm Horse 18-30

1920-1921

Traction Wheels: Four wheels, with two drive members in rear, 54x24.

No. of Plows Recommended: Three and four 14-in.

Length: 120 in.; **Width:** 84 in.; **Height:** 72 in.; **Weight:** 4800 lbs.; **Price:** $1685.

Turning Radius: 20 ft.; **Acres Plowed in 10-hr. Day:** 14.

Motor: Climax; 5 x 6½, vertical, 4 cylinders, cast en bloc.

Lubrication: Force feed.

Carburetor: Wilcox-Bennett, 1½ in.

Ignition System: Sevison.

Cooling System: Water and radiator.

Bearings: American roller in transmission and own on drive axle.

Transmission: Selective gear, 2½ to 3½ m.p.h. forward; 2 m.p.h. reverse.

Final Drive: Chain.

Belt Pulley: 14 x 8; 750 r.p.m. and 2500 feet per minute at normal engine speed.

FARM HORSE 18-30
Farm Horse Traction Works, Guttenberg, Ia.

FRANKLIN TRACTOR CO.
Greenville, Ohio

Franklin 15-30

1920-1921

Traction Wheels: Two crawlers; one on each side, 100 x 8.

No. of Plows Recommended: Two to three 14-in.

Length: 86 in.; **Width:** 52 in.; **Height:** 52 in.; **Weight:** 3500 lbs.

Turning Radius: 6 ft.

Motor: Buda, 4½ x 5½, vertical, 4 cylinders, cast enbloc.

Lubrication: Force feed.

Carburetor: Bennett, 1½ in.

Ignition System: Splitdorf high tension magneto.

Cooling System: Centrifugal pump, radiator and fan.

Bearings: New Departure ball in transmission.

Transmission: Sliding gear, 2 to 4 m.p.h. forward; 1¼ m.p.h. reverse.

Final Drive: Enclosed clutch.

Belt Pulley: 10 x 6; 1000 r.p.m. and 2618 ft. per minute at normal engine speed.

FRANKLIN 15-30
Franklin Tractor Co., Greenville, O.

The Simplest Tractor in America

The nine year success of the G-O Tractor with farmers throughout the country and its steady increase in sales are due to one basic fact—it is simpler. Farmers are justly terming it the simplest tractor in America.

Because of its advanced driving mechanism, giving six speeds forward and reverse, at belt or drawbar, a boy or a hired man can handle it in any work with ease. And because it has fewer parts, all gears enclosed, and no gears or chains on the rear wheels, it stays on the job longer with less need for service.

When service is required, the G-O Guarantee and the G-O Service Plan fill every need—keep the farmer satisfied and make him a booster for his G-O and the dealer who sold it to him.

If you are located where there is no G-O dealer and are in a position to take hold of a profitable tractor business, write for the G-O proposition. Drop a postal for any information you want.

THE GENERAL ORDNANCE COMPANY
2 West 43rd Street, N. Y. City

| Western Works and Sales Office | The G-O Co. of Texas | Eastern Works |
| Cedar Rapids, Iowa | Dallas, Texas | Derby, Conn. |

GENERAL ORDNANCE CO.
New York, New York

G. O. Model G 14-27   1920-1921

G-O MODEL G 14-27
General Ordnance Co., New York, N. Y.

Traction Wheels: Four wheels, two drive wheels in rear, 46 x 10.

No. of Plows Recommended: Three 14-in.

Length: 123 in.; **Width:** 71 in.; **Height:** 60 in.; **Weight:** 4,200 lbs.; **Price:** $1485.

Turning Radius: 6½ ft.; **Acres Plowed in 10-hr. Day:** 12 to 14.

Motor: Waukesha, 4½ x 5¾, vertical L-head, 4 cylinders. cast in pairs.

Lubrication: Force feed and splash system.

Carburetor: Kingston kerosene.

Ignition System: Kingston or Eisemann high tension magneto.

Lighting Equipment: Prestolite.

Cooling System: Perfex cellular radiator pump and fan.

Bearings: SKF ball on speed change gears and plain on drive axle.

Transmission: Friction, 1½ to 3¼ m.p.h. forward; 1½ to 3¼ m.p.h. reverse.

Final Drive: Spur gear.

Belt Pulley: 10 x 6½ in.; 600-1000 r.p.m., and 2600 f.p.m. at normal engine speed.

GENERAL TRACTORS, INC.
Chicago, Illinois

Monarch, Model M, 9-16   1920
Monarch, Model N, 18-30   1920

MONARCH, MODEL M, 9-16
General Tractors, Inc., Chicago, Ill.

Traction Wheels: Two crawlers, each 60 x 8.

No. of Plows Recommended: Two 14-in.

Length: 114 in.; **Width:** 65 in; **Height:** 72 in.; **Weight:** 6,200 lbs; **Price:** $1.650.

Turning Radius: 5 ft.

Motor: Own, 4 x 4, L-head, 4 cylinders, cast en bloc.

Lubrication: Combination splash and pump system.

Carburetor: Kingston, 1-in.

Ignition System: K-W, high tension magneto.

Lighting Equipment: Supplied to order.

Cooling System Circulating water pump to radiator.

Bearings: New Departure ball. in transmission.

Transmission: Enclosed 1½ to 3½ m.p.h. forward; 2 m.p.h. reverse.

Final Drive: Gears.

Belt Pulley: 14¾x6½; 665 r.p.m. and 2600 r.p.m. at normal engine speed.

The feature of Monarch construction which is mainly responsible for unusual performance is *Monarch traction*.

Engine power is valuable on a tractor only in so far as it can be converted into actual traction. This is accomplished on Monarch Tractors by the famous endless tracks which creep over the ground with an irresistible grip that laughs at hills and makes light of loads.

Monarch tracks are made of wear resisting Manganese steel. They are covered by a broad and absolute guarantee that the tracks will not wear out.

Monarch tractors have "inbuilt" power and strength, mechanical excellence in every detail. Most important of all **traction.** There is a Monarch Tractor for every farm need.

Monarch tractors are made in the following sizes: 16-9 H. P., 20-12 H. P. and 30-18 H. P.

General Tractors Incorporated

629 Old Colony Building   Chicago, Ill.

Monarch Tractors

NEVERSLIP

Traction Wheels: Two crawlers, 66 x 12 inches.
No. of Plows Recommended: Four 14-in.
Length: 126 in.; Width: 65 in.; Height: 75 in.; Weight: 7,400 lbs.; Price: $2700.
Turning Radius: 5½ ft.
Motor: Beaver, 4¾ x 6, valve-in-head, 4 cylinders, cast en bloc.
Lubrication: Combination splash and pump system.
Carburetor: Bennett, 1½-in.
Ignition System: K-W. high tension magneto.
Lighting System: Supplied to order.
Cooling System: Circulating water pump to radiator.
Bearings: Hyatt roller in transmission.
Transmision: Enclosed, 2 to 3 m.p.h. forward; 2 m.p.h. reverse.
Final Drive: Roller chain.
Belt Pulley: 16 x 8¾; 600 r.p.m. and 2600 f.p.m at normal engine speed.

MONARCH, MODEL N, 18-30
General Tractors, Inc., Chicago, Ill.

GOOLD, SHAPLEY & MUIR CO., LTD.

Brantford, Ontario, Canada

Beaver 12-24

1920

BEAVER 12-24
Goold, Shapley & Muir Co., Ltd., Brantford, Cntario, Canada.

Traction Wheels: Four wheel type; two in rear, 60x10, giving traction.
No. of Plows Recommended: Three 14-in.
Turning Radius: 18 ft.
Motor: Waukesha, 4½x6¾, vertical, 4 cylinders.
Lubrication: Force feed and splash.
Carburetor: Kingston, 1¼-in.
Ignition System: Splitdorf magneto.
Cooling System: Perfex radiator with pump circulation.
Bearings: Roller on rear axle and ball in transmission.
Transmission: Friction, own make.
Belt Pulley: 14x8; 800 r.p.m. and 2,600 feet per minute at normal engine speed.

G & O Radiators for tractors are specially designed and built for the hardest kind of duty. Square and round fin tubular and diagonal honeycomb types.

THE G & O MFG. CO.
New Haven, Conn.

HART-PARR CO.
Charles City, Iowa

Hart-Parr 30   1920-1924

Traction Wheels: Four-wheel tractor. with two drive members, 52 x 10, in rear.
No. of Plows Recommended: Three 14-in
Length: 141 in.; **Width:** 76 in.; **Height:** 61 in.; **Weight:** 5570 lbs.; **Price:** $1395.
Turning Radius: 13 ft.; **Acres Plowed in 10-hr. Day:** 10.
Motor: Own; 6½ x 7; horizontal, 2 cylinders, cast en bloc.
Lubrication: Madison-Kipp force feed lubricator.
Carburetor: Schebler.
Ignition System: K-W or Splitdorf high tension magneto with impulse starter.
Cooling System: Forced circulation with auto type radiator and fan.
Bearings: Hyatt roller and SKF ball in transmission and own on drive axle.
Transmission: Spur gear, 2 to 3 m.p.h. forward; 1.5 m.p.h. reverse.
Final Drive: Cast internal gear.
Belt Pulley: 14x8; 750 r.p.m. and 2750 feet per minute at normal engine speed.

HART-PARR 30
Hart-Parr Co., Charles City, la.

HOLT MANUFACTURING CO.
Peoria, Illinois

"Caterpillar" 5-Ton   1920-1924
"Caterpillar" 10-Ton   1920-1924

Tractor Wheels: Two caterpillar tracks, 91 in. long and 11 in. face.
No. of Plows Recommended: Four 14-in.
Length: 124 in.; **Width:** 63 in.; **Height:** 64 in.; **Weight:** 9400 lbs.
Turning Radius: 4 ft.
Motor: Own make, 4¾x6, vertical, 4 cylinders, cast in pairs.
Lubrication: Force feed system.
Carburetor: Schebler.
Ignition System: Eisemann high tension magneto.
Lighting Equipment: Northeast generator; Williard storage battery.
Cooling System: Modine radiator, pump and fan.
Bearings: Hyatt roller and Gurney throughout.
Transmission: Own make, selective gear, 1½-3-5.7 m.p.h. forward; 1.1 m.p.h. reverse.
Final Drive: Enclosed spur gear.
Belt Pulley: 12x8½; 1000 r.p.m. and 3140 f.p.m. at normal engine speed.

"CATERPILLAR" 5-TON
Holt Mfg. Co., Peoria, Ill.

280   1920

Traction Wheels: One caterpillar track on each side giving 3160 sq. in. of traction surface.

No. of Plows Recommended: Six 14-in.

Length: 146 in.; **Width:** 80 in.; **Height:** 81 in.; **Weight:** 18600 lbs.

Turning Radius: 5 1-6 ft.

Motor: Own; vertical, $6\frac{1}{2}$x7, 4 cylinders, cast singly.

Lubrication: Force feed.

Carburetor: Kingston.

Ignition System: K-W high tension magneto.

Lighting Equipment: Own; Northeast generator; Willard storage battery.

Cooling System: Radiator, fan and centrifugal pump.

Bearings: Hyatt and Gurney throughout.

Transmission: Selective gear; 1.65-3-4.78 m.p.h. forward; 1 m.p.h. reverse.

Final Drive: Enclosed spur gear.

Belt Pulley: 14x10$\frac{1}{2}$; 850 r.p.m. and 3120 f.p.m. at normal engine speed.

"CATERPILLAR" 10-TON
Holt Mfg. Co., Peoria, Ill.

HOOSIER WHEEL CO.

Franklin, Indiana

Hoosier 20-35   1920-1921

Traction Wheels: Four wheels with two, 48x12, in rear giving traction.

No. of Plows Recommended: Three 14-in.

Length: 136 in.; **Width:** 59 in.; **Height:** 51 in.; **Weight:** 3500 lbs.; **Price $1785.**

Turning Radius: 25 ft.

Motor: Midwest, $4\frac{1}{2}$x6, vertical, 4 cylinders, cast in pairs.

Lubrication: Force feed; gear pump.

Carburetor: Stromberg, 1$\frac{1}{4}$ in.

Ignition System: Eisemann high tension magneto.

Cooling System: Hooven radiator, fan and pump.

Bearings: Hyatt roller throughout.

Transmission: Foote Bros., Model B, 2.7 to 4 m.p.h. forward; 3 m.p.h. reverse.

Final Drive: Internal gear.

Belt Pulley: 10x8; 2600 ft. per minute at normal engine speed.

HOOSIER 20-35
Hoosier Wheel Co., Franklin, Ind.

ILLINOIS SUPER-DRIVE TRACTOR

MODEL C

Here is The Master Drive 3-4 Plow Tractor of AMERICA

The Illinois Super-Drive Tractor embodies exclusive features which are highly essential to dependability, economical operation, satisfactory performance and long life.

The Illinois Super-Drive Tractor is of unit construction—no frame to twist gears and bearings out of alignment. Its powerful kerosene burning motor, "Quick change" cross-over gears admitting of various speeds from $1\frac{3}{4}$ to 6 miles per hour without increasing the speed of the motor, its long wheel base distributing 75% of the weight on the rear wheels and 25% on the front wheels, its automobile type steering device and short turning radius, its extra large roomy platform with convenient controls for the operator, its over-size radiator, extra size fan and fan belt and motometer, together with its lightness of weight and powerful traction, make it an ideal all-around Farm Tractor and Road Building Tractor.

Its driving principle known as the Illinois Planetary Live Axle Spur Gear Drive, reduces friction to the minimum, provides for perfect lubrication and delivers 20% more engine power to the drawbar. The final drive of the Illinois Super-drive Tractor applies the power through driving spiders, sixteen cushion springs and eight sturdy V-shape arms, to the rims of the drive wheels and not to the hubs or spokes.

This final drive is aptly termed by an eminent engineer "A Master Stroke of Genius." Another eminent engineer termed the Illinois Super-Drive Tractor "The Most Modern of Farm Tractors."

Write for literature.

ILLINOIS TRACTOR COMPANY
BLOOMINGTON, ILLINOIS, U. S. A.

H. L. HURST MANUFACTURING CO.
Greenwich, Ohio

Hurst Cultiplow 2-4   1920

HURST CULTIPLOW 2-4
H. L. Hurst Manufacturing Co., Greenwich, O.

Traction Wheels: Two drive wheels, 28x4.

Length: 70 in.; **Width:** 22 in.; **Height:** 38 in.; **Weight;** 600 lbs.; **Price:** $385.

Lubrication: Splash system.

Carburetor: Schebler.

Ignition System: High tension magneto.

Cooling System: Water, with pump circulation.

Final Drive: Gear and chain to axle.

J. T. TRACTOR CO.
Cleveland, Ohio

J. T. 40   1920-1921

Traction Wheels: One "Planking Tread" crawler on each side, 57 x 10.

No. of Plows Recommended: Three and four 14-in.

Length: 126 in.; **Width:** 60 in.; **Height:** 62 in.; **Weight:** 7000 lbs.; **Price:** $2800.

Turning Radius: 5 ft.; **Acres Plowed In 10-hr. Day:** 10 to 14.

Motor: Chief; 4x6, vertical valve-in-head 4 cylinders, cast en bloc.

Lubrication: Force feed.

Carburetor: "J. T." special kerosene 1¼ in.

Ignition System: Kingston high tension magneto with impulse starter.

Cooling System: Water, Perfex radiator, fan and centrifugal pump.

Bearings: Hyatt and Timken roller.

Transmission: Selective gears, 1¼ to 5 m.p.h. forward; 1¼ m.p.h. reverse.

Final Drive: Enclosed internal gears.

Belt Pulley: 10x8; 1000 r.p.m. and 2600 feet per minute at normal engine speed.

J. T. 40
J. T. Tractor Co., Cleveland, O.

1920   283

KANSAS CITY HAY PRESS & TRACTOR CO.

Kansas City, Missouri

Prairie Dog, Model D, 15-30   1920

Traction Wheels. Two non-drive wheels, 32x5, in front with two drivers, 48 x 12, in rear.

No. of Plows Recommended: Three to four 14-in.

Length: 112 in.; **Width:** 70 in.; **Height:** 62 in.; **Weight:** 3850 lbs.

Turning Radius: 11 ft.; **Acres Plowed in 10 hr. Day** 10 to 12.

Motor: Waukesha, $4\frac{1}{2}$x$6\frac{1}{4}$, 4 cycle, 4 cylinders, cast in pairs.

Lubrication: Pressure feed.

Carburetor: Bennett, $1\frac{1}{2}$ in.

Ignition System: Splitdorf high tension magneto.

Cooling System: Perfex radiator, pump and fan.

Bearings: Hyatt high duty throughout.

Transmission: $2\frac{1}{2}$ to 4 m.p.h. forward; $2\frac{1}{2}$ m.p.h. reverse.

Final Drive: Internal gear.

Belt Pulley: 20x7; 350 r.p.m. and 2000 ft. per minute at normal engine speed.

PRAIRIE DOG, MODEL D, 15-30
Kansas City Hay Press & Tractor Co.,
Kansas City, Mo.

KARDELL TRACTOR & TRUCK CO.

St. Louis, Missouri

Kardell Utility 10-20   1920-1921

Traction Wheels: Four wheels with two drive members, 38x8, in rear.

No. of Plows Recommended: Two 14-in.

Length: 118 in.; **Width:** 58 in.; **Height:** 60 in.; **Weight:** 3500 lbs.

Turning Radius: 9 ft.; **Acres Plowed In 10-hr. Day:** 10.

Motor: Wisconsin, 4x5, vertical, 4 cylinders, cast en bloc.

Lubrication: Pressure feed.

Carburetor: Carter, 1-in.

Ignition System: Splitdorf high tension magneto with impulse starter.

Cooling System: Circulating pump.

Bearings: Gurney ball in transmission and Hyatt roller in rear axle.

Transmission: Shift gears; $2\frac{1}{4}$ to $3\frac{1}{2}$ m.p.h. forward; 2 m.p.h. reverse.

Final Drive: Live axle through differential.

Belt Pulley: 10x6; 1100 r.p.m. and 2600 ft. per minute at normal engine speed.

KARDELL UTILITY 10-20
Kardell Tractor & Truck Co., St. Louis, Mo.

284   1920

KECK-GONNERMAN CO.

Mt. Vernon, Indiana

Keck-Gonnerman 15-30   1920-1921

KECK-GONNERMAN 15-30
Keck-Gonnerman Co., Mt. Vernon, Ind.

Traction Wheels: Four wheels, with two traction members, 61×12, in rear.
No. of Plows Recommended: Three 14-in.
Length: 150 in.; **Width:** 78 in.; **Height:** 96 in.; **Weight:** 6500 lbs.; **Price:** $1500
Turning Radius: 30 ft.; **Acres Plowed in 10-hr. Day:** 10.
Motor: Own: $7\frac{1}{2} \times 8$, horizontal, 2 cylinders, cast en bloc.
Lubrication: Pump and splash system.
Carburetor: Schebler.
Ignition System: Bosch high tension magneto.
Cooling System: Radiator with pump and fan.
Bearings: Cast iron in transmission and cast iron and babbitt on drive axle.
Transmission: Sliding gears, 2 to 4 m.p.h. forward; 1 m.p.h. **reverse.**
Final Drive: Spur gears.
Belt Pulley: 12×8; 650 r.p.m. and 1004 f.p.m. at normal engine speed.

KNICKERBOCKER MOTORS, INC.

Poughkeepsie, New York

Knickerbocker, Jr., Kingwood Model, 5-10   1920

Traction Wheels: Four wheels; two traction in rear, 42x10.
No. of Plows Recommended: One 14-in.
Weight: 1,700 lbs.; **Price:** $750.
Motor: LeRoi, $3\frac{1}{8} \times 4\frac{1}{2}$, vertical, 4 cylinders, cast en bloc.
Lubrication: Piston plunger pump.
Carburetor: Kingston, $1\frac{1}{4}$-in.
Ignition System: Simms high tension magneto.
Cooling System: G. & O. honeycomb radiator, Pitter fan and force pump.
Bearings: Own, plain on rear axle.
Transmission: Selective, 3 m.p.h. forward.
Final Drive: Gear and pinion.
Belt Pulley: 7x5; 1,000 r.p.m. and 1,800 feet per minute at normal engine speed.

KNICKERBOCKER, JR., KINGWOOD MODEL, 5-10
Knickerbocker Motors, Inc., Poughkeepsie, N. Y.

WILLIAM KNUDSEN

Fremont, Nebraska

Knudsen 25-40   1920-1921

KNUDSEN 25-40
Wm. Knudsen, Fremont, Neb.

Traction Wheels: Two traction, 60x18, in rear with two non-drive, 28x14, in front.

No. of Plows Recommended: Four 14-in.

Length: 144 in.; **Width:** 72 in.; **Height:** 72 in.; **Weight:** 6000 lbs.

Turning Radius: 12 ft.; **Acres Plowed In 10-hr. Day:** 20.

Motor: Own, 5 x 9, vertical, 4 cylinders, cast singly.

Lubrication: Pump and splash.

Carburetor: Own, 1¾ in.

Ignition System: Kingston high tension magneto.

Cooling System: Water or oil; thermosyphon.

Bearings: Hyatt roller in transmission.

Transmission: Spur gear; 3 to 5 m.p.h. forward; 3 m.p.h. reverse.

Final Drive: Chain and sprocket.

Belt Pulley: 24 x 8½; 500 r.p.m. and 3600 ft. per minute at normal engine speed.

THE *Cotta* CLUTCH
MULTIPLE DISC

FOUND WHERE POWER + PERFECT PERFORMANCE IS DEMANDED 365 DAYS IN THE YEAR.

4 SUPERIOR POINTS AND THERE ARE OTHERS

1 - GREATER FRICTION SURFACE, REQUIRING LESS PRESSURE, THEREBY REDUCING WEAR.

2 - EASY AND POSITIVE ENGAGEMENT, ELIMINATING GRAB

3 - 1 SIMPLE ADJUSTMENT ONLY

4 - ALWAYS RELEASES

Cotta 117-29 MORGAN ST.

GEAR CO. ROCKFORD ILLINOIS

LA CROSSE TRACTOR CO.
La Crosse, Wisconsin

La Crosse, Model M, 7-12
La Crosse, Model G, 12-24

1920-1921
1920

Traction Wheels: Four wheel type; two traction, 48x7, in rear.

No. of Plows Recommended: One 14-in.

Length: 72 in.; **Width:** 62¼ in.; **Height:** 72 in.; **Weight:** 2350 lbs.; **Price:** $750.

Turning Radius: 8½ ft.

Motor: Own, 4 x 6, twin, 2 cylinders, cast en bloc.

Lubrication: Force feed.

Carburetor: Kingston, 1¼-in.

Ignition System: Atwater-Kent.

Cooling System: Hopper.

Bearings: S.K.F. and Hess-Bright ball in transmission.

Transmission: Friction 1½ to 3 m.p.h. forward; 2 m.p.h. reverse.

Final Drive: Roller pinion.

Belt Pulley: 10 x 5; 1000 r.p.m. and 2600 ft. per minute at normal engine speed.

LA CROSSE, MODEL M, 7-12
La Crosse Tractor Co., La Crosse, Wis.

LA CROSSE, MODEL G, 12-24
La Crosse Tractor Co., La Crosse, Wis.

Traction Wheels: Four wheels, with two 56 x 10 traction members in rear.

No. of Plows Recommended: Three 14-in.

Length: 135 in.; **Width:** 82½ in.; **Height:** 62 in.; **Weight:** 3800 lbs.; **Price:** $895.

Turning Radius: 9½ ft.; **Acres Plowed in 10-hr. Day:** 10.

Motor: Own; 6 x 7, 2 cylinders, cast en bloc.

Lubrication: Madison-Kipp force feed and own non-splash in motor.

Carburetor: Kingston, 1½-in.

Ignition Systems: Atwater-Kent dry cell battery.

Cooling System: Centrifugal pump and fan.

Bearings: Machined, bronze backed, die cast babbitt in motor and Hyatt roller throughout tractor.

Transmission: S. gear; 2¾ m.p.h. forward and 2½ m.p.h. reverse.

Final Drive: R. P. internal gears.

Belt Pulley: 11 x 7½; 900 r.p.m. and 2600 f.p.m. at normal engine speed.

JOHN LAUSON MANUFACTURING CO.

New Holstein, Wisconsin

Lauson 15-30　　　　　　　　　　　　　　　1920-1921
Lauson Road Tractor 15-30　　　　　　　　　1920-1921

Traction Wheels: Four-wheel type, with two traction members in rear, 54 x 12.

No. of Plows Recommended: Three and four 14-in.

Length: 136 in.; **Width:** 74 in.; **Height:** 62 in.; **Weight:** 6000 lbs.; **Price:** $2150

Turning Radius: 20 ft.; **Acres Plowed in 10-hr. Day:** 10 to 14.

Motor: Beaver $4\frac{3}{4}$ x 6, valve-in-head, 4 cylinders, cast en bloc.

Lubrication: Splash and force feed system.

Carburetor: Kingston.

Ignition System: Splitdorf high tension magneto.

Cooling System: Perfex radiator, fan and pump.

Bearings: Hyatt roller in transmission and on drive axle.

Transmission: Selective sliding gear, $2\frac{1}{2}$ and $1\frac{3}{4}$ m.p.h. forward; $1\frac{3}{4}$ m.p.h. reverse.

Final Drive: Gears, enclosed and running in oil.

Belt Pulley: 18 x 8; 475 r.p.m. and 2300 feet per minute at normal engine speed.

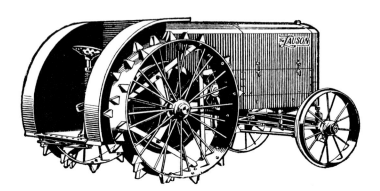

LAUSON 15-30
John Lauson Mfg. Co., New Holstein, Wis.

LAUSON ROAD TRACTOR 15-30
John Lauson Manufacturing Co., New Holstein, Wis.

Traction Wheels: Four wheels, two traction in rear, 54 x 16.

No. of Plows Recommended: Three to four 14-in.

Length: 136 in.; **Width:** 74 in.; **Height:** 62 in.; **Weight:** 9500 lbs.; **Price:** $2150.

Turning Radius: 20 ft.; **Acres Plowed in 10-hr. Day:** 10 to 14.

Motor: Beaver, $4\frac{3}{4}$ x 6, valve-in-head, 4 cylinders, cast en bloc.

Lubrication: Splash and force feed.

Carburetor: Kingston.

Ignition System: Splitdorf high tension magneto.

Cooling System: Perfex radiator, fan and pump.

Bearings: Hyatt roller in transmission and on rear axle.

Transmission: Selective sliding gear, $2\frac{1}{2}$ to $1\frac{3}{4}$ m.p.h. forward; $1\frac{3}{4}$ m.p.h. reverse.

Final Drive: Enclosed gears running in oil.

Belt Pulley: 18 x 8; 475 r.p.m. and 2300 ft. per minute at normal engine speed.

L. A. AUTO TRACTOR CO.
Los Angeles, California

"Little Bear" 4   1920-1921

"LITTLE BEAR" 4
L. A. Auto Tractor Co., Los Angeles, Cal.

Traction Wheels: Two solid web traction wheels in rear, 30 inches in height; two non-drive in front.

No. of Plows Recommended: One 14-in.

Length: 102 in.; **Width:** 58 in.; **Height:** 50 in.; **Weight:** 1,800 lbs.; **Price:** $795.

Turning Radius: 10 ft.; **Acres Plowed in 10-hr. Day:** 5 to 7.

Motor: Ford, 3¾x4, vertical, 4 cylinders, cast en bloc.

Lubrication: Gravity.

Carburetor: Holley, 1-in.

Ignition System: Ford.

Starting and Lighting Equipment: Ford.

Cooling System: Thermo syphon and Modine radiator.

Bearings: Own bronze in rear axle.

Final Drive: Bull Gear.

LEONARD TRACTOR CO.
Gary, Indiana

Leonard Four Wheel Drive 20-35   1920-1921

LEONARD FOUR WHEEL DRIVE 20-35
Leonard Tractor Co., Gary, Ind.

Traction Wheels: Drives on four wheels, front, 30 x 9, and rear, 50 x 12.

No. of Plows Recommended: Three 14-in.

Length: 144 in.; **Width:** 75 in.; **Height:** 68 in.; **Weight:** 5000 lbs.

Turning Radius: 8 1-6 ft.; **Acres Plowed in 10-hr. Day:** 10.

Motor: Buda; 4½x6, vertical, 4 cylinders, cast en bloc.

Lubrication: Force feed and splash system.

Carburetor: Zenith; 1¼-in.

Ignition System: Splitdorf high tension magneto.

Starting and Lighting Equipment: Optional.

Cooling System: Modine radiator and fan.

Bearings: SKF in transmission; Bower and SKF in axles and differentials.

Transmission: Selective gear, 2.6 to 4 m.p.h. forward; 2 m.p.h. reverse.

Final Drive: Internal gear, running in thin oil.

Belt Pulley: 16 x 8; 597 r.p.m. and 2500 feet per minute at normal engine speed.

MAGNET

"Remember The Name"

Then turn a few pages and examine its specifications.

You will find THE MAGNET TRACTOR a long step ahead with the niceties and refinements of its design.

You will find a big, husky four-cylinder motor driving the wheels through a three speed, auto type transmission, and a powerful, scientifically designed worm. You will find ball bearings throughout, forged cut and hardened gears, a system of control like you use in your automobile, a real leather upholstered spring seat, and a lot of other things that a real modern tractor should have. You will find that you will want to know this tractor better.

Send for Our Literature

MAGNET TRACTOR COMPANY
Minneapolis, Minn.

The LAUSON 15-30
DUST PROOF–ALL GEARS ENCLOSED

The extreme care used in manufacturing, the high quality of materials selected and the perfected design—without a basic change in five years, put the Lauson Tractor in a class by itself.

THE "PATTERN" TRACTOR

Tractor dealers and experts who have made a close study of what the farm tractor should be have voluntarily given the Lauson the title of the "Pattern" Tractor.

The Lauson has twenty-four Hyatt and Timken Roller Bearings—the most efficient type of bearings—at every point where wear comes.

Dealers who handle high quality farm machinery are requested to write for the Lauson Dealer Plan.

The John Lauson Manufacturing Co.
24 Monroe Street,   New Holstein, Wis.

For twenty-five years manufacturers of Lauson and Frost King Engines.

The LAUSON 15-30

LIBERTY TRACTOR CO.
Dubuque, Iowa

Klum, Model F, 16-32

1920

Traction Wheels: Four wheel type with two traction members in rear, 45x18.

No. of Plows Recommended: Three 14-in.

Length: 130 in.; Width: 69 in.; Height: 60 in.; Weight: 5200 lbs.

Turning Radius: 8 ft.

Motor: Climax, 5x6½, vertical, 4 cylinders, cast in pairs.

Lubrication: Pump and splash system.

Carburetor: Stromberg, 1½-in.

Ignition System: Splitdorf high tension magneto.

Cooling System: Hooven cellular radiator, fan and pump.

Bearings: Hyatt roller throughout.

Transmission: Enclosed gears running in oil, 2½ to 4 m.p.h. forward; 2½ m.p.h. reverse.

Final Drive: Spur gears.

Belt Pulley: 14x8; 700 r.p.m. and 2550 ft. per minute at normal engine speed.

KLUM, MODEL F, 16-32
Liberty Tractor Co., Dubuque, Ia.

LIBERTY TRACTOR CO.
Minneapolis, Minnesota

Liberty 18-32

1920-1921

Traction Wheels: Four wheel tractor with two traction wheels in rear.

No. of Plows Recommended: Four 14-inch.

Length: 144 in.; Width: 68 in.; Height: 60 in.; Weight: 5,500 lbs.

Turning Radius: 28 ft.; Acres Plowed in 10-hour day: 15.

Motor: Climax, 5 x 6½.; Vertical, 4 cylinders, cast in pairs.

Lubrication: Force feed.

Carburetor: Stromberg, 1½ in.

Ignition System: Splitdorf high tension magneto.

Cooling System: Shotwell-Johnson honeycomb radiator.

Bearings: Hyatt roller in transmission.

Transmission: Enclosed gears, 2½ to 4½ m. p. h. forward; 2½ m. p. h. reverse.

Final Drive: Spur gear.

Belt Pulley: 12 x 8; 900 r. p. m. and 2,600 feet per minute at normal engine speed.

LIBERTY 18-32
Liberty Tractor Co., Minneapolis, Minn.

MAGNET TRACTOR CO.

Minneapolis, Minnesota

Magnet 14-28   1920-1921

Traction Wheels: Four wheel type; two 48x12, tension wheels with straight line thrust on each spoke.

No. of Plows Recommended: Three 14-in.

Length: 142 in.; **Width:** 68 in.; **Height:** 62 in.; **Weight:** 4400 lbs.; **Price:** $1875.

Motor: Waukesha, $4\frac{1}{2}$x$6\frac{1}{4}$, vertical, 4 cylinders, cast in pairs.

Carburetor: Stromberg, $1\frac{1}{2}$-in.

Ignition System: Berling high tension magneto.

Cooling System: Honeycomb radiator, pump circulation.

Bearings: Hess-Bright ball in transmission.

Transmission: Sliding gear, 1.8 to 5 m.p.h. forward; 1.4 m.p.h. reverse.

Final Drive: Worm gear and live axle.

Belt Pulley: 14x7; 700 r.p.m. and 2600 ft. per minute at normal engine speed.

MAGNET 14-28
Magnet Tractor Co., Minneapolis, Minn.

MIDWEST ENGINE CO.

Indianapolis, Indiana

Midwest Utilitor $1\frac{1}{2}$-$3\frac{1}{2}$ 1920-1921

Traction Wheels. Two drive wheels, $24\frac{3}{4}$x3.

No. of Plows Recommended: One 7 or 8 in.

Length: 84 in.; **Width:** $29\frac{1}{2}$ in.; **Height:** 38 in.; **Weight:** 750 lbs.; **Price:** $380.

Turning Radius: 6 ft.; **Acres Plowed in 10-hr. Day:** 2.

Motor: Own, $3\frac{1}{2}$x$4\frac{1}{2}$ L-head, 1 cylinder.

Lubrication: Splash.

Carburetor: Kingston Model "Y," $\frac{3}{4}$-in.

Ignition System: Eisemann high tension magneto.

Cooling System: Water; thermo-syphon.

Bearings: Fafnir ball in transmission.

Transmission: Internal gear, $2\frac{1}{2}$ to 4 m.p.h. forward.

Final Drive: Internal gear.

Belt Pulley: $4\frac{1}{2}$x$3\frac{3}{4}$; 800 to 1200 r.p.m.

MIDWEST UTILITOR $1\frac{1}{2}$-$3\frac{1}{2}$
Midwest Engine Co., Indianapolis, Ind.

MINNEAPOLIS STEEL & MACHINERY CO.
Minneapolis, Minnesota

Twin City 12-20   1920-1926
Twin City 16-30   1920
Twin City 60-90   1920

TWIN CITY 12-20
Minneapolis Steel & Machinery Co., Minneapolis, Minn.

Traction Wheels: Four wheels, two in rear, 50x12, giving traction.

No. of Plows Recommended: Three 14-in.

Length: 134 in.; **Width:** 63 in.; **Height:** 63½ in.; **Weight:** 4000 lbs.

Turning Radius: 12½ ft.

Motor: Own make, 4 cylinders, 4½x6, vertical, cast en bloc.

Lubrication: Pressure feed.

Carburetor: Holley, 1¼-in.

Ignition System: Bosch high tension magneto with impulse starter.

Cooling System: Spirex radiator, centrifugal pump and fan.

Bearings: Hyatt roller in rear axle.

Transmission: Sliding gear; 2.2 to 2.9 m.p.h. forward.

Final Drive: Enclosed spur gear.

Belt Pulley: 16x6; 650 r.p.m. and 2700 f.p.m. at normal engine speed.

Traction Wheels: Four wheel tractor with two drives in rear, **54 x 12.**

No. of Plows Recommended Four **14-in.**

Length: 179 in.; **Width:** 70 in.; **Height:** 72 in.; **Weight:** 7,800 lbs.

Turning Radius: 16 ft.; **Acres Plowed in 10-hour day;** 12.

Motor: Own, 5 x 7½, L-head, 4 cylinders, cast en bloc.

Lubrication: Force and splash system.

Carburetor: Holley.

Ignition System: K-W. high tension magneto.

Starting and Lighting Equipment: Special.

Cooling System: Water circulation.

Bearings: Hyatt roller throughout.

Transmission: Spur gear, 2 to 2¾ m. p. h. forward, 2¾ m. p. h. reverse.

Final Drive: Internal bull gear.

Belt Pulley: 17 x 8, 528 r. p. m. and 2350 feet per minute at normal engine speed.

TWIN CITY 16-30
Minneapolis Steel & Machinery Co.,
Minneapolis, Minn.

TWIN CITY 60-90
Minneapolis Steel & Machinery Co.,
Minneapolis, Minn.

Traction Wheels: Four wheels with two traction members in rear, 84 x 30.

No. of Plows Recommended: Twelve 14-inch.

Length: 262 in.; Width: 114 in.; Height: 122 in.; Weight: 28,000 lbs.

Turning Radius: 24 ft. Acres Plowed In 10-hour day: 36.

Motor: Own, $7\frac{1}{4}$ x 9, L-head, 6 cylinders, cast singly.

Lubrication: Force and splash system.

Carburetor: Kingston.

Ignition System: K-W. high tension magneto.

Starting and Lighting Equipment: Special.

Cooling System: Water circulation.

Bearings: Babbitt throughout.

Transmission: Bevel and spur gear; 2 m. p. h. forward; 2 m. p. h. reverse.

Final Drive: External bull gear.

Belt Pulley: 23 x $10\frac{1}{2}$; 500 r.p.m. and 3,000 feet per minute at normal engine speed.

MINNEAPOLIS THRESHING MACHINE CO.

Hopkins, Minnesota

Minneapolis, All Purpose, 12-25	1920-1925
Minneapolis 22-44	1920-1928
Minneapolis 35-70	1920-1928

Traction Wheels: Four wheels with two drive wheels, 56 x 12, in rear.

No. of Plows Recommended: Three 14-in.

Length: 166 in.; Width: 86 in.; Height: 64 in.; Weight: 6400 lbs.

Motor: Own, $4\frac{1}{2}$ x 7, vertical L-head, 4 cylinders, cast en bloc.

Lubrication: Mechanical oil pump and splash.

Carburetor: Kingston kerosene burner.

Ignition System: K-W. high tension magneto.

Cooling System: Water, radiator, fan and water pump.

Bearings: Own make throughout.

Transmission: 2 1-5 to 3 m.p.h. forward; 2 1-5 m.p.h. reverse.

Belt Pulley: 15 x $6\frac{1}{2}$, 750 r. p. m.

MINNEAPOLIS, ALL PURPOSE, 12-25
Minneapolis Threshing Machine Co., Hopkins, Minn.

294

1920

MINNEAPOLIS 22-44
Minneapolis Threshing Machine Co., Hopkins, Minn.

Traction Wheels: Four wheels with two in rear, 66 x 20, providing traction.
No. of Plows Recommended: Four to six 14-inch.
Length: 167 in.; **Width:** 96 in.; **Height:** 110 in.; **Weight:** 12,000 lbs.
Motor: Own, 6 x 7, horizontal valve-in-head, 4 cylinders, cast in pairs.
Lubrication: Mechanical oil pump and splash.
Carburetor: Kingston kerosene burner.
Ignition System: K-W. high tension magneto.
Cooling System: Water, radiator, fan and water pump.
Bearings: Own make throughout.
Transmission: 2½ m.p.h. forward.
Belt Pulley: 20 x 10, 700 r. p. m.

Traction Wheels: Four wheel type with two rear wheels, 85 x 30, providing traction.
No. of Plows Recommended: Six to ten 14-inch.
Length: 206 in,; **Width:** 108 in.; **Height:** 136 in.; **Weight:** 22,500 lbs.
Motor: Own, 7¼ x 9, horizontal 4 cylinders, cast in pairs, valve-in-head.
Lubrication: Mechanical oil pump and splash.
Carburetor: Kingston kerosene burner.
Ignition System: K-W. high tension and batteries.
Cooling System: Water, radiator, fan and water pump.
Bearings: Own make throughout.
Transmission: 2 m.p.h. forward; 2 4-5 m.p.h. reverse.
Belt Pulley: 24 x 10¼; 500 r.p.m.

MINNEAPOLIS 35-70
Minneapolis Threshing Machine Co., Hopkins, Minn.

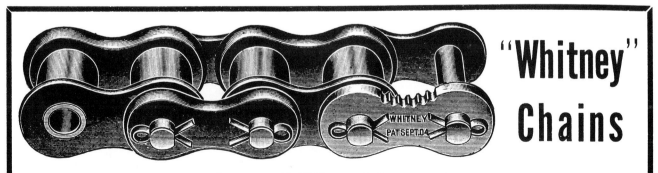

MINNESOTA-NILSON CORP.
Minneapolis, Minnesota

Nilson Junior 16-25

1920-1929

NILSON JUNIOR 16-25
Minnesota-Nilson Corp., Minneapolis, Minn.

Traction Wheels: Five - wheel tractor with three rear drive wheels, 50 x 16.
No. of Plows Recommended: Three 14-in.
Length: 148 in.; **Width:** 80 in.; **Height:** 66 in.; **Weight:** 5000 lbs.; **Price:** $1775.
Turning Radius: 16 ft.; **Acres Plowed In 10-hr. Day:** 10.
Motor: Waukesha, $4\frac{1}{4}$ x $5\frac{3}{4}$; vertical, 4 cylinders, cast in pairs.
Lubrication: Constant level splash system.
Carburetor: Kingston, $1\frac{1}{8}$-in.
Ignition System: K-W high tension magneto with impulse starter.
Cooling System: Radiator, fan and pump circulation.
Bearings: Hyatt roller throughout.
Transmission: Nilson special, $2\frac{1}{2}$ to 5 m. p. h. forward; $2\frac{1}{2}$ m. p. h. reverse.
Final Drive: Double roller chain.
Belt Pulley: 20 x 6; 360 r.p.m. and 2160 feet per minute at normal engine speed.

MONTANA TRACTOR CO.
Tinley Park, Illinois

Montana 15-20

1920-1921

Traction Wheels: Three wheels, all drive, 42x20.
Length: 158 in.; **Width:** 78 in.; **Weight:** 5000 lbs.; **Price:** $1300.
Turning Radius 10 ft.
Motor: Reliable, 6x7, horizontal, 2 cylinders, cast en bloc.
Lubrication: Detroit splash and pressure.
Carburetor: Reliable, $1\frac{1}{4}$ in.
Ignition System: Splitdorf high tension magneto.
Transmission: Own make, 2 to $3\frac{1}{2}$ m.p.h. forward; 2 m.p.h. reverse.
Final Drive: Enclosed chain.
Belt Pulley: Optional sizes.

MONTANA 15-20
Montana Tractor Co., Tinley Park, Ill.

The New Britain Tractor

THE New Britain Tractor does virtually all the work ordinarily done by a horse and a 6 H. P. stationary engine—and does it **better, faster** and **cheaper.** It is built of the best materials and is as carefully assembled as a fine motor car.

It fills a crying need on thousands of small farms, truck farms, seed farms, nurseries, orchards, vineyards and country estates. It is small, light, and economical to buy and run.

It is easy to operate—cranks in front like an automobile—no complicated levers—no letting go of handle bar to control spark. Tractor can be moved easily with clutch disengaged. Both wheels move uniformly. Rims easily removable by taking out six bolts.

Dealers who handle the New Britain Tractor are backed by the New Britain Machine Company, which for thirty-two years has been successfully building high grade machinery and fine precision tools.

A comprehensive national advertising campaign is under way. Sales and merchandising cooperation are at your call. The market waits. Write today.

THE NEW BRITAIN MACHINE CO.
New Britain, Conn.

Branches:

| New York Chicago | Philadelphia Cleveland | San Francisco Detroit |

1920

297

MOON TRACTOR CO.
San Francisco, California

Moon ''Pathmaker'' 12-25   1920

MOON "PATHMAKER" 12-25
Moon Tractor Co., San Francisco, Cal.

Traction Wheels: Two crawlers, 60 x 11.
No. of Plows Recommended: Three 14-in.
Length: 86 in.; Width: 55 in.; Height: 52 in.; Weight: 7500 lbs.; Price: $2875.
Turning Radius: 7 1-6 ft.; Acres Plowed in 10-hr. Day: 10.
Motor: Buda XTU, $4\frac{1}{4}$ x 6, vertical, 4 cylinders, cast in pairs.
Lubrication Force feed.
Carburetor: Stromberg, $1\frac{1}{2}$-in.
Ignition System: Eisemann magneto.
Cooling System: Fan, pump and radiator.
Bearings: Timken roller throughout.
Transmission: 1 to $2\frac{1}{4}$ m.p.h. forward; 1 m.p.h. reverse.
Final Drive: Worm and internal combination.
Belt Pulley: 11 x 5; 900 r.p.m. and 2600 ft. per minute at normal engine speed.

NEW BRITAIN MACHINE CO.
New Britain, Connecticut

New Britain, Model No. 1, 3-6   1920-1923
New Britain, Model N2, 3-6   1920-1924

Traction Wheels: Four wheel type; two traction, $26\frac{1}{2}$ x $3\frac{1}{2}$ or 6, in front.
No. of Plows Recommended: One 9-in.
Length: 96 in.; Width: 19 in.; Height: 36 in.; Weight: 650 lbs.; Price $400.
Acres Plowed in 10-hr. Day: $\frac{3}{4}$.
Motor: Own, $2\frac{3}{4}$ x 4, 4 cycle, 2 cylinders, cast en bloc.
Lubrication: Centrifugal-circulating and splash.
Carburetor: Kingston, $\frac{3}{4}$-in.
Ignition System: Splitdorf high tension magneto.
Cooling System: Thermo-Syphon, radiator and fan.
Bearings: Plain, bronze, roller and ball.
Transmission: Planetary, 1 to 3 m.p.h. forward.
Final Drive: Internal bull gear and pinion.
Belt Pulley: $5\frac{1}{2}$ x $4\frac{1}{4}$; 1500 r.p.m. and 2160 ft. per minute at normal engine speed.

NEW BRITAIN, MODEL No. 1, 3-6
New Britain Machine Co., New Britain, Conn.

Nilson Automatic Traction By Pull—Not Weight

Nilson Patented Lever Hitch The Harder the Pull the More Grip or Traction under Three Drive Wheels

Nilson Jr. Pulling a 4-Furrow Plow in Clover Sandy Loam Sod.

The Nilson JUNIOR Tractor will easily plow with 3-14 in. stubble bottoms practically anywhere; and with 4-14 in. bottoms where soil conditions are favorable. Write for catalog and specifications. Get our dealers contract.

MINNESOTA NILSON CORP.   **Minneapolis, Minn.**

NEW BRITAIN, MODEL N2, 3-6
New Britain Machine Co., New Britain, Conn.

Traction Wheels: Four wheel type; two traction, 32x4 or 6, in front.

No. of Plows Recommended: One 9-in.

Length: 98 in.; Width: 28 to 33 in.; Height: 39 in.; Weight: 750 lbs.; Price: $450.

Acres Plowed in 10-hr. Day: $\frac{3}{4}$.

Motor: Own, $2\frac{3}{4}$x4, 4 cycle, 2 cylinders, cast en bloc.

Lubrication: Centrifugal-circulating and splash.

Carburetor: Kingston, $\frac{3}{4}$-in.

Ignition System: Splitdorf high tension magneto.

Cooling System: Thermo-syphon, radiator and fan.

Bearings: Plain, bronze, roller and ball.

Transmission; Planetary, 1 to 2 m.p.h. forward.

Final Drive: Internal bull gear and pinion.

Belt Pulley: $5\frac{1}{2}$x$4\frac{1}{2}$; 1,500 r.p.m. and 2,160 feet per minute at normal engine speed.

OLDSMAR TRACTOR CO.

Oldsmar, Florida

Oldsmar Garden 2.5-4.6   1920-1923

Traction Wheels: Two traction, 32 x $4\frac{1}{2}$, in front, two non-drive, 24 x $4\frac{1}{2}$, in rear.

No. of Plows Recommended: One 8-in.

Length: 72 in.; Width: 36 in.; Height: 36 in.; Weight: 1100 lbs.; Price: $375.

Turning Radius: $4\frac{1}{2}$ ft.; Acres Plowed in 10-hr. Day: 1 to $1\frac{1}{2}$.

Motor: Own, 5 x $5\frac{1}{2}$, 1 cylinder.

Lubrication: Splash and gravity.

Carburetor: Schebler, Model D, $1\frac{1}{4}$-in.

Ignition System: Battery or magneto.

Cooling System: Air Cooled.

Belt Pulley: 5 x $3\frac{1}{2}$; 580 r. p. m.

OLDSMAR GARDEN 2.5-4.6
Oldsmar Tractor Co., Oldsmar, Fla.

"ONCE-OVER" TILLER CORP.

New York City, New York

"Once Over" Tiller 15-25

1920-1921

Traction Wheels: Two wheel type; both traction, 46 x 12, in front.
No. of Plows Recommended: Two 14-in.
Length: 166 in.; **Width:** 58 in.; **Height:** 60 in.; **Weight:** 4000 lbs.; **Price:** $1750.
Turning Radius: 15 ft.; **Acres Plowed In 10-hr. Day:** 9.
Motor: Buda, 4¼ x 5½, vertical, 4 cylinders, cast en bloc.
Lubrication: Force feed.
Carburetor: Bennett, 1¼-in.
Ignition System: Splitdorf magneto.
Cooling System: Shotwell-Johnson radiator, pump and fan.
Bearings: Hyatt roller in transmission.
Transmission: Sliding gear, 2½ to 4½ m.p.h. forward; 2 m.p.h. reverse.
Final Drive: Internal gear.
Belt Pulley: 10 x 7; 1000 r.p.m. at normal engine speed.

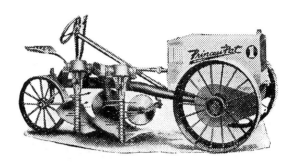

"ONCE OVER" TILLER 15-25
"Once-Over" Tiller Corporation, New York City, N. Y.

PARRETT MOTORS CORP.

Chicago, Illinois

Parrett Cultivating 6-12

1920-1921

PARRETT CULTIVATING 6-12
Parrett Motors Corp., Chicago, Ill.

Traction Wheels: Three wheels; two drive members, 44x6, in rear.
Length: 160 in.; **Width:** 104 in.; **Height:** 64 in.; **Weight:** 2800 lbs.; **Price:** $890.
Turning Radius 7 2-3 ft.; **Acres Cultivated in 10-hr. Day:** 15 to 24.
Motor: Le Roi, 3⅛x4½, vertical, 4 cylinders, cast en bloc.
Lubrication: Splash system.
Carburetor: Kingston, ⅞-in.
Ignition System: Kingston magneto.
Cooling System: Thermo-syphon.
Bearings: Hyatt roller in rear axle.
Transmission: Sliding gear; 1.25 to 3.3 m.p.h. forward and 1 m.p.h. reverse.
Final Drive: Internal gear and pinion.
Belt Pulley; 6x5; 900 r.p.m at normal engine speed.

The Plowman for Power and Performance.

For five years PLOWMAN Tractors have been conspicuous for service under average farming conditions. The very name suggests satisfaction. A PLOWMAN makes of the farmer a real plow man—able to do the work of three to four men and as many teams.

There is little saving over horses where only two plows are pulled. And tractor farmers have found that it takes more than one man to run a tractor larger than the PLOWMAN. So here is a machine that meets the test of practical farming.

Its price is right. Its work is right. And it has the backing of a skilled factory organization and a company of sound business men. Service troubles are practically unknown. You would be astonished to know how few repairs have been required for more than 1,800 machines now in operation.

SPECIFICATIONS OF PLOWMAN 15-30 H. P.

Steering Gear—Cut gear and worm enclosed in dustproof case and running in oil.

Clutch—Dry disc type, Raybestos lined and most simple to adjust.

Air Washer—Water type, no moving parts to get out of gear, giving a moist mixture, which is essential to a smooth running motor, and positively infallible in the removal of dirt, which is so essential.

Draw Bar Horse Power, 15. Belt Horse Power, 30.

Radiator—Perfex, extra size, non-freezable. Cooling—triple type, fan, pump and syphon.

Motor—Buda, Y. T. U., 4½-inch bore. 6-inch stroke. Lubrication—Full force-feed under pressure to all bearings. Cylinders—Four case en bloc.

Ignition—Highest grade high tension magneto, with fully automatic impulse starter.

Carburetor—Stromberg.

Governor—Our own special enclosed fly ball governor.

Transmission—Foote standard sliding gear, running in oil. Enclosed in dustproof case. Two speeds forward, one reverse.

Bearing—Long series Hyatt Roller Bearing throughout transmission.

Speeds—Normal driving speed, 3 m. p. h. Reverse speed, 2 m. p. h.

Gears—Drop forged, heat treated, hardened.

Clutch Shaft—11½-inch special alloy steel. Carrying clutch running between motor and transmission, capable of sustaining 6,500-pound load.

Rear Wheels—60-inch by 12-inch. Fitted with Hyatt Roller Bearings and dustproof hubs.

Front Wheels—30-inch by 5½-inch detachable rims, fitted with Hyatt Roller Bearings and dustproof hubs.

Brake—Raybestos lined band brake on differential drum.

Belt Pulley—8x14 inches, 590 r. p. m. Belt speed 2,600 feet per minute.

Front Axle—Oscillating, short turn, reinforced structural construction.

Frame—Heavy 5-inch steel channels, 11½ pounds to the foot.

Weight—Total, approximately 5,400 pounds. On front wheels, 1,980 pounds. On rear wheels, 3,420 pounds.

Turning Radius—Inside, approximately 15 feet.

Tread—Four feet 11 inches.

Dimensions—Height of tractor, 5¾ feet. Length over all, 13 feet. Width, 5½ feet. Wheel base, 99 inches.

PLOWMAN TRACTOR COMPANY

WATERLOO ∴ ∴ ∴ ∴ ∴ IOWA

PIONEER DEPENDABLE POWER
MEANS SERVICE

18  **36**

Equipped with a heavy duty $5\frac{1}{2}$x6 motor. Ample power for 28-inch Separator or four plows on intermediate speed. Three speeds, machine cut steel gears, running in oil. Timken roller bearings throughout.

PIONEER TRACTOR MFG. CO.

I Street

Winona, Minnesota

PLOWMAN TRACTOR CO.

Waterloo, Iowa

Plow Man 15-30

1920-1921

Traction Wheels: Four wheels, driven by two in rear, 60 x 10.
No. of Plows Recommended: Three or four 14-in.
Length: 156 in.; **Width:** 66 in.; **Height:** 69 in.; **Weight:** 4800 lbs.; **Price $1795.**
Turning Radius: 15 ft.
Motor: Buda; $4\frac{1}{2}$ x 6; vertical, 4 cylinders, cast en bloc.
Lubrication: Force feed.
Carburetor: Stromberg.
Ignition System: Splitdorf high tension magneto with impulse starter.
Cooling System: Perfex radiator.
Bearings: Hyatt roller throughout.
Transmission: Sliding gear; 2 to 3 m.p.h. forward.
Final Drive: Internal gear.
Belt Pulley. 14 x 8; 590 r.p.m. and 2150 feet per minute at normal engine speed.

PLOW MAN 15-30
Plowman Tractor Co., Waterloo, Ia.

1920

303

POPE MANUFACTURING CO.

Watertown, South Dakota

Dakota 15-27

DAKOTA 15-27
Pope Manufacturing Co., Watertown, S. D.

1920-1921

Traction Wheels: Open grip drive wheel, 5 feet wide.

No. of Plows Recommended: Three 14-in.

Length: 186 in.; **Width:** 89 in.; **Height:** 78 in.; **Weight:** 5700 lbs.; **Price:** $1750.

Turning Radius: 17 ft.; **Acres Plowed in 10-hr. Day:** 12.

Motor: Doman, $4\frac{3}{4}$ x 6, vertical, 4 cylinders, cast in pairs.

Lubrication: Force feed and splash.

Carburetor: Holley, $1\frac{1}{2}$ in.

Ignition System: K-W with impulse starter.

Cooling System: Water, S.-J. radiator, Oakes fan and belt driven pump.

Bearings: Own babbitt throughout.

Transmission: Own spur gear; 2.7 m.p.h. forward; 2.7 m.p.h. reverse.

Final Drive: Chains.

Belt Pulley: 14 x 7; 800 r.p.m. and 2700 feet per minute at normal engine speed.

PURITAN MACHINE CO.

Detroit, Michigan

New Elgin 12-25

NEW ELGIN 12-25
Puritan Machine Co., Detroit, Mich.

1920

Traction Wheels: Four wheels, two traction wheels in rear, 42 x 10.

No. of Plows Recommended: Two to three 14-in.

Length: 123 in.; **Width:** 60 in.; **Height:** 58 in.; **Weight:** 3400 lbs.

Turning Radius: 11 ft.; **Acres Plowed In 10-hr. Day:** 7 to 10.

Motor: Erd; 4 x 6, vertical, 4 cylinders, cast en bloc.

Lubrication: Pump and splash.

Carburetor: Kingston, $1\frac{1}{4}$ in.

Ignition System: Splitdorf high tension magneto with impulse starter.

Cooling System: Modine radiator, fan, water and pump.

Bearings: Hyatt roller in transmission and Timken roller on drive axle.

Transmission: Friction, $\frac{1}{4}$ to 6 m.p.h. forward and 1 m.p.h. reverse.

Final Drive: Double chain.

Belt Pulley: 9 x 8; 900 r.p.m.

RELIABLE TRACTOR & ENGINE CO.

Portsmouth, Ohio

Reliable 10-20   1920-1921

Traction Wheels: Four wheels, two drive, 48 x 10, in rear.

No. of Plows Recommended: Two 14-in.

Length: 116 in.; Width: 55 in.; Height: 60 in.; Weight: 3800 lbs.; Price $985.

Turning Radius: 14 ft.; Acres Plowed In 10-hr. Day: 5 to 8.

Motor: Own, 6 x 7, horizontal, 2 cylinders, cast en bloc.

Lubrication: Madison-Kipp force feed.

Carburetor: Own make, 1¼-in.

Ignition System: Splitdorf high tension magneto.

Cooling System: Centrifugal pump and water tank.

Bearings: Solid babbitt in transmission.

Transmission: Spur gear, 2 to 2½ m.p.h. forward; 2¼ m.p.h. reverse.

Final Drive: Roller pinion.

Belt Pulley: 18 x 6; 600 r.p.m. and 3000 ft. per minute at normal engine speed.

RELIABLE 10-20
Reliable Tractor & Engine Co., Portsmouth, O.

ROCK ISLAND PLOW CO.

Rock Island, Illinois

Heider Motor Cultivator 6-10   1920-1921

HEIDER MOTOR CULTIVATOR 6-10
Rock Island Plow Co., Rock Island, Ill.

Traction Wheels: Four wheels with two in rear, 46 x 5, furnishing traction.

No. of Plows Recommended: One 14-in.

Length: 132 in.; Width: 98 in.; Height: 62 in.; Weight: 2700 lbs.

Turning Radius: 8 ft.

Motor: Le Roi, 3⅛ x 4½, vertical, 4 cylinders, cast en bloc.

Lubrication: Circulating splash.

Carburetor: Kingston, ⅞-in.

Ignition System: Splitdorf high tension magneto.

Cooling System: Thermo-Syphon. Oakes fan and Perfex radiator.

Bearings: U. S. ball and Hyatt roller in transmission.

Transmission: Friction, 1½ to 3½ m.p.h. forward.

Final Drive: Bull gear.

Belt Pulley: 400 to 1000 r.p.m.

1842-
1920

This Year—
Demand
Reliable Farm Power

The world-wide shortage and high price of food demands *greater crops;* the shortage and higher cost of farm labor demands more and *more farm power*— tractors and threshers in particular.

Th shrewd farmer cannot afford to risk trouble, loss, delays and breakdowns with new or untried machines—or those rushed through the factory to meet a sped-up scale of production.

For 1920 Russell will build only a few more tractors and threshers than last year —but will *build them right*—true to "old reliable" standards of quality and service.

These are the only kind of machines you want to buy, sell or use—but get your order in early to guarantee prompt shipment.

Send now for Big New Russell Catalog.

THE RUSSELL & CO.   Massillon, O.

DISTRIBUTORS: THE RUSSELL & CO., Indianapolis, **Ind.**, Peoria, Ill. THE ARBUCKLE-RYAN CO., Toledo, O., Goshen, Ind. LINDSAY BROS., Milwaukee, Wis. GEO. O. RICH-ARDSON MACH'Y CO., St Joseph, Mo., Wichita, Kan. THE CLARK IMPLEMENT CO., Council Bluffs, Ia. THE F. P. HARBAUGH CO., St. Paul, Minn. THE MASSILLON ENGINE & THRESHER CO., Chattanooga, Tenn., Crowley, La., Stuttgart, Ark. THE A. H. AVERILL MACH. CO., San Jose, Calif., Portland, Ore., Spokane, Wash.

RUSSELL

THE OLD RELIABLE LINE

THE RUSSELL & CO.
Massillon, Ohio

Russell, Model B, 12-24	1920-1924
Russell Little Boss, Model B, 15-30	1920-1923
Russell, Model B, 20-35	1920-1923

Traction Wheels: Four wheels with two drive wheels, 53 x 12, in rear.

No. of Plows Recommended: Two to three 14-in

Length: 136 in.; **Width:** $52\frac{1}{2}$ in; **Height:** 79 in.; **Weight:** 4650 lbs.

Turning Radius: 13 ft.; **Acres Plowed in 10-hr. Day:** 8 to 10.

Motor: Waukesha, $4\frac{1}{2}$ x $5\frac{3}{4}$; vertical, 4 cylinders, cast in pairs.

Lubrication: Splash system.

Carburetor: Kingston double, $1\frac{1}{4}$-in.

Ignition System: Splitdorf magneto.

Cooling System: Modine honeycomb radiator.

Bearings: Timken roller in transmission and on drive axle.

Transmission: Gears, 2.4 to 3.7 m.p.h. forward: 2 m.p.h. reverse.

Final Drive: Gearing through rear wheels.

Belt Pulley: 12x6; 877 r.p.m., and 2755 f.p.m at normal engine speed.

RUSSELL, MODEL B, 12-24
The Russell & Co., Massillon, O.

Traction Wheels: Four wheels with two traction members, 56x10, in rear.

No. of Plows Recommended: Three to four 14-in.

Length: 145 in.; **Width:** 57 in.; **Height:** $82\frac{1}{2}$ in.; **weight:** 5590 lbs.

Turning Radius: 14 ft.; **Acres Plowed in 10-hr. Day:** 10 to 14.

Motor: Waukesha, $4\frac{3}{4}$x$6\frac{3}{4}$; L-head, 4 cylinders, cast in pairs.

Lubrication: Circulating splash.

Carburetor: Kingston, $1\frac{1}{4}$-in.

Ignition System: Splitdorf high tension magneto with impulse starter.

Cooling System: Modine honeycomb radiator.

Bearings: Babbitt.

Transmission: 2.4 to 3.7 m.p.h. forward; 2 m.p.h. reverse.

Final Drive: Spur gearing.

Belt Pulley: $12\frac{1}{2}$x7; 833 r.p.m. and 2725 f.p.m. at normal engine speed.

RUSSELL LITTLE BOSS, MODEL B, 15-30
The Russell & Co., Massillon, O.

RUSSELL, MODEL B, 20-35
The Russell & Co., Massillon, O.

Traction Wheels: Four wheel type with two rear wheels, 60 x 16, as traction members.
No. of Plows Recommended: Four to five 14-in.
Length: 162 in.; Width: 66 in.; Height: 90 in.; Weight: 7740 lbs.
Turning Radius: 15 ft.; Acres Ployed in 10-hr. Day: 14 to 18.
Motor: Model, $5\frac{1}{2}$ x 7; vertical, 4 cylinders, cast singly.
Lubrication: Force feed and splash system.
Carburetor: Kingston, $1\frac{1}{2}$-in.
Ignition System: Splitdorf magneto.
Cooling System: Perfex honeycomb radiator.
Bearings: Timken roller in transmission and on drive axle.
Transmission: Gearing, 2.4 to 3.75 m. p. h. forward; 2 m. p. h. reverse.
Final Drive: Gearing through rear wheels.
Belt Pulley: $12\frac{1}{2}$x8; 835 r.p.m., and 2732 f.p.m. at normal engine speed.

SAMSON TRACTOR CO.

Janesville, Wisconsin

Samson, Model D, "Iron Horse"   1920
Samson, Model M   1920-1922

SAMSON, MODEL D, "IRON HORSE"
Samson Tractor Co., Janesville, Wis.

Traction Wheels: Four wheel drive.
No. of Plows Recommended: One 14-in.
Turning Radius: 3 ft.
Motor: Valve-in-head, 171 cu. in. displacement, 4 cylinders.
Lubrication: Force feed and splash.
Carburetor: Zenith.
Ignition System: Simms high tension magneto.
Cooling System: Tubular radiator, rotary pump and Oakes fan.
Belt Pulley: 9x$4\frac{1}{2}$; 500 r.p.m.

Traction Wheels: Four-wheel type, with two rear wheels giving traction.
No. of Plows Recommended: Two 14-in.
Turning Radius: 13 ft.
Motor: Valve-in-head, 276 cu. in. displacement; 4 cylinders, cast en bloc.
Lubrication: Force feed.
Carburetor: Kingston.
Ignition System: Simms high tension magneto.
Cooling System: Tubular radiator, rotary pump and Oakes fan.
Final Drive: Bevel gear and pinion.
Belt Pulley: 18x6; 375 r.p.m.

SAMSON, MODEL M
Samson Tractor Co., Janesville, Wis.

SHELBY TRACTOR & TRUCK CO.
Shelby, Ohio

Shelby, Model D, 15-30

SHELBY, MODEL D, 15-30
Shelby Tractor & Truck Co., Shelby, O.

1920-1921

Traction Wheels: Four wheels; two traction, 48x12, in rear.
No. of Plows Recommended: Three 14-in.
Length: 131 in.; **Width:** 72 in.; **Height:** 60 in.; **Weight:** 4600 lbs.
Turning Radius: 7 ft. inside.
Motor: Erd, 4½x6, vertical, 4 cylinders, cast en bloc.
Lubrication: Internal pump and constant level splash.
Carburetor: Kingston, 1½-in.
Ignition System: Splitdorf high tension magneto.
Cooling System: Modine radiator, pump and fan.
Bearings: Hyatt and Timken roller.
Transmission: Sliding gear, 2¼ to 3¾ m.p.h. forward.
Final Drive: Enclosed spur gear.
Belt Pulley: 14x8; 600 to 750 r.p.m. at normal engine speed.

SOUTHERN MOTOR MANUFACTURING ASSOCIATION, LTD.

Houston, Texas

Ranger 8-16

1920-1921

Traction Wheels: Four-wheel drive; two front and two rear, 30x6½.

No. of Plows Recommended: One 14-in.

Length: 101 in.; Width: 85 in.; Height: 74 in.; Weight: 2600 lbs.; Price, $1100.

Turning Radius: 4 ft.; Acres Cultivated in 10-hr. Day: 20.

Motor: Le Roi, 3⅛x4½, vertical, 4 cylinders, cast en bloc.

Lubrication: Splash and force feed.

Carburetor: Holley, 1-in.

Ignition System: Splitdorf, high tension magneto.

Cooling System: Thermo syphon.

Bearings: Hyatt roller in transmission.

Transmission: Enclosed gear, 1½ to 2½ m.p.h. forward; 1½ to 2½ m.p.h. reverse.

Final Drive: Spur gear.

Belt Pulley: 12x4¾; 800 r.p.m. and 2500 feet per minute at normal engine speed.

RANGER 8-16
Southern Motor Mfg. Assn., Ltd., Houston, Tex.

STEARNS MOTOR MANUFACTURING CO.

Ludington, Michigan

Stearns Model Q 15-35

1920

Traction Wheels: Four wheels; two drive wheels in rear, 60 x 12.

No. of Plows Recommended: Three 14-in.

Length: 150 in.; Width: 73 in.; Height: 87 in.; Weight: 6800.

Turning Radius: 24 ft.

Motor: Own, 4¾ x 6½, vertical, valve-in-head, 4 cylinders, cast en bloc.

Lubrication: Force feed.

Carburetor: Lacharney.

Ignition System: Bosch magneto with impulse starter.

Cooling System: Perfex honeycomb radiator.

Transmission: Own spur gear.

Final Drive: Spur gears and live rear axle.

Belt Pulley: 16 x 8.

Bearings: SKF ball bearings throughout.

STEARNS MODEL Q 15-35
Stearns Motor Manufacturing Co., Ludington, Mich.

The Tapered Roller Bearing is *the* type of bearing that will function properly

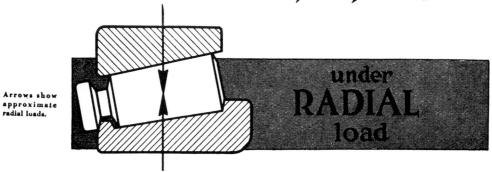

Arrows show approximate radial loads.

under RADIAL load

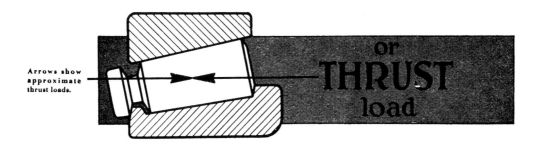

Arrows show approximate thrust loads.

or THRUST load

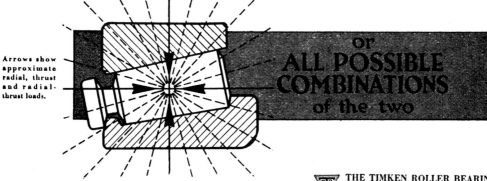

Arrows show approximate radial, thrust and radial-thrust loads.

or ALL POSSIBLE COMBINATIONS of the two

THE TIMKEN ROLLER BEARING CO.
CANTON, OHIO

PLANTS AT CANTON, OHIO; COLUMBUS, OHIO.
EUROPEAN FACTORIES, BIRMINGHAM, ENGLAND; PARIS, FRANCE.
GENERAL OFFICES, STEEL, ROLLING, AND TUBE MILLS, CANTON, OHIO.

TAPERED ROLLER BEARINGS FOR MOTOR CARS, MOTOR TRUCKS, FARM TRACTORS, FARM IMPLEMENTS, MACHINERY, AND INDUSTRIAL APPLIANCES

STANDARD PRACTICE

The use of Timken Bearings at points of hard service in the great majority of motor-vehicles is proof of leadership established on the tapered principle of design, quality of manufacture, performance on the road and service to the automotive industry.

TIMKEN BEARINGS

STINSON TRACTOR CO.
Superior, Wisconsin

Stinson Heavy Duty 18-36

1920-1921

STINSON HEAVY DUTY 18-36
Stinson Tractor Co., Superior, Wis.

Traction Wheels: Four wheels; two in rear, 60x12, furnishing traction.

No. of Plows Recommended: Four 14-in.

Width: 84 in.; **Weight:** 7100 lbs.; **Price:** $2250.

Turning Radius: 6 ft.; **Acres Plowed in 10-hr. Day:** 16.

Motor: Beaver, 4¾x6, vertical, 4 cylinders, cast en bloc.

Lubrication: Force feed and splash.

Carburetor: Kingston "L," 1⅜-in.

Ignition System: Splitdorf high tension magneto.

Cooling System: Pump, fan and radiator.

Bearings: Hyatt roller.

Transmission: Spur gear, 3 m.p.h. forward; 3 m.p.h. reverse.

Final Drive: Spur gear enclosed in oil.

Belt Pulley: 12x8; 950 r.p.m.

SUPERIOR TRACTOR CO.
Cleveland, Ohio

Superior 15-30

1920

SUPERIOR 15-30
Superior Tractor Co., Cleveland, O.

Traction Wheels: Four wheels with two traction in rear, 50x12.

No. of Plows Recommended: Three 14-in.

Length: 125 in.; **Width:** 66 in.; **Height:** 60 in.; **Weight:** 4500 lbs.

Turning Radius: 13 ft.; **Acres Plowed in 10-hr. Day:** 8.

Motor: Beaver, 4¾x6, overhead, 4 cylinders, cast en bloc.

Lubrication: Force feed and splash.

Carburetor: Kingston, 1½-in.

Ignition System: Eisemann magneto.

Cooling System: McCord radiator, centrifugal pump and Automotive fan.

Bearings: Hyatt roller throughout.

Transmission: 2.4 to 3.45 m.p.h. forward; 2.5 m.p.h. reverse.

Belt Pulley: 24x6½; 450 r.p.m. and 2600 feet per minute at normal engine speed.

TILLERMOBILE CO.
Minneapolis, Minnesota

Tillermobile 2-6   1920

Traction Wheels: Four wheels; two traction, 30x4, in front.

No. of Plows Recommended: One 8-in.

Length: 91 in.; **Width:** 22 in.; **Height:** 41 in.; **Wight:** 625 lbs.; **Price:** $385.

Motor: Veerac, 4x4, horizontal, 1 cylinder, cast singly.

Lubrication: Oil mixed with fuel.

Carburetor: Veerac, 1½-in.

Ignition System: Berling high tension magneto.

Cooling System: Air with fan.

Bearings: Bronze throughout.

Transmission: 1 to 3 m.p.h. forward.

Final Drive: Clutch in each wheel through reduction gears.

Belt Pulley: 11x4; 200 to 1200 r.p.m. at normal engine speed.

TILLERMOBILE 2-6
Tillermobile Co., Minneapolis, Minn.

TIOGA MANUFACTURING CO.
Philadelphia, Pennsylvania

Tioga "3" 15-30   1920

TIOGA "3" 15-30
Tioga Manufacturing Co., Philadelphia, Pa.

Traction Wheels: Two traction in rear 36x16; two non-drive in front, 30x5½

No. of Plows Recommended: Three to four 14-in.

Length: 120 in.; **Width:** 60 in.; **Height:** 60 in.; **Weight:** 4950 lbs.

Turning Radius: 12½ ft.

Motor: Wisconsin, $4^{1}/_{2}\times6$, vertical, 4 cylinders, cast en bloc.

Lubrication: Pressure.

Carburetor: Stromberg, 1¼-in.

Ignition System, Splitdorf high tension magneto.

Cooling System: G-O radiator, centrifugal pump and fan.

Bearings: Babbitt lined bronze, roller and ball in transmission and rear axle.

Transmission: Gear, 2.7 to 3.7 m.p.h. forward; 2.7 to 2.7 m.p.h. reverse.

Final Drive: Internal gear.

Belt Pulley: 12x7; 980 r.p.m. at normal engine speed.

TOPP-STEWART TRACTOR CO.
Clintonville, Wisconsin

Topp-Stewart 30-45

1920-1927

Traction Wheels: Drives on all four wheels, 42 x 12.

No. of Plows Recommended: Four to Six, 14-in.

Length: 167 in.; **Width:** 80 in.; **Height:** 77 in.; **Weight:** 8000 lbs.; **Price:** $3500.

Turning Radius: 11 ft.

Motor: Waukesha, $4\frac{3}{4}$ x $6\frac{3}{4}$; vertical, 4 cylinders, cast in pairs.

Lubrication: Automatic splash system.

Carburetor: Stromberg, $1\frac{1}{2}$-in.

Ignition System: Eisemann high tension magneto.

Cooling System: Centrifugal water pump.

Bearings: Hyatt roller in transmission.

Transmission: Sliding gear, $1\frac{3}{4}$ to $4\frac{1}{2}$ m.p.h. forward; $1\frac{3}{4}$ m.p.h reverse.

Final Drive: Internal gear, four-wheel.

Belt Pulley: 10 x 6 900 r.p.m. and 2600. f.p.m. at normal engine speed.

TOPP-STEWART 30-45
Topp-Stewart Tractor Co., Clintonville, Wis.

TORO MOTOR CO.
Minneapolis, Minnesota

Toro Tractor 12

1920-1924

Traction Wheels: Two traction wheels in rear, 42x6, and two non-drive wheels in front, 26x4.

No. of Plows Recommended: One 14-in.

Turning Radius: 8 1-3 ft.

Motor: Le Roi, $3\frac{1}{8}$x$4\frac{1}{2}$, vertical, 4 cylinders, cast en bloc.

Lubrication: Constant splash.

Carburetor: Kingston.

Ignition System: Eisemann high tension magneto.

Cooling System: Thermo-syphon, B. & W. radiator and fan.

Bearings: Own make on rear axle.

Transmission: Sliding gear.

Final Drive: Enclosed spur gear.

Belt Pulley: 8x$4\frac{1}{2}$; 1200 r.p.m. and 2500 feet per minute at normal engine speed.

TORO TRACTOR 12
Toro Motor Co., Minneapolis, Minn.

TRAYLOR ENGINEERING & MANUFACTURING CO.
Cornwells, Pennsylvania

Traylor 6-12

1920-1929

Traction Wheels: Four wheels, with two 38x10, traction members in rear.
No. of Plows Recommended: One 14-in.
Turning Radius: 11 ft.
Motor: Le Roi, $3\frac{1}{8}$x$4\frac{1}{2}$, vertical, 4 cylinders, cast en bloc.
Lubrication: Force feed.
Carburetor: Kingston, 1-in.
Ignition System: Splitdorf magneto.
Cooling System: Thermo-syphon. Pitter fan and G. & O. radiator.
Tranmission: Sliding Gear.
Final Drive: Open bull gear.
Belt Pulley: 8x$6\frac{1}{4}$; 1000 r.p.m.

TRAYLOR 6-12
Traylor Engineering & Mfg. Co., Cornwells, Pa.

TRIUMPH TRUCK & TRACTOR CO.
Kansas City, Missouri

Triumph 16-30

1920

Traction Wheels: Four wheels; two in rear, 48x10, giving traction.
No. of Plows Recommended: Three to four 14-in.
Weight: 4400 lbs.
Acres Plowed in 10-hr. Day: 8-10.
Motor: Climax, 5x$6\frac{1}{2}$, vertical, 4 cylinders, cast in pairs.
Lubrication: Pressure and pump.
Carburetor: Kingston, Model L .
Ignition System: Splitdorf high tension magneto.
Cooling System: Honeycomb radiator, fan and pump.
Bearings: Hyatt roller in transmission.
Transmission: Nuttall sliding gears, $2\frac{1}{2}$ to 4 m.p.h. forward; 2 m.p.h reverse.
Belt Pulley: 12x8; 820 r.p.m. and 2600 feet per minute at normal engine speed.

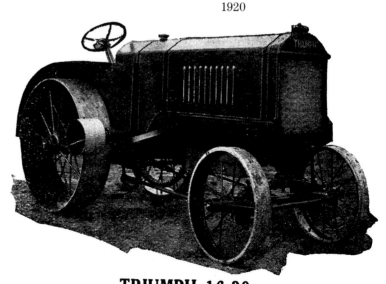

TRIUMPH 16-30
Triumph Truck & Tractor Co., Kansas City, Mo.

Sterling Spark Plugs

Here's a Sterling Plug for Motor Car, Truck or Tractor

There is a new snap, a new power you will notice as soon as you install Sterling Tractor Spark Plugs in your engine.

These new, strongly-built plugs deliver a spark as sharp and swift as a flash of lighting.

You will note the quick, ready response of your motor with these plugs feeding current to the cylinders. Sterling Tractor Plugs were developed to meet the extreme demands imposed by the high-heat producing internal combustion motors of farm tractors.

Naturally, since they meet the rigorous requirements of tractor engines, they cannot but be all the better for passenger car or motor truck.

Sterling Tractor Plugs are built for heavy duty—for gruelling, continuous work. The porcelain core is unusually heavy; the combustion chamber is extra deep, and the one-piece monel metal electrode will not warp.

Remember, Sterling plugs are separable and easily cleaned. Simply unscrew the gland nut, take out the porcelain core and wipe off the carbon. You can clean Sterling plugs clean.

Progressive garages and supply dealers everywhere sell and endorse Sterling plugs.

The Lockwood-Ash Motor Company

2060 Douglas Street.   Jackson, Michigan.

VICTORY TRACTOR CO.

Greensburg, Indiana

Victory 9-18

1920-1921

Traction Wheels: Three wheels; two rear traction wheels, 48x12.

No. of Plows Recommended: Two, 14-in.

Length: 130 in.; Width: 70 in.; Height: 56 in.; Weight: 3200 lbs.; Price: $1385.

Turning Radius: 7 2-3 ft.; Acres Plowed in 10-hr. Day: 9.

Motor: Gray, $3\frac{1}{2}$x5, vertical, 4 cylinders, cast en bloc.

Lubrication: Force feed from crankcase pump.

Carburetor: Carter, 1-in.

Ignition System: Splitdorf magneto.

Starting and Lighting Equipment: Special.

Cooling System: Jamestown radiator; thermo-syphon, fan.

Bearings: Annular ball and Hyatt roller throughout.

Transmission: Sliding gear; $1\frac{3}{4}$ to $4\frac{1}{2}$ m.p.h. forward and 2 m.p.h. reverse.

Final Drive: Worm and spur gear, live axle; enclosed.

Belt Pulley: 10x6; 1070 r.p.m. and 3000 f.p.m. at normal engine speed.

VICTORY 9-18
Victory Tractor Co., Greensburg, Ind.

VIM TRACTOR CO.

Schleisingerville, Wisconsin

Vim 10-20

1920-1921

VIM 10-20
Vim Tractor Co., Schleisingerville, Wis.

Traction Wheels: Four-wheel type; two in rear, 48x12, giving traction.

No. of Plows Recommended: Two to three 14-in.

Length: 120 in.; Width: 72 in.; Height: 66 in.; Weight: 3300 lbs.; Price: $1650.

Turning Radius: 12 ft.; Acres Plowed In 10-hr. Day: 10.

Motor: Waukesha, $3\frac{3}{4}$x$5\frac{1}{2}$, vertical, 4 cylinders, cast en bloc.

Lubrication: Splash and force feed.

Carburetor: Bennett, 1-in.

Ignition System: Splitdorf magneto with impulse starter.

Cooling System: Perfex radiator, centrifugal pump and Oakes fan.

Bearings: Gurney ball throughout.

Transmission: Sliding gear, 2 1-3 to 5 m.p.h. forward; 5 m.p.h. reverse.

Final Drive: Internal gear.

Belt Pulley: 10x$6\frac{1}{2}$; 1050 r.p.m. and 2500 feet per minute at normal engine speed.

WHARTON MOTORS CO.

Dallas, Texas

Wharton 12-22   1920-1923

WHARTON 12-22
Wharton Motors Co., Dallas, Tex.

Traction Wheels: Three-wheel pull. One in front, 30x8, and two in rear, 60x8.
Weight: 3680 lbs.
Turning Radius: 7 ft.
Motor: Erd, 4x6, vertical, 4 cylinders.
Lubrication: Force feed and splash.
Carburetor: Kingston, $1\frac{1}{4}$-in.
Ignition System: Splitdorf high tension magneto with impulse starter.
Cooling System: Perfex cellular radiator, fan and pump.
Bearings: Hyatt and Timken roller throughout.
Transmission: Sliding gear, $1\frac{1}{2}$ to 4 m.p.h. forward.
Belt Pulley: 12x8; 850 r.p.m.

WHEAT TRACTOR & TILLER CO., INC.

Buffalo, New York

Wheat Tractor 12-24   1920-1921

Traction Wheels: Two, 48x12, rear traction wheels and two front.
No. of Plows Recommended: Three 14-in.
Length: 132 in.; **Width:** 58 in.; **Height:** 58 in.; **Weight:** 4250 lbs.
Turning Radius: $9\frac{1}{2}$ ft.; **Acres Plowed In 10-hr. Day:** 10.
Motor: Erd; 4x6, valve-in-head, 4 cylinders, cast en bloc.
Lubrication: Force feed and splash.
Carburetor: Kingston, $1\frac{3}{4}$-in.
Ignition System: Splitdorf high tension magneto.
Cooling System: Fan, pump and radiator.
Bearings: Timken and Hyatt roller and New Departure ball.
Transmission: Foote Sliding gear; $2\frac{1}{2}$ to 4 m.p.h. forward; 2 7-10 m.p.h. reverse.
Final Drive: Internal spur gear.
Belt Pulley: 18x7; 600 r.p.m. and 2800 feet per minute at normal engine speed.

WHEAT TRACTOR 12-24
Wheat Tractor & Tiller Co., Inc., Buffalo, N. Y.

WHITNEY TRACTOR CO.
Upper Sandusky, Ohio

Whitney 9-18

WHITNEY 9-18
Whitney Tractor Co., Upper Sandusky, O.

1920-1922

Traction Wheels: Four wheels, driving from two rear wheels, 48 x 10.
No. of Plows Recommended: Two 14- in.
Length: 123 in.; **Width:** 56 in.; **Height:** 58½ in.; **Weight:** 3000 lbs: **Price:** $1175.
Turning Radius: 11 ft.; **Acres Plowed in 10-hr. Day:** 5 to 6.
Motor: Gile, 5½ x 6½.; opposed, two cylinders, cast separately.
Lubrication: Madison-Kipp force feed system.
Carburetor: Bennett.
Ignition System: Splitdorf high tension magneto.
Cooling System: Circulating pump and radiator.
Bearings: Timken roller in speed change gears and own roller on drive axle.
Transmission: Selective, 1½ to 4 m. p. h. forward; 3 m. p. h. reverse.
Final Drive: Chain.
Belt Pulley: 11 x 6¾; 750-900 r. p. m. and 2100 ft. per minute at normal engine speed.

WICHITA MOTORS CO.
Wichita Falls, Texas

Wichita 20-30

Traction Wheels: Four-wheel type; two traction in rear, 48x12.
No. of Plows Recommended: Three to four 14-in.
Length: 140 in.; **Width:** 74 in.; **Weight:** 5500 lbs.; **Price:** $2500.
Turning Radius: 25 ft.
Motor: 4½x6, valve-in-head, 4 cylinders, cast en bloc.
Lubrication: Pressure and splash.
Carburetor: Ensign, 1½-in.
Ignition System: High tension magneto.
Cooling System: Water and pump.
Transmission: 2½ to 3½ m.p.h. forward; 1.7 m.p.h. reverse.
Final Drive: Spur gear on axle.
Belt Pulley: 10x6; 950 r.p.m. and 2450 feet per minute at normal engine speed.

1920-1921

WICHITA 20-30
Wichita Motors Co., Wichita Falls, Tex.

WISCONSIN FARM TRACTOR CO.

Sauk City, Wisconsin

Wisconsin 16-30

1920-1921

Traction Wheels: Four wheels with two traction members, 52 x 12, in rear.
No. of Plows Recommended: Three or four 14 in.
Length: 130 in.; **Width:** 66 in.; **Height:** 65 in.; **Weight:** 5440 lbs.; **Price,** $2250.
Turning Radius: 11 ft.; **Acres Plowed in 10 hr. Day:** 10 to 15.
Motor: Climax, 5 x 6½; L-head, 4 cylinders, cast in pairs.
Lubrication: Force feed system.
Carburetor: Stromberg, 1½-in.
Ignition System: Eisemann high tension magneto.
Cooling System: Water, Perfex radiator and fan.
Bearings: Hyatt roller in transmission and babbitt on drive axle.
Transmission: Enclosed 2⅓ to 4 m. p. h. forward; 2 m. p. h. reverse.
Final Drive: Spur gear.
Belt Pulley: 16 x 8; 630 r. p. m. and 2640 ft. per minute at normal engine speed.

WISCONSIN 16-30
Wisconsin Farm Tractor Co., Sauk City, Wis.

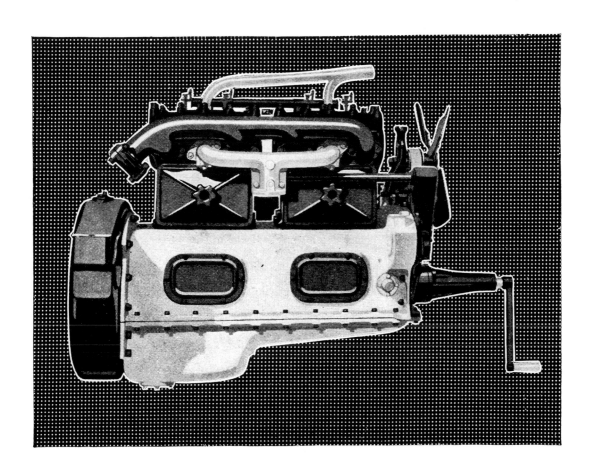

High Torque Motors

(Maximum Pull at Usable Speed)

Lower the Cost of Operation

The design of a tractor or truck engine has vital bearing on the cost of operation.

The high torque principle of construction embodied in Waukesha Motors proves this conclusively by performance.

For high torque (twistability) means maximum pull at usable speed—and usable speed means the number of revolutions a minute best suited to economy of operation and upkeep.

Also the ability of Waukesha High Torque Motors, to function perfectly, under conditions that would stall the average engine, offers assurance against costly delay.

An ever increasing number of tractor and truck manufacturers are specifying Waukesha Motors as their chief unit.

And in the same ratio, more and more users of automotive equipment, are demanding Waukesha High Torque Motors in the tractors or trucks they buy.

WAUKESHA MOTOR COMPANY, WAUKESHA, WIS.

The World's Largest Builders of Truck and Tractor Motors Exclusively   95

1921

In 1921, 44 models of 32 makes not included in 1920 were added.

AGRIMOTOR MANUFACTURING CO.

Wichita, Kansas

Mid-West 9-18   1921

MID-WEST 9-18
Agrimotor Mfg. Co., Wichita, Kan.

Traction Wheels: Four wheels, **two drive** wheels in rear, 56 x 10.

No. of Plows Recommended: Two or three 14-in.

Length: 128 in.; **Width:** 72 in.; **Height:** 61 in.; **Weight:** 3275 lbs.

Turning Radius 13 ft.

Motor: Gile, 5 x 6½, horizontal, 2 cylinders, cast singly.

Lubrication: Madison-Kipp force feed lubricator.

Carburetor: Kingston.

Ignition System: Atwater-Kent battery.

Cooling System: Perfex radiator, pump and fan.

Transmission: Sliding spur gear, 2¼ m.p.h.

Final Drive: Roller pinion.

Belt Pulley: 12 x 6, 750 r.p.m.

ALLIS-CHALMERS MANUFACTURING CO.
Milwaukee, Wisconsin

Allis-Chalmers Model B 6-12   1921
Allis-Chalmers 12-20   1921

ALLIS-CHALMERS MODEL B 6-12
Allis-Chalmers Mfg. Co., Milwaukee, Wis.

Traction Wheels: Two drive wheels in front.
Turning Radius: 9 11/12 ft.
Motor: Le Roi, $3\frac{1}{8} \times 4\frac{1}{2}$, vertical, 4 cylinders, cast en bloc.
Carburetor: Kingston, $\frac{7}{8}$-in.
Ignition System: High tension magneto.
Cooling System: Thermo-syphon.
Transmission: Own make; variable speeds.
Final Drive: Enclosed bevel gear.
Belt Pulley: $10 \times 5\frac{1}{2}$; 2,600 feet per minute at normal engine speed.

Traction Wheels: Four wheels; two in rear, 46 x 12, furnishing traction.
No. of Plows Recommended: Two to three 14-in.
Length: 135 in.; **Width:** 66 in.; **Height:** 62 in.; **Weight:** 4,400 lbs.
Turning Radius: 12 ft.
Motor: Midwest, $4\frac{1}{8} \times 5\frac{1}{4}$, vertical, 4 cylinders, cast in pairs.
Lubrication: Pressure.
Carburetor: Kingston.
Ignition System: High tension magneto.
Cooling System: Fin and tube radiator, fan and pump.
Transmission: $2\frac{1}{2}$ to $3\frac{1}{4}$ m.p.h. forward.
Final Drive: Bevel gear, enclosed.
Belt Pulley: $12\frac{1}{2} \times 6\frac{1}{2}$; 2,675 feet per minute at normal engine speed.

ALLIS-CHALMERS 12-20
Allis-Chalmers Mfg. Co., Milwaukee, Wis.

AVERY CO.

Peoria, Illinois

Avery 45-65	1921-1932
Avery 6-Cylinder Two-Row Motor Planter	1921
Avery 4-Cylinder Single-Row Motor Cultivator	1921
Avery 6-Cylinder Two-Row Motor Cultivator	1921-1925

Traction Wheels: Four-wheel, driving from two rear wheels, $87\frac{1}{2}$ x 24.

No. of Plows Recommended: Eight to ten 14-in.

Length: 215 in.; **Width:** $111\frac{1}{2}$ in.; **Height:** 121 in.; **Weight:** 22000 lbs.

Turning Radius: $20\frac{1}{2}$ ft.

Motor: Own; $7\frac{3}{4}$ x 8, opposed valve-in-head, 4 cylinders, cast en bloc.

Lubrication: Circulating splash.

Carburetor: Kingston double, 2-in.

Ignition System: K-W high tension magneto.

Starting System: Impulse starter.

Cooling System: Thermo-syphon.

Bearings: Own throughout.

Transmission: Spur gear, $1\frac{3}{4}$ to $3\frac{1}{3}$ m.p.h. forward; $1\frac{3}{4}$ to $2\frac{1}{8}$ m.p.h. reverse.

Final Drive: Double spur gear.

Belt Pulley: 26x10; 500-600 r.p.m.

AVERY 45-65
Avery Co., Peoria, Ill.

AVERY 6-CYLINDER TWO-ROW MOTOR PLANTER
Avery Co., Peoria, Ill.

Traction Wheels: Three wheels, driving from two rear wheels, 42 x 6.

Length: 184 in.; **Width:** 112 in.; **Height:** 67 in.; **Weight:** 3920 lbs.

Acres Planted in 10-hr. Day: 18 to 20.

Turning Radius: 9 1-3 ft.

Motor: Own; 3 x 4, vertical, 6 cylinders, cast en bloc.

Lubrication: Circulating splash, gravity to gearing.

Carburetor: Kingston, $\frac{3}{4}$-in.

Ignition System: K-W high tension magneto.

Starting System: Impulse starter.

Cooling System: Thermo-syphon.

Bearings: Hyatt roller and Bantam ball in transmission.

Transmission: Own, enclosed and sliding gear; 2 to $5\frac{1}{3}$ m.p.h. forward and 2 m.p.h. reverse.

Final Drive: Double spur gear.

Belt Pulley: 10x$5\frac{1}{4}$; 800 r.p.m.

Traction Wheels: Four wheels; two in rear, 42x5, giving traction.

Length: 118 in.; Width: 51 in.; Weight: 2650 lbs.

Motor: Own; vertical, 3x4, 4 cylinders, cast en bloc.

Lubrication: Circulating splash.

Carburetor: Kingston, ¾ in.

Ignition System: K-W high tension magneto.

Starting Equipment: K-W impulse starter.

Cooling System: Thermo syphon.

Bearings: Hyatt roller.

Transmission: Sliding gear, 2 to 5⅓ m.p.h. forward; 2 m.p.h. reverse.

Final Drive: Double spur gear, open.

Belt Pulley: 10x5¼; 800 r.p.m.

AVERY 6-CYLINDER TWO-ROW MOTOR CULTIVATOR

Avery Co., Peoria, Ill.

AVERY 4-CYLINDER SINGLE-ROW MOTOR CULTIVATOR

Avery Co., Peoria, Ill.

Traction Wheels: Three wheels, driving from two rear wheels, 42 x 6.

Length: 184 in.; Width: 112 in.; Height: 67 in.; Weight: 3450 lbs.

Turning Radius: 9 1-3 ft.

Acres Cultivated in 10-hr. Day: 18 to 20.

Motor: Own; 3x4, vertical, 6 cylinders, cast en bloc.

Lubrication: Circulating splash, gravity to gearing.

Carburetor: Kingston, ¾-in.

Ignition System: K-W high tension magneto.

Starting System: Impulse starter.

Cooling System: Thermo-syphon.

Bearings: Hyatt roller and Bantam ball in transmission.

Transmission: Own; enclosed sliding gear; 2 to 5⅓ m.p.h. forward and 2 m.p.h. reverse.

Final Drive: Double spur gear.

Belt Pulley: 10x5¼; 800 r.p.m.

BATES MACHINE & TRACTOR CO.

Joliet, Illinois

Bates Model H 15-25	1921-1925
Bates Steel Mule, Model F, 18-25	1921-1927
Bates Model G Industrial 25-35	1921-1927

Traction Wheels: Four wheel type; two traction in rear, 48x10.

No. of Plows Recommended: Three 14-in.

Length: 131 in.; Width: 63 in.; Height: 60 in.; Weight: 4000 lbs.

Acres Plowed in 10-hr. Day: 10.

Motor: Midwest, 4⅛x5¼, valve-in-head, 4 cylinders, cast in pairs.

Lubrication: Pressure.

Carburetor: Bennett, 1¼-in.

Ignition System: High tension magneto.

Cooling System: Perfex radiator, centrifugal pump and Automotive fan.

Bearings: Timken roller in transmission.

Transmission: Sliding gear; 2.5 to 3.5 m.p.h. forward; 2 m.p.h. reverse.

Final Drive: Enclosed spur gear.

Belt Pulley: 16x6½; 580 r.p.m. and 2450 feet per minute at normal engine speed.

BATES MODEL H 15-25
Bates Machine & Tractor Co., Joliet, Ill.

Traction Wheels: One crawler on each side, 58x10.
No. of Plows Recommended: Three 14-in.
Length: 105 in.; **Width:** 62 in.; **Height:** 58 in., **Weight:** 4850 lbs.
Turning Radius: $7\frac{1}{2}$ ft.; **Acres Plowed in 10-hr. Day:** 10.
Motor: Midwest; $4\frac{1}{8}$x$5\frac{1}{4}$, valve-in-head, 4 cylinders, cast in pairs.
Lubrication: Pressure.
Carburetor: Bennett.
Ignition System: Splitdorf high tension magneto.
Cooling System: Perfex radiator and gear driven pump circulation.
Bearings: Timken roller in transmission.
Transmission: Sliding gear, $2\frac{1}{4}$ to 4 m.p.h. forward; 2 m.p.h. reverse.
Final Drive: Enclosed gears running in oil.
Belt Pulley: 12x$8\frac{1}{2}$; 850 r.p.m. and 2650 feet per minute at normal engine speed.

BATES STEEL MULE, MODEL F, 18-25
Bates Machine & Tractor Co., Joliet, Ill.

BATES MODEL G INDUSTRIAL 25-35
Bates Machine & Tractor Co., Joliet, Ill.

Traction Wheels: Two wheels in front and two crawlers in rear.
Length: 125 in.; **Width:** $62\frac{1}{2}$ in.; **Height:** 63 in.; **Weight:** 6500 lbs.
Turning Radius: $6\frac{3}{4}$ ft.
Motor: Midwest, $4\frac{1}{2}$x6, Vertical, VH, 4 cylinders, cast in pairs.
Lubrication: Circulating under pressure.
Carburetor: Bennett, $1\frac{1}{2}$-in.
Ignition System: Bosch high tension.
Cooling System: Circulating pump, fan and radiator.
Bearings: Hyatt and Timken roller.
Transmission: Sliding gear, 2.4 to 3.5 m.p.h. forward; 2 m.p.h. reverse.
Final Drive: Enclosed gears.
Belt Pulley: 12x$8\frac{1}{2}$; 850 r.p.m. and 2650 feet per minute at normal engine speed.

C. L. BEST TRACTOR CO.

San Leandro, California

Tracklayer 30   1921-1924

326   **1921**

Traction Wheels: Two crawlers, 11½x61.

No. of Plows Recommended: Four 14-in.

Width: 53¼ in.; **Height:** 59 in.; **Weight:** 7400 lbs.; **Price:** $3,250.

Turning Radius: 5 ft.

Motor: Own, 4¾x6½, valve-in-head, 4 cylinders, cast singly.

Lubrication: Force feed to crank, cam and rocker arm.

Carburetor: Ensign, 1½ in.

Ignition System: Berling magneto.

Starting & Lighting Equipment: K-W generator.

Cooling System: Fan, centrifugal pump and radiator.

Bearings: Ball and roller throughout.

Transmission: Spur gear, 2 to 3 $\frac{1}{16}$ m.p.h. forward; 2½ m.p.h. reverse.

Final Drive: Spur gear.

Belt Pulley: 12x7; 800 r.p.m. and 2513 feet per minute at normal engine speed.

TRACKLAYER 30
C. L. Best Tractor Co., San Leandro, Cal.

BLEWETT TRACTOR CO.

Tacoma, Washington

Webfoot 25-40

1921

Traction Wheels: Crawler type, one crawler on each side, 12x66.

No. of Plows Recommended: Four to five 14-in.

Length: 112 in.; **Width:** 60 in.; **Height:** 64 in.; **Weight:** 8900 lbs.; **Price:** $4,000.

Turning Radius: 6 ft.

Motor: Beaver, 4¾x6, vertical, 4 cylinders, cast en bloc.

Lubrication: Force feed and splash.

Carburetor: Bennett, 1½-in.

Ignition System: Splitdorf high tension magneto.

Cooling System: Fan, pump and radiator.

Bearings: Timken throughout.

Transmission: Sliding gear, 1½ to 4 m.p.h. forward; 1½ to 4 m.p.h. reverse.

Final Drive: Internal gear.

Belt Pulley: 8x8; 4 speeds; 950 to 2630 feet per minute at normal engine speed.

WEBFOOT 25-40
Blewett Tractor Co., Tacoma, Wash.

BORING TRACTOR CORP.
Rockford, Illinois

Boring

1921-1922

BORING
Boring Tractor Corp., Rockford, Il.

Traction Wheels: Three wheels, two drive members, 54 x 10, in front.
No. of Plows Recommended: Two 14-in.
Length: 104 in.; Width: 74 in.; Height: 74½ in.; Weight: 4250 lbs.
Turning Radius: 8 2-3 ft.
Motor: Waukesha; 4⅜ x 5¾, L-head, 4 cylinders, cast in pairs.
Lubrication: Force feed.
Carburetor: Bennett 1½-inch.
Ignition System: High tension magneto.
Cooling System: Perfex radiator with fan and pump.
Bearings: Ball and roller throughout.
Transmission: Sliding gears, 3 m.p.h. forward; 2 m.p.h. reverse.
Final Drive: Enclosed chain.
Belt Pulley: 500 r.p.m.

CENTRAL TRACTOR CO.
Greenwich, Ohio

Centaur 2½-5

1921-1925

Traction Wheels: Two drive wheels, 28x4.
Length: 70 in.: Width: 25 in.; Height: 38 in.; Weight: 700 lbs.; Price $495.
Turning Radius: 8 ft.
Motor: New Way, vertical, 1 cylinder.
Lubrication: Splash System.
Carburetor: Schebler.
Ignition System: Bosch high tension magneto.
Cooling System: Air; fan in fly wheel.
Final Drive: Bevel and spur gears.

CENTAUR 2½-5
Central Tractor Co., Greenwich, O.

DAYTON-DOWD CO.
Quincy, Illinois

Leader, Model GU, 16-32

LEADER, MODEL GU, 16-32
Dayton-Dowd Co., Quincy, Ill.

1921-1923

Traction Wheels: Crawler type, running on Hyatt and New Departure ball bearings.

No. of Plows Recommended: Three to four 14-in.

Length: 126 in.; **Width:** 58 in.; **Height:** 54 in.; **Weight:** 7500 lbs.; **Price:** $2,775.

Turning Radius: 6 ft.

Acres Plowed in 10-hr. Day: 10 to 12.

Motor: Climax, 5x6½, vertical, 4 cylinders, cast in pairs.

Lubrication: Force feed to all bearings.

Carburetor: Stromberg, 1½ in.

Ignition System: Splitdorf high tension magneto.

Starting & Lighting Equipment: Optional.

Cooling System: Fan, circulating pump and radiator.

Bearings: Hyatt roller and New Departure ball.

Transmission: Sliding gear, 2¼ to 3½ m.p.h. forward; 2¾ m.p.h. reverse.

Final Drive: Chain, enclosed in oil.

Belt Pulley: 14x7; 800 r.p.m. and 2900 feet per minute at normal engine speed.

ELECTRIC WHEEL CO.
Quincy, Illinois

Allwork, Model G, 14-28

ALLWORK, MODEL G, 14-28
Electric Wheel Co., Quincy, Ill.

1921-1926

Traction Wheels: Four wheels; two traction in rear, 42x12, with pyramid lugs.

No. of Plows Recommended: Three 14-in.

Length: 120 in.; **Width:** 56 in.; **Height:** 57 in.; **Weight:** 4800 lbs.; **Price:** $1,875.

Turning Radius: 9½ ft.

Acres Plowed in 10-hr. Day: 11.

Motor: Own, 4¾x6, vertical, 4 cylinders, cast singly.

Lubrication: Constant level splash.

Carburetor: Kingston, 1½-in.

Ignition System: High tension magneto.

Starting Equipment: Impulse starter.

Cooling System: Pump, radiator and fan.

Bearings: Hyatt and Timken roller; S. K. F., Hess Bright and New Departure ball.

Transmission: Selective, sliding gear, 1¾ to 3⅞ m.p.h. forward; 1¾ m.p.h. reverse.

Final Drive: Enclosed spur gear.

Belt Pulley: 11x6; 900 r.p.m. and 2600 feet per minute at normal engine speed.

EMERSON-BRANTINGHAM IMPLEMENT CO.

Rockford, Illinois

E-B, Model Q, 12-20   1921-1928
E-B 16-32   1921-1928

Traction Wheels: Four-wheel tractor, with two drives in rear, 60 x 12.
No. of Plows Recommended: Three 14-in.
Length: 164 in.; **Width:** 81 in.; **Height:** 86 in.; **Weight:** 6500 lbs.
Turning Radius: 15 ft.; **Acres Plowed in 10-hr. Day:** 10.
Motor: Own; $4\frac{3}{4}$ x 5, vertical, 4 cylinders, cast in pairs.
Lubrication: Splash.
Carburetor: Bennett.
Ignition System: K-W high tension magneto.
Cooling System: Perfex radiator.
Bearings: Hyatt roller in transmission and on drive axle.
Transmission: Sliding gear, 1.64, 2.25 and 3.4 m.p.h. forward; 1.64 m.p.h. reverse.
Final Drive: Gear.
Belt Pulley: 12 x 8; 708 r.p.m. and 2225 feet per minute at normal engine speed.

E-B, MODEL Q, 12-20
Emerson-Brantingham Implement Co., Rockford, Ill.

Traction Wheels: Four wheels, with two traction members in rear, 72 x 16.
No. of Plows Recommended: Four 14-in.
Length: 192 in.; **Width:** 81 in.; **Height:** 124 in.; **Weight:** 9400 lbs.
Turning Radius: 22 ft.; **Acres Plowed in 10-hr. Day:** 14 to 16.
Motor: Own; $5\frac{1}{4}$x7, vertical, 4 cylinders, cast in pairs.
Lubrication: Splash system.
Carburetor: Bennett.
Ignition System: K-W high tension magneto.
Lighting Equipment: K-W.
Cooling System: Pump.
Bearings: Hyatt roller in transmission and plain on drive axle.
Transmission: Sliding gear, 1.71 to 2.26 m.p.h. forward; 2.26 m.p.h. reverse.
Final Drive: Gear.
Belt Pulley: $16\frac{1}{2}$x9; 600 r.p.m. and 2600 feet per minute at normal engine speed.

E-B 16-32
Emerson-Brantingham Implement Co., Rockford, Ill.

FOX RIVER TRACTOR CO.

Appleton, Wisconsin

Fox 20-40   1921

Traction Wheels: Four wheels; two drive in rear, 60x12.

No. of Plows Recommended: Four 14-in.

Length: 138 in.; **Width:** 72 in.; **Height:** 72 in.; **Weight:** 6700 lbs.; **Price:** $3,100.

Turning Radius: 14⅔ ft.

Motor: Own, 5½x7½, horizontal, valve-in-head, 4 cylinders, cast in pairs.

Lubrication: Mechanical force feed system.

Carburetor: Kingston, 1½-in.

Ignition System: Aero high tension magneto with impulse starter.

Cooling System: Pump, radiator and fan.

Bearings: Fifteen Hyatt roller.

Transmission: Selective, sliding gear, 1.6 to 3.86 m.p.h. forward; 1¾ m.p.h. reverse.

Final Drive: Enclosed spur gear.

Belt Pulley: 18x10; 650 r.p.m. and 3060 feet per minute at normal engine speed.

FOX 20-40
Fox River Tractor Co., Appleton, Wis.

FRANKLIN TRACTOR CO.

Greenville, Ohio

Creeping Grip 18-30   1921

Traction Wheels: Driven by crawler on each side.

No. of Plows Recommended: Four, 14-in.

Length: 114 in.; **Width:** 81 in.; **Height:** 72 in.; **Weight:** 9250 lbs.; **Price:** $4,000.

Turning Radius: 10 ft.

Motor: Climax, 5x6½, vertical, 4 cylinders, cast in pairs.

Lubrication: Pressure.

Carburetor: Zenith, with Donaldson air cleaner.

Ignition System: Eisemann.

Cooling System: Modine radiator, pump and fan.

Bearings: Standard ball bearings throughout.

Transmission: Own, 1 speed forward and one reverse.

Final Drive: Chain.

Belt Pulley: 12x8; 600 r.p.m. and 2250 feet per minute at normal engine speed.

CREEPING GRIP 18-30
Franklin Tractor Co., Greenville, O.

FRICK CO.

Waynesboro, Pennsylvania

Frick 12-20　　　　　　　　　　　　　　1921-1924
Frick 15-28　　　　　　　　　　　　　　1921-1924

FRICK 12-20
Frick Co., Waynesboro, Pa.

Traction Wheels: Four wheels; two drive wheels, 60 x 10, in rear.
No. of Plows Recommended: Three 14-in.
Length: 158½ in.; **Width** 77½ in.; **Height:** 66 in.; **Weight:** 5800 lbs.
Turning Radius: 12½ ft.; **Acres Plowed In 10-hr. Day:** 10.
Motor: Erd; 4 x 6, valve-in-head, vertical, 4 cylinders, cast en bloc.
Lubrication: Automatic splash system.
Carburetor: Kingston with Bennett air cleaner.
Ignition System: Kingston high tension magneto with impulse starter.
Cooling System: Perfex radiator with centrifugal pump and fan.
Bearings: Hyatt roller in transmission and babbitt on drive axle.
Transmission: Sliding gear, 2.3 to 3.8 m.p.h. forward; 2 m.p.h. reverse.
Final Drive: Master gear and pinions.
Belt Pulley: 13 x 7; 900 r.p.m. and 3075 feet per minute at normal engine speed.

Traction Wheels: Four wheels; two in rear, 60x12, giving traction.
No. of Plows Recommended: Three, 14-in.
Length: 158½-in.; **Width:** 81½ in.; **Height:** 66 in.; **Weight:** 6100 lbs.
Turning Radius: 12½ ft.; **Acres Plowed in 10-hr. Day:** 10.
Motor: Beaver, 4¼x6, valve-in-head, vertical, 4 cylinders, cast en bloc.
Lubrication: Automatic splash system.
Carburetor: Bennett, with Bennett air cleaner.
Ignition System: Splitdorf high tension magneto with impulse starter.
Cooling System: Perfex radiator with centrifugal pump and fan.
Bearings: Hyatt roller in transmission and babbitt on drive axle.
Transmission: Sliding gear, 2.3 to 3.8 m.p.h. forward; 2 m.p.h. reverse.
Final Drive: Master gear and pinions.
Belt Pulley: 13x7; 900 r.p.m. and 3075 feet per minute at normal engine speed.

FRICK 15-28
Frick Co., Waynesboro, Pa.

GOOLD, SHAPLEY & MUIR CO., LTD.

Brantford, Ontario, Canada

Beaver 15-30   1921

Traction Wheels: Two front, 34x6, and two drivers in rear, 60x12.
No. of Plows Recommended: Three to four, 14-in.
Length: 142 in.; **Width:** 78 in.; **Height:** 68 in.; **Weight:** 6300 lbs.
Turning Radius: 18 ft.; **Acres Plowed in 10-hr. Day:** 10 to 12.
Motor: Waukesha, 5x6¼, vertical, 4 cylinders, cast in pairs.
Lubrication: Pressure and splash.
Carburetors: Kingston, 1¼-in.
Ignition System: Splitdorf high tension.
Cooling System: Modine radiator with centrifugal pump.
Bearings: S K F ball and own roller.
Transmission: Friction, 2½ to 3½ m.p.h. forward; 2½ to 3½ m.p.h. reverse.
Final Drive: Internal gear.
Belt Pulley: 14x7; 790-980 r.p.m. and 2900-3600 feet per minute at normal engine speed.

BEAVER 15-30
Goold, Shapley & Muir Co., Ltd.,
Brantford, Ontario, Canada.

HART-PARR CO.

Charles City, Iowa

Hart-Parr 20   1921-1924

HART-PARR 20
Hart-Parr Co., Charles City, Ia.

Traction Wheels: Four wheels; two traction in rear, 46x10.
No. of Plows Recommended: Two 14-in.
Weight: 3800 lbs.; **Price:** $1,195.
Motor: Own, 5¼x6½, horizontal, 2 cylinders, cast en bloc.
Lubrication: Madison-Kipp, force feed.
Carburetor: Schebler, 1¼-in.
Ignition System: K-W high tension magneto.
Cooling System: Honeycomb radiator, centrifugal pump and fan.
Bearings: Own make on axles.
Transmission: Selective, sliding gear, 2 to 3 m.p.h. forward.
Final Drive: Internal spur gears.
Belt Pulley: 13x6; 800 r.p.m. and 2700 feet per minute at normal engine speed.

HICKS-PARRETT TRACTOR CO.

Chicago Heights, Illinois

Hicks-Parrett, Model K, 15-30   1921
Hicks 25-35   1921

HICKS-PARRETT, MODEL K, 15-30
Hicks-Parrett Tractor Co., Chicago Heights, Ill.

Traction Wheels: Four wheel type; two traction in rear, 60x10.
No. of Plows Recommended: Three, 14-in.
Turning Radius: 11 1/12 ft.
Motor: Own, $4\frac{1}{2}$x6, vertical, 4 cylinders, cast en bloc.
Lubrication: Force feed, own system.
Carburetor: Kingston, $1\frac{3}{8}$-in.
Ignition System: Eisemann high tension magneto.
Cooling System: Oakes fan, centrifugal pump and Perfex radiator.
Bearings: Own plain, S K F ball and Hyatt roller in transmission.
Transmission: Selective gear, 2.75 to 4.7 m.p.h. forward.
Final Drive: Spur gear.
Belt Pulley: 12x$7\frac{1}{2}$; 1000 r.p.m. and 3141.6 feet per minute at normal engine speed.

Traction Wheels: Two crawlers, 60x8.
No. of Plows Recommended: Four, 14-in.
Weight: 7850 lbs.
Turning Radius: 13 feet.
Motor: W. S. M., $4\frac{3}{4}$x6, vertical, 4 cylinders, cast en bloc.
Lubrication: Full pressure feed.
Carburetor: Kingston, $1\frac{1}{2}$-in.
Ignition System: Eisemann high tension magneto.
Starting & Lighting Equipment: Optional.
Cooling System: Fan, pump and radiator.
Bearings: Ball.
Transmission: Gear, 2.4 to 3.4 m.p.h. forward; 2.4 m.p.h. reverse.
Final Drive: Gear.
Belt Pulley: 22x$8\frac{1}{2}$; 485 r.p.m. and 2600 feet per minute at normal engine speed.

HICKS 25-35
Hicks-Parrett Tractor Co., Chicago Heights, Ill.

PIERCE Governors

Make Tractors Last Longer

YOU have probably noticed that some tractors never seem to give the owners any trouble whatever, while those of other makes, costing as much and apparently as well built, can't do half a day's steady plowing without something going wrong.

Investigate closely and you will find that tractors which are continually in the repair shop, and which reach a premature old age, are either provided with inadequate governors, or with no governor at all. Pierce Governors positively prevent rapid depreciation and excessive upkeep cost—which inevitably result when the speed of tractor motors is not automatically controlled.

That's why Pierce Governors are standard equipment on so many tractors. If efficient and economical service means anything to you, see that the manufacturer has provided a Pierce Governor before you buy any tractor.

The Pierce Governor Company
WORLD'S LARGEST
GOVERNOR BUILDERS

Anderson   Indiana

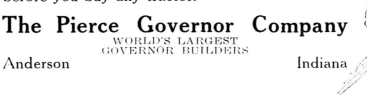

HUBER MANUFACTURING CO.
Marion, Ohio

Huber Super Four 15-30   1921-1925

Traction Wheels: Four wheel type; two traction in rear, 60x10.
No. of Plows Recommended: Three 14-in.
Length: 150 in.; **Width:** 82½ in.; **Height:** 69 in.; **Weight:** 5800 lbs.; **Price:** $1.885.
Turning Radius: 12 ft.; **Acres Plowed in 10-hr. Day:** 10 to 14.
Motor: Midwest, 4½x6, valve-in-head, 4 cylinders, cast in pairs.
Lubrication: Force feed, variable as to load and not speed of engine.
Carburetor: Kingston, 1¼-in.
Ignition System: Kingston high tension magneto with impulse starter.
Cooling System: Water, circulated by propulsion-rotary pump; Perfex radiator.
Bearings: Hyatt roller, Gurney ball and own plain.
Transmission: Selective sliding gear, 2 to 5 m.p.h. forward; 2¼ m.p.h. reverse.
Final Drive: Bull wheel in each driver, shielded.
Belt Pulley: 13x7; 1000 r.p.m. and 3060 feet per minute at normal engine speed.

HUBER SUPER FOUR 15-30
Huber Mfg. Co., Marion, O.

MASSEY-HARRIS CO., LTD.
Toronto, Ontario, Canada

Massey-Harris No. 2 12-22   1921

Traction Wheels: Four wheels; two traction, 60x10 in rear.
No. of Plows Recommended: Three, 14-in.
Length: 146 in.; **Width:** 76 in.; **Height:** 68 in.; **Weight:** 5400 lbs.; **Price:** $1,500.
Turning Radius: 12 ft.; **Acres Plowed in 10-hr. Day:** 10.
Motor: Buda HTU, 4¼x5½, vertical, 4 cylinders, cast en bloc.
Lubrication: Force feed.
Carburetor: Kingston, 1¼-in.
Ignition System: Kingston magneto.
Cooling System: Oakes fan, centrifugal pump and Perfex radiator.
Bearings: Hyatt, SKF and U. S. ball and roller; plain in wheels.
Transmission: Sliding spur gear, 1.83 to 2.68 m.p.h. forward; 1.9 m.p.h. reverse.
Final Drive: Spur gear and pinion to drive wheels.
Belt Pulley: 12x7; 1000 r.p.m.

MASSEY-HARRIS No. 2 12-22
Massey-Harris Co., Ltd., Toronto, Ontario, Canada.

MASTER TRACTOR CO.
Minneapolis, Minnesota

Master Jr. 6-12

MASTER JR. 6-12
Master Tractor Co., Minneapolis, Minn.

1921

Traction Wheels: 30x4.
No. of Plows Recommended: One 12-in.
Length: 60-in.; Width: 30 in.; Height: 32 in.; Weight: 1000 lbs.; Price: $585.
Turning Radius: 3¼ ft.; Acres Plowed in 10-hr. Day: 1½.
Motor: Le Roi, 3⅛x4½, vertical, 4 cylinders, cast en bloc.
Lubrication: Pump and splash.
Carburetor: Kingston, 1-in.
Ignition System: Berling magneto.
Cooling System: Cellular copper radiator.
Bearings: Hyatt.
Transmission: Selective gear, 1 to 2½ m.p.h. forward; 1½ m.p.h. reverse.
Final Drive: Gear, through live axle.
Belt Pulley: 8x4: 1000 r.p.m.

MINNEAPOLIS STEEL & MACHINERY CO.
Minneapolis, Minnesota

Twin City 20-35

1921-1926

Traction Wheels: Four wheels; two drivers in rear, 60x20.
No. of Plows Recommended: Five to six, 14-in.
Length: 152 in.; Width: 88 in.; Height: 73 in.; Weight: 8100 lbs.
Turning Radius: 15 ft.
Motor: Own, 5½x6¾, vertical, valve-in-head, 4 cylinders, cast in pairs.
Lubrication: Pressure feed.
Carburetor: Holley, 2-in.
Ignition System: High tension magneto with impulse starter.
Starting & Lighting Equipment: Special.
Cooling System: Modine tubular radiator, centrifugal pump and fan.
Bearings: Hyatt throughout.
Transmission: Sliding gear, 2.2 and 2.9 m.p.h. forward; 1.85 m.p.h. reverse.
Final Drive: Enclosed spur gear.
Belt Pulley: 21x8½; 466 r.p.m. and 2560 feet per minute at normal engine speed.

TWIN CITY 20-35
Minneapolis Steel & Machinery Co., Minneapolis, Minn.

1921

337

MINNEAPOLIS THRESHING MACHINE CO.

Hopkins, Minnesota

Minneapolis General Purpose 17-30

1921-1923

MINNEAPOLIS GENERAL PURPOSE 17-30
Minneapolis Threshing Machine Co.,
Hopkins, Minn.

Traction Wheels: Four wheels, two drivers, 54x12, in rear.

No. of Plows Recommended: Three to four 14-in.

Length: 132 in.; **Width:** 74 in.; **Height:** 70 in.; **Weight:** 6000 lbs.; **Price:** $2,000.

Turning Radius: $13\frac{1}{2}$ ft.

Motor: Own, $4\frac{3}{4}$x7, vertical, valve-in-head, 4 cylinders, cast en bloc.

Lubrication: Mechanical oil pump and splash.

Carburetor: Kingston, $1\frac{3}{4}$-in.

Ignition System: Splitdorf high tension magneto with impulse starter.

Cooling System: Water, radiator, fan and pump.

Bearings: Hyatt roller, SKF ball and own bronze, babbitt lined.

Transmission: Sliding gear, 2.6 to 2.7 m.p.h. forward; 1.97 m.p.h. reverse.

Final Drive: Spur gear.

Belt Pulley: $15\frac{1}{2}$x$7\frac{1}{2}$; 775 r.p.m.

MONARCH TRACTOR CO.

Watertown, Wisconsin

Monarch 20-30

1921-1925

Traction: Crawler on each side, 12x66.

No. of Plows Recommended: Four, 14-in.

Length: 126 in.; **Width:** 66 in.; **Height:** 75 in.; **Weight:** 8350 lbs.; **Price:** $3500.

Turning Radius: $7\frac{1}{2}$ ft.

Motor: Beaver, $4\frac{3}{4}$x6, vertical, 4 cylinders, cast en bloc.

Lubrication: Force feed.

Carburetor: Kingston, $1\frac{1}{2}$-in.

Ignition System: K-W high tension magneto.

Lighting Equipment: Extra, K-W generator.

Cooling System: Perfex radiator, pump and Automotive fan.

Bearings: Hyatt roller throughout.

Transmission: Selective, sliding gear, $1\frac{1}{2}$ to $3\frac{1}{2}$ m.p.h. forward; $1\frac{1}{4}$ m.p.h. reverse.

Final Drive: Chain.

Belt Pulley: 16x8; 637 r.p.m. and 2600 feet per minute at normal engine speed.

MONARCH 20-30
Monarch Tractor Co., Watertown, Wis.

THE HOLLEY
KEROSENE CARBURETOR

The Holley Kerosene Carburetor will use successfully any liquid fuel whose final boiling point is not over 600 degrees Fahrenheit, thus making possible in one engine the use of kerosene, gasoline, California distillate, alcohol or benzol.

These results are obtained by the correct application of the heat of the exhaust, which turns the fuel into vapor and gives maximum power, smooth running, quick get-away and freedom from troubles due to carbon accumulation and oil dilution.

15,000 NOW IN USE.

Holley Carburetor Co.
DETROIT   MICHIGAN

1921

NICHOLS & SHEPARD CO.
Battle Creek, Michigan

Nichols & Shepard 20-42

1921-1926

NICHOLS & SHEPARD 20-42
Nichols & Shepard Co., Battle Creek, Mich.

Traction Wheels: Four wheels; two 64x 20, in rear giving traction.

No. of Plows Recommended: Three to five 14-in.

Length: 185 in.; **Width:** 90 in.; **Height:** 110 in.; **Weight:** 13500 lbs.

Motor: Own make; 2 cylinders, 8x10, horizontal, cast singly.

Lubrication: Force feed.

Carburetor: Kingston.

Ignition System: High tension magneto.

Cooling System: Perfex radiator, centrifugal pump and fan.

Bearings: Plain, own make.

Final Drive: Bevel gear.

Belt Pulley: 22x8; 500 r.p.m. at normal engine speed.

OHIO TRACTOR CO.
Columbus, Ohio

Ohio 15-30

1921

Traction Wheels: Two, 42x12, equipped with spuds or cleats.

No. of Plows Recommended: Three, 14-in.

Length: 120 in.; **Width:** 66 in.; **Height:** 56 in.; **Weight:** 4,550 lbs.; **Price:** $2,800.

Turning Radius: 18 ft.; **Acres Plowed in 10-hr. Day:** 10.

Motor: Wisconsin, 4½x6, vertical, 4 cylinders, cast en bloc.

Lubrication: Force feed.

Carburetor: Schebler, 1¼-in.

Ignition System: Eisemann magneto with impulse starter.

Starting & Lighting Equipment: Optional, 12 volt system.

Cooling System: Pump.

Bearings: Thirty-one, taper and ball, Timken, SKF and New Departure.

Transmission: Sliding gear, three speeds forward and one reverse, 1¼ to 5 m.p.h. forward; 2½ m.p.h. reverse.

Final Drive: Double reduction of worm and internal gear.

Belt Pulley: 10 or 12x7; 1,000 r.p.m.

OHIO 15-30
Ohio Tractor Co., Columbus, O.

PACIFIC POWER IMPLEMENT CO.

Oakland, California

All-In-One 12-25

1921

ALL-IN-ONE 12-25

Pacific Power Implement Co., Oakland, Cal.

Traction Wheels: Three wheel type; two traction in rear, 52x8.

No. of Plows Recommended: Two to three 14-in.

Length: 180 in.; **Width:** 74 in.; **Height:** 75 in.; **Weight:** 4800 lbs.; **Price:** $1,975.

Turning Radius: 8 ft.; **Acres Plowed in 10-hr. Day:** $7\frac{1}{2}$ to 10.

Motor: Weidely, $3\frac{3}{4}x5\frac{1}{2}$, vertical, 4 cylinders, cast en bloc.

Lubrication: Force feed through crank shaft.

Carburetor: Kingston, $1\frac{1}{4}$-in.

Ignition System: Berling high tension.

Starting & Lighting Equipment: Impulse starter; K-W generator for lighting.

Cooling System: Modine radiator, housed in Oakes fan, built in centrifugal pump, auxiliary water tank with automatic radiator filler.

Bearings: Two Timken in front wheel, four Hyatt in drive wheels, six ball in transmission, with four ball and two Hyatt in differential and jack shaft.

Transmission: Sliding gear, $2\frac{1}{2}$ to $3\frac{1}{2}$ m.p.h. forward; $1\frac{1}{2}$ m.p.h. reverse.

Final Drive: Internal gear, enclosed or opened manganese roller pinion, run dry.

Belt Pulley: 8x8; 1,200 r.p.m. and 2,600 feet per minute at normal engine speed.

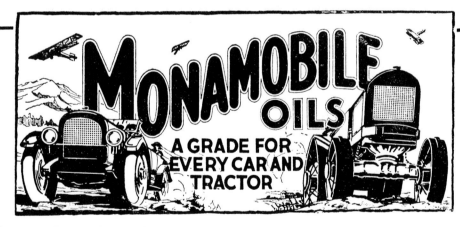

QUALITY AND ECONOMY

MONAMOBILE OILS represent the highest *quality* possible, which guarantees to the user a real *economy* in lubrication, regardless of price.

The High Quality of Monamobile Oils has attracted the attention of the largest manufacturers of Trucks, Tractors and Automobiles.

Protect your investment in automotive equipment by insisting upon Monamobile Oils.

WRITE FOR OUR ATTRACTIVE PROPOSITION.

MONARCH MANUFACTURING COMPANY

High Grade Oils and Greases

COUNCIL BLUFFS, IA.   SAN FRANCISCO, CAL.   TOLEDO, OHIO

POST-WHITNEY CO.
Cleveland, Ohio

Whitney 9-18

1921

Traction Wheels: Four wheels, driving from two rear wheels, 48 x 10.

No. of Plows Recommended: Two 14- in.

Length: 123 in.; **Width:** 56 in.; **Height:** $58\frac{1}{2}$ in.; **Weight:** 3000 lbs.

Turning Radius: 6 ft.; **Acres Plowed in 10- hr. Day:** 6.

Motor: Own, $5\frac{1}{2}$x$6\frac{1}{2}$; opposed, horizontal, two cylinders, cast separately.

Lubrication: Madison-Kipp force feed system.

Carburetor: Kingston.

Ignition System: Splitdorf high tension magneto.

Cooling System: Circulating pump and radiator.

Bearings: Hyatt and Timken.

Transmission: Sliding gear, three speeds, $1\frac{3}{4}$ to 4 m.p.h. forward; 2 m.p.h. reverse.

Final Drive: Chain.

Belt Pulley: 11x7; 750 r.p.m. and 2200 ft. per minute at normal engine speed.

WHITNEY 9-18
Post-Whitney Co., Cleveland, O.

REED FOUNDRY & MACHINE CO.
Kalamazoo, Michigan

Reed, Model A, 15-30

1921-1923

Traction Wheels: Four wheels; two drive wheels in rear.

No. of Plows Recommended: Three to four 14-in.

Weight: 4000 lbs.; **Price:** $2250.

Motor: Doman; $4\frac{3}{4}$x6, vertical L-head, head, 4 cylinders, cast en bloc.

Lubrication: Splash system.

Carburetor: Holley.

Ignition System: Splitdorf high tension magneto.

Cooling System: Pump, fan and Modine radiator.

Bearings: Hyatt roller in speed change gears.

Transmission: Selective gears, $2\frac{1}{2}$ to $3\frac{1}{4}$ m. p. h. forward.

Final Drive: External bull gear.

Belt Pulley: 16x8; 756 r.p.m.

REED, MODEL A, 15-30
Reed Foundry & Machine Co., Kalamazoo, Mich.

1842-1921

Russell Machines are Pedigreed

Like blooded live-stock they are the result of painstaking selection and steady improvement over many years.

Russell Kerosene Tractors

are backed by our successful experience in making Reliable tractors ever since 1875. Composed only of true and proven features; *built up* to Old Reliable standards, not *down* to a price—and with a big surplus of Durability and Power. Made in 4 sizes, with 4 cylinders and 4 wheels. A size for every farm.

Russell Steam Traction Engines

never did have a real rival for smooth, even flow of abundant power. Operate threshers at just the right speed to get out most grain with least wear and tear. Unequaled for road hauling and heavy power jobs.

Russell Threshers

are the world's best. Exclusive features include the big easy-running 15-bar Cylinder that works tooth-and-nail with the High-finger Grate and gets out most of the grain *right there;* and the patented Distributing Beater that plunges into the straw, spreads it evenly full width across the rack and gets out the very last kernels.

No other thresher has these features—and none other can equal the Russell for saving and cleaning all the grain. Made in six sizes including the 20x34 for Individual farm or Community use.

Send now for the big New Russell Catalog

The Russell & Co. Factory and General Offices **Massillon, O.**

Russell Giant 30-60 hp.

Russell Kerosene Tractors. This type are made in 12-24, 15-30, 20-35.

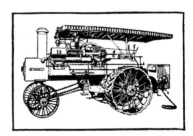

Russell Traction Engines are made in 5 sizes.

RUSSELL
THE OLD RELIABLE LINE

STROUD MOTOR MANUFACTURING ASSOCIATION
San Antonio, Texas

Stroud "All-In-One" 18-30

1921

STROUD "ALL-IN-ONE" 18-30
Stroud Motor Mfg. Ass'n, San Antonio, Texas.

Traction Wheels: Four wheels; two open type, built-up, traction in rear, 60x12.

No. of Plows Recommended: Three to four 14-in.

Width: 70 in.; **Weight:** 6500 lbs.

Turning Radius: 10 ft.

Motor: Climax, 5x6½, vertical, 4 cylinders, cast in pairs.

Lubrication: Pressure feed through drilled crank shaft.

Carburetor: Stromberg, 1-in.

Ignition System: Splitdorf magneto with impulse starter.

Cooling System: Honeycomb radiator and pump.

Bearings: Hyatt roller in transmission.

Transmission: Sliding gear, 2⅝ to 3⅝ m.p.h. forward; 2¼ m.p.h. reverse.

Final Drive: Master gears, enclosed.

Belt Pulley: 26x7½; 345 r.p.m. and 2600 feet per minute at normal engine speed.

TIOGA TRACTOR CO.
Baltimore, Maryland

Tioga "3" 18-32

1921-1928

TIOGA "3" 18-32
Tioga Tractor Co., Baltimore, Md.

Traction Wheels: Two traction in rear 36x16; two non-drive in front, 30x5½.

No. of Plows Recommended: Three to four 14-in.

Length: 120 in.; **Width:** 60 in.; **Height:** 55 in.; **Weight:** 4950 lbs.; **Price:** $2625.

Turning Radius: 9 ft.

Motor: Midwest, 4½x6, vertical, 4 cylinders, cast in pairs.

Lubrication: Pressure.

Carburetor: Stromberg, 1¼-in.

Ignition System, Splitdorf high tension magneto.

Cooling System: G-O radiator, centrifugal pump and fan.

Bearings: Babbitt lined bronze, roller and ball in transmission and rear axle.

Transmission: Gear, 2.7 to 3.7 m.p.h. forward; 2.7 to 2.7 m.p.h. reverse.

Final Drive: Internal gear.

Belt Pulley: 12x7; 980 r.p.m. at normal engine speed.

UNITED TRACTORS CORP.

New York, New York

Mohawk 8-16   1921

Traction Wheels: Two-wheel type; both traction, located in front, 40 x 8.

No. of Plows Recommended: One to two 14-in.

Length: 120 in.; **Width:** 40 in.; **Height:** 48 in.; **Weight:** 2150 lbs.; **Price:** $785.

Turning Radius: 4 ft.; **Acres Plowed In 10-hr. Day:** Six.

Motor: Light "H;" 3¼ x 4½, 4 cylinders, cast en bloc.

Lubrication: Pump and splash system.

Carburetor: Kingston, ⅞-in.

Ignition System: Simms high tension magneto.

Starting and Lighting Equipment: Optional.

Cooling System: Rex radiator and fan.

Bearings: Roller throughout.

Transmission: Gear, 2½ to 3 m.p.h. forward; 2 m.p.h. reverse.

Final Drive: Enclosed spur gear.

Belt Pulley: 8 x 4; 600 r.p.m.

MOHAWK 8-16
United Tractors Corp., New York, N. Y.

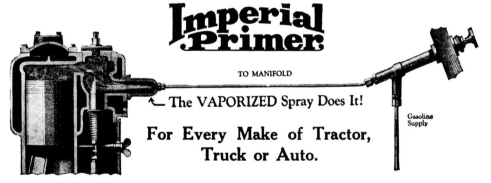

Starts Your Motor Easily and Quickly

Imperial Primer

TO MANIFOLD

The VAPORIZED Spray Does It!

Gasoline Supply

For Every Make of Tractor, Truck or Auto.

You do not have to "Spin" the most stubborn motor in winter or summer if you put on an Imperial Primer—one or two lifts of the crank and it will invariably start!

Easily and quickly installed, low in price.

Full description of this popular device and full line of up-to-date Priming Cups, Shut-Off Cocks, Three-Way Cocks, Tube Couplings, Gasoline Strainers, Etc., is given in our new catalog No. 103—write for copy today.

IMPERIAL BRASS MFG. CO., 520 So. Racine Ave., Chicago

1922

In 1922, 26 models of 20 makes not included in 1921 were added.

ALLIS-CHALMERS MANUFACTURING CO.

Milwaukee, Wisconsin

Allis-Chalmers 15-25
Allis-Chalmers 20-35

1922-1927
1922-1929

Traction Wheels: Four wheels; two in rear, 46 x 12, furnishing traction.

No. of Plows Recommended: Three 14-in.

Length: 135 in.; **Width:** 66 in.; **Height:** 62 in.; **Weight:** 4,400 lbs.

Turning Radius: 12 ft.

Motor: Midwest, $4\frac{1}{8}$x$5\frac{1}{4}$, vertical, 4 cylinders, cast in pairs.

Lubrication: Pressure.

Carburetor: Kingston.

Ignition System: High tension magneto.

Cooling System: Fin and tube radiator, fan and pump.

Transmission: $2\frac{1}{2}$ to $3\frac{1}{4}$ m.p.h. forward.

Final Drive: Internal gear, enclosed.

Belt Pulley: $12\frac{1}{2}$x$6\frac{1}{2}$; 2,675 feet per minute at normal engine speed.

ALLIS-CHALMERS 15-25
Allis-Chalmers Mfg. Co., Milwaukee, Wis.

346

1922

Traction Wheels: Four-wheel type; two traction in rear, 50x12.

No. of Plows Recommended: Four 14-in.

Turning Radius: 15 ft.

Motor: Own, vertical, 4 cylinders, cast en bloc.

Lubrication: Pressure.

Carburetor: Kingston, $1\frac{1}{2}$-in.

Ignition System: High tension magneto.

Cooling System: Fan, centrifugal pump and radiator.

Bearings: Hyatt roller in transmission and rear axle.

Transmission: Shifting gear, $2\frac{1}{2}$ to $3\frac{1}{4}$ m.p.h. forward.

Final Drive: Pinion and internal gear.

Belt Pulley: $13x7\frac{1}{2}$; 930 r.p.m. and 3,160 feet per minute at normal engine speed.

ALLIS-CHALMERS 20-35
Allis-Chalmers Mfg. Co., Milwaukee, Wis.

ARO TRACTOR CO.

Minneapolis, Minnesota

Aro 3-6   1922-1923

Traction Wheels: Two drive wheels in front, 30x4.
No. of Plows Recommended: One 10-in.
Length: 43 in.; **Width:** 28 in.; **Height:** 45 in.; **Weight:** 1,000 lbs. Price $465.
Turning Radius: 4 ft. **Acres Plowed in 10-hr. Day:** 2.
Motor: Own, $4\frac{1}{2}x5$, 4-cycle, 1 cylinder.
Lubrication: Pump and splash.
Carburetor: Schebler, $1\frac{1}{4}$-in.
Ignition System: Berling magneto with impulse starter.
Cooling System: S-J radiator and Automotive fan.
Bearings: Hess-Bright ball on crankshaft.
Transmission: Worm and gear; 1 to 3 m.p.h. forward.
Final Drive: Worm gear.
Belt Pulley: $6x4\frac{1}{2}$; 900 r.p.m. and 1,400 feet per minute at normal engine speed.

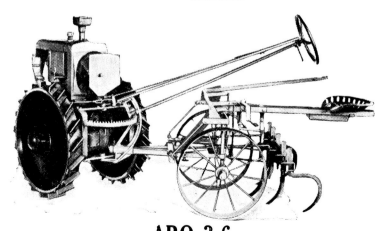

ARO 3-6
Aro Tractor Co., Minneapolis, Minn.

AVERY CO.

Peoria, Illinois

Avery Track Runner   1922-1925
Avery 12-20   1922

AVERY TRACK RUNNER
Avery Co., Peoria, Ill.

Traction Wheels: Two crawlers in rear running on rollers; two non-drive wheels in front, 26x3.

No. of Plows Recommended: Three to four 14-in.

Length: 108 in.; **Width:** 48 in.; **Height:** 58 in.; **Weight:** 5,000 lbs.

Turning Radius: Within its own length.

Motor: Own, 4x5½, vertical, 4 cylinders, cast en bloc.

Lubrication: Force feed.

Carburetor: Kingston double, 1¼-in.

Ignition System: Splitdorf double head magneto.

Starting and Lighting Equipment: Westinghouse.

Cooling System: Oakes fan, centrifugal pump and Perfex radiator.

Bearings: Roller and ball throughout.

Transmission: Selective gear, 1½ to 3½ m.p.h. forward.

Final Drive: Enclosed gear.

Belt Pulley: 12x8½; 1,100 r.p.m. at normal engine speed.

AVERY 12-20
Avery Co., Peoria, Ill.

Traction Wheels: Four wheels; two rear drivers, 50x12.

No. Plows Recommended: Two to three 14-in.

Length: 130 in.; **Width:** 56 in.; **Height:** 78 in.; **Weight:** 5500 lbs.

Turning Radius: 11 ft.

Motor: Own, 4⅜x6, opposed, valve-in-head, 4 cylinders, cast en bloc.

Lubrication: Circulating splash.

Carburetor: Kingston double, 1¼-in.

Ignition System: K-W high tension.

Starting & Lighting Equipment: K-W impulse starter.

Cooling System: Thermo-syphon.

Bearings: Gurney ball throughout.

Transmission: Spur gear, 2⅜ to 3 m.p.h. forward on low; 3½ to 4 m.p.h. forward on high; 2⅜ to 3 m.p.h. reverse.

Final Drive: Double spur gear.

Belt Pulley: 16x7; 800-900 r.p.m.

70% of All Power Garden Cultivators Now Use This Engine

COMPACTNESS, light weight, economy of operation and thorough dependability have given the Basco Type P. Motor premier place in the garden tractor field. And these same qualities, plus its unique proportions, make it applicable to any equipment that does not require much in excess of $1\frac{1}{2}$ H. P. Upward of fifty thousand of these motors are giving unfailing service in these other uses.

High-grade automobile engine materials and construction. Air-cooled—never overheats—will run steadily 10 or 12 hours a day under load in hot weather without a murmur. Uses only 1 1/5 pints of gasoline and 1/10 pint of oil per hour. Continuous all-day operation costs about 30c.

Circular "P" gives full details—write for it.

·4-cycle — air-cooled — built-in-magneto — drop forged chrome nickel steel gears and shafts. Weighs only 45 lbs.

Another Proved Power Unit for Farm Work

The Basco "Full-Power" engine is a full half horsepower condensed into 40 lbs. Operates 10 hours on 1 gallon of gas. Light weight and compactness make it an ideal integral unit of any machine requiring up to $\frac{1}{2}$ H. P. May also be used separately for operating pumps, churns, milkers, grinders, cream separators, washing machines, etc.

Same general construction as the Basco Type "P" engine. Conforms to Underwriters' specifications—safe to use anywhere.

A wide demand is being developed through Farm Paper advert'sing. Write for circular and proposition.

4-cycle—air cooled—magneto and starter equipped—high-grade automobile engine materials and construction throughout. Weighs only 40 lbs.

Briggs & Stratton Co.
Milwaukee, Wisconsin
BASCO PRODUCT

BEEMAN TRACTOR CO.
Minneapolis, Minnesota

Beeman Jr.

1922-1925

BEEMAN JR.
Beeman Tractor Co., Minneapolis, Minn.

Traction Wheels: Drives on two wheels, $16\frac{1}{2}$x$2\frac{1}{2}$.

Turning Radius: 2 ft.

Motor: Briggs & Stratton, vertical, $2\frac{1}{2}$x $2\frac{1}{2}$, 1 cylinder.

Lubrication: Pump.

Carburetor: Briggs & Stratton, $\frac{1}{2}$-in.

Ignition System: Briggs & Stratton high tension magneto.

Cooling System: Air cooled.

Bearings: Plain.

Transmission: $\frac{3}{4}$ to 3 m.p.h. forward.

Final Drive: Open; gears to drive wheels.

Belt Pulley: 4x$1\frac{5}{8}$; 125 to 250 r.p.m.

C. L. BEST TRACTOR CO.
San Leandro, California

Best Tracklayer 60

1922-1924

Traction Wheels: Two crawlers, each 88x20.
No. of Plows Recommended: Nine 14-in.
Length: 140 in.; **Width:** 90 in.; **Height:** $76\frac{1}{2}$ in.; **Weight:** 17500 lbs.; **Price:** $5,750.
Motor: Best, $6\frac{1}{2}$x$8\frac{1}{2}$, valve-in-head, 4 cylinders, cast singly.
Lubrication: Splash system.
Carburetor: Ensign.
Ignition System: Bosch.
Cooling System: Fan, pump and radiator.
Bearings: Anti-friction throughout.
Transmission: Sliding gear.
Final Drive: Internal gear.
Belt Pulley: 16x12; 650 r.p.m. and 2720 feet per minute at normal engine speed.

BEST TRACKLAYER 60
C. L. Best Tractor Co., San Leandro, Calif.

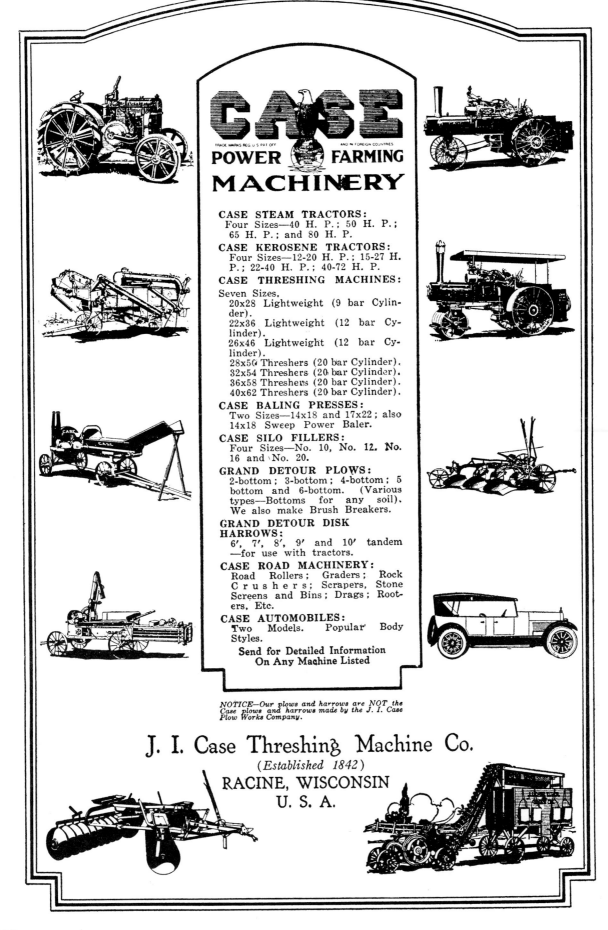

CASE

POWER FARMING MACHINERY

CASE STEAM TRACTORS:
Four Sizes—40 H. P.; 50 H. P.; 65 H. P.; and 80 H. P.

CASE KEROSENE TRACTORS:
Four Sizes—12-20 H. P.; 15-27 H. P.; 22-40 H. P.; 40-72 H. P.

CASE THRESHING MACHINES:
Seven Sizes.
20x28 Lightweight (9 bar Cylinder).
22x36 Lightweight (12 bar Cylinder).
26x46 Lightweight (12 bar Cylinder).
28x50 Threshers (20 bar Cylinder).
32x54 Threshers (20 bar Cylinder).
36x58 Threshers (20 bar Cylinder).
40x62 Threshers (20 bar Cylinder).

CASE BALING PRESSES:
Two Sizes—14x18 and 17x22; also 14x18 Sweep Power Baler.

CASE SILO FILLERS:
Four Sizes—No. 10, No. 12. No. 16 and No. 20.

GRAND DETOUR PLOWS:
2-bottom; 3-bottom; 4-bottom; 5 bottom and 6-bottom. (Various types—Bottoms for any soil). We also make Brush Breakers.

GRAND DETOUR DISK HARROWS:
6', 7', 8', 9' and 10' tandem —for use with tractors.

CASE ROAD MACHINERY:
Road Rollers; Graders; Rock Crushers; Scrapers, Stone Screens and Bins; Drags; Rooters, Etc.

CASE AUTOMOBILES:
Two Models. Popular Body Styles.

Send for Detailed Information On Any Machine Listed

NOTICE—Our plows and harrows are NOT the Case plows and harrows made by the J. I. Case Plow Works Company.

J. I. Case Threshing Machine Co.
(Established 1842)
RACINE, WISCONSIN
U. S. A.

J. I. CASE THRESHING MACHINE CO.

Racine, Wisconsin

Case 12-20
Case 40-72

1922-1926
1922-1923

CASE 12-20
J. I. Case Threshing Machine Co., Racine, Wis.

Traction Wheels: Four wheels, two drive wheels in rear, 42 x 12.

No. of Plows Recommended: Two to three 14-in.

Length: 109 in.; **Width:** $58\frac{5}{16}$ in.; **Height:** $55\frac{1}{2}$ in., **Weight:** 4232 lbs.; **Price:** $1,050.

Turning Radius: 24 ft.

Motor: Own; $4\frac{1}{8}$ x 5, vertical valve-in-head, 4 cylinders, cast en bloc.

Lubrication: Pressure feed through drilled crank shaft.

Carburetor: Kingston, $1\frac{1}{4}$-in.

Ignition System: Berling high tension magneto with impulse starter.

Cooling System: Pump, fan, radiator and thermostat.

Bearings: Hyatt roller in transmission.

Transmission: Sliding gear, 2.2 to 3 m.p.h. forward.

Final Drive: Enclosed spur gears.

Belt Pulley: $14\frac{1}{2}$ x $6\frac{3}{8}$; 1050 r.p.m.

CASE 40-72
J. I. Case Threshing Machine Co., Racine, Wis.

Traction Wheels: Four wheels; two drive wheels in rear, 72x20.

No. of Plows Recommended: Eight to ten 14-in.

Length: 200 in.; **Width:** 105 in.; **Height:** 110 in.; **Weight:** 21200 lbs.; **Price:** $5,200.

Acres Plowed in 10-hr. Day: 25.

Motor: Own, 7x8, vertical, valve-in-head, 4 cylinders, cast in pairs.

Lubrication: Pressure feed through drilled crankshaft; force to cylinders.

Carburetor: Kingston, $2\frac{1}{2}$-in.

Ignition System: High tension magneto with impulse starter.

Cooling System: Fan, pump and radiator.

Bearings: Hyatt and Timken.

Transmission: Sliding gear, 2.07 to 2.97 m.p.h. forward.

Final Drive: Enclosed spur gears.

Belt Pulley: $19\frac{1}{2}$x$10\frac{1}{2}$; 750 r.p.m. and 3,827 feet per minute at normal engine speed.

CLEVELAND TRACTOR CO.
Cleveland, Ohio

Cletrac "F" 9-16   1922-1923
Cletrac 12-20   1922-1929

CLETRAC "F" 9-16
Cleveland Tractor Co., Cleveland, O.

Traction Wheels: Two crawlers, 48x5½.

No. of Plows Recommended: Two, 12-in.

Length: 83 in.; Width: 43 in.; Height: 50 in.; Weight: 1865 lbs.; Price $595.

Turning Radius: 8 ft.; Acres Plowed in 10-hr. Day: 8.

Motor: Own, 3¼x4½, vertical, 4 cylinders, cast en bloc.

Lubrication: Circulating splash.

Carburetor: Tillotson, 1-in.

Ignition System: Eisemann or Teagle high tension magneto.

Cooling System: Tube type radiator, pump and fan.

Bearings: Plain and ball.

Transmission: Sliding gear; 1 to 3 m.p.h. forward; 1 to 3 m.p.h. reverse.

Final Drive: Live axle shaft.

Belt Pulley: 7½x6; 1,600 r.p.m. and 3,000 feet per minute at normal engine speed.

Traction Wheels: One crawler on each side.

No. of Plows Recommended: Three 12-in.

Length: 96 in.; Width: 50 in.; Height: 52 in.; Weight: 3455 lbs.; Price: $1,345.

Turning Radius: 6 ft.; Acres Plowed in 10-hr. Day: 8 to 10.

Motor: Own, 4x5½, 4-cycle, 4 cylinders, cast en bloc.

Lubrication: Force feed system.

Carburetor: Kingston, 1⅛ in.

Ignition System: Teagle or Eisemann magneto.

Starting System: Impulse starter on magneto.

Cooling System: Water pump, radiator and fan.

Bearings: Plain, ball and roller.

Transmission: Sliding gear, 1 to 3½ m. p.h. forward; 2 m.p.h. reverse.

Final Drive: Internal gear and pinion.

Belt Pulley: 8x6; 1265 r.p.m. and 2500 feet per minute at normal engine speed.

CLETRAC 12-20
Cleveland Tractor Co., Cleveland, O.

EAGLE MANUFACTURING CO.

Appleton, Wisconsin

Eagle, Model F, 12-22   1922-1924
Eagle, Model F, 16-30   1922-1924

Traction Wheels: Four wheels, two rear, 48 x 12, affording traction.

No. of Plows Recommended: Three 14-in.

Length: 132 in.; **Width:** 65 in.; **Height:** 76 in.; **Weight:** 5850 lbs.

Turning Radius: 13 ft; **Acres Plowed in 10-hr. Day:** 8 to 9.

Motor: Own; 7 x 8, valve-in-head, 2 cylinders, cast en bloc.

Lubrication: Madison-Kipp force feed.

Carburetor: Schebler.

Ignition System: Splitdorf high tension magneto with impulse starter.

Cooling System: Perfex radiator, circulating pump and fan.

Bearings: Hyatt roller in transmission and plain on drive axle.

Transmission: Sliding gear, 2 to 3 m.p.h. forward; 1¾ m.p.h. reverse.

Final Drive: Spur gear, geared to both rear wheels.

Belt Pulley: 20 x 8½; 450 r.p.m. and 2356 feet per minute at normal engine speed.

EAGLE, MODEL F, 12-22
Eagle Mfg. Co., Appleton, Wis.

Traction Wheels: Four wheels, two rear, 52 x 12, affording traction.

No. of Plows Recommended: Four 14-in.

Length: 141 in.; **Width:** 70 in.; **Height:** 78 in.; **Weight:** 7100 lbs.

Turning Radius: 14 ft.; **Acres Plowed in 10-hr. Day:** 11-12.

Motor: Own; 8 x 8, valve-in-head, 2 cylinders, cast en bloc.

Lubrication: Madison-Kipp force feed.

Carburetor: Schebler.

Ignition System: Splitdorf high tension magneto with impulse starter.

Cooling System: Perfex radiator, fan, circulating pump.

Bearings: Hyatt roller in transmission and plain on drive axle.

Transmission: Sliding gear, 2 to 3 m.p.h. forward; 1¾ m.p.h. reverse.

Final Drive: Spur gear to both rear wheels.

Belt Pulley: 24 x 10; 450 r.p.m. and 2800 feet per minute at normal engine speed.

EAGLE, MODEL F, 16-30
Eagle Mfg. Co., Appleton, Wis.

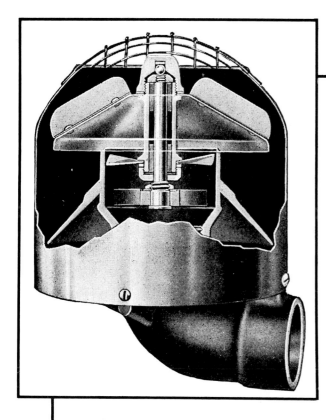

UNITED AIR CLEANER

EJECTOR TYPE

(SELF-CLEANING)

This instrument removes, from the air used by tractor, truck or motor car, all injurious foreign matter.

Operated automatically by the ingoing air, it requires no attention whatever. The dust separated is instantly ejected to the open air—never accumulating.

The UNITED is not affected by changes in weather, freezing, etc. Back firing cannot harm it or cause any dust to pass it.

Its application to any engine causes no loss of power.

Equipped with oilless bearings, simple (one moving part) highly efficient, silent, durable, inexpensive.

Write for Full Particulars

UNITED MANUFACTURING AND DISTRIBUTING COMPANY

536 LAKE SHORE DRIVE   CHICAGO, ILLINOIS

GRAY TRACTOR CO., INC.
Minneapolis, Minnesota

Gray 20-36   1922

GRAY 20-36
Gray Tractor Co., Inc., Minneapolis, Minn.

Traction Wheels: Two non drive wheels in front, 40x8, and one rear drum, 54x 54, giving traction.
No. Plows Recommended: Four, 14-in.
Length: 174 in.; **Width:** 81 in.; **Height:** 63 in.; **Weight:** 6300 lbs.; **Price:** $1,975.
Turning Radius: 20 ft.; **Acres Plowed in 10-hr. day:** 15.
Motor: Waukesha, $4\frac{1}{2}$x$6\frac{1}{4}$, L-head, 4 cylinders, cast in pairs.
Lubrication: Force feed.
Carburetor: Bennett, $1\frac{1}{2}$-in.
Ignition System: Bosch high tension magneto.
Cooling System: Shotwell-Johnson radiator, centrifugal pump and fan.
Bearings: Hyatt and New Departure roller and ball in transmission.
Transmission: Sliding gear; 2.4 to 3 m.p.h. forward; 2.4 m.p.h. reverse.
Final Drive: Chains.
Belt Pulley: $11\frac{1}{2}$x8; 1000 r.p.m. and 3000 feet per minute at normal engine speed.

HOLT MANUFACTURING CO.
Peoria, Illinois

''Caterpillar'' T-35   1922

Traction Wheels: Two caterpillar tracts giving 1000 sq. in. traction surface.
Length: 103 in.; **Width:** 48 in.; **Height:** 52 in.; **Weight:** 4000 lbs.
Turning Radius: 5 ft.
Motor: Own, 4x$5\frac{1}{2}$, overhead camshaft, 4 cylinders, cast en bloc.
Lubrication: Full force feed.
Carburetor: Kingston, $1\frac{1}{2}$ in.
Ignition System: Eisemann high tension magneto.
Starting & Lighting Equipment: "N. E." (Special equipment.)
Cooling System: Fan, centrifugal pump and tubular radiator.
Bearings: Ball and roller in transmission.
Transmission: Selective sliding gear; ($2\frac{1}{8}$. 3 and $5\frac{1}{4}$ m.p.h. forward; $2\frac{3}{8}$ m.p.h. reverse.
Final Drive: Spur gear, enclosed.
Belt Pulley: $11\frac{1}{2}$x$6\frac{1}{2}$; 820 r.p.m. and 3000 feet per minute at normal engine speed.

"CATERPILLAR" T-35
Holt Mfg. Co., Peoria, Ill.

For the Lighter Jobs

The "Caterpillar's"* field of usefulness is by no means limited to the lighter jobs. There is a "Caterpillar"* of size and capacity for every power need. On farm or ranch, in the mining, oil and lumber industries, for snow removal and other civic work —wherever power and endurance are at a premium, the "Caterpillar"* has no real competitor.

In the "Caterpillar"* T-35, Holt brings to industry and to agriculture a small compact tractor embodying the same dependable qualities found in the larger "Caterpillars."* The T-35 fits in with the road making and road maintenance programs of every city, town, county, and township. Its range of speeds, short-turning, and ability to operate in any weather or soil, gives it definite and pronounced advantages over teams or other methods of road-dragging and patrol maintenance. For quickly and economically handling the lighter jobs, road contractors, engineers, and industrial users find the T-35 invaluable. For the farmer, the T-35 fills the need for a long-lived easily operated engine, able under all conditions, to plow, seed, and harvest, do hauling and belt work at a lower cost than can be done by any other method.

*THERE IS BUT ONE "CATERPILLAR"—HOLT BUILDS IT

Reg.U.S. Pat.Off.

HOLT
PEORIA, ILL.
STOCKTON, CALIF.

THE HOLT MFG. CO., Inc.
Peoria, Ill.   Stockton, Calif.

Export Division: 50 Church St., New York

BRANCHES AND SERVICE STATIONS ALL OVER THE WORLD

KROYER MOTORS CO.

Los Angeles Harbor
San Pedro, California

Wizard 4-Pull 20-35

1922-1924

WIZARD 4-PULL 20-35

Kroyer Motors Co., Los Angeles Harbor, San Pedro, Cal.

Traction Wheels: Drives on all four wheels, each 43x13½.

No. of Plows Recommended: Four to five, 14-in.

Length: 112 in.; **Width:** 66 in.; **Height:** 57 in.; **Weight:** 6800 lbs.; **Price:** $3250.

Turning Radius: 6 ft.; **Acres Plowed in 10-hr. Day:** 14.

Motor: Own, 5¼x6½, vertical, 4 cylinders, cast in pairs.

Lubrication: Full pressure feed.

Carburetor: Ensign, 1½-in.

Ignition System: Bosch high tension magneto.

Starting and Lighting Equipment: Optional as extra.

Cooling System: Liberty tubular radiator, centrifugal pump and fan.

Bearings: Hess Bright ball and Timken roller.

Transmission: Selective; 2¼ to 4 m.p.h. forward; 2 m.p.h. reverse.

Final Drive: Chain, enclosed and running in oil.

Belt Pulley: 12x10; 850 r.p.m. and 2,600 feet per minute at normal engine speed.

LA CROSSE TRACTOR CO.

La Crosse, Wisconsin

La Crosse, Model H, 12-24

1922-1923

Traction Wheels: Four wheels, with two 56 x 10 traction members in rear.

No. of Plows Recommended: Three 14-in.

Length: 135 in.; **Width:** 82½ in.; **Height:** 62 in.; **Weight:** 3800 lbs.

Turning Radius: 9½ ft.; **Acres Plowed in 10-hr. Day:** 10.

Motor: Own; 6 x 7, 2 cylinders, cast en bloc.

Lubrication: Own non-splash in motor.

Ignition Systems: Dry cell battery.

Cooling System: Centrifugal pump and fan.

Bearings: Machined, bronze backed, die cast babbitt in motor and roller throughout tractor.

Transmission: S. gear; 2¾ m.p.h. forward and 2½ m.p.h. reverse.

Final Drive: R. P. internal gears.

Belt Pulley: 11 x 7½; 900 r.p.m. and 2600 f.p.m. at normal engine speed.

LA CROSSE, MODEL H, 12-24

La Crosse Tractor Co., La Crosse, Wis.

Allwork
KEROSENE TRACTORS

"Supreme in the Orchard"

Kerosene tractors with unusual possibilities because built better, and known everywhere for their surplus power, dependable service and durability. Ample power for three plows, 28-inch thresher and 16-inch ensilage cutter. Backed by a well-known company, strong financially and of undoubted integrity. You can pin your faith to an Allwork.

"8 Years of Service"

Write for Catalog Today

ELECTRIC WHEEL CO., BOX 404A   QUINCY, ILL.

JOHN LAUSON MANUFACTURING CO.
New Holstein, Wisconsin

Lauson 12-25   1922-1925

LAUSON 12-25
John Lauson Mfg. Co., New Holstein, Wis.

Traction Wheels: Four wheels; two in rear. 48×12, giving traction.
No. of Plows Recommended: Three 14-in.
Weight: 4500 lbs.; **Price:** $1495.
Turning Radius: $12\frac{3}{4}$ ft.; **Acres Plowed in 10-hr. Day:** 9.
Motor: Lauson-Midwest, $4\frac{1}{8}$x$5\frac{1}{4}$, vertical, 4 cylinders, cast in pairs.
Lubrication: Force feed.
Carburetor: Kingston, $1\frac{1}{4}$-in.
Ignition System: Splitdorf high tension magneto with impulse starter.
Cooling System: Cellular radiator, fan and pump.
Bearings: Hyatt and Timken.
Transmission: Selective, sliding gear $3\frac{1}{4}$ m.p.h. forward; $2\frac{1}{2}$ m.p.h. reverse.
Final Drive: Spur gear.
Belt Pulley: 16x7; 650 r.p.m. and 2857 feet per minute at normal engine speed.

LONDON MOTOR PLOW CO.
Springfield, Ohio

London Motor Plow "S" 12-25   1922-1923

Traction Wheels: Four wheels; two traction in rear 48x12.
No. of Plows Recommended: Three, 12-in.
Length: 168 in.; **Width:** 72 in.; **Height:** 60 in.; **Weight:** 4600 lbs.
Turning Radius: 9 ft.; **Acres Plowed in 10-hr. Day:** 13.
Motor: Midwest, valve-in-head, $4\frac{1}{8}$x$5\frac{1}{4}$, 4 cylinders, cast en bloc.
Lubrication: Force feed.
Carburetor: Columbia, $1\frac{1}{4}$-in.
Ignition System: K-W magneto with impulse starter.
Cooling System: Shotwell-Johnson radiator and Hytex fan.
Transmission: Selective, 2.7 to 5.6 m.p.h. forward; 2.5 m.p.h. reverse.
Final Drive: Internal spur gear and live axle.
Belt Pulley: 14x8; 1,000 r.p.m. and 3,665 feet per minute at normal engine speed.

LONDON MOTOR PLOW "S" 12-25
London Motor Plow Co., Springfield, O.

MIDWEST ENGINE CO.

Indianapolis, Indiana

Midwest Utilitor Model 50I   1922-1923
Midwest Utilitor Model 50I-A   1922-1923

MIDWEST UTILITOR MODEL 50I
Midwest Engine Co., Indianapolis, Ind.

Traction Wheels. Two drive wheels, $24\frac{3}{4}$x 4.

No. of Plows Recommended: One 10-in.

Length: 84 in.; **Width:** $17\frac{1}{2}$-$30\frac{1}{2}$ in.; **Height:** 36 in.; **Weight:** 750 lbs.; **Price:** $295.

Turning Radius: 6 ft.; **Acres Plowed in 10-hr. day:** $\frac{1}{2}$.

Motor: Own, $3\frac{1}{2}$x$4\frac{1}{2}$ L-head, 1 cylinder.

Lubrication: Combination splash and ring oiler.

Carburetor: Holley, $\frac{7}{8}$-in.

Ignition System: Eisemann high tension magneto.

Cooling System: Water; thermo-syphon.

Bearings: Fafnir ball in transmission.

Transmission: Internal gear, $2\frac{1}{2}$ to 4 m. p.h. forward.

Final Drive: Internal gear.

Belt Pulley: $4\frac{5}{8}$x$3\frac{3}{4}$; 600 to 1,200 r.p.m.

Traction Wheels: Two drive wheels, $24\frac{3}{4}$x4.

No. of Plows Recommended: One, 10-in.

Length: 88 in.; **Width:** 27-42 in.; **Height:** 36 in.

Turning Radius: 6 ft.; **Acres Plowed in 10-hr. Day:** 2.

Motor: Own, $3\frac{1}{2}$x$4\frac{1}{2}$, 4 cycle, 1 cylinder.

Lubrication: Combination splash and ring oilers.

Carburetor: Holley, $\frac{7}{8}$-in.

Ignition System: Eisemann high tension magneto.

Cooling System: Thermo-syphon.

Bearings: Babbitt.

Final Drive: Internal gear.

Belt Pulley: $4\frac{5}{8}$x$3\frac{3}{4}$; 1,000 r.p.m.

MIDWEST UTILITOR MODEL 50I-A
Midwest Engine Co., Indianapolis, Ind.

MOTOR MACULTIVATOR CO.

Toledo, Ohio

Motor Macultivator $1\frac{1}{2}$ 1922-1924

Traction Wheels: Two wheels, $19\frac{1}{2}$x3, with gear drive on both.

Length: 54 in.; **Width:** $17\frac{1}{2}$ in.; **Height:** 32 in.; **Weight:** 210 lbs.; **Price:** $195.

Turning Radius: Pivot.

Motor: Own, $2\frac{3}{4}$x$3\frac{1}{2}$, vertical, 1 cylinder.

Lubrication: Splash.

Carburetor: Float type, $\frac{3}{4}$-in.

Ignition System: High tension magneto.

Cooling System: Air cooled.

Bearings: Die cast babbitt.

Transmission: Spur gear.

Final Drive: Bull gear and pinion.

MOTOR MACULTIVATOR $1\frac{1}{2}$
Motor Macultivator Co., Toledo, O.

PARRETT TRACTOR CO.

Chicago Heights, Illinois

Parrett 16-28   1922

Traction Wheels: Four wheels; two in front 46x4, and two traction in rear 60x10.

No. of Plows Recommended: Three, 14-in.

Length: 158 in.; **Width:** $77\frac{1}{2}$ in.; **Height:** $67\frac{1}{2}$ in.; **Weight:** 5000 lbs.; **Price:** $1390.

Turning Radius: 11 ft.; **Acres Plowed in 10-hr. Day:** 12.

Motor: Midwest No. 402, $4\frac{1}{8}$x$5\frac{1}{4}$, vertical, 4 cylinders, cast in pairs.

Lubrication: Force feed.

Carburetor: Kingston, $1\frac{1}{4}$-in.

Ignition System: Eisemann magneto.

Cooling System: Fan, centrifugal pump and Perfex radiator.

Bearings: Hyatt roller and S. K. F. ball in transmission.

Transmission: Sliding gear, 2.1 to 4.5 m.p.h. forward; 1.75 m.p.h. reverse.

Final Drive: Internal gear.

Belt Pulley: 12x$7\frac{1}{2}$; 1,200 r.p.m. and 3,770 feet per minute at normal engine speed.

PARRETT 16-28
Parrett Tractor Co., Chicago Heights, Ill.

Heider

Tractors and Motor Cultivators

MODEL IC 12-20

MODEL ID 9-16

FOR 14 YEARS Heider Tractors have been in the field helping the farmers of this country get their work done quicker and better than they had ever been able to do it before.

There are many reasons for the popularity of the Heider. The famous Heider friction transmission eliminates clutch, transmission and bevel gears. **This means** no gear stripping and does away with a lot of parts.

This transmission also allows 7 speeds forward and 7 reverse for either traction or belt. Easy to operate, easy to control. Equipped with 4 cylinder Waukesha motor, Dixie magneto, Kingston carburetor, Perfex radiator, Bennett air cleaner. Burns kerosene or gasoline.

Heider Motor Cultivators

Unit control. The gangs and front wheels are moved simultaneously, which means positive control and quick action. You simply guide the gangs over the corn, the front end takes care of itself. It's a feature the farmers appreciate. Equipped with LeRoi motor, Hyatt roller and U. S. ball bearings, Dixie magneto, Kingston carburetor, Bennett air cleaner. 5-10 H. P.

Made in two sizes—
    Model M two row
    Model M-2 single row

Besides the tractors and motor cultivators, the Rock Island Plow Co. also manufactures

POWER FARMING TOOLS
    Including
ROCK ISLAND TRACTOR PLOWS
    2, 3 or 4 bottoms

ROCK ISLAND TRACTOR DISCS
    6, 7, 8 or 10-foot cut
ROCK ISLAND TRACTOR LISTERS
    As well as a complete line of
HORSE DRAWN IMPLEMENTS

Write for catalogs, giving complete details, prices and terms.

ROCK ISLAND PLOW COMPANY, Rock Island, Ill.

BRANCHES:

| Minneapolis, Minn. | Indianapolis, Ind. | Dallas, Tex. | St. Louis, Mo. |
| Sioux Falls, S. D. | Kansas City, Mo. | Omaha, Nebr. | Denver, Colo. |

1922

363

ROCK ISLAND PLOW CO.

Rock Island, Illinois

Heider Motor Cultivator 5-10   1922-1927

Traction Wheels: Four wheels with two in rear, 46x6, furnishing traction.

Length: 132 in.; **Width:** 98 in.; **Height:** 62 in.; **Weight:** 2700 lbs.

Turning Radius: 7 11/12 ft.

Motor: Le Roi, $3\frac{1}{8}$ x $4\frac{1}{2}$, vertical, 4 cylinders, cast en bloc.

Lubrication: Circulating splash.

Carburetor: Kingston, $\frac{7}{8}$-in.

Ignition System: Splitdorf high tension magneto.

Cooling System: Thermo-Syphon. Hy-Duty fan and Perfex radiator.

Bearings: U. S. ball and Hyatt roller in transmission.

Transmission: Friction, $1\frac{1}{2}$ to $3\frac{1}{2}$ m.p.h. forward.

Final Drive: Bull gear.

Belt Pulley: 400 to 1000 r.p.m.

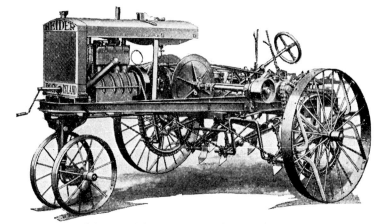

HEIDER MOTOR CULTIVATOR 5-10
Rock Island Plow Co., Rock Island, Ill.

WILSON TRACTOR MANUFACTURING CO.

Ottumwa, Iowa

Wilson 12-20   1922

WILSON 12-20
Wilson Tractor Mfg. Co., Ottumwa, Ia.

Traction Wheels: Drives from four wheels, 40x12.

No. of Plows Recommended: Two to three, 14-in.

Length: 112 in.; **Width:** 71 in.; **Height:** 56 in.; **Weight:** 3705 lbs.

Turning Radius: 7 ft.; **Acres Plowed in 10-hr. Day:** 10 to 14.

Motor: Weidley, $4x5\frac{1}{2}$, vertical, 4 cylinders.

Lubrication: Pump system.

Carburetor: Kingston, $1\frac{1}{4}$-in.

Ignition System: Eisemann magneto.

Cooling System: Perfex radiator, centrifugal pump and fan.

Bearings: New Departure and Hyatt roller thrust.

Transmission: Own, planetary, $1\frac{3}{4}$ to 3.6 m.p.h. forward; $1\frac{3}{4}$ m.p.h. reverse.

Final Drive: Bull gears to rear wheels, chain to front.

Belt Pulley: 8x8; 800-1,265 r.p.m. and 2,650 feet per minute at normal engine speed.

YUBA MANUFACTURING CO.

Marysville, California

Yuba Ball Tread 25-40   1922-1930

Traction Wheels: Two crawlers in rear; one front wheel.

No. of Plows Recommended: Six 14-in.

Length: 157 in.; **Width:** 73½ in.; **Height:** 61 in.; **Weight:** 10250 lbs.; **Price:** $4250.

Turning Radius: 9 ft.

Motor: Wisconsin, 5¾ x 7; T-head, 4 cylinders, cast in pairs.

Carburetor: Stromberg, 1½-in.

Ignition System:.. Bosch high tension magneto.

Lighting: K-W system.

Cooling System: Fan, pump and Modine radiator.

Bearings: Hyatt roller in transmission.

Transmission: Sliding gear, 2¼ to 3¼ m. p.h. forward.

Final Drive: Internal gear.

Belt Pulley: 10, 12 or 14 x 8½, optional.

YUBA BALL TREAD 25-40
Yuba Mfg Co., Marysville, Cal.

1923

In 1923, 16 models of 12 makes not included in 1922 were added.

AUSTIN MANUFACTURING CO.

Chicago, Illinois

Austin 12-20   1923

Traction Wheels: Four-wheel drive, each wheel 40x12.
No. of Plows Recommended: Three 14-in.
Width: 70 in. **Weight:** 4600 lbs.
Turning Radius: 7 ft.
Motor: Weidley, Model M, 4x5½, overhead valve, 4 cylinders, cast en bloc.
Lubrication: Centrifugal pump.
Carburetor: Kingston, 1¼-in.
Ignition System: Eisemann magneto.
Cooling System: Centrifugal pump, Perfex radiator and Oakes fan.
Bearings: New Departure and Hyatt.
Transmission: Selective, 2 to 3¾ m.p.h. forward; 2 m.p.h. reverse.
Final Drive: Chain to front wheels; bull gear and pinion to rear.
Belt Pulley: 8x8; 1265 r.p.m. and 2650 ft. per minute at normal engine speed.

AUSTIN 12-20
Austin Manufacturing Co., Chicago, Ill.

366   1923

The Tractors That Build Business— and Make Daily Profits for Dealers

Avery Track-Runner

Profit by Others' Experience!

Everywhere, dealers looking toward the future of their business, are selling the Avery Line of Motor Farming, Threshing, Hauling and Road Building Machines.

New Avery 15 H. P. Tractor

These dealers know that Avery Machines are dependable. They know that they are the products of experienced and successful manufacturers —that they embody certain valuable and exclusive service features—and they know also that every buyer appreciates the fact that Avery Machines represent full value—are reasonably priced and render an enduring and economical service.

Wherever sold, Avery Machines have proved their efficiency—dependability—reserve power —ease of handling—economy—and ready adaptability.

Write for New Avery Book

Illustrates complete line of Avery Power Machines, points out the many desirable features and new improvements which have helped to make the Avery contract such a profitable one to dealers. Also brings prices and facts proving why other dealers are building such a substantial business the Avery way. Write today.

Avery Company, Factory and Main Office, Peoria, Ill.

Branch Houses, Distributors and Service Stations covering every state in the Union

AVERY

Tractors, Trucks Motor Cultivators, Threshers, Plows, etc.

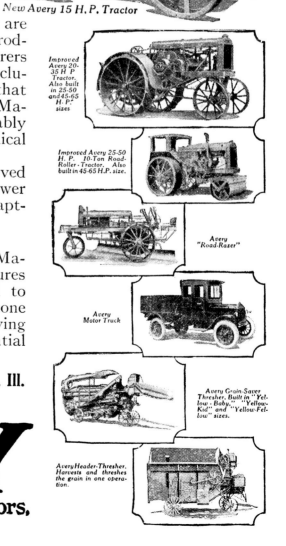

Improved Avery 20-35 H P Tractor. Also built in 25-50 and 45-65 H. P. sizes

Improved Avery 25-50 H. P. 10-Ton Road-Roller-Tractor. Also built in 45-65 H.P. size.

Avery "Road-Razer"

Avery Motor Truck

Avery Grain-Saver Thresher. Built in "Yellow-Baby," "Yellow-Kid" and "Yellow-Fellow" sizes.

Avery Header-Thresher. Harvests and threshes the grain in one operation.

AVERY CO.
Peoria, Illinois

Avery 20-35   1923-1927
Avery 25-50   1923-1932

AVERY 20-35
Avery Co., Peoria, Ill.

Traction Wheels: Four wheels, driving from two rear wheels, 60x16.

No. of Plows Recommended: Three to four 14-in.

Length: 152 in.: **Width:** 68 in.; **Height:** 80 in.; **Weight:** 7500 lbs.

Turning Radius: 12 ft.

Motor: Own, $4\frac{7}{8}$ x 7. horizontal opposed, valve in head, 4 cylinders. cast en bloc.

Lubrication: Madison-Kipp full force feed.

Carburetor: Kingston double, $1\frac{1}{4}$-in.

Ignition System: K-W high tension magneto.

Starting System: Impulse starter.

Cooling System: Cellular radiator, pump and fan.

Bearings: Hyatt roller in differential.

Transmission: Spur gear; $2\frac{1}{3}$ to $3\frac{1}{2}$ m. p.h. forward.

Final Drive: Double spur gear.

Belt Pulley: $16x7\frac{1}{2}$; 700-900 r.p.m. at normal engine speed.

Traction Wheels: Four wheels, driving from two rear wheels, 69 x 20.

No. of Plows Recommended: Five to six 14-in.

Length: 176 in.; **Width:** $90\frac{1}{2}$ in.; **Height:** 108 in.; **Weight:** 12500 lbs.

Turning Radius: 20 ft.

Motor: Own, $6\frac{1}{2}$ x 8, opposed valve-in-head, 4 cylinders; cast in pairs.

Lubrication: Madison-Kipp full force feed.

Carburetor: Kingston double, 2 in.

Ignition System: K-W high tension magneto.

Starting System: Impulse starter.

Cooling System: Cellular radiator, pump and fan.

Bearings: Own throughout.

Transmission: Spur gear, $2\frac{1}{2}$ to $4\frac{2}{3}$ m. p.h. forward; $2\frac{1}{2}$ to 3 m.p.h. reverse.

Final Drive: Double spur gear.

Belt Pulley: $22x8\frac{1}{2}$; 600-700 r.p.m.

AVERY 25-50
Avery Co., Peoria, Ill.

The Bear Tractor

Just Compare These Features
With Those of Any Other Tractor

Light Weight

6,400 lbs. net; 6,900 lbs. with fuel, oil and water —3.5 to 3.9 lbs. ground pressure per square inch— 2 tons lighter than competing tractors.

Extreme Compactness

Over-all dimensions: 125¼ inches long; 62½ inches wide; 54 inches high; 6 feet turning radius. The photographic illustrations show the extreme compactness of the Bear.

The track grips the ground whether going over rises or depressions.

Once-a-month Oiling

Oiled throughout from reservoirs—no waste of time each day with "greasing up"—not a grease cup on the tractor.

Remarkable Drawbar Horse-Power

80% of the engine's power is delivered at the drawbar, actually available for pulling—an efficiency never before equalled.

Compensating Track Roller System

This system equally distributes the weight of the tractor so that the track conforms to the irregularities of the ground, and maintains uniform traction. Observe this feature in the pictures.

Heavy Duty Engine

Heavy duty, valve-in-the-head engine—made especially for hard tractor work—its 2⅞-inch crank shaft of chrome nickel reflects its quality.

Steel Cable Drawbar

A *resilient* drawbar! Attached to the track frame forward of center and below center of gravity— pulls down in front and increases traction.

Ball Bearing Throughout

Here's one reason for so little waste of power in the Bear—annular ball bearings—*36 of them!* No plain bearings and no adjustments.

Welded Fuel Tank

The fuel tank is welded—not riveted—and is non-leakable. It holds 42 gallons. The fuel line is of airplane metallic hose.

Great Flexibility

The flexibility of the Bear is shown by the accompanying pictures. The extreme ranges of the Oscillating Bar and the Compensating Track Rollers give the Bear a mobility heretofore not approached.

No-trouble Track

Of all the exclusive features that make up its excellence, perhaps none distinguishes the Bear more than the Bear Track—it causes *so little trouble* and *so little expense.* It is adjusted by a single lever.

Easy Control and Comfortable Seat

It is as easy to operate a Bear Tractor as an automobile—and equally comfortable. The control is essentially the same as on a standard car.

Write us regarding dealer opportunities.

BEAR TRACTORS, Inc., 5329 Park Place, NEW YORK CITY

The Bear is extremely flexible—adaptable to varied conditions.

BEAR TRACTORS, INC.

New York, New York

Bear 25-35

1923-1925

BEAR 25-35
Bear Tractors, Inc., New York, N.Y.

Traction Wheels: Two crawlers, 64x12.

No. of Plows Recommended: Four, 14-in.

Length: 125¼ in.; Width: 62½ in.; Height: 54 in.; Weight: 6000 lbs.; Price: $4250.

Turning Radius: 6 ft.

Motor: Stearns, 4¾x6½, valve-in-head, 4 cylinders, cast en bloc.

Lubrication: Force feed.

Carburetor: Schebler, 1¾.

Ignition System: Bosch magneto.

Cooling System: Fan, centrifugal pump and spiral sectional radiator.

Bearings: Standard ball throughout.

Transmission: Selective gear; 5.9-3.4 to 2.1 m.p.h. forward; 2 m.p.h. reverse.

Final Drive: Internal gear.

Belt Pulley: 12x9; 1190 r.p.m. and 3800 ft. per minute at normal engine speed.

J. I. CASE PLOW WORKS CO.

Racine, Wisconsin

New Wallis OK 15-27

1923-1926

Traction Wheels: Four wheels with two, built up, traction in rear, 48x12.

No. of Plows Recommended: Three 14-in.

Length: 132 in.; Width: 61 in.; Height: 65 in.; Weight: 3630 lbs.

Turning Radius: 15 ft.

Motor: Own, 4¼x5¾, valve-in-head, 4 cylinders, cast en bloc.

Lubrication: Circulating-splash.

Carburetor: Bennett, 1¼-in.

Ignition System: Bosch high tension magneto, with impulse starter.

Cooling System: Modine radiator, centrifugal pump and fan.

Bearings: Timken roller in rear axle.

Transmission: Selective gear, 2½ to 3½ m.p.h. forward; 2½ m.p.h. reverse.

Final Drive: Spur gear.

Belt Pulley: 18½x7; 475 r. p. m. and 2,300 feet per minute at normal engine speed.

NEW WALLIS OK 15-27
J. I. Case Plow Works Co., Racine, Wis.

ELECTRIC WHEEL CO.
Quincy, Illinois

Allwork 20-38   1923

Traction Wheels: Two rear drive wheels, 48x14, with 6-in. extension rims.

No. of Plows Recommended: Four 14-in.

Length: 126 in.; **Width:** 85 in.; **Height:** 72 in.; **Weight:** 6500 lbs.; **Price:** $1695.

Turning Radius: 12½ ft.; **Acres Plowed in 10-hr. Day:** 13½.

Motor: Own; 5x7, vertical, 4 cylinders, cast singly.

Lubrication: Force feed oiling to all bearings.

Carburetor: Kingston, 1½-in.

Ignition System: High tension magneto with impulse starter.

Cooling System: Perfex radiator, centrifugal pump and fan.

Bearings: Die cast, babbitt lined, bronze backed shell bearings.

Transmission: Selective, sliding gear, 2 to 4¼ m.p.h. forward; 2 m.p.h. reverse.

Final Drive: Enclosed spur gears.

Belt Pulley: 13¾x8; 900 r.p.m. and 3000 feet per minute at normal engine speed.

ALLWORK 20-38
Electric Wheel Co., Quincy, Ill.

GRAY TRACTOR CO., INC.
Minneapolis, Minnesota

Gray 22-40   1923

Traction Wheels: Two non drive wheels in front, 40x8, and one rear drum, 54x54, giving traction.

No. Plows Recommended: Four, 14-in.

Length: 173 in.; **Width:** 80 in.; **Height:** 64½ in.; **Weight:** 6900 lbs.

Turning Radius: 17 ft.; **Acres Plowed in 10-hr. day:** 15.

Motor: Waukesha, 5x6¼, L-head, 4 cylinders, cast en bloc.

Lubrication: Pressure.

Carburetor: Bennett, 1½-in.

Ignition System: Bosch DU-4 high tension magneto.

Cooling System: Shotwell-Johnson radiator, centrifugal pump and fan.

Starting and Lighting Equipment: Impulse starter.

Bearings: Hyatt and New Departure roller and ball in transmission.

Transmission: Sliding gear; 2.4 to 3 m.p.h. forward; 2.4 m.p.h. reverse.

Final Drive: Chains.

Belt Pulley: 11⅜x8⅛; 950 r.p.m. and 2850 feet per minute at normal engine speed.

GRAY 22-40
Gray Tractor Co., Inc., Minneapolis, Minn.

Get in on the Ground Floor of a Great Tractor Success

WHEN *McCormick - Deering Tractors* came out into the power farming world a little while ago they met a ready-made demand that absorbed them fast enough to keep the dealers clamoring for shipments. These tractors started with the advantage of McCormick-Deering reputation, and they showed the public such a combination of features, built into an attractive, up-to-the-minute design, that many a dealer has found himself on the defensive against farmers who knew what they wanted, and wanted it bad. Speedier production had to come to the rescue.

Power farming is ready for great strides ahead. In two or three years there should be huge numbers of McCormick-Deering 15-30 and 10-20 h.p. tractors on the farms. Every dealer who plays his part in keeping abreast of the movement will reap great rewards. If you want to get a good early start, get in touch with the Harvester branch house.

INTERNATIONAL HARVESTER COMPANY
of America
(Incorporated)

606 S. Michigan Ave.   **Chicago, Illinois**

McCormick-Deering Tractor Features —

Ball and Roller Bearings at 28 points.

All wearing parts, including cylinder walls, replaceable.

Entire main frame in one sturdy unit.

All wearing parts enclosed, running in oil.

All parts easily accessible, easily removed.

Alemite lubricating system.

Throttle governor.

Large belt pulley.

Adjustable drawbar.

Water air cleaner.

Three forward speeds.

Comfort and safety features, such as platform, wide fenders, adjustable seat and foot levers.

For Every Power Need

The "Caterpillar's"* field of usefulness is practically unlimited. There is a "Caterpillar"* of size and capacity for every power need. On farm or ranch, in the mining, oil and lumber industries, for snow removal and other civic work—wherever tractive power and endurance are at a premium, the "Caterpillar"* has no real competitor.

There is no phase of road-making, heavy-duty hauling or power farming which the *"Caterpillar"** has not bettered and made more economical. Its great power and endurance have enabled it to establish performance records which are accepted as standard by leading road officials, engineers, contractors and farmers. More miles of good roads are being built and maintained by *"Caterpillars"** than by any other method or machine. The *"Caterpillar"** has plowed thousands of acres of land more effectively, and seeded and harvested crops at the lowest cost. There is a size and type of *"Caterpillar"** for every power need. For the lighter jobs the 2-ton (T-35) possesses every quality required for speedy, low-cost working. **For** moderate power demands the 5-ton is the choice of the most experienced users. The 10-ton is supreme in the heavy-duty field. Write for our special Co-operative Dealer Plan!

HOLT
PEORIA, ILL.
STOCKTON, CALIF.

*THERE IS BUT ONE "CATERPILLAR" —HOLT BUILDS IT

THE HOLT MFG. CO., Inc.
Peoria, Ill.   Stockton, Calif.
Export Division: 50 Church St , New York

BRANCHES AND SERVICE STATIONS ALL OVER THE WORLD

THE HOLT MANUFACTURING CO., INC.

Peoria, Illinois and Stockton, California

"Caterpillar" 2-Ton   1923-1924

Traction Wheels: Two self-laying tracks; 51-in. ground contact; 10-in. wide.
No. of Plows Recommended: Three 14-in.
Length: 103 in.; **Width:** 48 in.; **Height:** 52 in.; **Weight:** 4000 lbs.
Turning Radius: 5½ ft.
Motor: Own, 4x5½, overhead camshaft, 4 cylinders, cast en bloc.
Lubrication: Full force feed.
Carburetor: Kingston, 1¼ in.
Ignition System: Eisemann high tension magneto.
Lighting Equipment: "N. E." (Special equipment.)
Cooling System: Fan, centrifugal pump and tubular radiator.
Bearings: Ball and roller in transmission.
Transmission: Selective, sliding gear; 2⅛, 3 and 5¼ m.p.h. forward; 2⅜ m.p.h. reverse.
Final Drive: Spur gear, enclosed.
Belt Pulley: 11½x6½; 1000 r. p. m. and 3000 feet per minute at normal engine speed.

"CATERPILLAR" 2-TON
The Holt Mfg. Co., Inc., Peoria, Ill. and Stockton, Cal.

INTERNATIONAL HARVESTER CO.

Chicago, Illinois

McCormick Deering 10-20   1923-1934
McCormick Deering 15-30   1923-1929

Traction Wheels: Four wheels, two traction in rear, 42x12.

No. of Plows Recommended: Two, 14-in.

Length: 123 in.; **Width:** 60 in.; **Height:** 62 in.; **Weight:** 3700 lbs.

Turning Radius: 15 ft.

Motor: Own; 4¼x5, vertical, valve-in-head, 4 cylinders, cast en bloc.

Lubrication: Splash and force feed.

Carburetor: Ensign, 1¼-in.

Ignition System: Aero high tension magneto.

Cooling System: Thermo-syphon.

Bearings: Own make roller in transmission and rear axle.

Transmission: Selective; 2 to 4 m.p.h. forward; 2¾ m.p.h. reverse.

Final Drive: Spur gear.

Belt Pulley: 15¼x7; 645 r.p.m. and 2575 ft. per minute at normal engine speed.

McCORMICK-DEERING 10-20
International Harvester Co., Chicago, Ill.

WHY BALL BEARINGS

Mean Uninterrupted Performance

THE farmer's time is too valuable to run the chances of having to make any major adjustments during a busy season.

Bearings, securely housed to exclude dirt and grit, especially in change speed mechanism, should be wear-proof and, hence, non-adjustable.

That point, together with its superior efficiency — permitting the freer flow of power from engine to drawbar — makes New Departure ball bearings the logical choice in any tractor or power-driven farm implement.

Have you received your copy of the Tractor Manual?

THE NEW DEPARTURE
MANUFACTURING COMPANY
Bristol, Conn.
Detroit   Chicago

New Departure
Ball Bearings

Traction Wheels: Four wheel type, two in rear, 50x12, giving traction.

No. of Plows Recommended: Three 14-in.

Length: 133 in.; **Width:** 65 in.; **Height:** 61 in.; **Weight:** 5750 lbs.

Turning Radius: 15 ft.

Motor: Own, $4\frac{1}{2}$x6, vertical, valve-in-head, 4 cylinders, cast en bloc.

Lubrication: Splash and force feed.

Carburetor: Ensign, $1\frac{1}{2}$-in.

Ignition System: Aero high tension magneto.

Cooling System: Thermo-syphon.

Bearings: Own make roller in transmission and rear axle.

Transmission: Selective; 2 to 4 m.p.h. forward; $2\frac{3}{4}$ m.p.h. reverse.

Final Drive: Spur gear.

Belt Pulley: $6\frac{3}{4}$x8; 595 r.p.m. and 2600 ft. per minute at normal engine speed.

McCORMICK-DEERING 15-30
International Harvester Co., Chicago, Ill.

KEYSTONE IRON & STEEL CORP.

Los Angeles, California

Keystone 20-35   1923

Traction Wheels: Two tracks, 1728 sq. in. traction surface.

No. of Plows Recommended: Three 14-in.

Length: 132 in.; **Width:** 72 in.; **Height:** 54 in.; **Weight:** 9850 lbs.

Turning Radius: $5\frac{1}{2}$ ft.

Motor: Waukesha, 5x$6\frac{1}{4}$, 4 cylinders.

Lubrication: Gear pump to all bearings.

Carburetor: Halley, $1\frac{1}{2}$-in.

Ignition System: Splitdorf high tension magneto.

Cooling System: Centrifugal pump, Oakes fan and Perfex radiator.

Bearings: Hyatt and Timken roller.

Transmission: Sliding spur gears, $1\frac{1}{4}$ to 5 m.p.h. forward; $2\frac{1}{2}$ m.p.h. reverse.

Final Drive: Gear and pinion to crawler drive sprockets.

Belt Pulley: 16x8; 600 r.p.m.

KEYSTONE 20-35
Keystone Iron & Steel Corp., Los Angeles, Cal.

"Keystone" - "20-35"

NOTE THE FLEXIBLE TRACKS

NOTE THE CENTER WHEEL DRIVE

The Big Ideas are

all small rollers and wheels are **eliminated** from its **Track Mechanism**. They are **not there** to wear and give trouble. Power is applied in **center** of **tracks** at **top** and **bottom** through the **large center Bull Wheel**, consequently **no strain** on **track shoe** or **pin**.

Built by KEYSTONE IRON & STEEL CORP., Los Angeles, Cal.
WRITE FOR DEALERS PROPOSITION.

Run Your Belts Slack Without Slip

Every belt user wants a slack belt, but slack belts slip.

If you will give your belts an occasional treatment with Cling-Surface preservative they will not slip and you can run them all slack and pull full loads.

While Cling-Surface will keep them pliable, waterproof and long-lived.

It contains no resin. For over 25 years it has been used all over the world, and is the only treatment giving these results.

Buy in pint, quart, half or full gallon cans from your dealer, or come to us if he fails you.

CLING-SURFACE CO., 1018 Niagara St., Buffalo, New York

LOMBARD AUTO TRACTOR-TRUCK CORP.

New York, New York

Lombard 60   1923-1925
Lombard 100   1923-1925

Traction Wheels: Two crawlers at rear, 86x12.

No. of Plows Recommended: Ten to fourteen, 14-in.

Length: 175 in.; **Width:** 51¾ in.; **Height:** 72 in.; **Weight:** 12,000 lbs.

Turning Radius: 20 ft.

Motor: Special make, 5⅛x6¾, vertical, 4 cylinders, cast en bloc.

Lubrication: Force feed through drilled crankshaft.

Carburetor: Stromberg, 1¾-in.

Ignition System: Simms.

Starting and Lighting Equipment: Leece-Neville.

Cooling System: Pump, radiator and Oakes fan.

Bearings: Special.

Transmission: Special; 2-4 to 6 m.p.h. forward; 1½ m.p.h. reverse.

Final Drive: Bevel gear.

LOMBARD 60
Lombard Auto Tractor-Truck Corp., New York City, New York.

LOMBARD 100
Lombard Auto Tractor-Truck Corp., New York City, New York.

Traction Wheels: Two crawlers at rear, 84x12.

No. of Plows Recommended: Twelve to sixteen, 14-in.

Length: 336 in.; **Width:** 77 in.; **Height:** 78 in.; **Weight:** 19000 lbs.

Turning Radius: 28 ft.

Motor: Special make, 5¾x7, vertical, 6 cylinders, cast in pairs.

Lubrication: Force feed through drilled crankshaft.

Ignition System: Simms magneto, impulse starter.

Starting and Lighting Equipment: Leece-Neville.

Cooling System: Pump, radiator and Oakes fan.

Bearings: Special.

Transmission: Special; 2-4-6 to 8 m.p.h. forward; 1½ m.p.h. reverse.

Final Drive: Worm.

**The Genuine,
Original
Robert Bosch
Products**
consist of
the following:

*Magnetos
Spark Plugs
Spot Lights
Electric Horns
Lighting Generators
Starting Motors
Impulse Starter
    Couplings
Flexible Adjustable
    Couplings
Storage Batteries
Hydrometers
Mechanical Lubri-
    cators
Lamps
Magneto-Generator
    Units*

**Send for interesting
"Bosch Facts" and
full details of our
proposition**

A Typical
Genuine Bosch
Product

ZU4 Magneto

Quick Short Spurts

or long, steady grinds are all the same—if the ignition system is thoroughly dependable. Whether the tractor is pulling up a long, stiff hill, or the motor truck traveling a long route over the highways, there is always a constant, even flow of power if the ignition system is the genuine, *original* Bosch—

Robert Bosch Magnetos and Spark Plugs

The live merchant who handles this—the largest line of quality automotive accessories in the world—has an indestructible asset— the selling franchise that grows more valuable year after year.

Robert Bosch Magneto Co., Inc.

Otto Heins, President

123 West 64th St.   **New York**

Chicago Branch: 1302 South Wabash Ave.

Several Hundred U. S. Service Stations—Representatives the World Over

No connection whatsoever with the American Bosch Magneto Corporation

M. B. M. MANUFACTURING CO.
Milwaukee, Wisconsin

Red E Garden   1923-1925

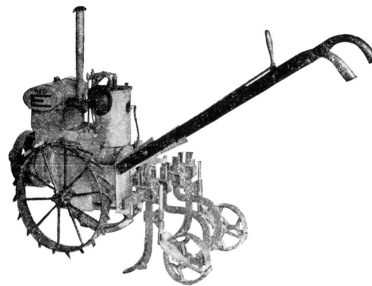

RED E GARDEN
M. B. M. Manufacturing Co., Milwaukee, Wis.

Traction Wheels: Two wheels, both traction, 20x3.

No. of Plows Recommended: One 8 in.

Length: 73 in.; **Width:** 17 in.; **Height:** 36 in.; **Weight:** 420 lbs.; **Price:** $250.

Turning Radius: 2 ft.

Motor: Own, vertical, 3¾x4, 1 cylinder.

Lubrication: Special splash.

Carburetor: Holley, ⅞ in.

Ignition System: Bosch high tension magneto.

Cooling System: Air; fan in fly wheel.

Bearings: Ball and roller.

Transmission: Worm; 1 to 4 m.p.h. forward.

Final Drive: Worm.

Belt Pulley: 3x3½; 1200 r.p.m.

MONARCH TRACTORS, INC.
Watertown, Wisconsin

Monarch Ind. Model E 4-40   1923-1925
Monarch Ind. Model D 6-60   1923-1925

Traction Wheels: Crawler on each side, 12x67¼.

Length: 134 in.; **Width:** 83⅜ in.; **Height:** 79 in.; **Weight:** 12,000 lbs.; **Price,** $4,200.

Turning Radius: 7 ft.

Motor: Beaver, 4¾x6; 4 cylinders, cast in pairs.

Lubrication: Splash and pump.

Carburetor: Stromberg, 1¾-in.

Ignition System: American Bosch magneto.

Cooling System: Centrifugal Pump, Modine radiator, and Automotive fan.

Bearings: Hyatt roller in transmission.

Transmission: Sliding gear; 2¼ to 5 m.p.h. forward.

Final Drive: Chain.

Belt Pulley: 16x8¾; 800 r.p.m.

MONARCH INDUSTRIAL MODEL E 4-40
Monarch Tractors, Inc., Watertown, Wis.

The Double Market Doubles Profits on this Complete Line

CRAWLER construction and ample power fit the Cletrac for both farm and industrial work. The two models—the "W" and its more recent tractor-mate, the "F"—make up a *complete* tractor line.

With no other crawler tractors of moderate price on the market, and with the Cletrac's double sales opportunities, the Cletrac dealer has a big lead over his nearest competitor. Model "W" has a steady, month-in and month-out demand from the farm market and, in addition, an ever-increasing demand from manufacturers, road builders, contractors and all sorts of industries.

In Model "F" the Cletrac dealer can offer a *new principle* in crawler tractors—a two-plow tractor which does *all* farm jobs including *cultivation*. Model "F" is made in three sizes with varying widths and clearances. It works *between* the rows or *straddling* the rows, and cultivates corn, potatoes, cotton, or other row crops. Two leading implement manufacturers are building one and two row cultivators which hitch behind Cletrac "F" and make horses unnecessary on any cultivating job.

Make the most of this opportunity for double profit in your territory. Write for full information and our offer to responsible dealers.

THE CLEVELAND TRACTOR COMPANY
Largest Producers of Crawler Tractors in the World

19215 Euclid Avenue   **Cleveland, Ohio**

MODEL F   Cletrac REG. U.S. PAT. OFF   MODEL W

9-16 H. P.   12-20 H. P.

MONARCH INDUSTRIAL MODEL D 6-60
Monarch Tractors, Inc., Watertown, Wis.

Traction Wheels: Crawler on each side, $12 \times 89\frac{1}{4}$.

Length: 140 in.; **Width:** $83\frac{3}{8}$ in.; **Height:** 79 in.; **Weight:** 15500 lbs.; **Price:** $5,500.

Turning Radius: 8 ft.

Motor: Beaver, $4\frac{3}{4} \times 6$, 6 cylinders, cast in pairs.

Lubrication: Splash and pump.

Carburetor: Stromberg D, $1\frac{3}{4}$-in.

Ignition System: American Bosch magneto.

Starting and Lighting Equipment: American Bosch (Special equipment).

Cooling System: Centrifugal Pump, Modine radiator, and Automotive fan.

Bearings: Hyatt roller in transmission.

Transmission: Sliding gear; $2\frac{1}{4}$ to 5 m.p.h. forward.

Final Drive: Chain.

Belt Pulley: $16 \times 8\frac{3}{4}$; 800 r.p.m.

Important Reasons For the Waterloo Boy's Success on Farms

1. From the bottom up the Waterloo Boy is built for the heavy, continuous, day-in and day-out duty on farms. Sturdy and strong throughout, it lasts longer and costs less for upkeep.

2. A real kerosene tractor. Its engine, specially built for burning kerosene, utilizes this low priced fuel with real economy. In many competitive tests and on thousands of farms its fuel economy has been proved.

3. Its simple, two-cylinder engine—an engine with fewer but larger parts—having a large bore and long stroke, develops 12 H.P. at the drawbar and 25 H.P. on the belt, at the low operating speed of 750 R.P.M.

4. Easy to get at. The motor parts, the transmission, the differential are all readily accessible from a standing position. It is comparatively easy to keep the Waterloo Boy in good running order —a feature every user highly appreciates.

5. Because of its simplicity, the Waterloo Boy is easy to understand, easy to operate. The farmer doesn't need to be a mechanic to keep it going.

6. At the present price to the farmer— a price far below the pre-war price, the Waterloo Boy makes an unusually profitable investment for farmers in your territory.

Remember, the Waterloo Boy is a full-fledged three-plow tractor—and for belt work it gives the farmer sufficient power to operate a complete battery of belt machinery. It fills completely the power needs on the majority of farms.

John Deere Plow Company
Kansas City   **Omaha**

1924

In 1924, 14 models of 10 makes not included in 1923 were added.

ALLIS-CHALMERS MANUFACTURING CO.

Milwaukee, Wisconsin

A-C Orchard 15-25   1924-1925
A-C Special Road Maintainer   1924-1925

Traction Wheels: Two 42x12, located in rear.

No. of Plows Recommended: Three 14-in.

Length: 135 in.; **Width:** 68½ in.; **Height:** 50 in.; **Weight:** 4700 lbs.

Turning Radius: 12 ft.

Motor: Own, 4⅛x5¼, V-head, 4 cylinders, cast in pairs.

Lubrication: Pressure.

Carburetor: Kingston, 1¼ in.

Ignition System: Dixie 46-C high tension magneto.

Cooling System: Fan, pump and radiator.

Bearings: Plain, ball and roller.

Transmission: Selective gear; 2¼ to 3 m.p.h. forward; 3 m.p.h. reverse.

Final Drive: Spur pinion and internal gear.

Belt Pulley: 12½x6½; 817 r.p.m and 2675 feet per minute at normal engine speed.

A-C ORCHARD 15-25
Allis-Chalmers Mfg. Co., Milwaukee, Wis.

This Aeroplane view shows the Milwaukee factory of Allis-Chalmers—126 acres of equipment, manned by an organization second to none in engineering ability.

20-35 Size

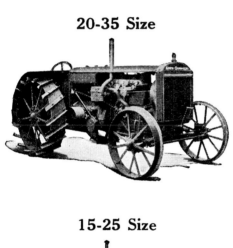

15-25 Size

Better Built by Better Builders

ALLIS-CHALMERS MFG. CO.

Builders of Power for 69 Years

Tractor Division

MILWAUKEE   WISCONSIN

BRANCHES

Wichita and Liberal, Kans.; Enid, Okla.; Amarillo, Texas; Lincoln, Neb.; Fargo, N. D.; Des Moines, Ia. Illinois Farm Equipment Co., Bloomington, Ill.; Banting Mfg. Co., Toledo, Ohio.

The Right Tractor
The Right Factory
The Right Sales Plan

Allis-Chalmers tractor dealers are making money now, made money in the past and can look forward to a prosperous future with every confidence. The importance of upholding the reputation of the great Allis-Chalmers institution is the dealer's protection.

The ability of Allis-Chalmers to build good machinery is known the world over; their disposition to build a good tractor has been demonstrated by eight years past performance of tractors now in the field.

A MONEY MAKING FRANCHISE

Liberal territory arrangements, full co-operation in sales, financing, advertising and service by factory, branch and individual "block men," keep Allis-Chalmers tractors moving.

The Allis-Chalmers plan of selling and helping the dealer sell is as practical as the tractor, as broad and effective as the institution behind it.

You want the proof. We have it. Without obligating yourself, you may write us for the complete plan.

Traction Wheels: Two 46x15 in rear; especially heavy for road work.

Length: 135 in.; Width: 70 in.; Height: 64 in.; Weight: 5600 lbs.

Turning Radius: 12 ft.

Motor: Own, $4\frac{1}{8}$x$5\frac{1}{4}$, V-head, 4 cylinders, cast in pairs.

Lubrication: Pressure.

Carburetor: Kingston, $1\frac{1}{4}$ in.

Ignition System: Dixie 46-C high tension magneto.

Cooling System: Fan, pump and radiator.

Bearings: Plain, ball and roller.

Transmission: Selective gear; $2\frac{1}{2}$ to $3\frac{1}{4}$ m.p.h. forward; $3\frac{1}{4}$ m.p.h. reverse.

Final Drive: Spur pinion and internal gear.

Belt Pulley: $12\frac{1}{2}$x8; 817 r.p.m. and 2675 feet per minute at normal engine speed.

A-C SPEC. ROAD MAINTAINER
Allis-Chalmers Mfg. Co., Milwaukee, Wis.

ARO TRACTOR CO.

Minneapolis, Minnesota

Aro 4-8   1924-1927

ARO 4-8
Aro Tractor Co., Minneapolis, Minn.

Traction Wheels: Two drive wheels in front, 30x4.

No. of Plows Recommended: One 10-in.

Length: 43 in.; Width: 28 in.; Height: 45 in.; Weight: 1,000 lbs. Price $450.

Turning Radius: 4 ft. Acres Plowed in 10-hr. Day: 2.

Motor: Own, $4\frac{3}{4}$x5, 4-cycle, 1-cylinder.

Lubrication: Pump and splash.

Carburetor: Schebler, $1\frac{1}{4}$-in.

Ignition System: Berling magneto with impulse starter.

Cooling System: S-J radiator and Automotive fan.

Bearings: Hess-Bright ball on crankshaft.

Transmission: Worm and gear; 1 to 3 m.p.h. forward; 1 reverse.

Final Drive: Worm gear.

Belt Pulley: 6x$4\frac{1}{2}$; 900 r.p.m. and 1,400 feet per minute at normal engine speed.

AVERY CO.

Peoria, Illinois

Avery 15-30   1924-1925

AVERY 15-30
Avery Co., Peoria, Ill.

Traction Wheels: Four wheels; two non-drive in front and two in rear 50x12 giving traction.

No. Plows Recommended: Three 14-in.

Length: 125 in.; **Width:** 60 in.; **Height:** 66 in.; **Weight:** 5500 lbs.

Turning Radius: 9 ft.

Motor: Own, $4\frac{1}{2}$x6, horizontal opposed, 4-cylinders, removable cylinder walls.

Lubrication: Multiple feed pressure pump.

Carburetor: Stromberg, $1\frac{1}{4}$ in.

Ignition System: K-W high tension.

Cooling System: Radiator, fan and pump.

Bearings: Ball and roller.

Transmission: Spur gear; $2\frac{3}{4}$ to $3\frac{3}{4}$ m.p.h. forward; $2\frac{1}{4}$ m.p.h. reverse.

Final Drive: Rear axle drive.

Belt Pulley: 16x$6\frac{3}{4}$; 950 r.p.m.

BATES MACHINE & TRACTOR CO.

Joliet, Illinois

Bates Industrial 20-25   1924-1926
Bates Industrial 30-40   1924-1926

BATES INDUSTRIAL 20-25
Bates Machine & Tractor Co., Joliet, Ill.

Traction Wheels: Two crawlers full length of tractor, 10-in. wide and 64-in. long.

Length: 103 in.; **Width:** 60 in.; **Height:** 58 in.; **Weight:** 6500 lbs.

Turning Radius: 6 ft.

Motor: Beaver, $4\frac{1}{4}$x6, valve-in-head, 4-cylinders, cast en bloc.

Lubrication: Force feed system.

Carburetor: Kingston, $1\frac{1}{4}$ in.

Ignition System: High tension magneto.

Cooling System: Pump.

Bearings: Ball and roller.

Transmission: Sliding gear; $2\frac{1}{2}$ to $3\frac{1}{2}$ m.p.h. forward; 2 m.p.h. reverse.

Final Drive: Spur gear, enclosed and running in oil.

Belt Pulley: 12x$8\frac{1}{2}$; 850 r.p.m. and 2600 feet per minute at normal engine speed.

BATES INDUSTRIAL 30-40
Bates Machine & Tractor Co., Joliet, Ill.

Traction Wheels: Two crawlers. 84x12. full length of tractor.
Length: 122 in.; **Width:** 66 in.; **Height:** 66 in.; **Weight:** 9500 lbs.
Turning Radius: 7 ft.
Motor: Waukeska, 5x6¼, L-head, 4-cylinders, cast in pairs.
Lubrication: Force feed.
Carburetor: Kingston, 1½ in.
Ignition System: High tension magneto.
Cooling System: Pump.
Bearings: Ball and roller.
Transmission: Sliding gear; 1.4 to 4½ m. p.h. forward; 3¼ m.p.h. reverse.
Final Drive: Spur gear, enclosed and running in oil.
Belt Pulley: 12x8½; 850 r.p.m. and 2600 feet per minute at normal engine speed.

ELECTRIC WHEEL CO.

Quincy, Illinois

Allwork Kerosene 16-30   1924-1926
Allwork 20-35   1924-1929
Allwork 22-40   1924-1929

ALLWORK KEROSENE 16-30
Electric Wheel Co., Quincy, Ill.

Traction Wheels: Four wheels, two traction wheels in rear, 48 x 12.
No. of Plows Recommended: Three 14-in
Length: 125 in.; **Width:** 76 in.; **Height:** 69 in.; **Weight:** 5200 lbs.; **Price:** $1295.
Turning Radius: 12 ft.; **Acres Plowed In 10-hr. Day:** 11.
Motor: Own; 5 x 6, vertical, 4 cylinders, cast separately.
Lubrication: Constant level splash.
Carburetor: Kingston, 1½-in.
Ignition System: High tension magneto.
Starting Equipment: Impulse starter.
Cooling System: Pump, radiator and fan.
Bearings: Hyatt and American roller.
Transmission: Selective sliding gear, 2 to 4¼ m.p.h. forward; 2 m.p.h. reverse.
Final Drive: Enclosed spur gears.
Belt Pulley: 13¾x7½; 700 to 900 r.p.m. and 3000 feet per minute at normal engine speed.

ALLWORK 20-35
Electric Wheel Co., Quincy, Ill.

Traction Wheels: Two rear drive wheels, 48x14, with 6-in. extension rims.

No. of Plows Recommended: Four 14-in.

Length: 126 in.; Width: 85 in.; Height: 72 in.; Weight: 6500 lbs.; Price $1695.

Turning Radius: 14 ft. Acres Plowed in 10-hr. Day: $13\frac{1}{2}$.

Motor: Own; 5x7, vertical, 4 cylinders, cast singly.

Lubrication: Force feed oiling to all bearings.

Carburetor: Kingston, $1\frac{1}{2}$-in.

Ignition System: High tension magneto with impulse starter.

Cooling System: Perfex radiator, centrifugal pump and fan.

Bearings: Die cast, babbitt lined, bronze backed shell bearings.

Transmission: Selective, sliding gear, 2 to $4\frac{1}{4}$ m.p.h. forward; 2 m.p.h. reverse.

Final Drive: Enclosed spur gears.

Belt Pulley: $13\frac{3}{4}$x$7\frac{1}{2}$; 900 r.p.m. and 2800 feet per minute at normal engine speed.

Traction Wheels: Four wheels; two in rear 48x14 with 6 in. extension rims giving traction.

No. of Plows Recommended. Four to five 14-in.

Length: 126 in.; Width: 88 in.; Height: 73 in.; Weight: 8000 lbs.; Price $2200.

Turning Radius: 14 ft.; Acres Plowed in 10-hr. Day: $13\frac{1}{2}$ to 18.

Motor: Own, $5\frac{1}{2}$x7, vertical; 4-cylinders, cast singly.

Lubrication: Force feed oiling to all bearings.

Carburetor: Kingston, $1\frac{3}{4}$ in.

Ignition System: High tension magneto with impulse starter.

Cooling System: Perfex radiator, centrifugal pump and fan.

Bearings: Die cast, babbitt lined, bronze backed shell bearings.

Transmission: Selective sliding, 2 to $4\frac{1}{4}$ m.p.h. forward; 2 m.p.h. reverse.

Final Drive: Enclosed spur gears.

Belt: Pulley: $13\frac{3}{4}$x$9\frac{1}{2}$; 700-900 r.p.m. and 2900 feet per minute at normal engine speed.

ALLWORK 22-40
Electric Wheel Co., Quincy, Ill.

FEDERAL FOUNDRY SUPPLY CO.

Cleveland, Ohio

Merry Garden Auto Cultivator   1924

MERRY GARDEN AUTO CULTIVATOR
Federal Foundry Supply Co., Cleveland, O.

Traction Wheels: Two wheels, both traction, 20x3.

Weight: 260 lbs.; **Price:** $230.

Motor: Evinrude; $2\frac{5}{8}$x$2\frac{1}{2}$, 2-cylinders.

Ignition System: Bosch magneto.

Cooling System: Thermo-syphon.

Belt Pulley: 6x2; 200 r.p.m.

GILSON MANUFACTURING CO.

Port Washington, Wisconsin

Bolens Power Hoe 1.4   1924-1925

Traction Wheels: Two wheels, 15x3.

Weight: 200 lbs.; **Price:** $180.

Turning Radius: $1\frac{1}{2}$ ft.

Motor: Briggs & Stratton, $2\frac{1}{2}$x$2\frac{1}{2}$, vertical, 4-cycle, 1-cylinder, cast en bloc.

Lubrication: Combination pump and splash.

Carburetor: Zenith, $\frac{1}{2}$ in.

Ignition System: High tension magneto in fly wheel.

Cooling System: Air blower in fly wheel.

Bearings: Babbitt and bronze.

Transmission: Eight to one gear reduction in motor; patented belt drive to jack shaft; chain from jack shaft to bull wheels. Five to one reduction.

Final Drive: Chain.

Belt Pulley: 6x2; 310 r.p.m. and 105 feet per minute at normal engine speed.

BOLENS POWER HOE 1.4
Gilson Mfg. Co., Port Washington, Wis.

Creators of Farm Wealth—
They Sell Well and Stay Sold

Power applied to Farm Implements creates the wealth of the farm, from which all other wealth is derived. Not a business in the world could survive in its present state, if power was withdrawn from the implements, which produce the food we eat.

Mechanical power controls the world of production today. Agriculture is right now in the midst of a revolution caused by the movement of mechanical power onto the farm. The wind mill, stationary engine, lighting plant, automobile, truck and the tractor are each a unit in the new plan of farm crop production through mechanical power, which increases the productive power of one man, solves the hired help problem, saves time, increases the amount of crop production and lowers the cost per unit. Mechanical power is a creator and a saver of farm wealth.

Selling Tractor Power to the Farmer is the big business of farm equipment dealers this year. The movement of tractor power to the farm is on the upward swing right now. Look over the line of KEROSENE BURNING HART-PARR TRACTORS on the opposite page. They deliver the goods for both the farmer and the dealer. They sell well and stay sold.

Round out your line of farm equipment by adding the famous line of HART-PARR KEROSENE BURNING TRACTORS, built by the oldest concern in the industry. Write for our selling plan. The experience of a generation of tractor manufacturing and merchandising is back of this plan. It pays.

HART-PARR COMPANY
Founders of the Tractor Industry

Department "A"   Charles City, Iowa

Many of the old Hart-Parrs that plowed the virgin prairies of the Northwest are still in use today. The great grand-daddy of all Tractors was old Hart-Parr No. 1, built in 1901.

1924   391

HART-PARR CO.
Charles City, Iowa

Hart-Parr 40   1924-1925

Traction Wheels: Four wheels; two in front, 28x5; two traction in rear. 52x13.

No. of Plows Recommended: Four 14-in.

Length: 140 in.; Width: 96 in.; Height: 67 in.; Weight: 7500 lbs.; Price $2250 f.o.b. factory.

Turning Radius. 13 ft.

Motor: Own, $5\frac{1}{2}$x$6\frac{1}{2}$; horizontal; 4-cylinder, cast in pairs.

Lubrication: Madison-Kipp force feed.

Carburetor: Schebler. $1\frac{1}{2}$ in.

Ignition System: K-W high tension magneto with impulse starter.

Cooling System: Centrifugal pump, fan and radiator.

Bearings: Roller and ball in transmission and own on drive axle.

Transmission: Selective, sliding spur gear, 2 to 3 m.p.h forward.

Final Drive: Internal gear and master pinions.

Belt Pulley: 14x8; 750 r.p.m. and 2750 feet per minute at normal engine speed.

HART-PARR 40
Hart-Parr Co., Charles City, Ia.

THE RUSSELL & CO.
Massillon, Ohio

Russell, Model B, 20-40   1924

Traction Wheels: Four wheel type with two rear wheels, 60 x 16, as traction members.

No. of Plows Recommended: Four to five 14-in.

Length: 164 in.; Width; 88 in.; Height: 87 in.; Weight: 7740 lbs.

Turning Radius: $16\frac{3}{4}$ ft.; Acres Plowed in 10-hr. Day: 14 to 18.

Motor: Climax, $5\frac{1}{2}$x7; vertical, 4 cylinders, cast in pairs.

Lubrication: Force feed.

Carburetor: Kingston, $1\frac{1}{2}$-in.

Ignition System: Splitdorf magneto with impulse starter.

Cooling System: Modine honeycomb radiator.

Bearings: Timken roller in transmission and on drive axle.

Transmission: Gearing, 2.4 to 3.75 m. p. h. forward; 2 m. p. h. reverse.

Final Drive: Gearing through rear wheels.

Belt Pulley: $12\frac{1}{2}$x8; 833 r.p.m., and 2732 f.p.m. at normal engine speed.

RUSSELL, MODEL B, 20-40
The Russell & Co., Massillon, Ohio

392   1924

YUBA MANUFACTURING CO.

Marysville, California

Yuba Ball Tread 15-25   1924

YUBA BALL TREAD 15-25
Yuba Mfg. Co., Marysville, Cal.

Traction Wheels: Two crawlers, ball tread, 36x12.
Length: 142 in.; **Width:** 54 in.; **Height:** 55½ in.; **Weight:** 5680 lbs.; **Price:** $2750.
Turning Radius: 8 ft.
Motor: Wisconsin UA, 4¼x6, vertical, 4 cylinders, cast en bloc.
Lubrication: Force feed.
Carburetor: Stromberg M, 1¼-in.
Ignition System: Bosch high tension magneto.
Cooling System: Modine radiator, automotive fan and centrifugal pump.
Bearings: Hyatt roller.
Transmission: Disk and planetary; 3¼ m.p.h. forward; 2 m.p.h. reverse.
Final Drive: Enclosed gear.
Belt Pulley: 12x6½; 900 r.p.m.

RAJAH GIANT, $1.25
Special for Tractor Service. Recommended for Rumely.

RAJAH
SPARK PLUGS

The GIANT is a sturdy plug that will stand the most gruelling motor service in any tractor.

Can be taken apart for cleaning or replacing of porcelain. Nothing to wear out. Lasts indefinitely—a Rajah terminal goes with each plug without extra charge.

If your dealer cannot supply you order direct. Send for our catalog of Plugs, Terminals, etc.

RAJAH AUTO SUPPLY CO.
BLOOMFIELD, NEW JERSEY
U. S. A.

1925

By 1925, the tractors were more conventional in appearance and operation, lessening operational and repair problems, and mechanic's schools and individual experience relieved the repair problem. The 1925 listing includes 36 models of 24 makes not shown in 1924.

ADVANCE-RUMELY THRESHER CO., INC.
La Porte, Indiana

Oil Pull "L" 15-25   1925-1927
Oil Pull "M" 20-35   1925-1927
Oil Pull "S" 30-60   1925-1927

OIL PULL "L" 15-25
Advance-Rumely Thresher Co., Inc., La Porte, Ind.

Traction Wheels: Four wheels, with two in rear, 48x12, giving traction and two non-drive in front, 30x6.
No. of Plows Recommended: Three 14-in.
Length: 136 in.; **Width:** $55\frac{3}{4}$ in.; **Height:** $62\frac{1}{2}$ in.
Turning Radius: 15 ft.
Motor: Own; $5\frac{13}{16}$x7, horizontal; valve-in-head, 2 cylinders, loose sleeve.
Lubrication: Mechanical oiler and splash.
Carburetor: Own—Secor Higgins, $1\frac{13}{16}$ in.
Ignition System: Bosch high tension magneto.
Starting: Mechanical.
Cooling System: Pump circulation; oil in system.
Bearings: New Departure, Timken and bronze.
Transmission: Spur gear; 2, $2\frac{1}{2}$ and 3 m. p. h. forward; $2\frac{1}{2}$ m. p. h. reverse.
Final Drive: Spur gear—enclosed in transmission.
Belt Pulley: 16x$7\frac{1}{2}$; 755 r.p.m. and 3000 feet per minute at normal engine speed.

More power *for actual work*

No friction to steal away your power
in this smooth-running ball-bearing transmission

In the *Light-Weight* OilPull, Rumely engineers have achieved another distinct triumph in tractor engineering. Power loss in bearings and gears has been reduced to practically nothing. *Friction,* the power thief—the cause of deterioration—of breakdowns—of lost time—of heavy repair expense and many other ills—*has been shackled.*

This has been done, *first,* by means of a *Ball-Bearing* Transmission. All shafts in the transmission of this OilPull Tractor are mounted upon smooth-running, *annular ball bearings.* The rear axle is likewise ball-bearing mounted. Each bearing is housed individually and packed in grease. *Second,* every gear inside the transmission is machine cut, with case-hardened teeth. And the complete transmission is enclosed in a dustproof case and operates in a bath of oil.

Frictionless construction is only one feature of the *Light-Weight* OilPull which assures *more power* for plowing, discing, culti-packing and many other drawbar and belt jobs—*at less cost.*

WRITE TODAY FOR CATALOG

In this *Light-Weight* OilPull, Triple Heat Control, Oil Cooling, Dual Lubrication and all the famous OilPull principles of construction have been retained. It is still the famous OilPull, with many improvements and refinements.

The design is small, light, compact, easy to handle and maneuver.

The OilPull has stood for the best in tractor construction for over 14 years. It is the *proved* "quality" tractor. Its record for reliable daily power service—fuel economy—low upkeep and long life stands unduplicated. Write today for complete catalog. Address Dept. A.A.A.

ADVANCE-RUMELY
THRESHER CO., INC., LA PORTE, IND.
(Incorporated)
Serviced Through 33 Branches and Warehouses

Light-Weight
OilPull
The 10-Year Tractor

The Advance-Rumely line includes kerosene tractors, steam engines, grain and rice threshers, husker-shredders, alfalfa and clover hullers, bean hullers, silo fillers, corn shellers, motor trucks and tractor winches.

Traction Wheels: Two drive wheels in rear, 52x16, and two non-drive in front, 34x7.
No. of Plows Recommended: Four 14-in.
Length: 151 in.; Width: 71½ in.; Height: 70½ in.
Turning Radius: 17 ft.
Motor: Own; 6⅛x8¼, horizontal, valve-in-head, 2 cylinders, loose sleeve.
Lubrication: Mechnical oiler and splash.
Carburetor: Own—Secor Higgins, 2⅛ in.
Ignition System: Bosch high tension magneto.
Starting Equipment: Mechanical.
Cooling System: Pump circulation; oil in system.
Bearings: New Departure, Timken and bronze.
Transmission: Spur gear; 2, 2½ and 3 m. p. h. forward; 2½ m. p. h. reverse.
Final Drive: Spur gear enclosed in transmission.
Belt Pulley: 18¾x8½; 635 r.p.m. and 3000 feet per minute at normal engine speed.

OIL PULL "M" 20-35
Advance-Rumely Thresher Co., Inc., La Porte, Ind.

OIL PULL "S" 30-60
Advance-Rumely Thresher Co., Inc., La Porte, Ind.

Traction Wheels: Four wheel type; two in rear, 64x24, giving traction and two in front, 44x10.
No. of Plows Recommended: Eight to ten 14-in.
Length: 191 in.; Width: 100 in.; Height: 88¼ in.
Turning Radius: 22 ft.
Motor: Own; 9x11, horizontal, valve-in-head, 2 cylinders, loose sleeve.
Lubrication: Mechanical oiler and splash.
Carburetor: Own—Secor Higgins, 2¾ in.
Ignition System: Bosch high tension magneto.
Starting Equipment: Mechanical.
Cooling System: Pump circulation; oil in system.
Bearings: New Departure, Timken and bronze.
Transmission: Spur gear; 2, 2½ and 3 m. p. h. forward; 2½ m. p. h. reverse.
Final Drive: Spur gear enclosed in transmission.
Belt Pulley: 25x10; 470 r.p.m. and 3000 feet per minute at normal engine speed.

AMERICAN SWISS MAGNETO CO.
Toledo, Ohio

Motor Macultivator 1

1925-1926

MOTOR MACULTIVATOR 1
American Swiss Magneto Co., Toledo, O.

Traction Wheels: Two wheels, $21\frac{1}{2}$x3.

Price: $162.50.

Turning Radius: Pivot.

Motor: Briggs & Stratton "P B"; $2\frac{1}{2}$x$2\frac{1}{2}$; four cycle; 1 cylinder.

Lubrication: Splash and pump feed.

Ignition System: High tension magneto; fly wheel type.

Cooling System: Blowers.

Transmission: Worm and gear.

Final Drive: Worm and gear, enclosed.

J. I. CASE PLOW WORKS CO.
Racine, Wisconsin

Wallis OKO 15

1925-1926

Traction Wheels: Four wheels; two in rear, 42x12, giving traction, and two in front, 28x$6\frac{1}{4}$.

No. of Plows Recommended: Three 14-in.

Length: 127 in.; **Width:** 56 in.; **Height:** 50 in.; **Weight:** 3,820 lbs.

Turning Radius: $13\frac{1}{2}$ ft.

Motor: Own; $4\frac{1}{4}$x$5\frac{3}{4}$, valve-in-head, 4 cylinders, cast en bloc.

Lubrication: Circulating splash.

Carburetor: Bennett, $1\frac{1}{4}$-in.

Ignition System: Bosch high tension magneto with impulse starter.

Cooling System: Modine tubular radiator, centrifugal pump and fan.

Bearings: Timken roller on rear axle.

Transmission: Selective gear; $2\frac{1}{2}$ to $3\frac{1}{2}$ m. p. h. forward; $2\frac{1}{2}$ m. p. h. reverse.

Final Drive: Spur gear.

WALLIS OKO 15
J. I. Case Plow Works Co., Racine, Wis.

J. I. CASE THRESHING MACHINE CO.
Racine, Wisconsin

Case 18-32
Case 25-45

1925-1928
1925-1930

Traction Wheels: Four wheels, with two drive wheels, 52 x 14, in rear.

No. of Plows Recommended: Three to four 14-in.

Length: 127 in.; **Width:** 72 in.; **Height:** 68 in.; **Weight:** 6500 lbs.; **Price:** $1350.

Turning Radius: 13½ ft.; **Acres Plowed in 10-hr. Day:** 10 to 14.

Motor: Case; 4½ x 6, 4 cylinders, cast en bloc.

Lubrication: Pressure feed through drilled crank shaft.

Carburetor: Kingston, 1⅝.

Ignition System: Bosch high tension magneto with impulse starter.

Cooling System: Pump, radiator and fan.

Bearings: Hyatt roller in transmission and rear axle.

Transmission: Selective sliding gear, 2.50 to 3.33 m. p. h. forward; 1.80 m. p. h. reverse.

Final Drive: Spur gear, enclosed.

Belt Pulley: 16x7½; 1000 r.p.m. and 4180 feet per minute at normal engine speed.

CASE 18-32
J. I. Case Threshing Machine Co., Racine, Wis.

Traction Wheels: Four wheels with two drive wheels, 56 x 16, in rear.

No. of Plows Recommended: Four to five 14 in.

Length: 153 in.; **Width:** 82½ in.; **Height:** 90 in.; **Weight:** 10,065 lbs.; **Price:** $2750.

Turning Radius: 20¼ ft.;

Motor: Own, vertical, 5½ x 6¾, 4 cylinders, cast in pairs.

Lubrication: Force feed through drilled crankshaft. Madison-Kipp force feed auxiliary oiler for cylinders.

Carburetor: Kingston, 2 in.

Ignition System: Bosch high tension magneto.

Cooling System: Pump, radiator and fan.

Bearing: Hyatt roller, Timken roller and New Departure ball.

Transmission: Selective sliding gear, 2.2 to 3.2 m. p. h. forward; 1.4 m. h. p. reverse.

Final Drive: Spur gear, enclosed.

Belt Pulley: 16½ x 8½; 850 r. p. m. and 3669 feet per minute at normal engine speed.

CASE 25-45
J. I. Case Threshing Machine Co., Racine, Wis.

398

1925

IT HAS MADE HISTORY

Tractive power applied to agriculture has reached its highest development in the "Caterpillar" Tractor. Over fifteen years ago the "Caterpillar" obsoleted all existing ideas of how "traction" could be obtained on the softest soils, in sand and in snow. International leadership quickly followed and it has been continuously maintained, because no matter what the soil, climate, road or through roadless country, the "Caterpillar" has proved its superior economy, as well as its enormous pulling power.

It is the adaptability of the "Caterpillar" to every climate and working condition that marks it as the world's foremost producer of reliable power. For orchard, vineyard and farm use; on engineering projects and public works; in the oil, mining and lumber industries—wherever there is need for the utmost in tractive power and endurance, "Caterpillars" are indispensable because they perform tasks impossible for any other machine or method.

CATERPILLAR TRACTOR CO.

Peoria, Ill.   San Leandro, Calif.   Stockton, Calif.

CATERPILLAR
Reg.U.S.   Pat.Off.

1925   399

CATERPILLAR TRACTOR CO.

Peoria, Illinois, San Leandro and Stockton, California

"Caterpillar" 60   1925-1930
"Caterpillar" 2-Ton   1925-1928
"Caterpillar" 5-Ton   1925-1926
"Caterpillar" 10-Ton   1925

Traction Wheels: Two crawlers, each 89x20.

No. of Plows Recommended: Nine 14-in.

Length: 156 in.; **Width:** 95 in.; **Height:** 78 in.; **Weight:** 19,000 lbs.

Motor: Best, 6½x8½, valve-in-head, 4 cylinders, cast singly.

Lubrication: Force feed.

Carburetor: Stromberg, 2 in.

Ignition System: Bosch magneto.

Cooling System: Fan, pump and radiator.

Bearings: Ball and roller throughout.

Transmission: Sliding gear.

Final Drive: Spur gear.

Belt Pulley: 16x10; 650 r.p.m. and 2640 feet per minute at normal engine speed.

"CATERPILLAR" 60
Caterpillar Tractor Co., Peoria, Ill., San Leandro and Stockton, Cal.

Traction Wheels: Two self-laying tracks; 51-in. ground contact; 10-in. wide.

No. of Plows Recommended: Three 14-in.

Length: 108 in.; **Width:** 52 in.; **Height:** 53 in.; **Weight,** 4,700 lbs.

Turning Radius: 5½ ft.

Motor: Own, 4x5½, overhead camshaft, 4 cylinders, cast en bloc.

Lubrication: Full force feed.

Carburetor: Zenith, 1¼-in.

Ignition System: Eisemann high tension magneto.

Lighting Equipment: "N. E." (Special equipment.)

Cooling System: Fan, centrifugal pump and tubular radiator.

Bearings: Ball and roller in transmission.

Transmission: Selective, sliding gear; 2⅛, 3 and 5¼ m.p.h forward; 2⅜ m.p.h. reverse.

Final Drive: Spur gear, enclosed.

Belt Pulley: 11⅝x6½; 1000 r.p.m. and 3000 feet per minute at normal engine speed.

"CATERPILLAR" 2-TON
Caterpillar Tractor Co., Peoria, Ill., San Leandro and Stockton, Cal.

"CATERPILLAR" 5-TON

Caterpillar Tractor Co., Peoria, Ill., San Leandro and Stockton, Cal.

Traction: Two self-laying tracks, 75 in. ground contact and 12 in. wide.

No. of Plows Recommended: Four to six 14-in.

Length: 124 in.; **Width:** 61 in.; **Height:** 65½ in.; **Weight:** 10,400 lbs.

Turning Radius: 7 ft.

Motor: Own make, 4¾x6, vertical, 4 cylinders. cast in pairs.

Lubrication: Full force feed.

Carburetor: Kingston, 1½-in.

Ignition System: Eisemann high tension magneto.

Lighting Equipment: Northeast generator; Willard storage battery. (Special equipment.)

Cooling System: Radiator, centrifugal pump and fan.

Bearings: Ball and roller.

Transmission: Own make, selective sliding gear, 1.75-3-4.25 m. p. h. forward; 2 m. p. h. reverse.

Final Drive: Enclosed spur gear.

Belt Pulley: 13½x8½; 1000 r.p.m. and 3530 f.p.m. at normal engine speed.

Traction: Two self-laying tracks; 101 in. ground contact, 15 in. wide.

No. of Plows Recommended: Six 14-in.

Length: 151 in.; **Width:** 81 in.; **Height:** 111 in.; **Weight:** 20,000 lbs.

Turning Radius: 9 ft.

Motor: Own; vertical, 6½x7, 4 cylinders, cast singly.

Lubrication: Full force feed.

Carburetor: Zenith, 1¾-in.

Ignition System: Eisemann high tension magneto.

Lighting Equipment: Northeast generator; Willard storage battery. (Special equipment.)

Cooling System: Radiator, fan and centrifugal pump.

Bearings: Ball and roller.

Transmission: Own make; selective, sliding gear; 1.67-2.2-3 m. p. h. forward; other speeds optional with 4.78 m.p.h. high; 1.25 m.p.h. reverse.

Final Drive: Enclosed spur gear.

Belt Pulley: 14x9; 850 r.p.m. and 3140 f.p.m. at normal engine speed

"CATERPILLAR" 10-TON

Caterpillar Tractor Co., Peoria, Ill., San Leandro and Stockton, Cal.

THE FAMOUS EAGLE TRACTORS

Powerful medium speed motor, large friction clutch pulley for belt work, driven direct from crankshaft in a position to assure plenty of belt clearance.

Hulling
Threshing
Hay Baling
Silo Filling
Corn Shelling
Feed Grinding

Discing
Seeding
Plowing
Harrowing
Harvesting
Road Grading

Three Sizes: 13-25, 16-30, 20-40 Model "H."

A tractor for all needs, SIMPLE, STRONG and DURABLE.

EASY TO OPERATE AND ECONOMICAL

If interested, write for further information, also on the NEW ALL-STEEL EAGLE SILO FILLER equipped with Timken roller bearings.

THE EAGLE MFG. CO.   APPLETON, WISCONSIN

DEERE & CO.
Moline, Illinois

John Deere 15-27   1925-1927

Traction Wheels: Four wheels with two traction members, 46x12, in rear.

No. of Plows Recommended: Three 14 in.

Length: 109 in.; **Width:** 63 in.; **Height:** 56 in.; **Weight:** 3900 lbs.

Turning Radius: 12 ft.; **Acres Plowed in 10-hr. Day:** 12 to 14.

Motor: Own, $6\frac{1}{2}$x7; horizontal, 2 cylinders, cast en bloc.

Lubrication: Force feed; gear pump; drilled crankshaft.

Carburetor: Schebler, $1\frac{1}{2}$-in.

Ignition System: Splitdorf high tension magneto.

Cooling System: Thermo siphon, Modine radiator and fan.

Bearings: Hyatt roller in differential; Timken roller on axles.

Transmission: Sliding gears $2\frac{1}{2}$ to $3\frac{1}{4}$ m. p. h. forward; 2 m. p. h. reverse.

Final Drive: Double roller chain.

Belt Pulley: 15x$7\frac{1}{2}$; 800 r.p.m. and 3200 ft. per minute at normal engine speed.

JOHN DEERE 15-27
Deere & Co., Moline, Ill.

EAGLE MANUFACTURING CO.
Appleton, Wisconsin

Eagle, Model H, 13-25   1925-1928
Eagle, Model H, 16-30   1925-1933
Eagle, Model H, 40   1925-1928

Traction Wheels: Four wheels, two rear, 48 x 12, affording traction.

No. of Plows Recommended: Three 14-in.

Length: 132 in.; **Width:** 65 in.; **Height:** 76 in.; **Weight:** 5,800 lbs.

Turning Radius: 13 ft; **Acres Plowed in 10-hr. Day:** 8 to 9.

Motor: Own; 7 x 8, valve-in-head, 2 cylinders, cast en bloc.

Lubrication: Madison-Kipp force feed.

Carburetor: Schebler.

Ignition System: Splitdorf high tension magneto with impulse starter.

Cooling System: Perfex radiator, circulating pump and fan.

Bearings: Hyatt roller in transmission and plain babbitt on drive axle.

Transmission: Sliding gear, 2 to 3 m.p.h. forward; $1\frac{3}{4}$ m.p.h. reverse.

Final Drive: Enclosed spur gear, geared to both rear wheels.

Belt Pulley: 20 x $8\frac{1}{2}$; 450 r.p.m. and 2350 feet per minute at normal engine speed.

EAGLE, MODEL H, 13-25
Eagle Mfg. Co., Appleton, Wis.

1925   403

EAGLE, MODEL H, 16-30
Eagle Mfg. Co., Appleton, Wis.

Traction Wheels: Four wheels, two rear, 52 x 12, affording traction.

No. of Plows Recommended: Four 14-in.

Length: 141 in.; **Width:** 70 in.; **Height:** 78 in.; **Weight:** 7100 lbs.

Turning Radius: 14 ft.; **Acres Plowed in 10-hr. Day:** 11-12.

Motor: Own; 8 x 8, valve-in-head, 2 cylinders, cast en bloc.

Lubrication: Madison-Kipp force feed.

Carburetor: Schebler.

Ignition System: Splitdorf high tension magneto with impulse starter.

Cooling System: Perfex radiator, fan, circulating pump.

Bearings: Hyatt roller in transmission and plain babbitt on drive axle.

Transmission: Sliding gear, 2 to 3 m.p.h. forward; 1¾ m.p.h. reverse.

Final Drive: Enclosed spur gear to both rear wheels.

Belt Pulley: 24 x 10; 450 r.p.m. and 2800 feet per minute at normal engine speed.

Traction Wheels: Four wheel type; two traction in rear, 52x12.

Length: 146 in.; **Width:** 70 in.; **Height:** 78 in.; **Weight:** 7400 lbs.

Turning Radius: 15 ft.

Motor: Own, 8x10, horizontal, 2 cylinders, cast en bloc.

Lubrication: Madison-Kipp force feed.

Carburetor: Schebler, 1¾-in.

Ignition System: Splitdorf high tension magneto with impulse starter.

Cooling System: Water, Automotive fan, Perfex radiator and centrifugal pump.

Bearings: Hyatt roller in transmission; plain babbitt in rear axle.

Transmission: Sliding gear; 2 to 3 m.p.h. forward; 1¾ m.p.h. reverse.

Final Drive: Enclosed spur gear direct to wheels.

Belt Pulley: 24x10; 450 r.p.m. and 2800 feet per minute at normal engine speed.

EAGLE, MODEL H, 40
Eagle Manufacturing Co., Appleton, Wis.

FEDERAL FOUNDRY SUPPLY CO.
Cleveland, Ohio

Federal Garden Tractor   1925-1931

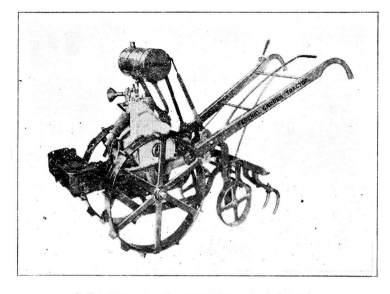

FEDERAL GARDEN TRACTOR
Federal Foundry Supply Co., Cleveland, O.

Traction Wheels: Two cast iron wheels, 20x3 and ¾-in. lugs.

Price: $195.

Motor: Four cycle, vertical, 2½x2½, 1 cylinder.

Lubrication: Splash and pump feed.

Carburetor: Float feed, set jet type.

Ignition System: High tension magneto built in flywheel.

Cooling System: Air current guided to hot part of cylinder from blower on flywheel.

FRICK CO., INC.
Waynesboro, Pennsylvania

Frick 15-30   1925-1926

Traction Wheels: Four wheels; two in rear, 60x12-14, giving traction.
No. of Plows Recommended: Three, 14-in.
Length: 158½-in.; Width: 81½ in.; Height: 66 in.; Weight: 7100 lbs.
Turning Radius: 12½ ft.; Acres Plowed in 10-hr. Day: 10.
Motor: Beaver, 4¾x6, valve-in-head, vertical, 4 cylinders, cast en bloc.
Lubrication: Splash and force feed.
Carburetor: Zenith for gas; Ensign for kerosene; water injection.
Ignition System: Splitdorf high tension magneto with impulse starter.
Cooling System: Perfex radiator with centrifugal pump and fan.
Bearings: Hyatt roller in transmission and babbitt on drive axle.
Transmission: Sliding gear, 2.1 to 3.25 m. p.h. forward; 2 m.p.h. reverse.
Final Drive: Spur gear, enclosed.
Belt Pulley: 13x7; 900 r.p.m. and 3075 feet per minute at normal engine speed.

FRICK 15-30
Frick Co., Inc., Waynesboro, Pa.

1925   405

More than 3,000,000
ORIGINAL BOSCH
Magnetos are in use

Starting is easy when a Fordson has the Original Bosch Magneto System

STARTING troubles are cured now, once, and for all, by installing the ORIGINAL BOSCH Magneto System on the Fordson.

The ORIGINAL BOSCH Magneto has an impulse coupling which "boosts" the spark and makes starting easy and quick—even in the coldest weather.

Any user will tell you how this world-famous magneto saves time, annoyance and repair bills. It is waterproof, dustproof and eliminates the use of coils and timers. Installation is simple.

Robert Bosch Magneto Co., Inc., 119A West 64th Street, New York, N. Y. Chicago Branch: 1302 South Wabash Avenue.

In buying an ORIGINAL BOSCH Magneto System or other original Bosch Products make sure you see the full name "Robert Bosch" and the trademark shown above—only then can you be sure of getting ORIGINAL BOSCH quality as known the world over since 1887.

ORIGINAL BOSCH Products

ORIGINAL BOSCH products include magnetos, spark plugs, horns, generators, magneto-generators, Fordson magneto attachment, Ford magneto attachment, starters, switches, hydrometer for radio batteries, impulse couplings, etc.

Write for descriptive literature on the products in which you are interested

CLING-SURFACE

The Most Widely Used and Successful Belt Treatment

Every dealer has calls for, or is selling, a belt dressing.

And yet few customers are really satisfied.

Why? Because they want results which the belt dressings do not give, but which Cling-Surface for nearly thirty years has been giving to thousands of threshermen and plants all over the world.

Cling-Surface in one grade can be used for all kinds of belts. It makes and keeps them pliable, waterproof and preserved and stops all slipping so all belts can be run slack and pull full loads.

Threshermen are ordering from us in every mail because you, their dealers, haven't it.

If you will write us for information and special introductory offer you can get a permanent business on these goods —which satisfied customers give.

Cling-Surface Co., 1018 Niagara St., Buffalo, N. Y.

GRAY TRACTOR CO.

Minneapolis, Minnesota

Canadian special 22-40   1925-1930

Traction Wheels: Two non-drive wheels in front, 40x8, and one drum in rear, 54x54, giving traction.

No. of Plows Recommended: Four, 14-in.

Price: $2385.

Motor: Waukesha; 5x6¼; 4 cylinders.

Lubrication: Force feed.

Carburetor: Bennett, 1½ in.

Ignition System: Bosch DU-4 high tension magneto.

Cooling System: Shotwell-Johnson radiator, centrifugal pump and fan.

Bearings: Hyatt roller and New Departure ball in transmission.

Transmission: Sliding gears; 2.4 to 3 m.p.h. forward; 2.4 m.p.h. reverse.

Final Drive: Chain.

Belt Pulley: 11⅜x8⅛; 950 r.p.m. and 2850 feet per minute at normal engine speed.

CANADIAN SPECIAL 22-40
Gray Tractor Co., Minneapolis, Minn.

The first Pierce-Arrow, built in 1902.

Old Hart-Parr No. 3, built in 1902 and still alive and kicking.

Both Were New in 1902

The HART-PARR is Still Giving Service

In 1902, the year of the first Pierce-Arrow, HART-PARR founded the tractor industry by building fifteen successful gasoline traction engines. Old HART-PARR No. 3, pictured above, was sold to an Iowa farmer who operated it continuously for twenty-three busy years. Today, it and six others of the original fifteen are still giving service on American farms.

As In the Past, HART-PARRS are Built for L-a-s-t-i-n-g Service

The modern kerosene-burning HART-PARR, though vastly improved and simplified, is still built with old-fashioned thoroughness to give enduring service. The **improved** models for 1925, with enclosed drive, disc clutch, greater power, stronger construction and **detachable power take-off,** represent a quarter of a century of knowing how. When you sell a HART-PARR you sell l-a-s-t-i-n-g satisfaction. It is not "just a tractor," but a year in and year out investment for its buyer.

HART-PARR CO., 149 Lawler St., Charles City, Iowa

KEROSENE TRACTORS - STATIONARY ENGINES - FEED MILLS

HART-PARR

FOUNDERS OF THE TRACTOR INDUSTRY

WASHING MACHINES - AIR COMPRESSORS - COMMERCIAL CASTINGS

GREAT WESTERN MOTORS, INC.
San Jose, California

Fageol 10-15   1925-1926

Traction Wheels: Four wheels; two walking type in rear, 48x8½, giving traction.

No. of Plows Recommended: Two, 14-in.

Length: 119 in.; **Width:** 55 in.; **Height:** 52 in.; **Weight:** 3,800 lbs.; **Price:** $1320.

Turning Radius: 13½ ft.; **Acres Plowed in 10-hr. Day:** 7.

Motor: Lycoming, 3¾x5, L-head, 4 cylinders, cast en bloc.

Lubrication: Full force feed.

Carburetor: Zenith L-4, 1-in.

Ignition System: Splitdorf high tension magneto.

Cooling System: Thermo-syphon or centrifugal pump; optional.

Bearings: Strom ball and Timken roller in transmission.

Transmission: Bevel and spur gear; 2½ m. p. h. forward; 2½ m. p. h. reverse.

Final Drive: Spur gear; live axle; no differential.

Belt Pulley: 6x6½; 1,200 r.p.m. and 2,700 feet per minute at normal engine speed.

FAGEOL 10-15
Great Western Motors, Inc., San Jose, Cal.

HART-PARR CO.
Charles City, Iowa

Hart-Parr 12-24   1925-1927
Hart-Parr 16-30   1925-1926
Hart-Parr 40   1925-1926

HART-PARR 12-24
Hart-Parr Co., Charles City, Ia.

Traction Wheels: Four wheels; two traction in rear, 46x10.

No. of Plows Recommended: Two to three 14-in.

Length: 116 in.; **Width:** 66 in. **Height:** 56 in.; **Weight:** 4,250 lbs.

Turning Radius: 11 ft.; **Acres Plowed in 10-hr. Day:** 7½.

Motor: Own, 5½x6½, horizontal, 2 cylinders, cast en bloc.

Lubrication: Madison-Kipp, force feed.

Carburetor: Schebler, 1½-in.

Ignition System: Robert Bosch high tension magneto with impulse starter.

Cooling System: Radiator, centrifugal pump and fan.

Bearings: Own make on axles.

Transmission: Selective, sliding spur gear. 2½ to 3½ m.p.h. forward, 1½ m.p.h reverse.

Final Drive: External gear, enclosed.

Belt Pulley: 13x8; 800 r.p.m. and 2,722 feet per minute at normal engine speed.

Traction Wheels: Four-wheel tractor, with two drive members, 52 x 10, in rear.

No. of Plows Recommended: Three 14-in.

Length: 132 in.; **Width:** 74 in.; **Height:** 67 in.; **Weight:** 5,050 lbs.

Turning Radius: 13 ft.; **Acres Plowed in 10-hr. Day:** 10.

Motor: Own; $6\frac{1}{2}$x7; horizontal, 2 cylinders, cast en bloc.

Lubrication: Madison-Kipp force feed lubricator.

Carburetor: Schebler, $1\frac{1}{2}$-in.

Ignition System: Robert Bosch high tension magneto with impulse starter.

Lighting Equipment: To order.

Cooling System: Radiator, centrifugal pump and fan.

Bearings: Roller and ball in transmission and own on drive axle.

Transmission: Selective, sliding spur gear, 2 to 3 m.p.h. forward; 1.5 m.p.h. reverse.

Final Drive: External gear, enclosed.

Belt Pulley: 14x9; 750 r.p.m. and 2,700 feet per minute at normal engine speed.

HART-PARR 16-30
Hart-Parr Co., Charles City, la.

HART-PARR 40
Hart-Parr Co., Charles City, la.

Traction Wheels: Four wheels; two in front, 28x5; two traction in rear, 52x13.

No. of Plows Recommended: Four 14-in.

Length: 140 in.; **Width:** 96 in.; **Height:** 67 in.; **Weight:** 7500 lbs.; **Price** $2250 f.o.b. factory.

Turning Radius. 13 ft.

Motor: Own, $5\frac{1}{2}$x$6\frac{1}{2}$; horizontal; 4-cylinder, cast in pairs.

Lubrication: Madison-Kipp force feed.

Carburetor: Schebler, $1\frac{1}{2}$ in.

Ignition System: Robert Bosch high tension magneto with impulse starter.

Cooling System: Centrifugal pump, fan and radiator.

Bearings: Roller and ball in transmission and own on drive axle.

Transmission: Selective, sliding spur gear, 2 to 3 m.p.h forward.

Final Drive: Internal gear and master pinions.

Belt Pulley: 14x9; 800 r.p.m. and 2750 feet per minute at normal engine speed.

McCormick-Deering
INDUSTRIAL Tractor

for

**Road and
Industrial
Work**

Dependable, Economical, Convenient Power

for Industrial, Municipal or Commercial Service

THE McCormick-Deering Tractor is built with ample power for all kinds of industrial, municipal, and commercial service. In road building and maintenance, in industrial plants, etc., where these tractors are in daily use, they are giving such satisfactory service that the demand for them is rapidly increasing. The dispatch with which a McCormick-Deering enables work to be done helps to account for the increasing demand. The three forward speeds give a choice suitable for long, hard pulls, or for a quick move from one location to another.

Modern Design: The McCormick-Deering Industrial Tractor embodies the most modern developments in tractor design and construction. The engine is of the valve-in-head, four-cylinder, heavy-duty type. Its working parts are thoroughly protected from dust and dirt, which makes it well adapted to all kinds of road construction and maintenance work. The main frame forms

a rigid and substantial foundation for the engine and a dust and dirt-proof housing for working parts.

Other Outstanding Features: These tractors are equipped with the famous two-bearing crankshaft which is guaranteed against breakage for the life of the tractor, and the crankshaft ball bearings are guaranteed against breaking, wearing out, or burning out for the life of the tractor. The cylinders are removable and should one become scored or worn it can be easily replaced with a new one. The clutch is of the multiple-disk dry-plate type and has ample friction surface to insure proper transmission of power and prevent grabbing. The tractor is spring-mounted in front which protects the engine from shocks.

Disk wheels are used both front and rear, equipped with solid rubber tires. Special wheel equipment can be supplied to meet conditions. Where power is needed for belt work a pulley attachment can be used. The power take-off can also be applied and enables the tractor to deliver power at the rear for running the pulled machine or for driving more than one machine at a time.

COMPLETE DETAILS FURNISHED ON REQUEST

INTERNATIONAL HARVESTER COMPANY
OF AMERICA
(INCORPORATED)

606 SO. MICHIGAN AVE.   CHICAGO, ILL.

1925   411

INTERNATIONAL HARVESTER CO.
Chicago, Illinois

McCormick-Deering Industrial   1925-1933

Traction Wheels: Four wheels; two traction in rear, rubber tires; two non-drive in front, 27x3½.

Length: 118 in.; **Width:** 59 in.; **Height:** 61 in.; **Weight:** 4,430 lbs.

Turning Radius: 14 ft.

Motor: Own; 4½x5, valve in head, 4 cylinders, removable cylinder.

Lubrication: Splash and force circulation.

Carburetor: Ensign.

Ignition System: K-W.

Cooling System: Thermo-syphon.

Bearings: New Departure.

Transmission: 2, 4 and 10 m.p.h. forward; 3.8 m.p.h. reverse.

Final Drive: Spur gear, live axle.

Belt Pulley: 15¼x7; 645 r.p.m. and 2575 feet per minute at normal engine speed.

McCORMICK-DEERING INDUSTRIAL
International Harvester Co., Chicago, Ill.

J. T. TRACTOR CO.
Cleveland, Ohio

"J-T" 25-40   1925

Traction Wheels: Two crawlers, 110x11.

No. of Plows Recommended: Three 14-in.

Length: 137 in.; **Width:** 60 in.; **Height:** 68½ in.; **Weight:** 9,400 lbs.; **Price:** $3500.

Turning Radius: 5 ft.

Motor: Climax K U, 5x6½, vertical, 4 cylinders, cast in pairs.

Lubrication: Pressure system; geared oil pump.

Carburetor: Zenith, 1½-in.

Ignition System: K-W magneto with impulse starter.

Lighting Equipment: Prestolite system.

Cooling System: McCord tubular radiator, Oakes fan and centrifugal pump.

Transmission: Selective; 1⅓ to 5 m.p.h. forward; 1¼ m.p.h. reverse.

Final Drive: Internal ring gear and bull pinion.

Belt Pulley: 10x8; 900 r.p.m. and 2350 feet per minute at normal engine speed.

"J T" 25-40
J. T. Tractor Co., Cleveland, O.

412   1925

LITTLE GIANT CO.

Mankato, Minnesota

Little Giant, Model B, 12-22
Little Giant, Model A, 18-35

1925-1927
1925-1926

Traction Wheels: Four wheels with two drivers in rear, 54×14.

No. of Plows Recommended: Three or four 14-inch.

Length: 144 in.; **Width:** 52 in.; **Height:** 59 in.; **Weight:** 5,200 lbs.; **Price:** $1000.

Turning Radius: 14 ft.; **Acres Plowed In 10-hour day:** 10 to 15.

Motor: Own; $4\frac{1}{2}$ x 5, L-head, 4 cylinders, cast in pairs.

Lubrication: Force feed and splash combined.

Carburetor: Kingston.

Ignition System: Kingston high tension magneto.

Cooling System: Water and pump system.

Bearings: Hyatt roller throughout.

Transmission: Sliding gear, $1\frac{1}{2}$, 3 and 6 m. p. h. forward; $1\frac{1}{2}$ m. p. h. reverse.

Final Drive: Direct gear drive.

Belt Pulley: 9 x 7; 900 r. p. m. and 2,120 feet per minute at normal engine speed.

LITTLE GIANT, MODEL B, 12-22
Little Giant Co., Mankato, Minn.

LITTLE GIANT, MODEL A, 18-35
Little Giant Co., Mankato, Minn.

Traction Wheels: Four wheels with two drivers in rear, 66 x 20.

No. of Plows Recommended: Four to six 14-inch.

Length: 168 in.; **Width:** 75 in.; **Height** 73 in.; **Weight:** 8,700 lbs.; **Price:** $1500.

Turning Radius: 16 ft.; **Acres Plowed In 10-hour day:** 15 to 25.

Motor: Own; $5\frac{1}{2}$ x 6, L-head, 4 cylinders, cast in pairs.

Lubrication: Force feed and splash combined:

Carburetor: Kingston.

Ignition System. Kingston high tension magneto.

Cooling System: Water and pump system.

Bearings: Hyatt roller throughout.

Transmission: Sliding gear, $1\frac{1}{2}$, 3 and 6 m. p. h. forward, $1\frac{1}{2}$ m. p. h. reverse.

Final Drive: Direct gear drive.

Belt Pulley: 13 x 9; 750 r. p. m. and 2,520 feet per minute at normal engine speed

The Nilson Junior Tractor
for Power *and* Durability

THE NILSON JUNIOR TRACTOR will pull a 3-bottom 14-inch stubble plow in average soil at a speed of $2\frac{1}{4}$ to $2\frac{1}{2}$ miles per hour with ease. Farmers are demanding a tractor that will stand up under all conditions. They want a tractor that will give year 'round service —one that is equally efficient at the draw bar and the belt. In the **NILSON** you will find these advantages and many more. At the draw bar it will pull 3000 lbs. at plowing speed. It develops 25 horse power at the belt.

Read the specifications published in this book. Then write us for full details of our attractive dealer proposition.

MINNESOTA NILSON CORPORATION
27th Avenue South and 27th Street   MINNEAPOLIS, MINN.

Traction by Pull — Not by Weight

The NILSON is a proven tractor with plenty of reserve power. It is durable and light in weight. It does the same work as a machine of much greater weight. It is flexible and economical to operate. All NILSON machines are sold under an iron-clad guarantee. Let us tell you more about it.

Aggressive Dealers Wanted In All Localities.

Price
790.⁰⁰
F. O. B., Mpls.

MEAD-MORRISON MANUFACTURING CO.
East Boston, Massachusetts

Bear "55"   1925

Traction Wheels: Crawlers; flexible track; dry type.
No. of Plows Recommended: Four, 14-in.
Length: 124 in.; **Width:** 65 in.; **Height:** 95 in.; **Weight:** 8,700 lbs.
Turning Radius: 6 ft.; **Acres Plowed In 10-hr. Day:** 17.
Motor: Stearns, $4\frac{3}{4}$x$6\frac{1}{2}$, vertical, overhead valves, 4 cylinders, cast en bloc.
Lubrication: Pressure feed to all crankshaft, piston pin, camshaft and rocker shaft bearings.
Carburetor: Schebler, $1\frac{3}{4}$-in.
Ignition System: Bosch magneto with impulse starter.
Lighting Equipment: Optional.
Cooling System: Spirex sectional radiator, pump circulation, 60 gal. per min., 24 in. fan and silent chain drive.
Bearings: Guerney ball bearings in transmission.
Transmission: Selective spur gear; 2 to 5 m.p.h. forward; $1\frac{1}{2}$ m.p.h. reverse.
Final Drive: Internal gear to track through driving sprocket.
Belt Pulley: 12x9; 1000 r.p.m. and 3140 feet per minute at normal engine speed.

BEAR "55"
Mead-Morrison Mfg. Co., East Boston, Mass.

MINNESOTA-NILSON CORP.
Minneapolis, Minnesota

Nilson Jr., 16-25   1925-1928

Traction Wheels: 50 inches diameter and 30 inches total width.
No. of Plows Recommended: Three and four 14-in.
Length: 147 in.; **Width:** 72 in.; **Height:** 62 in.; **Weight:** 5000 lbs.; **Price:** $790.
Turning Radius: 16 ft.
Motor: Waukesha, $4\frac{1}{4}$x$5\frac{3}{4}$, L-head, 4 cylinders, cast in pairs.
Lubrication: Force and splash.
Carburetor: Kingston, $1\frac{1}{2}$-in.
Ignition System: High tension magneto.
Starting and Lighting Equipment: Optional.
Cooling System: Perfex radiator, pump and fan.
Bearings: Hyatt roller throughout.
Transmission: Selective; $1\frac{1}{2}$ to $2\frac{1}{4}$ m.p.h. forward.
Final Drive: Chain.
Belt Pulley: 20x6; 360 r.p.m. and 1900-2100 feet per minute at normal engine speed.

NILSON JR., 16-25
Minnesota-Nilson Corp.,
Minneapolis, Minn.

ROCK ISLAND PLOW CO.
Rock Island, Illinois

Heider 15-27

1925-1927

Traction Wheels: Four wheels; two in rear, 57x10, giving traction and two non-drive in front, 30x5.

No. of Plows Recommended: Three, 14-in.

Length: 144 in.; Width: 74 in.; Height: 96 in.; Weight: 6,000 lbs.

Turning Radius: $12\frac{1}{2}$ ft.; Acres Plowed in 10-hr. Day: 12.

Motor: Waukesha, $4\frac{3}{4}$x$6\frac{3}{4}$, L-head, 4 cylinders, cast in pairs.

Lubrication: Circulating splash.

Carburetor: Kingston, L-4, $1\frac{1}{2}$-in.

Ignition System: Splitdorf high tension magneto.

Cooling System: Centrifugal pump, fan and Perfex radiator.

Bearings: U. S. ball in transmission.

Transmission: Friction; 1 to 4 m.p.h. forward; 1 to 4 m.p.h. reverse.

Final Drive: Gears.

Belt Pulley: 14x7; 100 to 900 r.p.m. and 2200 feet per minute at normal engine speed.

HEIDER 15-27
Rock Island Plow Co., Rock Island, Ill.

THE RUSSELL & CO.
Massillon, Ohio

Russell, Model C, 20-40

1925-1926

RUSSELL, MODEL C, 20-40
The Russell & Co., Massillon, Ohio

Traction Wheels: Four wheel type with two rear wheels, 60×16, as traction members.

No. of Plows Recommended: Four to five 14-in.

Length: 164 in.; Width; 68 in.; Height: 87 in.; Weight: 7740 lbs.

Turning Radius: $16\frac{3}{4}$ ft.; Acres Plowed in 10-hr. Day: 14 to 18.

Motor: Climax, $5\frac{1}{2}$x7; vertical, 4 cylinders, cast in pairs.

Lubrication: Force feed.

Carburetor: Kingston, $1\frac{1}{2}$-in.

Ignition System: Bosch magneto with impulse starter.

Cooling System: Modine tubular radiator.

Bearings: Timken roller in transmission and on drive axle.

Transmission: Gearing, 2.4 to 3.75 m. p. h. forward; 2 m. p. h. reverse.

Final Drive: Gearing through rear wheels.

Belt Pulley: $12\frac{1}{2}$x8; 835 r.p.m., and 2732 f.p.m. at normal engine speed.

416

1925

QUALITY Piston Rings for QUALITY ENGINES

The tradename **QUALITY** was selected as the only word suitable to fully express the actual values in each ring that bears this name.

THE performance of any engine will be no better than the performance of its piston rings.

Over one hundred leading manufacturers of quality engines recognize this fact by using **QUALITY** Piston Rings for initial installation. They know that every ring in every cylinder will function exactly the same as all the others, and that the result will be a fine, smooth and efficient performance.

And for replacement, **QUALITY** Piston Rings are the logical choice as well. Accurately built to the proper oversizes, they can be installed in worn cylinders with the full assurance that they will hold compression, prevent oil leaking and render faithful, dependable service over a long and trouble free period.

As a mark of identification and a guarantee of quality, each ring is stamped with the name "QUALITY." Oversize rings for replacement have, in addition, their oversize plainly marked on each ring.

The Piston RING COMPANY
Muskegon, Michigan

TORO MANUFACTURING CO.
Minneapolis, Minnesota

Toro Tractor 10

1925-1927

Traction Wheels: Two traction wheels in rear, 42x6, and two non-drive wheels in front, 26x4.

No. of Plows Recommended: One 14-in.

Length: 105 in.; **Width:** 44 in.; **Height:** 54 in.; **Weight:** 2,600 lbs.; **Price:** $850.

Turning Radius: 8 1-3 ft.

Motor: Le Roi, $3\frac{1}{8}$x$4\frac{1}{2}$, vertical, 4 cylinders, cast en bloc.

Lubrication: Constant splash.

Carburetor: Kingston.

Ignition System: Eisemann high tension magneto.

Cooling System: Thermo-syphon, Shotwell-Johnson radiator and fan.

Bearings: Hyatt roller, SKF and Nice ball.

Transmission: Sliding gear. 2.6 to 3.75 m.p.h. forward and 3 m.p.h. reverse.

Final Drive: Enclosed bull gear.

Belt Pulley: 8x$4\frac{1}{4}$, 1200 r.p.m. and 2500 feet per minute at normal engine speed.

TORO TRACTOR 10
Toro Manufacturing Co., Minneapolis, Minn.

TOWNSEND TRACTOR CO.
Janesville, Wisconsin

Townsend 2-Plow 20 h.p.
Townsend 20-40

1925-1928
1925-1928

TOWNSEND 2-PLOW 20 H. P.
Townsend Tractor Co., Janesville, Wis.

Traction Wheels: Four wheels; two in rear, 45x10, giving traction and two non-drive in front, 25x5.

No. of Plows Recommended: Two, 14-in.

Length: 112 in.; **Width:** 54 in.; **Height:** 54 in.; **Weight:** 4000 lbs.

Turning Radius: 8 ft.

Motor: Own, $7\frac{1}{2}$x9, horizontal, valve-in-head, 1 cylinder.

Lubrication: Force feed oiler.

Carburetor: Own, $2\frac{1}{4}$ in.

Ignition System: High tension magneto.

Starting and Lighting Equipment: Extra.

Cooling System: Radiator.

Bearings: Plain babbitt.

Transmission: Spur gear; $2\frac{1}{2}$ to $3\frac{1}{2}$ m.p.h. forward; 2 m.p.h. reverse.

Final Drive: Spur gear.

Belt Pulley: 14x7; 475 to 600 r.p.m.

Traction Wheels: Four wheels; two non-drive in front, 32x8, and two traction in rear, 56x18.

No. of Plows Recommended: Four, 14-in.

Length: 140 in.; Width: 78 in.; Height: 78 in.; Weight: 6500 lbs.

Turning Radius: 12 ft.

Motor: Own, $7\frac{1}{2}$x9, horizontal, valve in head, 2 cylinders, cast en bloc.

Lubrication: Force feed oiler.

Carburetor: Own, $2\frac{1}{4}$-in.

Ignition System: High tension magneto.

Starting and Lighting Equipment: Extra.

Cooling System: Radiator.

Bearings: Plain babbitt.

Transmission: Spur gear; $2\frac{1}{2}$ to 3 m.p.h. forward; 2 m.p.h. reverse.

Final Drive: Spur gear.

Belt Pulley: 20x8; 450 to 500 r.p.m.

TOWNSEND 20-40
Townsend Tractor Co., Janesville, Wis.

THE UTILITOR CO.

Indianapolis, Indiana

Midwest Utilitor Model 502   1925-1937

Traction Wheels. Two drive wheels, $24\frac{3}{4}$x4.

No. of Plows Recommended. One 8-in.

Length: 84 in.; Width: $17\frac{1}{2}$-$30\frac{1}{2}$ in.; Height: 36 in.; Weight: 750 lbs.

Turning Radius: 6 ft.; Acres Plowed In 10-hr. Day: 1.

Motor: Own, $3\frac{1}{2}$x$4\frac{1}{2}$ L-head, 1 cylinder.

Lubrication: Splash.

Carburetor: Kingston, 1-in.

Ignition System: Eisemann high tension magneto.

Cooling System: Water; thermo-syphon.

Bearings: Fafnir ball in transmission.

Transmission: Internal gear, $2\frac{1}{2}$ to 4 m.p.h. forward.

Final Drive: Internal gear.

Belt Pulley: $4\frac{5}{8}$x$3\frac{3}{4}$; 600 to 1,200 r.p.m.

MIDWEST UTILITOR MODEL 502
The Utilitor Co., Indianapolis, Ind.

WIZARD TRACTOR CORP.
Los Angeles, California

Wizard 4-Pull 20-35   1925-1930

Traction Wheels: Drives on all four wheels, each $43 \times 13\frac{1}{2}$.

No. of Plows Recommended: Four to five, 14-in.

Length: 112 in.; **Width:** 66 in.; **Height:** 57 in.; **Weight:** 6800 lbs.; **Price** $3100.

Turning Radius: 6 ft.; **Acres Plowed in 10-hr. Day:** 16.

Motor: Own, $5\frac{1}{4} \times 6\frac{1}{2}$, vertical, 4 cylinders, cast in pairs.

Lubrication: Full pressure feed.

Carburetor: Ensign, $1\frac{1}{2}$-in.

Ignition System. High tension magneto.

Starting and Lighting Equipment: Optional as extra.

Cooling System: Tubular radiator, centrifugal pump and fan.

Bearings: Hess Bright ball and Timken roller.

Transmission: Selective; $2\frac{1}{8}$ to 3 m.p.h. forward; 2 m.p.h. reverse.

Final Drive: Chain, enclosed and running in oil.

Belt Pulley: 12×10; 850 r.p.m. and 2,600 feet per minute at normal engine speed.

WIZARD 4-PULL 20-35
Wizard Tractor Corp., Los Angeles, Cal.

FORDSON TRACTOR MOTOR NUMBERS BY MONTHS—1918-1928
(UNITED STATES PRODUCTION)

	JAN	FEB	MAR	APR	MAY	JUNE	JULY	AUG	SEPT	OCT	NOV	DEC
1918	260	617	1732	3083	7609	9581	11938	15226	18638	22248	26288	29979
1919	34427	39555	44783	50962	53080	53111	55305	60865	68056	74810	81363	88088
1920	100001	100193	102295	104760	121592	124732	138087	151505	154891	158178	—	—
1921	—	—	—	158327	158971	—	159454	159888	—	170244	170395	170891
1922	—	201026	202522	208633	216081	225029	234356	244017	252533	252762	257908	262825
1923	268583	276350	284255	295532	306915	318011	327012	333682	342100	349497	357850	365191
1924	370351	375182	382282	390744	400862	410891	418073	423636	429656	435905	442805	448201
1925	453360	460452	469850	481488	492801	502798	511497	519303	527103	534603	542703	549901
1926	557608	568303	579111	590385	600305	608948	616685	623159	629830	—	—	645610
1927	645611	—	—	—	—	—	—	—	—	—	—	739582
1928	739583	—	—	—	—	—	—	—	—	—	—	747583

UNITS BUILT IN CORK, IRELAND	
1929	747682 to 757368
1930	757369 to 772564
1931	772565 to 776065
1932	776066 to 779153

UNITS BUILT IN DAGENHAM, ENGLAND	
1933	779158 to 781965
1934	781966 to 785547
1935	785548 to 794702
1936	794703 to 807581
1937	807582 to 826778
1938	826779 to 830000

INDEX

426

List of Manufacturers' Early Advertisements

(Not inclusive of all manufacturers contained herein or advertisements within the *Cooperative Tractor Catalog*).